Mostly Good and Competent Men

SECOND EDITION

Robert P. Howard

Revised and Updated by
Peggy Boyer Long and Mike Lawrence

THE INSTITUTE FOR
PUBLIC AFFAIRS

University of Illinois at Springfield, Springfield, Illinois

Library of Congress Cataloging-in-Publication Data

Howard, Robert P.
    Mostly good and competent men / by Robert P. Howard. -- 2nd ed. /
  revised and updated by Peggy Boyer Long and Mike Lawrence.
        p.   cm.
    Includes bibliographical references and index.
    ISBN 0-938943-15-4
    1. Governors--Illinois--Biography.   2. Illinois--Biography.
  3. Illinois--Politics and government.   I. Long, Peggy Boyer, 1946-
  . II. Lawrence, Mike, 1942-   . III. Title.
  F540.H69 1999
  977.3'04'0922--dc21
  [b]
                                                              98-50866
                                                                  CIP

ISBN: 0-938943-15-4

This book is a revised and updated edition of *Mostly Good and Competent Men: Illinois
Governors 1818 to 1988*, published in 1988 by *Illinois Issues* and the Illinois State
Historical Society, Springfield, Illinois.

Unless otherwise indicated, all photos are courtesy of the Illinois State Historical
Library and *Illinois Issues* magazine.

Designer: Diana L. C. Nelson
Printer: United Graphics
Back cover photos: Shadrach Bond, Edward Coles, and Ninian Edwards, courtesy
    of the Illinois State Historical Library
Front cover photos: Jim Thompson, courtesy of the Illinois State Historical Library;
    Jim Edgar, courtesy of the Office of the Governor; and George Ryan, courtesy of
    the Office of the Secretary of State

Printed in the United States of America

10 9 8 7 6 5 4 3 2 1

The Institute for Public Affairs
P.O. Box 19243
University of Illinois at Springfield
Springfield, IL 62794-9243

Phone: 217-206-6502 • Fax: 217-206-7257 • e-mail: wojcicki@uis.edu
Web site: http://www.uius.edu/~ipapu/ipapu.html

Contents

Preface to the Second Edition

In 1988 Robert Howard suggestively called this collection of biographies of the Illinois governors *Mostly Good and Competent Men* — a title that reflects the pushes and pulls he must have felt as a top-notch newspaperman and a respected amateur historian. The old reporter in him probably would have favored a more headline-splashing title, but the academic in him encouraged a title that would connote the longer, more thoughtful pose of the historian. The "*mostly* good" compromise satisfied both sides of his psyche. Howard's title is at once an accurate assessment of the group that has held the state's highest office, a typical example of midwestern phraseology, and — of course — an invitation to find out which men were neither competent nor good.

Concerned with the governors rather than the governorship, this second edition of *Mostly Good and Competent Men* is a specialized book designed to tell about the men who held this state's highest office. Who were they? Where did they come from? How did they rise to leadership? How did they respond to the responsibilities and opportunities of the governorship, and what happened to them afterward? Most of the governors were important or colorful, or both. Too many have faded from memory. Some are remembered for the wrong reasons.

The gestation period of these biographies began in 1933 when a young Associated Press correspondent, a stranger in Springfield, wondered about the personalities and problems of the former governors (there were 27 of them then) whose portraits hung in a double tier along the walls of Henry Horner's reception room and private office. At the time, Howard could not have anticipated that he would spend 50 years as a front row observer of Illinois government and know 10 governors personally. During that time, he realized that the lack of a historical background was an occupational handicap for a newspaperman involved with state officials, legislatures, and elections. Sometime after 1950 Howard struck upon the idea of a book on the governors, and he began preserving the scraps of information that finally blossomed into the first edition of this text. When Robert Howard died in 1989, he left *Mostly Good and Competent Men* and *Illinois: A History of the Prairie State* as a legacy to students of Illinois political history.

I hope that Robert Howard would be pleased with the Institute for Public Affairs' decision to breathe new life into *Mostly Good and Competent Men* by publishing this edition. I hope, too, that he would appreciate my attempts to clarify (and in some instances to correct) his work. I know that he would be proud of the contributions that his fellow journalists Ed Wojcicki, Peggy Boyer Long, and Mike Lawrence made to this edition. Wojcicki is the publisher of *Illinois Issues* magazine, the state's leading monthly magazine of public affairs, supported by the University of Illinois at Springfield. In this text, he provides the initial glimpse of Governor George Ryan. Boyer Long, the editor of *Illinois Issues,* magazine graciously and deftly picked up where Howard left off. She is responsible for writing the story of the Illinois governors from 1988 to 1998 – Jim Thompson and Jim Edgar. Her chapter on Edgar is the seminal post-gubernatorial analysis of his career and administration. Lawrence, now at the Public Policy Institute at Southern Illinois University, brings his experience to his analysis of the changing role of the governorship in the last 30 years. Lawrence, a veteran newspaperman, worked for the *Galesburg Register-Mail,* the *Quad-City Times,* and the *Chicago Sun-Times.* He also served as press secretary to Governor Jim Edgar.

Illinois is a robust, ever-changing state. Her governors are as much a reflection of the hopes of her citizens as they are the captains of her destiny. Robert Howard captured the vitality of the men who have occupied the governor's mansion. With this second edition, we have done our best to remain true to his vision. In this small way, we hope to revitalize Robert Howard's legacy to the people of this state.

Rodd Whelpley
Associate Editor
University of Illinois at Springfield
Institute for Public Affairs

Acknowledgments

Certainly the lion's share of the credit for the second edition of *Mostly Good and Competent Men* belongs to author Robert P. Howard. Although Howard died shortly after the publication of the first edition, his diligent scholarship provided the foundation for this edition. Of course, Howard did not work alone on the first edition. So it is appropriate here to acknowledge those who contributed to the original text: Their work surely informs this edition.

Robert Howard himself said that this book would not have been written had it not been for his father, J. R. Howard, a lifetime observer of the political process; Dr. C. F. Littell, professor of political science at Cornell College; and Paul M. Angle, who first encouraged him to read Illinois history. Howard never forgot Milburn P. Akers, an Associated Press associate, who presided over his indoctrination to Springfield.

Special thanks go to Mrs. Mildred V. Schulz, who during her last years as reference librarian at the Illinois State Historical Library kept telling Howard to hurry up. J. Michael Lennon, publisher of *Illinois Issues,* and Michael Devine, state historian for the Illinois State Historical Society published the first edition. Beverley Scobell, with assistance from Marilyn Huff and Cheryl Peck, did the editing. Janice Petterchak and Mary Michals supplied the photographs. Marcia Plasters and Stan Warman transformed Perfect Writer diskettes into a usable electronic manuscript and continued their technical support throughout the editing process.

The entire first edition manuscript was read by Fred H. Bird, Jr., Cullom Davis, William L. Day, Samuel K. Gove, and James D. Nowlan. Some chapters were read by John R. Chapin, Irving Dilliard, Daniel Egler, Harold E. Gibson, Raymond H. Hammes, David Kenney, Thomas B. Littlewood, and Mark Plummer. Others who helped with information and advice included Carl R. Baldwin, John D. Buenker, Janet Cornelius, Rodney O. Davis, William W. Downey, Paul M. Green, John Hoffmann, Daniel D. Holt, Robert W. Johannsen, Donald F. Lewis, Michael Maher, Archie Motley, Taylor Pensoneau, John Y. Simon, and Robert Sutton, along with Michael Devine, state historian and Illinois Historic Preservation Agency director, and staff members of the State Historical, Lincoln, and Sangamon State University libraries.

Finally, the first edition might not have been finished had not Robert's wife Beth believed that at age 78 he needed a word processor.

The second edition would not be possible without the foresight of Nancy Ford, director of the Institute for Public Affairs at the University of Illinois at Springfield and the Institute's Editorial Board who saw the need for an update. Ed Wojcicki, publisher of *Illinois Issues*, then took responsibility for publishing the project on behalf of the Institute. Wojcicki and Jon N. Austin, the executive director of the Illinois State Historical Society, took care of transferring the copyright from *Illinois Issues* and the State Historical Society to the Institute for Public Affairs.

The Institute's editorial and book production team put in the effort that transformed the idea of a second edition into a bona fide book. Charlene Lambert, Jackie Wright, and Kim Allen did early preparation of the manuscript. Rodd Whelpley developed the manuscript, and Jill Barfield copyedited it. Jill also helped pick photographs. Diana Nelson designed the text and the cover. Bud Bartlett added his marketing expertise to the project. Beverley Scobell was on board every step of the way. She was involved in manuscript preparation, fact checking, and photo selection, and she provided a bridge from the first edition to the second.

Kathryn M. Harris, director of the Illinois State Historical Library, and her entire staff were nothing but gracious and helpful. Particular thanks go to Mary Michals who opened the library's photo files.

Charles N. Wheeler III read portions of the text and checked facts. Kevin Flanagan, assistant librarian at the American Legion, helped verify some facts about Governor Stelle. Greg Koos of the McLean County Historical Society verified some facts about Governors Hamilton, Fifer, and Stevenson. Phil Germann of the Historical Society of Quincy and Adams County supplied facts about Governor Wood. Bill Harris at McKendree College supplied information on Governor French, and Catherine "Kay" Schlichting at Ohio Wesleyan helped track down facts about Governor Hamilton. Bill Barnhart, co-author of a forthcoming book on Otto Kerner, shared information to make this edition's biography of that governor more accurate. Governor Jim Edgar granted Peggy Boyer Long an interview during the last hectic days of his administration and provided invaluable insight. Edgar Press Secretary Eric Robinson gave copies of valuable documentation, and Rosalie Warren helped research the Thompson and Edgar administrations. Dave Joens read through the entire text and made many helpful suggestions and corrections.

Introduction

The unwritten job specifications for governor of Illinois call for a melding of the best qualities of a statesman, an administrator, and a politician. The governor should understand what the people want and what they can afford. He or she should act evenhandedly and promptly in establishing priorities and managing the dozens of agencies in an expanding bureaucracy, and he or she should be a leader who can win the legislature's cooperation and the public's support. The ideal person rarely exists, and certainly cannot appear on a ballot every four years.

From 1818 to 1998, 38 men have occupied the office of the governor, with George Ryan becoming the 39th in 1999. No one pretends that the chief executives represent a cross-section of Illinois citizenry. All have been white males. In the state's first 180 years, only one woman, Dawn Clark Netsch, ran as a major-party candidate for governor, and only one black man, Roland Burris, entered his name in a major party's primary race for the state's highest office. All but Samuel H. Shapiro trace their ancestry to western or northern Europe. William H. Bissell and Edward F. Dunne were Roman Catholics, and Shapiro and Henry H. Horner were Jews. Otherwise, active or nominal Protestants have had a monopoly on the office.

Yet within this seemingly narrow demographic, the governors have been men of diverse backgrounds, talents, and philosophies. Three governors – Edward Coles, Ninian Edwards, and Adlai Stevenson – came from elitist families with a tradition of public service. They are far outnumbered, however, by those who rose from obscurity and made their way upward, in the Abraham Lincoln tradition, by hard work, brains, and personality, with good luck always an additional factor. In that category are such prominent figures as William H. Bissell, Richard J. Oglesby, John M. Palmer, John P. Altgeld, and Frank O. Lowden. Some governors were reared in political atmospheres. When they ran for the top office, Stevenson, William G. Stratton, and Otto Kerner were emulating fathers who had been state officials. Shelby M. Cullom was the son of a state legislator. And the state's twenty-second governor, Richard Yates, followed directly in his father's footsteps. (Richard Yates, Sr. was governor during the Civil War.) Edward F. Dunne and Richard B. Ogilvie's fathers were business executives. Charles S. Deneen was the son of a Latin professor. Len Small and James R. Thompson grew up in the homes of doctors. At the other extreme, the underprivileged Thomas Ford was reared in poverty by a twice-widowed mother. Some acquired considerable wealth, with Governor Lowden apparently not the only millionaire. As time passed, the governors tended to be better educated. The recent ones are all college graduates. As to intelligence, some were obviously quite bright, and some were slower in their capacity to understand and evaluate difficult situations.

Politically, Illinois has had 21 Republican governors, 14 Democrats, and one Whig. (The first three preceded the arrival of political parties in Illinois.) The net result, through 1998, is that Republicans have served as chief executive for 110 years, and Democrats for 54 years. The Republican advantage in number and in years served was built up between the Civil War and the Depression, and there has been a Republican mini-boom since the mid-1970s.

The Constitution of 1970 requires only that governors be United States citizens who are at least 25 years old and have been residents of the state for three years. Along with some detail about the mechanics of the office, the constitution without qualification or elaboration states that "the governor shall have the supreme executive power, and shall be responsible for the faithful execution of the laws." In real life, however, there are limitations on the executive. Naturally, a governor with a legislative agenda must work with members of the General Assembly to frame the laws that put the administration's policies into practice. But executive decisions are not the sole preserve of the governor. In Illinois, the governor must share the responsibility and prestige of the executive branch with other officials – the attorney general, secretary of state, comptroller, and treasurer – who are accountable only to the people and may be affiliated with a different party than the governor. These other executive branch officers may be more concerned with personal ambition than with the harmonious operation of state government.

Even so, Illinois has never lacked applicants for the underpaid office in which there is no assurance that good work will be rewarded with a four-year extension of tenure. Indeed, the rise of the multiple-term governor is a relatively modern phenomenon. Under the 1818 and 1848 constitutions, governors were prohibited from immediate reelection. Since the direct reelection of governors was permitted by the 1870 constitution, only Lowden, who had presidential ambitions, and Louis L. Emmerson, who was 69 years old, retired voluntarily after one term. For governors who want more than one term, the easy way is to concentrate on reelection and leave the hard decisions for the future – or for the last term. A more difficult road is to follow Governor Horner's example of imposing a necessary retail sales tax in 1933 and then – somehow – winning a second term in 1936. Like Horner, Governor Ogilvie used determination, time, party loyalty, the logic of necessity, and official favors to break down resistance to putting in place a state income tax. His foresight, however, was not so handsomely rewarded, and he yielded his office to Dan Walker, a governor so confrontational that his own party chose not to renominate him after his term in office. (In fact, when Walker became a non-organization Democratic governor, Chicago Mayor Richard J. Daley publicly regretted that Republican Ogilvie had not been reelected.)

Former Illinois governors have a limited political future. The office has not turned out to be a warm-up for the White House, and only Stevenson was nominated for president by a united major political party. (Governor Lowden's name was placed in nomination, but he didn't win the nod and Governor John Palmer was the nominee of an anti-Bryan Gold Democratic faction in 1896.) Charles S. Deneen in 1924 was the last governor to reach the U.S. Senate. None has been appointed to a president's cabinet, although Stevenson as ambassador to the United Nations had cabinet rank. In addition to Stevenson, only Cullom and Lowden became nationally prominent. Former governors who went on federal payrolls were Kerner, a judge of the U.S. Court of Appeals, and Joseph W. Fifer, an interstate commerce commissioner nearly a century ago. In terms of longevity in office, as a rule U.S. Senators and congressmen have more durable careers than governors. (Being less visible, holders of the lower state offices can also hope for repeated reelection.)

Thus, the governorship of this state has represented the pinnacle of the public service careers of the 38 men who have held the job. But, many Illinoisans would be hard-pressed to name more than a handful of them. While there is no Abraham Lincoln or Stephen A. Douglas on the roster, the life stories of these men are worth knowing. Through them, we can draw inferences about the evolving nature of political power and leadership and understand the personalities of the men who shaped our state.

The fundamental question is whether Illinois' governors were good men who effected good public policy. A large majority – possibly three-quarters – have been men of good will, character, and competence who deserve the respect of the generations that did not know them. Nearly a dozen would qualify as statesmen whose wisdom, vision, and leadership provided showpieces of good government, often in difficult times. Most Illinois governors left behind reputations for probity and honesty. Their stories are lessons on the proper measure of courage and ability in service of the public.

But it would be unrealistic to expect any state, especially one with a short attention span for reform movements, to routinely elect superstatesmen. If we remember that large-scale land title frauds involved prominent territorial figures and that Illinois qualified for statehood with a dishonest census, we must assume that some of our early governors would not be exempt from the scandals that too often have given state and local government a bad name. So the best men are not always elected, which is a characteristic of democracies, and the state's top office occasionally has been filled by chairwarmers and crooks. Since the middle of the 20th century, governors Kerner and Walker, some executive branch officials, and a number of legislators, have gone to prison for various financial crimes that, with one exception, involved official business. (Walker's troubles grew out of private investments after he left office.) Most convictions were obtained by federal prosecutors, which might be a reflection on state law enforcement. Two earlier governors, Joel A. Matteson and Len Small, had narrow escapes when they came under intrastate investigation. To be blunt about it, the inaugural oath has been administered to two governors who went to prison, two others who might have, two or more incompetents, and an oddball. Another was constitutionally unqualified for the office. The stories of these men are lessons of power gone awry.

This book will acquaint you with the faces and names of the men – both good and bad – who have brought Illinois to the new millennium. Today, perhaps more than ever before, we face questions about the abilities and the moralities of our elected officials. With every election, we judge how candidates will handle the precarious demands of gathering power, governing efficiently, and retaining personal integrity. And soon, perhaps the demographics of our pool of chief executives will expand to include women and minorities. But, we have no crystal balls to guide us. Instead our state offers to us the lessons of a rich and colorful history punctuated by the life stories of the mostly good and competent men who have been the governors of Illinois.

1st Governor

Shadrach Bond
1773-1832

1773 – Born, Nov. 14, near Baltimore, Maryland.
1809 – Illinois becomes a territory separate from the Indiana Territory.
1810 – Marries Achsah Bond, a distant cousin.
1812 – Becomes Illinois Territory representative to Congress.
1814 – Settles near Kaskaskia, worked as receiver of public money.
1818 – Illinois Constitutional Convention adopts a state constitution and selects
Kaskaskia as the state capital, Aug. 6; Bond becomes first governor of Illinois,
Oct. 6; President Monroe signs congressional resolution making Illinois the 21st
state.
1820 – General Assembly declares Vandalia the state capital for 20 years.
1822 – Term as governor ends; becomes record keeper at Kaskaskia land office.
1826 – Makes a failed bid for Congress.
1830 – Makes a failed bid for Senate.
1832 – Dies at his farm, April 12.

Held office
October 6, 1818 to December 5, 1822

The first governor of the state of Illinois was a big, gregari
ous farmer with limited education and average ability. He
owned land, slaves, and foxhounds, and he held desirable
public offices most of his adult life. Shadrach Bond was Illinois'
first representative to Congress as nonvoting territorial delegate.
He became governor in 1818. To both offices he was elected without opposition.

For his time, Bond was an adequate governor who accepted
his only opportunity to play a statesman's role. As a member of
the state Council of Revision, he joined the Supreme Court justices in vetoing a bill to establish an uncapitalized and unregulated state bank. The veto was overridden, and the bank turned out
to be one of the worst mistakes ever made by an Illinois legislature. When the new state found itself deeply in debt, it wasn't
Bond's fault. Statehood had arrived prematurely, and the Bond
administration marked time while waiting for a flood of settlers to
come down the Ohio River and across from Kentucky. The governor was busier before and after his term of office when, by presidential appointment, he was receiver and then registrar of the
federal land office at Kaskaskia.

The Bonds of the Indiana Territory

Shadrach Bond was born November 14, 1773, somewhere in Maryland. According to his tombstone, a family-inspired biography, and some historians, the birthplace was Frederick, Fredericktown, or Frederick County, which are synonymous. Local historians there have never heard of him, however, and a Maryland genealogist who is a Bond family specialist believes that he probably was born in the Back River Upper Hundred, which is part of Baltimore County. His father paid taxes there in 1773; most of the Bonds lived in the Baltimore vicinity; and there is no evidence that Nicodemus and Rachel Stevenson Bond, Shadrach's parents, lived or visited in Frederick that year. Originally from England, by way of Virginia, the Bonds were prolific, minor members of the plantation and slave-owning class. Opportunities were limited, and Shadrach, the sixth of ten children, headed for the frontier in 1794.

Two Shadrach Bonds, uncle and nephew, were an early first family of Illinois, when Illinois was still part of the Indiana Territory. The elder, known as Shadrach Senior or Judge Bond, had been a civilian scout with George Rogers Clark's "Illinois regiment" in the Revolutionary War and was one of the first English-speaking frontiersmen to make a home on the American Bottom.

The future governor was the nephew, Shadrach Junior. Under his uncle's tutelage, Bond became a landowner and farmer at the New Design community. In 1810 at Nashville, Tennessee, Shadrach was married to a distant cousin, Achsah Bond, a native of the Baltimore vicinity. They had five daughters and two sons.

The two Bonds steadily advanced in political prominence, sitting in both houses of the Indiana territorial legislature and in local courts as appointed judges. When the court system was reorganized, the younger Bond was a justice of the peace. When Illinois was part of the Indiana Territory, the Bonds generally were factional allies of Governor William Henry Harrison. Their opponents included Kaskaskia's richest men, John Edgar and Robert Morrison, who were not pleased that Harrison supported investigations of land grant frauds. (Neither Bond was ever accused of obtaining land fraudulently.)

Bond's Public Service to the Illinois Territory

When Illinois became a separate territory in 1809, Bond showed little interest in asserting leadership. He usually sided with

Jesse B. Thomas, who had been instrumental in achieving separation from Indiana, and against Ninian Edwards, Illinois' territorial governor, who would later become the state's third governor. That was especially true after Edwards did not appoint Bond commander of the St. Clair County militia.

Contrary to two published biographies, the first governor was neither an Indian fighter nor a hero of the War of 1812. He declined an opportunity to run for colonel against William B. Whiteside, a member of a prominent family of Indian fighters. In 1812 Edwards made him one of four aides-de-camp. But late that year, when Edwards personally led an expedition against Indian villages at Peoria, Bond was on his way to Washington, by horseback and stage, to serve as the Illinois Territory's first nonvoting delegate to Congress. Also contrary to legend, Bond did not participate in the defense of Washington when it was burned by the British on August 14, 1814. By that time he was back in Illinois with a political plum, a presidential appointment as receiver of public money for the Kaskaskia land office.

The only record of the 1812 vote that sent Bond to Congress is a petition "complaining of the undue election of Bond." He served in Washington for 15 months. He worked for a bill to raise 10 companies of mounted rangers, and also proposed that a road connect Shawneetown and Kaskaskia.

In 1814, after he became a land office official, Bond moved to a farm west of Kaskaskia, the territorial capital, and built a two-story brick house that was regarded as palatial. Men of his position needed slaves for field and house work, and the 1820 census showed that the governor owned "14 Negroes." When he died in 1832, he bequeathed nine blacks, total value $1,210, to his wife and daughters.

Bond as State Governor

At the approach of statehood, in a factional truce prominent Democrats Ninian Edwards and Jesse B. Thomas took for themselves the state's two U.S. senatorships. Bond announced his candidacy for the single congressional seat, against John McLean, a Thomas partisan, and Daniel Pope Cook, an Edwards kinsman. For unstated reasons, Bond announced a month before the election that he would rather be governor of the new state. The official returns have been lost, but the *Illinois Intelligencer* said Bond received 3,628 votes, with only a handful being cast for some other man. When the legislature met, his majority was officially given as 3,427. Legislative journals contain no details.

A justice of the peace swore in Bond and Lieutenant Governor Pierre Menard, the only elected state officials, on October 6, 1818. In his inaugural message, he declared that the treasury was empty and the state's credit impaired. As a temporary solution, he recommended borrowing rather than increasing taxes. As one source of income, he proposed that the state lease its salt works outside Shawneetown and the two sections of land that had been donated by Congress for a seminary.

Because the best transportation was by water, Bond was justified in asking for internal improvements, especially the digging of a canal between the Illinois River and Lake Michigan. He also asked for a revision of the territorial code and more humane criminal laws. He wanted to abolish whipping and confinement in stocks and pillory for minor offenses and death sentences for arson, horse stealing, murder, and rape. He proposed that counties be required to build strong and substantial jails, and that the state, when it could afford it, should build a prison where convict labor could pay part of the operating costs.

More than most other early governors, Bond had some success in dealing with the legislature. Because of a funding shortage, it authorized the borrowing of $50,000. But the legislature also approved private lottery schemes to finance river and drainage improvements. (These failed because of the shortage of money.)

Midway in his term, when the Second General Assembly met in the new capital at Vandalia, Bond announced that the treasury was solvent. He recommend that a "seminary of learning" be built near Vandalia. He chose not to veto a "black code" patterned after the laws of slave states.

Taking the unpopular side of the chief pocketbook issue – the shortage of money in the Western country – the governor objected to proposals to manufacture prosperity by creating state banks with the authority to issue paper money and make unsecured loans. He warned that the result could be "a state of things still more embarrassing," but the legislature ignored him. The General Assembly overrode his vetoes of the bank bill and a "stay" law that gave settlers a legal excuse not to pay their debts. As he predicted, the state soon faced a monetary crisis, a heavy debt, and echoes of scandal.

Back to the Land Office

Two months after Bond's term ended, President James Monroe appointed him to the Kaskaskia land office as registrar, or record keeper. President John Quincy Adams re-appointed him to the prestigious position four years later. Always a politician, the former governor took his turn in 1826 at trying to defeat Congressman Daniel P. Cook, who had beaten John McLean twice and Elias Kent Kane once. Running as a supporter of William H. Crawford for the presidency, he polled approximately a third of the vote. In 1830, when a Senate vacancy was filled, only nine legislators voted for him. (The state legislature elected Senators at that time.)

The elder statesman was the first grand master of the first Masonic lodge in Illinois. Appointed by the legislature, he served on the commission that built the first state penitentiary at Alton. When a second state bank was created, he was made a director of its Edwardsville branch. He served on the governing boards of private companies chartered to dig a canal from the Illinois River to Chicago and to improve the Kaskaskia River. Both ventures failed.

Still holding the land office job, Bond died of pneumonia in his farm home on April 12, 1832. The inventory of his estate included "several farms," nine slaves, livestock, and a barrel of "very old" whiskey valued at $14.

In 1879, his remains were moved from the family cemetery on the farm to Evergreen Cemetery atop a hill in Chester, the new county seat. Two years later Kaskaskia and the farm were swept downstream when the flooded Mississippi changed its course.

2nd Governor

Edward Coles
1786-1868

1786 – Born, Dec. 15, Albemarle County, Virginia.

1814 – Writes letter to Thomas Jefferson urging him to head an emancipation movement.

1815 – Travels west, buys land near Edwardsville.

1818 – Returns to Illinois, attends the constitutional convention.

1822 – Coles elected governor with only 33 percent of the vote as proslavery candidates split the majority vote; inaugurated Dec. 5.

1824 – Voters refuse to call a convention aimed at amending the 1818 constitution to allow slavery. Coles leads this victorious antislavery movement.

1830 – Makes a failed bid for Congress.

1832 – Moves to Philadelphia, Pennsylvania; continues his antislavery work.

1835 – Appointed head of Illinois' state board of canal commissioners.

1862 – President Lincoln signs the Emancipation Proclamation, Sept. 22; Cole's son Roberts, a slave-owning plantation owner in Virginia and Confederate captain, is killed in battle.

1868 – Coles dies on July 7.

Held office
December 5, 1822 to December 6, 1826

Edward Coles became governor by a minority vote only three years after he migrated to Illinois. He lacked rapport with the public and never attracted a personal following during the 11 years he lived in Illinois. But during his term in office Coles played the leading role in preventing Illinois from becoming a slave state. Only Thomas Ford, who became governor two decades later, did as much to influence the course of Illinois history.

In 1824 Governor Coles responded quickly to the legislature's proslavery majority order of a referendum calling for a constitutional convention that would have legalized the *de facto* human bondage that existed in early Illinois. Lacking power to veto the resolution, he assumed leadership in defining the issue, raised money for publicizing his views, and mobilized public sentiment against supporting the proslavery movement. In what had seemed to be a hopeless campaign, the cause of freedom triumphed – 6,640 to 4,972.

The Young Abolitionist

Enniscorthy plantation in Albemarle County, Virginia, was an unusual spawning ground for an abolitionist. John Coles, who had been a Revolutionary War colonel, and Rebecca, Edward's parents, moved in a social circle that included presidents and governors. Patrick Henry and Dolly Madison were their cousins. They had extensive property holdings, obtained in part through grants from the British crown. The Coles sons and sons-in-law were influential, and Isaac, one of Edward's brothers, had been called "the most perfect gentleman in America" when he was Thomas Jefferson's private secretary.

Edward Coles was born December 15, 1786, the eighth of 12 children in his family. His education – at Hampden Sidney College and then at the College of William and Mary – was impeccable. Bishops and professors taught that slavery might be wrong in principle but that it must be tolerated because of the difficulty of getting rid of it. Because of the "peltings and upbraidings of conscience," young Coles could not accept that reasoning. In a brief autobiography, he wrote decades later that "at William and Mary I imbibed the belief that man could not of right hold property in his fellow man and under this conviction determined to remove the chain of slavery and to emigrate to and reside with my colored people in one of the new states or territories." Shortly before graduation he was called home to help supervise the plantation during his father's final months. Soon he inherited 782 acres and 20 slaves. Had his father known that he planned to free them, they would have been bequeathed to someone else.

Upon hearing of his plans to free the slaves, Coles' shocked family begged him not to be impetuous. Virginia law required that freed slaves leave the state within a year, and the plantation could not be sold in the economic situation before the War of 1812. So Coles accepted James Madison's invitation to become his private secretary, in part because it provided an opportunity to collect information about the free country beyond the Alleghenies. A major item in antislavery literature is an 1814 letter in which Coles urged Thomas Jefferson to head a movement for emancipation of Virginia slaves and to "put into practice the hallowed principles contained in the renowned Declaration of Independence of which you are the immortal author." Jefferson declined because of advanced years but encouraged Coles to follow his own conscience. Three years earlier Coles had been the go-between who arranged the reconciliation of Jefferson and John Adams.

During his White House years, Coles never wavered in his determination to leave Virginia, as his autobiography reveals:

> The existence of war, and the difficulty of selling, and when sold, of collecting the money made me remain in this situation for six years. On peace being made, I resigned the secretaryship and set out for the western country to seek a permanent home in Ohio, Indiana or Illinois.

Coles Moves West

Accompanied by a slave, he traveled westward in 1815. That year he bought 6,000 acres near Edwardsville. "Were I a married man, I think I could set myself down and be very happy in the Illinois Territory," Coles wrote. "I do not think I am extravagant in my calculation when I say that $10,000 in the hands of a tolerably judicious man will in five or six years be worth $100,000 by the gradual and certain increase in the value of property."

A trip to Russia, made at Madison's request, delayed his settlement in Illinois. Traveling in the first American war ship to enter the Baltic Sea, Coles straightened out a misunderstanding with Czar Alexander I and then leisurely toured the continent and the British Isles.

On a second journey to Illinois in 1818, Coles carried a letter of introduction from President James Monroe to Ninian Edwards, the territorial governor, and attended the constitutional convention at Kaskaskia. He knew that some delegates wanted Illinois to be a slave state, but he didn't think it would happen.

National politics also was involved. In early maneuvering for the 1824 presidential election, Coles supported Treasury Secretary William H. Crawford as the most able (if least popular) man in a crowded field. Thomas Ford wrote that Coles was sent to Illinois to counteract the influence of Edwards, who favored John C. Calhoun.

Returning to Virginia, Coles finally collected the debt for the plantation sale. In a dramatic scene on two Ohio River flatboats lashed together, Coles announced to his blacks (two aged women had been left behind, with provision for their care) that they were free, immediately and unconditionally. He gave each family a quarter section of land. He hired some to work on his Edwardsville farm, while the others found jobs nearby or in St. Louis.

In Illinois, Coles was both a farmer and a federal official, for Monroe had appointed him receiver, or money collector, of the land office at Edwardsville. Courteous and helpful to land buyers, always well-dressed in a rough environment, he was soon known by reputation in much of the state. As the Bond administration drew to a close, slavery became a political issue, and in 1822 the aristocrat became a candidate for governor.

A Rocky, but Principled Governorship

Without public announcement, slavery advocates planned to call a constitutional convention after the 1822 election. Joseph Phillips was the choice of the dominant faction led by Jesse B. Thomas, one of the Illinois Territory's early representatives to Congress. Phillips was so confident that he would be elected the second governor of Illinois that he resigned from the Illinois Supreme Court in 1822. In a two-man race he would have defeated Coles easily, but political parties did not exist in the Old Northwest, and the two chief factions, both of which favored slavery, divided their vote between Phillips and another Supreme Court justice, Thomas C. Browne, backed by Ninian Edwards' supporters. A fourth candidate, James B. Moore, did little campaigning. The proponents of slavery were shocked by the outcome. With only 33 percent of the vote, Coles was elected by a plurality of 167 over Phillips. Together the two slavery candidates polled 59 percent. In his disappointment, Phillips left Illinois.

The new governor was a polished gentleman, tall, and handsome. But he was also stiff, slightly awkward, and he lacked personal magnetism. He did not consult legislators and opposition leaders about his plans for the state, and he never hesitated to be blunt when he criticized them in public messages. His inaugural speech was a diplomatic failure, especially in its outspoken treatment of the racial issue. Demanding justice and humanity for all, he asked that the indenture system and a black code be abolished, that the kidnapping of free blacks be stopped, and that freedom be granted to the descendants of slaves who had been brought to Illinois during the French period. Hooper Warren, the crusading editor of the *Edwardsville Spectator*, accused the governor of precipitating a crisis. And this was not altogether untrue: A week later a legislative committee recommended that a constitutional convention consider the governor's requests. The report did not specifically ask for legalized slavery, but the inference was clear.

By high-handedly reversing a contested election, the proslavery forces obtained the necessary two-thirds vote in the House of Representatives. Several hours after the final vote to reverse the representative's election, a raucous and alcoholic celebration broke out outside the governor's rooming house. John Reynolds, himself a leader in the anti-Coles forces, wrote in later years that the legislature's action "looked revolutionary, and was condemned by all honest and reflecting men."

Approval of the referendum to call for a new, proslavery constitutional convention seemed inevitable at the start of the unusually bitter 18-month campaign. Coles quickly met friendly legislators and issued a call to arms. In the campaign he worked long hours, wrote extensively, and contributed more than the $4,000 that was his four-year salary. Coles bought the *Illinois Intelligencer* and contributed almost weekly articles. Morris Birkbeck, who with George Flower had established English colonies on the prairie near the Wabash River, expressed regret that he could not pay for the printing of pamphlets he wrote under the name of Jonathan Freeman. Financial help and other pamphlets came from Nicholas Biddle, president of the Bank of United States, and Roberts Vaux of Philadelphia, whom Coles had known since his White House days. They emphasized that slavery was unprofitable and cruel, and quoted the opinions of men who had lived in the South.

In heavy balloting August 2, 1824, Coles' supporters cast 57 percent of the vote and won, 6,640 to 4,972. Had the result been reversed, Illinois would have been in turmoil for years: The proslavery faction undoubtedly would have written a Southern-style constitution and made every effort to put it into effect. With multiplying controversies, their attempt to override the Ordinance of 1787 – which had prohibited slavery in the Northwest Territory, that then included Illinois – would have been challenged in the federal courts and Congress. And the character of immigration would have changed, with Easterners hesitating to come to Illinois. As it was, pseudoslavery existed almost until the Civil War, and the black code was not repealed until the war was over. Had Illinois been a slave state, Abraham Lincoln probably would have launched his political career elsewhere.

Coles Faces the Fallout for Sticking to his Convictions

Thereafter, Coles encountered petty persecution. When he gave his slaves certificates stating that he was restoring their inalienable right to liberty, he had not known of a month-old law requiring a $1,000 bond for each free black to prevent them from becoming a public charge. Vindictive Madison County officials obtained a $2,000 judgment against the governor, but the legislature, which after 1824 had an antislavery majority, canceled the penalty. Supreme Court Justice John Reynolds, who presided at the trial level during the court hearing, had refused to admit Coles' evidence, ruling against him on all points. In other litigation, a libel suit was dropped, probably because the governor was anxious to go to court on the issue. The Senate meanwhile refused to confirm the appointment of Morris Birkbeck as secretary of state after he had served three months. The chamber had previously rejected Cole's nomination of William H. Hamilton for secretary.

Without success, Coles advocated tax-supported schools. During the 1825 legislative session, Senator Joseph Duncan, who would become governor in nine years, sponsored a bill that would enable counties to levy a tax to support free schools open to whites between five and 21 years. On paper, the law placed Illinois ahead of other states, but the bill contained an out clause: No person could be taxed for schools without his consent. Since no one would consent to be taxed voluntarily, Duncan's law was soon repealed. Schools continued on a subscription basis for 30 years.

Coles criticized the legislature for having created an uncapitalized and unregulated state bank and for allowing borrowers to postpone debt payments. The people would be better off, he said, if forced to rely on their own industry and economy.

Coles and his lieutenant governor, Adolphus Frederick Hubbard, an uneducated lawyer from Shawneetown, were opposites. When Ninian Edwards resigned from the U.S. Senate, Coles scornfully rejected two Hubbard schemes: that the governorship be turned over to Hubbard, who would appoint Coles to the Senate; or that Coles appoint Hubbard senator. Coles, who refused to "sneak into the senate," wrote that "the more I see and know of the politicians in this state, the less respect and confidence I have in them."

Hubbard sought revenge the next summer by claiming that the governor had forfeited his office by taking a trip east. Contending that he was the legal chief executive during the rest of the term, Hubbard announced the appointment of William Lee D. Ewing, a future governor, as militia paymaster general. Both the legislature and the Supreme Court rejected Hubbard's pretensions. Coles might have been unpopular, but his opponents were not ready to put an obviously unqualified man in his place.

When left alone to do his job, Coles was a detail-oriented administrator. He wrote his own state papers, including the copies that went into the archives, in a small precise hand. He gave close attention to details of state business, such as management of saline lands, the settlement of French claims at Peoria, the location of seminary townships, and revenues from school sections.

An Active Retirement Away From Illinois

After his term ended, the electorate snubbed Coles and his antislavery followers, but the losers in the 1824 referendum were rewarded with senatorships and other high offices. Almost to a man, the new leaders of the old Jesse B. Thomas faction lined up behind Andrew Jackson and benefited from his frontier popularity. Many of those who backed Coles on the slavery issue also were receptive converts to Jackson's Democratic Party.

The governor had lost friends in 1824 by supporting Crawford for the presidency. When the legislature elected a senator to succeed Edwards, Coles, who never wavered in his criticism of Jackson, received only four votes on the first ballot and one on the tenth. In his final candidacy, he ran for Congress in 1830 and finished third.

With no prospect for again attaining influential office, Coles left Illinois. In the autumn of 1832 he moved to Philadelphia, a city of culture where he had a widening acquaintance. A year later he married Sally Logan Roberts, 24, a member of a prominent Quaker family. They had two sons and a daughter.

When Governor Duncan visited Philadelphia in 1838, he went with Coles "to a literary club where I met many of the first citizens and spent a delightful evening." Three years earlier Duncan had appointed Coles to the presidency of the state board of canal commissioners, hoping that he could borrow $500,000 to complete the waterway. Because the state was unwilling to pledge its faith in repayment of a loan, Eastern investors were not interested in the canal.

As a private citizen, Coles maintained an interest in politics and corresponded extensively with public men, including historians and former presidents. One of his letters urged Madison to free his slaves. In 1854 he started a small flap with Stephen A. Douglas, who was arguing that extension of slavery into the terri-

tories should be left to popular sovereignty. Coles in an open letter insisted that the Ordinance of 1787 made slavery illegal in the
Old Northwest. Douglas published a vehement reply citing
Indiana and Illinois indenture laws and saying that, where it existed, slavery was local in character and not attributable to Congress.

Two years later, in a paper read before the Historical Society
of Pennsylvania, Coles replied:

> Of course, the continuance of the remnant of the French
> slaves for so long a time in Illinois rose from the fact of its
> being quietly acquiesced in, and not brought to the decision
> of the courts of justice. If the question had even been
> brought before me as governor of the state, I would not have
> hesitated for a moment to decide, and if necessary to have
> enforced that decision, that slavery did not legally exist in
> Illinois, and of course held all in service, as such, were enti-
> tled to their freedom. This opinion I expressed in my inau-
> gural address, and in messages to the legislature.

The former governor was wealthy, with a major part of his
income coming from valuable blocks in downtown St. Louis. At
one time he had title to 23 sections of bounty land in the Military
Tract, a favorite area for speculation by some governors. He was
paying taxes on part of it in his final years. Prairieland Farm in
Madison County covered 474 acres. Coles also owned 4,890 acres
in Missouri, a house and four lots in Edwardsville, and three houses in Philadelphia. At the start of the Civil War, he held leases on
holdings of nearly 1,000 acres in Virginia. Philanthropies included
longtime support of the American Colonization Society, which
sought resettlement of blacks in Africa.

In 1861, he closed his autobiographical letter by writing:

> The longer I live, the more I see and hear of the disgraceful
> proceedings of the present day, the more pleasing the con-
> solation I feel in reflecting on the efforts and agency I had in
> our succeeding efforts in the cause of freedom and against
> the curse of slavery and its expansion over the lovely state of
> Illinois. But I must stop, or my nervous headache, always
> made worse by writing, will drive me mad.

During his final years Coles wrote that he never expected to be happy again. His younger son, Roberts Coles, had bought a plantation in Albemarle County and had become a slaveowner. When the Civil War broke out, Coles wanted his son to return to Philadelphia or go abroad as a neutral. Instead, Roberts, as a Confederate captain, was killed in 1862 while defending Roanoke Island in unimportant fighting. Governor Coles lingered past his 81st birthday. He died July 7, 1868, but he lived long enough to know that all slaves had been freed.

3rd Governor

Ninian Edwards
1775-1833

1775 – Born, March 17, Mount Pleasant, Maryland.

1790 - 1791 – Attends Dickinson College.

1794 – Sent to Kentucky to look after his grandfather's holdings, quickly becomes politically active and is twice elected a state representative.

1803 – Marries Elvira Lane, a cousin; becomes a circuit judge.

1806 – Withdraws from congressional contest; becomes a member of the Kentucky Court of Appeals.

1808 – Becomes Chief Justice of the Kentucky Court of Appeals.

1809 – James Madison appoints Edwards governor of the newly created Illinois Territory, April 24.

1812 – Edwards calls for a referendum to make Illinois a territory of the second grade; voting rights are granted to all white males over 21 who pay taxes and who have lived in the territory over a year.

1812 - 1814 – Edwards serves disastrously in the War of 1812, leading an unimpressive campaign against friendly Native Americans; he is forced to allow officers from other territories to command troops in the Illinois territory.

1818 – Ends his term as territory governor; begins term as a U.S. Senator.

1824 – Resigns from the Senate in the wake of the "A.B. Plot," a smear campaign in which Edwards ("A.B.") charged Treasury Secretary William Crawford with gross negligence.

1826 – Becomes governor of the state of Illinois.

1830 – Retires from the office of governor.

1832 – Makes a failed bid for Congress.

1833 – Dies on July 20 in cholera epidemic.

Held Office
December 6, 1826 to December 6, 1830
(Territorial Governor April 24, 1809 to October 6, 1818)

The imposing Ninian Edwards was governor of Illinois for 13 years, nine as the presidentially appointed governor of the territory of Illinois from 1809 to 1818, and, beginning in 1826, four more years as the popularly elected chief executive of the state. In the interval he was U.S. Senator. Regarded by contemporaries as one of the great men of the Western country, Edwards was the leader of one of two early political factions in Illinois. A fluent orator and writer, he was an authority on frontier government and a businessman whose enterprises included farming, merchandising, banking, and land speculation. In addition, he was a man of compassion to whom the moneyless went for free medical consultation.

His term as the state's third governor came at the end of a controversial career. His popularity had peaked at the end of the territorial period, when he willingly surrendered his office and helped his constituents get the greater political privileges that went with statehood. Thereafter, he was less effective.

Though Edwards was a man of commanding appearance and superior intellect, he lost major battles with political rivals. He was pompous, vain – some thought him arrogant and overbearing – and he was guilty of errors in judgment. So part of his biography is a recital of failure to meet expectations. Nevertheless, John Francis Snyder, a 19th century physician and author, believed that Edwards was the most able man in Illinois.

Edwards as Kentucky Politician and Lawyer

In his native Maryland, the future governor was reared in an elite, intellectual household. He was born March 17, 1775, the oldest son of Benjamin and Margaret Beall Edwards, at Mount Pleasant, their farm home in Montgomery County. The father, a native of Virginia, was a merchant and farmer who served in the Maryland House of Delegates, represented his district in the state convention that ratified the federal Constitution, and was elected to a two-month vacancy in the Third Congress. His brother, John Edwards, was elected from Kentucky to both houses of Congress. His mother's family, the Bealls, were also an important Maryland family.

Young Ninian was educated by private tutors, one of whom was William Wirt, a future attorney general of the United States, and he attended Dickinson College for the 1790-1791 school year. Edwards was a member of the Dickinson class of 1792, though he did not graduate. Ninian Wirt Edwards, the governor's son, wrote that "it was required of the law class that they should read, for one-half of the time, history, but young Edwards having, under the instruction of his father, become a good historian, devoted that portion of the time required for that study to the reading of medicine."

Like many other seaboard planters, the Edwards family moved to better land in the newly opened West. When he was 19, the family sent Ninian to Kentucky to take charge of his grandfather's holdings and find land for other family members. In Nelson County, he opened and improved land, built distilleries and tanyards, and generally displayed a capacity for business. Beginning a political career, he was elected state representative before he was twenty-one and was reelected almost unanimously. In his early Kentucky period, young Edwards drank too much and became an unsuccessful gambler. He reformed and thereafter was opposed to gambling, profane swearing, and Sabbath breaking.

In 1799, Edwards moved to Russellville in Logan County, where he developed a law practice serving Kentucky and western Tennessee. He acquired more than 2,000 acres and became militia major and presiding judge of the General Court. In 1803 he became a circuit judge and married Elvira Lane, a cousin from Maryland. In 1804, as a presidential elector, he voted for Thomas Jefferson. Two years later, facing certain defeat, he withdrew from a congressional contest. In 1806 he was a member of the Court of Appeals, the highest in the state, and two years later advanced, at the age of thirty-three, to the chief justiceship. His prospects were for a long career of judicial eminence and increasing wealth in Kentucky, but his tenure as chief justice lasted only one year.

The Territorial Governor Takes the First Step Toward Statehood

When the Illinois Territory became separate from the Indiana Territory in 1809, John Boyle, one of Edwards' associates, was appointed governor and collected a $138.88 salary for twenty-one days. Then they traded jobs: Boyle resigned and became chief justice of the Kentucky Court of Appeals, and President Madison appointed Edwards to replace him, on the recommendation of Henry Clay, William Wirt, and Senator John Pope, an uncle.

Edwards, one month past his 34th birthday, was younger than any of the chief executives elected after statehood. Appointed for a three-year term, he was commander in chief of the militia, superintendent of Indian affairs, and superintendent of the government-owned salines that were the frontier's chief source of salt. A cousin, Nathaniel Pope, as secretary of the territory, was the new governor's right-hand man. Completing the official hierarchy were three federal judges with whom the governor shared legislative power. One was Jesse B. Thomas, an experienced Indiana-Illinois political in-fighter who for two decades would be Edwards' associate and rival. Each territorial governor received a 1,000-acre land grant, and Edwards, who arrived with his slaves and livestock herds three months after appointment, settled on the American

Bottom between Kaskaskia and Prairie du Rocher. He named his farm Elvirade, in honor of his wife.

Included in the welcoming speeches when Edwards arrived at the capital were pleas for patronage. These were followed by conflicting private advice as to who deserved preference. The governor, who hoped he would not have to become a partisan, retained civil employees who had received emergency appointments from Pope. For the militia, he canceled all appointments and proclaimed that company officers would be elected by the men and the regimental staff by the captains, with the understanding that he would commission the winners. It was both a means of involving the public in the democratic process and of avoiding tough decisions. His uncle, a Kentucky senator, told Edwards he should accept his full legal responsibility. Thereafter, Edwards made his own appointments and became the head of one of the two major factions in Illinois politics. In the new alignment, Jesse B. Thomas took over leadership of the anti-Edwards group.

The governor and the judges proclaimed that Indiana statutes not otherwise inconsistent would be effective in Illinois. To meet Western conditions, they followed the example of Indiana and did not hesitate to borrow from the codes of newer states, especially Kentucky, even though it was contrary to the guidelines of the Northwest Ordinance of 1787.

The governor solved the dilemma over the extension of suffrage to the Illinois frontier: a major factor in the march toward statehood. The law gave him responsibility for determining if and when a majority of the populace wished to advance to second-grade government, which would permit election of a legislature and a delegate to Congress. The Ordinance of 1787 permitted voting only by freeholders who owned fifty acres and had lived two years in the territory. That would have been obnoxious in Illinois, where the complexities of fraudulent land grant titles had delayed the sale of the public domain. As a result, settlement was largely by squatters, and only an estimated ten percent of the adult men could qualify as freeholders. In early 1812 Edwards called for an April referendum on the question of advancing to second grade government. It carried overwhelmingly. Then he waited five months before setting an October date for the election of the legislature and delegate. Meanwhile, at his request, Congress extended the right of suffrage in Illinois to all white males of twenty-one years who paid a county or territorial tax and had lived in the territory one year. As a result, Illinois was the most democratic of the territories, and Edwards had kept the richest men at Kaskaskia, John Edgar and Robert Morrison, from getting control of the legislature. Shadrach Bond won the position as delegate to Congress. Bond was not an Edwards' ally, but he worked with him.

Edward's Farcical War of 1812

During the War of 1812 it was important for Illinois to have a man in Washington. However, for Edwards the war was a personal disaster. He was both an alarmist who was afraid that white settlements would be overrun by Indian hordes and a patriot who spent his private funds to buy presents for Indian chiefs and help build blockhouses and equip mounted ranger companies. The governors of Indiana and Missouri also expected trouble, but Edwards overstated his case. In complex sentences and almost endless paragraphs, he sent letter after letter to Washington warning of attacks that never came. Secretary of War William Eustis trusted his own sources of information. Edwards believed that the Madison administration did not appreciate the situation, especially after a massacre at Fort Dearborn in which nearly 75 men, women, and children lost their lives. Meanwhile, the delay of his reappointment increased the governor's insecurity.

Edwards, who never forgot that he commanded the Illinois militia, was offended when William Henry Harrison, the hero of Tippecanoe, was made a brigadier general and given command of operations from Indiana westward. Accepting at face value rumors that at Lake Peoria, four days away, the natives were massing a large force, Edwards took the offensive. At Fort Russell, which guarded Edwardsville, he collected 350 rangers and mounted volunteers whom he personally led northward. Near Peoria they burned several villages, killed two dozen Indians, captured four others and eighty horses, and returned in eighteen days with one man wounded. Constituents were impressed, but not officials at Washington; the burned villages belonged to Jack Partridge, who had befriended the whites at Fort Dearborn, and Gomo, who had been an intermediary in diplomatic efforts to confine the Indians to a neutral role.

The governor came into even greater disrepute after he sent an expedition by boat to the small French settlement at Peoria. Captain Thomas Craig, an Indian-hater from Shawneetown, was ransacking the nearly deserted town when Thomas Forsyth, a highly regarded government agent, returned and assured Craig that the few Indians there were powerless and at least potentially friendly. A few days later, when a shot was fired at one of Craig's boats, the white force raided the settlement, destroyed considerable property, and took captive Forsyth and some forty Frenchmen. In midwinter they were released below Alton without food.

The administration soon showed its displeasure. Benjamin Howard resigned as governor of Missouri and, as a brigadier general, led a federal force into Edwards' territory. At Peoria he built the 100-foot square Fort Clark. Having forfeited his last chance for an army command, Edwards left Illinois to visit his family, which he had sent to Kentucky a year earlier for safety. He complained to Secretary of State James Monroe that during the war Madison had given him neither instructions on what to do nor thanks for arduous work. "I have not till the present time been one day absent from my post since the indians [sic] first commenced their depredations – and with a constitution very delicate indeed I do believe that I have since August last undergone as much fatigue and hardship as any soldier in the army," he wrote.

As hostilities ended and immigration speeded up, Edwards was appointed one of three commissioners to negotiate treaties on the Indiana, Illinois, and Missouri frontiers. With Governor William Clark of Missouri and Auguste Choteau of St. Louis as co-negotiators, he prevailed upon tribesmen to give up title to more than eight million acres, for which the Native Americans received $18,400. Fort Edwards, which had an eight-year existence on the Mississippi River at present day Warsaw, was named for the governor who never became a military hero.

On to Statehood

Friction between the federally appointed judges and other officials was common. In 1812 the governor suspected that his character was being besmirched, and he and Jesse B. Thomas were on the verge of a duel. There were complaints that the judges, holding court infrequently, were not earning their salaries. The judges retorted that frontier travel was a hardship. The legislature went to the extreme of passing laws to govern the jurisdiction and procedures of federal courts. Congress settled the controversy with a law that backed up the legislature.

To avoid charges that he was a tyrant, Edwards went out of the way to avoid vetoes. Nevertheless, as a matter of principle, the legislature in 1814 petitioned for abolition of the absolute veto. His only veto, which prevented the abolition of de facto slavery, was amazing for its inconsistencies. Edwards said he personally opposed slavery, but he refused to let the legislature abolish the indenture system under which it existed in Illinois. In practice, Edwards not only bought and sold indentured servants, but also rented out some people for their forced labor. Later, in the U.S. Senate, he voted for the Missouri Compromise of 1820, which let Maine enter the union as a free state and Missouri enter as a slave state. He held that extending slavery into Missouri would dilute its evil.

In 1818 the territorial congressional delegate Nathaniel Pope guided a measure to grant Illinois statehood through both houses. Once the enabling act passed, a constitutional convention convened on August 3, and finished its work 23 days later.

The Controversial Senator Edwards

Edwards' career as a United States senator was a disappointment. With the arrival of statehood, he and Jesse B. Thomas, old-time enemies, took for themselves, in what was a political deal, the two Senate seats. When the new legislature met, he was elected senator on the first ballot. Not until the fourth ballot did Thomas get the necessary majority vote of the two houses. Then Edwards' luck turned bad. When the two senators drew straws, Thomas won the six-year term, and Edwards had to stand for reelection in four months. By that time their political deal had expired, and Edwards barely defeated Michael Jones, an early land office official.

On patronage matters, President Monroe favored Thomas, who also got a prized assignment to the public lands committee. As slaveholders, both senators voted for the Missouri Compromise, which was sponsored by Thomas. The July 4, 1820 *Edwardsville Spectator* accused Edwards of a conflict of interest, saying he owned twenty-two blacks whom he had hired out in Missouri.

The senator, a land speculator, placed his private interests over those of his constituents when he opposed an 1820 law that reduced government land prices to $1.25 from $2.00 an acre and allowed purchases of eighty acres, half the previous figure. Because it abolished credit sales, Edwards insisted that settlers were being unfairly treated. He ignored the point that speculators did not want price-cutting by the government. Henceforth, that vote was used as a political issue against Edwards.

A controversy known as the "A. B. Plot," which for two years occupied the attention of federal officials and partisan newspapers, forced Edwards to return to Illinois as a private citizen. He caused trouble for himself by writing several *Washington Republican* articles that he signed "A.B." in which he accused Treasury Secretary William H. Crawford of malfeasance in his official dealings with unstable Western banks. Edwards, in 1818, had helped organize the Bank of Edwardsville and had used his influence to have it made a land office depository. Finding the bank in trouble, he resigned as a director in 1821 before the bank's failure cost the government $46,800. At the heart of the A.B. controversy was whether Crawford had been notified that Edwards believed government money should be withdrawn from the bank.

Politics at the national level was involved. In advance of the 1824 campaign, many regarded Crawford as the strongest candidate for president. As was customary, the two Illinois senators split, with Thomas backing Crawford and Edwards supporting John C. Calhoun, who was, not coincidentally, backed by the *Washington Republican.*

Edwards told the governor-historian Thomas Ford that he made the original charges against Crawford under a promise of support from President Monroe, Calhoun, Andrew Jackson, and John Quincy Adams. But when he was unable to get supporting evidence in the A.B. dispute, Edwards became unhappy in the Senate. He wanted to become minister to Mexico but Monroe nixed the idea. Adams later made the appointment. While Edwards was on his way to his new post, William H. Crawford told the House that he had never been advised of the Edwardsville bank's condition. Called back to testify before a House committee, Edwards proffered formal charges but could not substantiate them. When the committee exonerated Crawford, Edwards had no option but to resign his diplomatic post.

Edwards the State Governor

That Edwards could be elected governor in 1826, a watershed year, was a political miracle. Newer settlers had little interest in retaining the Edwards family in office. His record in the Senate was tainted. And after his ministerial position fell through, the state legislature – now dominated by his factional enemies – refused to send him back to the Senate. He had lost favor with President John Quincy Adams and could not expect another federal post. He could not run for Illinois' one seat in Congress because it was held by Daniel Pope Cook, his son-in-law and ally. The new Western hero was Andrew Jackson, whose followers were incensed because Cook had cast Illinois' vote for Adams when the House of Representatives elected the President in 1825. Edwards refrained from criticizing Jackson but was not accepted by the Jacksonians.

Like Edward Coles four years earlier, Edwards would have been defeated had the opposition centered on one candidate. Adolphus Frederick Hubbard, the unqualified lieutenant governor, insisted on running for governor, even though Thomas Sloo Jr., a state senator of good reputation but small acquaintance, was backed by a majority of the disorganized Jacksonian Democrats. Edwards won a single-handed, one-issue campaign by boldly telling the frontiersmen that his enemies were responsible for the state's financial dilemma. He blamed them for creating a worthless bank, for the law that required that depreciated bank notes be received at par for payment of taxes and other bills, for auditors' warrants worth one-third of face value, for an enormous state debt, and for a real estate tax system that would continue annual deficits. He won with slightly less than half of the vote, with Sloo finishing only 447 votes behind.

In office, Governor Edwards had a four-year running fight with the legislature, chiefly over the management of the Bank of Illinois, which it had established in 1821. His main opposition came from the 1826-1827 legislature, which a history published in 1874 called "one of the worst that has ever been inflicted on the state." (The unofficial "worst legislature" citation has been frequently awarded in most states, but not in Illinois in recent decades.) In his inaugural address he berated officers of the branch bank at Edwardsville, accusing them of fraud and perjury and recommending impeachment and trial. Specific charges followed in special messages that named some of the state's most powerful politicians, all enemies of the governor. Heading the list was Theophilus T. Smith, who was both a Supreme Court justice and cashier of the Edwardsville bank. Others named included Shadrach Bond, who had been governor eight years earlier, and Thomas Carlin, who would be in 12 more years.

The legislature exonerated the men involved. Today, it seems probable that Edwards had right on his side — Thomas Ford believed that the investigating committee was stacked — but the governor's belligerence and self-righteous air helped spoil his case. John Reynolds noted that Edwards was not gifted with prudence and tact. Ford criticized Edwards for the scatter-gun charges that weakened his case by naming some men of good reputation.

Edwards retracted some of his critical statements, so that his administration made some progress in straightening out the financial situation. The legislature passed a law that would tighten bank regulation. It also abolished five circuit judgeships and assigned the Supreme Court justices to do their work, an economy measure the governor advocated. Another law granted some relief to debtors; however, like Bond and Coles, Edwards protested.

His midterm message introduced a new States' Rights Doctrine. The verbose governor asserted that all public lands within its borders belonged to the state and that the federal government could only own land needed for forts, naval facilities, and necessary public buildings. Both Congress and the electorate ignored him but the legislature, just to be on the safe side, petitioned Congress to accept the governor's assertion.

Edwards the Man

During his busy political career, Edwards also carried on several business ventures. Historian John Moses called Edwards the foremost merchant in the state. He was said by his son to have established eight or ten stores at such places as Kaskaskia, Belleville, Carlyle, Alton, and Springfield, Illinois, and at St. Louis, Franklin, and Chariton, Missouri. Edwards also established saw and grist mills. To some extent, his business affairs suffered because he had to leave hired managers in charge for long periods. The agriculture of Illinois benefited from the improved breeds of horses, cattle, and sheep he brought to the state and from choice fruit trees, grapes, and shrubbery he imported.

Edwards moved from his Elvirade farm outside Kaskaskia to Edwardsville in 1818 and to Belleville in 1825. Belleville, which had been made the county seat in 1814 when it was only a cornfield, was one of his many speculations. The governor bought the townsite a few years later and offered to sell lots for $60, soon to be increased to $100, with special concessions to blacksmiths and other craftsmen. In addition to townsite speculations, some with his son-in-law Daniel Cook as a partner, he had heavy holdings in agricultural land that usually was offered for resale with hope of a quick, if not large, profit.

Edwards, who never was good at organizing campaigns and who never condescended to the common low arts of electioneering, made one more effort to re-enter public life. In 1832 he belatedly became a candidate for Congress and finished second in a three-man field.

Thomas Ford described Edwards as a large, well-made man, with a noble, princely appearance. He was credited with major virtues, among them humor, compassion, truth, and charity. He was an amateur doctor with a sizable charitable practice. When General Winfield Scott came to northern Illinois to fight the Black Hawk War, he brought along with his troops a cholera epidemic that spread down the Mississippi River and reached Belleville. Caring for stricken neighbors, Edwards refused to flee from his home. On July 20, 1833, the epidemic numbered the former governor as one of its victims.

The governor's first grave was at Belleville. He was twice reburied at Springfield, at Hutchinson's Cemetery in 1855 and at Oak Ridge Cemetery in 1866.

4th Governor

John Reynolds
1788-1865

1788 – Born, Feb. 26, Montgomery County, Pennsylvania.

1800 – Comes to the Illinois Territory with his family.

1812 – Serves as an advance guard for Gov. Edward's Quixotic Lake Peoria Indian campaign.

1816 – Becomes judge advocate of the militia's second regiment.

1818 – Defeated in a bid to become a constitutional convention delegate.

1818 - 1825 – Serves as a justice of the Illinois Supreme Court.

1823 – Makes unsuccessful bid for Senate.

1827 - 1830 – Serves in the 5th and 6th General Assemblies.

1830 – Defeats Lt. Gov. William Kinney, becomes governor.

1831 – Treaty of Chicago, the last Indian treaty pertaining to Illinois land, is signed.

1832 – The Black Hawk War precipitated when Black Hawk refuses to stay west of the Mississippi; after the war all Native American tribes are ordered out of Illinois.

1834 – Resigns governorship before his term expires to serve in the U.S. House.

1836 – Loses his bid for reelection to the U.S. House.

1839, 1840 – Wins elections to the U.S. House.

1853 - 1855 – Speaker of the Illinois House.

1858 – Loses election for superintendent of public instruction.

1865 – Dies, May 18, at his home in Belleville.

Democrat
December 6, 1830 to November 16, 1834

John Reynolds, the "Great Oddball" of Illinois officialdom, realized that he lacked the intellectual stature to serve as governor, Supreme Court justice, congressman, and speaker of the state House of Representatives. Still, he didn't let that stop him from running for – and winning election to – all those offices. A compulsive campaigner, the state's fourth governor also many times found himself on the short side of the vote tally.

Reynolds called himself the "Old Ranger," to remind people that he had served in the War of 1812. Highly prejudiced and a man of many idiosyncrasies, he avoided extreme positions in important political contests. Thomas Ford, a contemporary, described how Reynolds, a collector of friendships, adopted the protective coloration of frontier society:

> No one would suppose from hearing his conversation and public addresses that he ever learned more than to read and

write and cypher to the rule of three....He had been a farmer, a lawyer, and a soldier, a judge, and a member of the legislature. He had passed his life on the frontiers among a frontier people; he had learned all the bye-words, catch-words and figures of speech invented by the vulgar ingenuity and common among a back woods people; to these he had added a copious supply of his own, and had diligently compounded them into a language peculiar to himself, which he used on all occasions, both public and private. He was a man of remarkably good sense and shrewdness for the sphere in which he chose to move, and he possessed a fertile imagination, a ready eloquence, and a continual mirthfulness while mingling with the people.

Undereducated, eccentric, and opinionated, he normally espoused only policies that were popular among the frontiersmen upon whose votes he depended. However, on major controversies such as banking and finance, he cannily avoided future embarrassment by eavesdropping or cautious questioning when in the presence of his intellectual superiors. Hints thus acquired were translated into official policy with the result, all things considered, that he had a respectable administration. He wasn't an executive, but the state's shaky fiscal condition improved somewhat during his four years in office. It could have been worse.

The Rise of the Old Ranger

The future governor was born February 26, 1788, in Montgomery County, Pennsylvania, six months after his Protestant Irish parents, Robert and Margaret Moore Reynolds, landed at Philadelphia. He was soon taken to Tennessee, and reached Illinois when he was 12, driving one of his father's two teams of horses. The Reynolds were headed for upper Louisiana but settled outside Kaskaskia at the urging of a land speculator involved in the wholesale frauds. He spent part of his boyhood in the Goshen neighborhood east of Edwardsville, and a one-year stint at a seminary in Knoxville, Tennessee, got him a pseudoclassical education. Back in Illinois under the informal procedures of the pre-statehood period, he was accepted into the ranks of the attorneys. (Proving that not all self-schooled lawyers were of Lincoln's caliber.)

His law practice was unimportant, but he became well to-do early in life as an associate of a cousin, Joseph A. Beaird. Like many prominent men of his time, he speculated in land, apparently quite successfully, although he left no details. He did reveal that he had bought and sold two stores worth $10,000 each. Once he offered a $50 reward for an escaped slave, which could have indicated that he had been in the business of buying and selling blacks. He believed that slavery was morally and legally right.

His military career was long enough for him to have a service record and safe enough to ensure that he would one day live to be an *Old* Ranger. He was a member of a spy (advance guard) company on Ninian Edwards' unimpressive Lake Peoria expedition in late 1812. "I never fired a gun, as I saw no occasion for it," he recalled. He did confiscate a sack of corn, soon abandoned because it became rain-soaked, and he saw Governor Edwards unhorsed in a deep mudhole. Later he was a member of a Missouri-Illinois force that built Fort Clark at Peoria. He saw no action, but he wrangled a sergeancy for himself. Three years later he was judge advocate of the militia's second regiment, which was a political appointment. Thereafter, he was continually running for office, almost any office.

A Lifetime of Campaigning Begins

Reynolds hated many people, especially Jesse B. Thomas, who defeated him for election as a delegate to the 1818 constitutional convention. Reynolds went to the opening session of the General Assembly when officials were being elected. He probably would have taken a job as door keeper, but he was elected an associate justice of the Illinois Supreme Court, a $1,000-a-year job he claimed not to have asked for.

During his term as a Supreme Court justice (1818-1825), Reynolds took the unpopular side on one important issue. He joined the 3-to-2 majority in attempting to veto the 1822 bill that created a state bank that left the new state heavily in debt. Normally, he would have voted to please the great mass of uninformed voters who believed that the uncapitalized bank would insure prosperity. On other court business, the few opinions he wrote were undistinguished. Sitting at the trial level, he ruled against Governor Coles on all counts in the Madison County case involving bonding of freed slaves. On appeal, the other Supreme Court justices ruled for Coles.

Reynolds was denied reelection at the end of his Supreme Court term. When the legislature created five new circuit judgeships, his name was absent. Seeking both opportunity and revenge, he ran for the U.S. Senate in 1823, while he was still on the bench, but lost to Jesse B. Thomas, 16 to 26.

With nothing better being available, he then ran for state representative, losing once and winning twice. In the legislature his major interest was establishment of a state penitentiary and abolition of flogging and the pillory as punishment for crime.

The Governor

Considering the alternative, Illinois was fortunate that Reynolds, a "milk and cider" or moderate Jacksonian Democrat, was its fourth chief executive. In 1830, no more men of the caliber of Ninian Edwards, the retiring governor, were available. The "whole hog" Jacksonians wanted his successor to be Lieutenant Governor William Kinney, a convivial Baptist preacher whose administrative incompetence would be demonstrated when the legislature put him in charge of construction of state-owned railroads. Sued for funds he hadn't accounted for, Kinney left a bankrupt estate. By contrast, Reynolds' public and private lives were scandal free and his home life exemplary. He did not use alcohol, although he freely bought it to treat voters. For many of his virtues, credit goes to the bad example of his father, who once created a drunken disturbance in his son's courtroom and who, in the investigation of territorial land frauds, was indicted on 17 counts of perjury and forgery.

The choice was difficult. Kinney, who was said to have campaigned with a Bible in one hand and a bottle in the other, undiplomatically criticized church people who weren't Baptists. Reynolds never went to church and in his conversation was habitually profane, perhaps more so than any other Illinois governor. Because they expected Kinney to carry the state handily, the remnants of the Edwards faction and the Henry Clay Whigs did not enter a candidate. Reynolds won easily by virtue of the anti-Kinney vote.

In the 1830 campaign, Reynolds said he had always been against the disastrous state bank and, echoing Edwards, blamed Kinney and other bank officials for the heavy tax burden. In reply, the Jacksonians pointed out that he had borrowed from the bank. Reynolds allowed Edwards, a former enemy, to write his inaugural speech and thus passed up an opportunity to lead a movement for debt repudiation. He called for winding up the bank's affairs as rapidly as possible and set a precedent for Governor Thomas Ford's stand for fiscal responsibility 10 years later. In his book *My Own Times*, Reynolds said little in justification of his stands on this and other issues. If public sentiment was divided, he usually kept still.

In his messages to the legislature, like other governors, he was for education and public improvements. He did not stir up trouble by engaging in crusades, however. In 1830 he supported the proposition to build a canal from the Illinois River to Chicago over Kinney's protest that it would bring more Yankees to Illinois.

In the Black Hawk War, he waited to determine that expulsion of Indians was a popular cause before he called out the militia and asked for the help of federal troops. Accompanied by a staff of colonels, he used the commander in chief's prerogative to go along on two military expeditions into northwest Illinois. His personal bravery became suspect when a combined federal-state force of 2,500 men reached Vandruff's Island on which Indians might be concealed. Suddenly ill, the governor went below decks.

Reynolds did sign two Indian treaties. In the summer of 1831, he and General Edmund P. Gaines met with 30 Sac chiefs who confirmed an 1804 land cession and agreed to stay west of the Mississippi River. The next year he and General Winfield Scott signed the Treaty of Fort Armstrong that for all practical purposes ended the Indian occupation of Illinois.

An Early Departure to Greener Pastures

Reynolds left the governor's seat just days before the end of his term to begin an intermittent career in Congress. Writing of his service in Washington, John Quincy Adams in his diary called Reynolds untruthful, vulgar, and knavish. In his first term he switched positions on a tariff issue, ultimately opposing it. In 1836 he lost to Adam W. Snyder, a perennial rival. He was later elected again and served from 1839 to 1843.

During one of his out-of-office intervals, Reynolds lost $17,000 as the principal investor in the first Illinois railroad, a six-mile, wooden-railed line from the American Bottom bluffs, where he owned coal land, to the Mississippi River opposite St. Louis. It used horsepower and crossed a lake on a rickety bridge.

If Reynolds ever had been a statesman, he forfeited that rating in 1839. The legislature authorized Governor Thomas Carlin to borrow $4 million to finance the Illinois and Michigan Canal. Reynolds was totally unqualified for the assignment, but he talked Carlin into sending him to Europe as a special commissioner. With three associates, he made ill-advised and bungling deals that caused heavy losses to the state.

The European junket was a honeymoon tour at state expense for Reynolds and his second wife, Sarah Wilson, whom he had met while a congressman and married in 1836. She was tall, stately, and 20 years younger. He bought an expensive home for her in Belleville, where he had moved in 1831. His first wife, Catherine Manegle, daughter of Julien Dubuque, the Canadian Indian trader, had died in 1834 after 17 years of marriage. Reynolds, who had no children by either marriage, acted as a father to his first wife's three children.

Reynolds was elected for the last time when he ran for state representative in 1853 and was rewarded with the speakership.

The Old Ranger Passes On

In his later years, he became a prolific author whose chief talent was a remarkable if disorganized memory for names, faces, dates, and places. Two of his books have merit. *The Pioneer History of Illinois* (1852) ends with statehood in 1818. Reynolds got help for this volume from John Mason Peck and John Russell. *My Own Times* (1855) is an autobiographical sequel. Together they contain details not found elsewhere about settlement and people. The author's prejudicial thoughts about morals, religion, politics, history, and science fill a plotless novel, *The Life and Adventures of John Kelly* (1853). A trip to a New York exposition resulted in *Sketches of the Country* (1856). And he wrote *Friendship's Offering* in 1858 as a tribute to his friend Peck. Reynolds wrote rapidly and never corrected or interlined the words he scrawled on a pad held on his knee. Unemployed printers set books and occasional newspapers on a secondhand press in the law office in the back of his Belleville home. But Reynolds himself learned to set type and could quickly issue broadsides that gave his views on current events. His final book turned out to be *The Balm of Gilead*, a 48-page defense of slavery.

With the approach of the Civil War, Reynolds was a Copperhead who hated Stephen A. Douglas even more than he hated Abraham Lincoln. He openly sympathized with the South and blamed abolitionists and "black Republicans" for sectional strife. He ran for office the last time in 1858 on the Buchanan ticket as a candidate for superintendent of public instruction, finishing third and last. In 1860 he was a John C. Breckenridge delegate to the Democratic National Convention at Charleston but was denied a seat. During the war his outspoken support of secession attracted considerable attention, but old age and past prominence saved him from military arrest. He outlived Lincoln by a month.

Reynolds, an agnostic to his final hour, died of pneumonia May 18, 1865, at his Belleville home. When a minister called to tell the Old Ranger of his last chance for repentance, he contemptuously gasped, "The hell you say."

5th
Governor

William Lee Davidson Ewing
1796-1846

1796 – Born, March 1, Logan County Kentucky.

1818 – Reaches Shawneetown, Illinois.

1830 – Elected state representative, becomes speaker of the 7th General Assembly.

1832 – Elected state senator, is chosen speaker of the senate, serves until 1837.

1833 – Becomes acting lieutenant governor on March 1, when Lt. Governor Zodok Casey leaves his post to become a member of Congress.

1834 – Becomes governor on Nov. 17 when Reynolds leaves to serve in the U.S. House before his term expires; leaves office on Dec. 3 when Governor-elect Duncan is sworn into office; returns to his Illinois Senate seat.

1835 - 1837 – Serves as U.S. Senator from Illinois while also serving in the Illinois Senate. (He is appointed to fill the seat vacated upon the death of Senator Elias Kent Kane on December 12.)

1839 - 1843 – After defeating Lincoln for the speakership of the Illinois House in 1838, serves as speaker for the 11th and 12th General Assemblies.

1843 - 1846 – Is the auditor of public accounts (an office eventually dissolved by the 1970 Illinois Constitution and in 1973 resurrected as comptroller); dies in office, March 25.

Democrat
November 17, 1834 to December 3, 1834

Williiam Lee Davidson Ewing, governor for 16 days, completed the unexpired term of John Reynolds, who resigned as chief executive so that he could go to Washington as a newly elected congressman. Later Ewing was a United States Senator for two years, again filling a vacancy.

A friendly Scotch-Irishman who held an unusual sequence of public offices, mostly minor, Ewing was an attorney who lived in Vandalia and seldom practiced law. He had little to do during his half-month as governor. At the start of Governor Joseph Duncan's administration, he sent a message to the legislature that loyally followed Jacksonian doctrine by criticizing the Bank of the United States. Already reelected to the state Senate, he advocated another effort to establish a state bank but didn't say how it should differ from the disastrous Bank of Illinois created by the 1821 legislature. Loyalty to the Jackson political creed helped in his pursuit of patronage jobs and public office.

Ewing's Early Years

His signature read Wm. Lee D. Ewing, and he was named for his maternal grandfather, a general who was killed in the Revolutionary War. He was born March 1, 1796, in Logan County, Kentucky, the son of Finis and Margaret Davidson Ewing. His father, a Presbyterian minister, was one of four men who organized the Cumberland Presbyterian Church in 1810.

Details of his early life are vague, but the future governor seems to have become a lawyer before he reached Shawneetown sometime in 1818. Early in 1821 he was appointed one of eight trustees of Vandalia, the new capital. When the government opened a land office at Vandalia in 1820, Ewing was appointed receiver, a job he lost as the result of a robbery of the Bank of Illinois three years later. He kept two sacks of specie [coins] in his house because it was safer there than in any other house in town. Government regulations called for land office receipts, minus expenses, to be deposited in the Bank of Illinois at Shawneetown, which was a long way off. He then asked Ninian Edwards to help him get a government job as a surveyor in Iroquois County. Early in his Vandalia career Ewing married Caroline Berry, daughter of Elijah Berry, the first state auditor. They had six children, of whom two daughters reached adulthood.

The poverty of his early Vandalia years was not permanent. Ewing, who later lived in a good house in Vandalia, became a land speculator. There is a record that he bought 54 quarter sections and sold 101 in the Military Tract before 1833. Incomplete land office records about purchases would account for the discrepancy. In 1830 the census showed that he owned two slaves.

One of the few militia officers who performed creditably during the Black Hawk War of 1832, he was major of a spy battalion that did advance patrol work in pursuing Indians out of Illinois, across Wisconsin, and into the Mississippi River at Bad Axe.

The Career Path of a Seat Warmer

In a unique political career, he was elected speaker for three of the terms he served in the Illinois House of Representatives. The path upward started in 1826 with two terms as clerk of the House. He then was elected state representative in 1830 and senator in 1832.

Not only did Ewing back into the governorship – he did so absolutely. Ewing was not elected lieutenant governor, but as

Senate leader he was next in line when Lieutenant Governor Zodok Casey resigned after his election to Congress. Then, when Governor Reynolds resigned for the same reason, Ewing became governor for half a month, after which he automatically resumed his seat in the Senate.

He was appointed to fill Illinois' U.S. Senate seat upon the death of Elias Kent Kane on December 12, 1835. Late in 1836, when more influential Democrats wanted to assure a future vacancy in the Senate, Republican Abraham Lincoln and a group of anti-Jackson men perversely maneuvered Ewing's reelection. True to form, he lost that Senate seat in two years, but almost at once returned to the Illinois House to serve two terms as speaker. Again without interruption, he was back in his starting job as clerk of the House in 1842. He soon prevailed upon his colleagues in the legislature to elect him state auditor, a position he held until his death on March 25, 1846.

Perhaps Ewing's greatest political triumph is that he twice defeated Lincoln for the speakership of the Illinois House. The first time, in 1838, the Whigs had a nominal majority, but three were absent and party discipline not being important, several from neighboring districts found reason to vote for the Vandalia resident.

A few months later, when he was trying to prevent the removal of the state capital to Springfield, Ewing called Lincoln a "coarse and vulgar fellow" and a "low and obscure colleague." Today, of course, Governor Ewing is not so easily remembered, while the vulgar Mr. Lincoln is somewhat less obscure.

6th Governor

Joseph Duncan
1794 - 1844

1794 – Born, Feb. 22, Paris, Kentucky.

1812 – 1814 – Served in the War of 1812.

1824 – Elected to the first of two terms for the Illinois Senate.

1826 – Elected to the first of four terms in Congress.

1831 – Begins his service as a major general in the Black Hawk War.

1834 – Elected governor while in Washington.

1837 – The legislature votes to move the state capital from Vandalia to Springfield, March 3; A mob in Alton kills Elijah P. Lovejoy, editor of the abolitionist paper, the *Alton Observer.*; Financial panic of 1837 hits the state, severely hampers the internal improvements initiative to build railroads and the Illinois and Michigan Canal.

1838 – Ends his term as governor.

1841 – Federal government sues Duncan, the signer of a surety bond for his brother-in-law, for losses resulting from his brother-in-law's defaults.

1842 – Runs as the Whig nominee for governor; gets 45 percent of the vote.

1844 – Duncan dies, Jan. 15.

Whig
December 3, 1834 to December 7, 1838

Joseph Duncan, the only Whig governor of Illinois, was elected in absentia by voters who assumed that he was still a Democrat. The four-term congressman stayed in Washington until after the 1834 election, made no campaign speeches, and still won with 54 percent of the vote in a four-man field. Meanwhile, he had changed from an admirer to a critic of President Andrew Jackson, an act which caused Duncan to suffer politically and financially.

Like Jackson, Duncan was a Western man with a military background. He might have had a long career as a Jacksonian Democrat, but he refused to be stampeded by the great Western mass movement that swept Jackson into the White House in 1828. Instead, in Washington, the Democrat found himself more comfortable as a follower of John Quincy Adams and Henry Clay.

Duncan did not publicly announce that he was changing parties. The political leaders got the message when Duncan voted to override vetoes of bills to improve the Wabash River and the Chicago harbor and defied Jacksonian policy by introducing an amendment to recharter the Bank of the United States. But, the informality of election procedures and the slowness of frontier communication permitted Duncan's surprise election. Congress did not adjourn until July 1, and then his wife's illness delayed their return to Illinois until after the election one month later. Not until inauguration day December 3 did the rank-and-file realize that the new governor was a Whig – not the reliable Jackson man they thought they sent to Washington. At the time, a formal Whig Party organization did not exist in Illinois.

After Duncan's election, Jackson supporters – the lineal descendants of Thomas Jefferson's Democratic Republicans – organized their Democratic party at the state level. Thereafter, they made certain that election-day support centered on a single slate of candidates. With Jackson's name as their inspiration and Stephen A. Douglas as their tactician, Democrats controlled Illinois politics for two decades, until party alignments were fractured by the uproar over slavery that brought on the Civil War.

The new governor denied that he was an apostate, saying he held steadfastly to the principles on which Jackson was first elected in 1828. Duncan still believed in one-term presidencies, in economy and reform, and in keeping the spoils system out of government. But the legislature, dominated by Jacksonian Democrats, was even more unfriendly than it had been toward Coles, Edwards, and Reynolds.

Among the governors of Illinois, Duncan deserves honorable mention for his opposition to ill-timed and expensive programs for the construction of state-owned railroads and the chartering of another state bank that brought on Illinois' severest financial crisis. Time soon demonstrated that he was the best of the four men in the campaign for governor. Had the voters realized that Duncan was not a true Jacksonian, William Kinney, the "whole hog" extremist whom John Reynolds had defeated for governor four years earlier, would likely have been elected. Thomas Ford, who defeated Duncan for the governorship in 1842, held a high opinion of the man. Ford said that the Whig governor "had a sound judgment, a firm confidence in his own convictions of right, and a moral courage in adhering to his convictions which is rarely met with."

Military Service and Early Political Career

Born in Paris, Kentucky, on February 22, 1794, the future governor was the third son of Joseph and Anna Maria McLaughlin Duncan, Virginians of Scotch and Scotch-Irish lineage. His father, an army major who had built a 20-room stone inn among the log cabins at Paris, died when Joseph was 12. Three years later, his mother married an army captain who died in two more years. His older brothers had been educated at Yale and at Transylvania University in Kentucky, but instead of going to college, young Joseph assumed responsibility for his mother's finances. At 21, he was appointed guardian for his sister and two younger brothers.

At the start of the War of 1812, he enlisted in the army and in a council of war voted to defend Fort Stephenson, which had been ordered abandoned. Later he commanded a detachment that kept a British force in Canada under winter surveillance.

He migrated to Illinois because an uncle and a brother had ties to Territorial Governor Ninian Edwards. His uncle, Robert K. McLaughlin, had been appointed territorial treasurer. At Edwards' request, Joseph's brother Mathew, a Kentucky newspaperman, printed the Illinois territorial laws. Mathew Duncan then moved to Kaskaskia, edited *The Herald*, and published the first book printed in Illinois. At Brownsville in Jackson County, Joseph Duncan farmed and operated a mill. Before statehood he was appointed a justice of the peace. Governor Bond commissioned him a major general of militia, an honor both military and political. His formal education had been limited, but Duncan radiated intelligence and leadership qualities. Erect, taller than most men, he had dark eyes and striking features.

Midway in the Coles administration he was elected state senator, where he introduced the first bill for free common school education for all children. Duncan was a director and later president of the 1821 state bank's branch at Brownsville. A report during the Edwards administration showed that he had borrowed $2,000 from the bank and repaid $275. Other officers and directors had similar records.

In 1826, as a comparative newcomer, he challenged Edwards' son-in-law, the popular Daniel Pope Cook, by running for the state's only seat in Congress. He won easily, and as a Jackson man had no difficulty winning three more terms. In Congress he served on the public lands committee and gave his attention to Western causes such as preemption, early completion of surveys, sale of the public domain at low prices, and the prohibition of tollgates on the National Road.

During his first term, at a dinner given by President Adams, the Illinois congressman met socialite Elizabeth Caldwell Smith, a semi-invalid, who was four-feet, five inches tall. In her diary she wrote that Henry Clay told her that Duncan "was not only a good looking fellow but was a good son and brother, having taken care of his mother and educated his sister and two brothers." The next year they honeymooned in Illinois and established their residence at Jacksonville, where Duncan ordered construction of the first frame house.

In 1831, the first year of the Black Hawk War, on Governor Reynolds' appointment, as a major general Duncan commanded a mounted militia force of 1,500 that destroyed an abandoned Indian village near Rock Island. Congressional duties kept him from participating in the second year of the war.

The Split With Jackson

Early in the Jackson administration, Duncan began to have doubts about the man for whom he had campaigned in 1824 and 1828. He was disappointed in Jackson's cabinet, and he objected to the president's appointment of a Tennessee man to superintend the Galena lead mines. Duncan, who had rigid views about keeping politics out of civil service, refused to endorse his brother's application for a federal job as an Indian agent. The congressman continued to believe in single terms, economy and retrenchment, and governmental reforms. He was disappointed when the president abandoned his original causes in the process of mobilizing public opinion behind new programs. Duncan thought that rechartering the Bank of the United States, which Jackson vetoed, was essential to the nation's economy. He returned to Illinois and, more than a year in advance, announced that he was a candidate for governor in 1834.

In the election, Jackson supporters split their strength between two "whole hog" candidates. A Belleville caucus backed William Kinney, while a group at Vandalia entered Robert K. McLaughlin, Duncan's uncle, a lawyer who had been territorial and state treasurer, served in both houses of the legislature, and married a niece of Shadrach Bond. An unimportant fourth candidate was anti-Jackson. Backed by Whigs and "milk and cider" Democrats, the absent Duncan won easily.

Building Infrastructure in a Faltering Economy

At his inauguration the governor criticized Jacksonian doctrine, advocated tax-supported education, and said that "to keep the government poor, and the people rich, is a political maxim which ought never to be forgotten." Much of the speech expressed concern about a grassroots demand that the state enter the transportation and banking businesses. When the legislature disregarded his advice, financial disaster followed. The period of prosperity marked by optimism and inflated real estate prices at the start of the Duncan administration was followed by the Panic of 1837, caused when President Van Buren restructured the over-inflated easy-credit banking system.

Of the three expensive projects undertaken during his administration, Duncan favored only the Illinois and Michigan Canal, connecting the Illinois River with Chicago, which had been advocated by all governors since Shadrach Bond. In his inaugural address, Duncan asked for a waterway wide enough for steamboats to pass, with the federal government to provide financing through a larger land grant or a direct appropriation. Congress never helped, but before the economic crash, the legislature put up enough money for digging to start at Bridgeport on July 4, 1836. During the financial crisis, Edward Coles, the former governor, could not borrow funds in the East because Illinois had not pledged its faith for repayment. Later, Duncan paid his own way to New York in a partially successful effort to raise funds.

Duncan opposed the 1837 internal improvements legislation under which Illinois undertook construction of an extensive network of state-owned railroads. The Supreme Court justices joined him in a veto that was promptly overridden. Duncan believed in railroads as well as the canal, but he insisted that the work be done by private corporations and that the state's participation be limited to purchase of part of the capital stock. With the onset of the 1837 panic, Duncan urged a special legislative session to repeal the internal improvements law. The lawmakers ignored his advice, which Duncan repeated at the end of his term.

Had the other members of the Council of Revision supported him, he would have followed Shadrach Bond's example and vetoed an 1837 bill that, repeating the 1821 mistake, chartered another State Bank of Illinois. Because Andrew Jackson had put the Bank of the United States out of business, Stephen Douglas and other Democrats in Illinois supposed that Duncan would approve state banks. The governor, accepting the Whig doctrine that the United States needed a well-regulated national banking system, announced in his inaugural message that he would look with disfavor upon another state bank. With the help of some Democrats, the state bank bill was barely passed by inconsistent

Whigs, chiefly from the Alton area, who hoped to become rich by diverting Mississippi River trade from St. Louis. Bank stock soon sold at a premium and the belief spread that dividends could pay for the projected canal and railroads. Duncan approved an investment of not more than $100,000, but shortly before the crash the legislature raised the state's share of bank capital to $2 million.

The panic forced the closing of state banks, and Duncan placed the blame on former President Jackson. His final I-told-you-so message to the legislature reminded the state that it would not be in financial trouble if his banking and internal improvement recommendations had been followed. When he took office, the state debt was $217,276. Four years later it was $6,688,784, and the retiring governor couldn't be blamed.

Duncan as a Temperate, Anti-Abolitionist

Duncan was consistent in a conservative stand on the slavery question. He denounced as outrageous the murder of Elijah Lovejoy, an abolitionist editor, but simultaneously blamed the violence and discord on antislavery agitators. He was ready to resign as a trustee of Illinois College under the impression that the president and most professors were abolitionists, but he was told it was not true. He held that "it is wrong, morally and politically, for any citizen or public institution to teach or advocate doctrines or principles in this country which cannot be carried into practice peaceably without violating the constitution of the United States, or forcibly without civil war." The 1820 census listed Duncan as owning two slaves in Jackson County.

The abolitionism issue was involved in a dispute that led to efforts by Duncan and others to organize a second Presbyterian church at Jacksonville. When it failed, he transferred his membership to Pisgah. For years he was a trustee of Illinois College. He was the first president of the board of trustees of the Illinois Institution for the Education of Deaf Mutes. A prohibitionist, Duncan regretted the "dreadful ravages and baneful effects of intemperance." During his four years as governor, he donated half of his $1,000 salary to support an Illinois temperance paper.

Another attempt for the Governor's Office

In the 1838 election the Whigs ran Cyrus Edwards who narrowly lost to Thomas Carlin. But in 1842, the Whigs nominated Duncan again for governor, largely in a play for the Mormon vote, which two years prior had gone to Whigs. Missouri Democrats drove Joseph Smith from that state, and the Mormons founded Nauvoo on the Illinois side of the Mississippi in 1839. As the city grew — by 1845 it would be the state's largest city — it obtained incredible political power. Its city charter, granted by the legislature in 1840, gave the city unique rights, such as the power to make laws contrary to the state and federal constitution, the ability to raise its own militia, and annexation authority. Even so, Governor Carlin honored requests from the Missouri governor to have Smith arrested. But, Democrats in the judiciary saved Smith from extradition. The Mormon leader urged Mormons to vote Democrat in 1842. The Whigs countered by nominating Duncan, perhaps as an appeal to tradition. But when Democratic candidate Adam W. Snyder died just prior to the election, the Democrats ran Thomas Ford, a Supreme Court justice who had no connection with recent Mormon controversies. Thus, Ford won their vote.

A Riches to Rags Retirement

Before and during his term as governor, Duncan was wealthy as a result of years of land speculations. No record of his total holdings has been preserved, but Duncan's daughter said he had personal investments "in Chicago, Sandusky, Michigan City, Jacksonville and lands through out central Illinois." He also was involved in the promotion of villages that never became cities. He paid $450,000 for a quarter interest in Oquawka, which was platted after the Black Hawk War. He also invested in Illiopolis, Marshall, and Warsaw. As the geographical center of the state, Illiopolis was promoted as a possible successor to Vandalia as the state capital in 1837, but there has been no intimation that the governor used his official position in an effort to gain financially.

Ongoing federal litigation came to a head to cloud the 1842 gubernatorial campaign. His only sister, Polly Ann, had married William Linn, a personable scoundrel who, while Duncan was in Congress, was appointed receiver at the Vandalia land office. Duncan also appointed his brother-in-law as a canal commissioner. (Democrats criticized him for that inconsistency in his views on patronage.) Because he had signed Linn's bond as one of nine sureties, the governor was liable when Linn defaulted on land office collections. That gave the Jackson administration the opportunity to punish Duncan for turning Whig, and in 1841 three federal court judgments totaling $76,714 were issued. During litigation that dragged on for several years, Duncan claimed that Linn had been appointed to a second term after discovery of the defalcation (which Abraham Lincoln in an 1839 speech said totaled $55,000). Not knowing of the shortage, Duncan had signed a second bond. Apparently the result of official connivance, the other sureties turned out to be insolvent, and Duncan was sued for the entire amount.

Claiming he was being persecuted, Duncan in 1841 said that he had been put to the expense of defending four suits in federal courts, two of which were appealed to the Supreme Court, and asked "that I may be allowed to pay the debt without ruinous sacrifice of our property in times like the present." But the government insisted on forced sales that, at depression prices, wiped out Duncan's fortune. Court records no longer exist, but a daughter wrote that the government realized only $35,000 when:

> thousands of acres of the best and most carefully selected lands in Illinois were sold at 10¢ an acre. Some of the handsomest residential property in Jacksonville was sold at $3 or $4 a lot, and nearly forty acres comprising Duncan's Addition to Chicago, now in the heart of the city, were sold at from $5 to $7 a lot.

Survived by his widow and seven children, Duncan died January 15, 1844, in his Jacksonville home after a short illness. Except for a trust fund, he left his widow penniless. Two decades later the Duncan family was resisting efforts in court to break the trust. Mrs. Duncan, who was remembered as "a delicate, kindly little lady, always dressed in black silk and lace, and always expecting to be waited on," once sold a cow so that a daughter could attend a St. Louis concert by "the Swedish Nightingale," Jenny Lind. The former first lady lived until 1876.

7th Governor

Thomas Carlin
1786-1852

1786 – Born, July 18, near Fankfort, Kentucky.
1821 – Becomes first sheriff of Greene County.
1825 - 1833 – Served in the Senate in the 4th - 7th General Assemblies.
1831 - 1832 – Captain of Greene County militia companies in Black Hawk War.
1838 – The first Democrat nominated at a state convention, Carlin wins gubernatorial election.
1840 – Nauvoo Charter gives the Mormon settlement unique rights, including the right to raise its own militia, to make laws contrary to the state and federal Constitution, and to annex surrounding territory.
1844 – Loses an election to Congress to Stephen A. Douglas.
1849 – Serves an unexpired term in the state legislature.
1852 – Dies, Feb. 14.

Democrat
December 7, 1838 to December 8, 1842

Two years after Andrew Jackson left the White House, Illinois Democrats, accepting the advice of young Stephen A. Douglas, began holding nominating conventions and finally elected a governor who was a "whole hog" Jacksonian. Thomas Carlin, a farmer who barely won the 1838 election, was an uncompromising partisan. Since he wasn't a party leader and hadn't recently been involved with state government, he couldn't be held responsible for the mistakes of the previous few years. Thus he was the first guinea pig testing out a briefly held Democratic theory that nonleaders make preferred candidates. The theory was valid with the election in 1842 of Thomas Ford, who was one of Illinois' great governors, and in 1846 of Augustus C. French, who was adequate. Carlin, however, rates at or near the bottom of the roster of chief executives.

The first convention-nominated governor, Carlin has been characterized as honest but ignorant by two historians, Theodore C. Pease and R. Carlyle Buley. John F. Snyder, a contemporary, said Carlin was "not brilliant." Other writers made a point of crediting him with nonintellectual virtues, but no one dissented from the basic premise that he lacked the background and capacity to govern a major state, especially one in financial difficulty. His personal integrity and his complete loyalty to Jackson were never questioned. Baffled by the complexities he faced, Carlin accepted

conflicting advice that led to shifting policies. Both content and literary style indicate that his state papers were written by a changing cast of advisers.

Carlin, a muscular man with sandy hair, a thin face, and fair
complexion, was the last of the Indian-fighter governors. In the
War of 1812, he had been a member of a spy company on Ninian
Edwards' Peoria expedition. In both years of the Black Hawk War
he was the captain of Greene County militia companies that did-
n't see action.

Joseph Gillespie, an Edwardsville judge with a long memory,
recalled that Carlin had great physical prowess and personal
courage, that he was always ready for a rough-and-tumble fight,
and that as a fine horseman, woodsman, and marksman he was an
invaluable member of frontier society. "He was always intensely
proslavery, or at least Negro-hating," Gillespie concluded. "He
hated banks and he was suspicious of Yankees, unless they were
Democrats."

The Road to the Governorship

Of Irish ancestry, the future governor was born July 18, 1786,
near Frankfort, Kentucky, the son of Thomas and Elizabeth Evans
Carlin. The family moved to Missouri in 1803. Carlin's father died
seven years later, leaving his widow and seven children, of whom
Tom was the oldest. Educational opportunities were limited, and
he did not learn to read during his boyhood. He came to Illinois
in time to serve as a mounted ranger in the War of 1812, married
Rebecca Huitt in 1814, built a log cabin opposite the mouth of the
Missouri River, and operated a ferry for four years. He was the
first sheriff when Greene County was organized in 1821.
Carrollton, the county seat, was located on his property, and he
donated land for public buildings. He served two terms as state
senator and in 1834 was appointed receiver for the land office at
Quincy, where he lived during his term as governor.

Carlin was the Democrats' second choice for governor in
1838. The first Democratic convention nominated James W.
Stephenson of Galena, a land office official who withdrew when it
was discovered that his accounts were delinquent. As a good
Jacksonian, Carlin promised in the campaign that rigid compli-
ance with bank charter requirements would be profitable for the
state. He was against monopolies and wanted the state to own and
operate all railroads. The Whig candidate, Cyrus Edwards, a busi-

nessman at upper Alton who was the youngest brother of the former governor, ran as a friend of internal improvements and lost by 926 votes, the closest a Whig candidate came to carrying the state.

Inconsistent Treatment of the Mormons

Carlin, who had joined in a bipartisan welcome to Mormon refugees from Missouri, routinely signed the charter that gave almost unlimited local governmental powers to Joseph Smith and his associates at Nauvoo. Later, he approved Missouri warrants for the extradition of Smith as a fugitive from justice. Smith, who did not suspect that trouble was ahead, was arrested a few hours after he had been treated with respect when he called at the governor's home. The political and legal situation surrounding the Mormon controversy was increasing in complexity when the time came to transfer responsibility to Governor Ford.

Infrastructure Financing Pulls State Into the Red

The departing Governor Duncan recommended scrapping the 1837 internal improvements program that provided public funding for waterway improvements and the Illinois Central Railroad system. But, Carlin optimistically opened his administration by ignoring the financial panic that had closed banks and stifled commerce. He had vague reservations about a large-scale railroad program on which the state had spent $2 million, but he was confident about the future. The public wanted railroads, the legislature agreed, and projects totaling $1 million were added to the transportation program. Within a year all hands, including the governor, realized that it was impossible for the young state to finance and construct that many railroads. Reversing his position, Carlin called a special session of the legislature that abandoned the internal improvements pipe dream but left a stupendous debt.

The Illinois and Michigan Canal to Chicago required bond financing, and the 1839 legislature authorized the governor to borrow $1 million. Duncan ignored a Whig suggestion that he negotiate with financial houses. Not knowing how to get the capital, Carlin appointed former Governor John Reynolds to be his official agent in Europe. But Reynolds used a European junket more as a vacation than as a mission to find financial backers. At Philadelphia and in Europe, the incompetent Reynolds borrowed money on unfavorable terms, with the state losing more than $150,000 on two transactions. One contract was with the London banking house of Wright and Company, which went bankrupt while Carlin debated whether he should approve it. Illinois' financial condition sunk even lower when the state sold bonds with a face value of $804,000 for only $261,500, their current market value. The selling of these bonds, the Macalister and Stebbins bonds, remained a political controversy for nearly 20 years. Because of money woes, canal construction was suspended in 1842.

The Jacksonian governor blamed the state bank and the Bank of Illinois at Shawneetown for his financial headaches. In his inaugural message he warned that banks become enmeshed in politics, resist regulation, encourage speculation, and add to the hardships of frontier farming. The state bank came under the control of Whigs, who lost money by investing in Alton interests. When there was bipartisan support for state purchase of an additional $3 million of stock in expectation that dividends would pay the entire bill for canal and internal improvements interest, Carlin warned against it and was supported by the Senate committee on banks. As a partial solution, the General Assembly levied an inadequate one-mill property tax to be applied to bond interest.

An Undistinguished End

Four years as governor made Carlin a pessimist. His final despondent message to the legislature again blamed the banks for economic ills that Duncan had traced to Jackson's veto of the Bank of the United States and his order that settlers must pay for their farms with gold or silver. Because it wasn't Democratic party policy, Carlin recommended that Illinois not accept a share of the proceeds from federal land sales. However, he wanted Congress to donate more land for the canal. He didn't know how the interest on the state debt could be paid, since taxes were unpopular and therefore couldn't be increased. The message, a jumble of inconsistencies, recommended that the legislature repeal the charters of the state and Shawneetown banks. Carlin had promised Thomas Ford, the incoming governor, that he would not ask for the repeal. Ford wrote that his predecessor "had not the genius to see how money might be raised to complete it [the canal] except by petitioning Congress for an increased donation of land, then certain never to be granted."

Out of office, Carlin returned to Greene County and spent the rest of his life as a farmer. Still ambitious politically, well in advance of the 1844 election, he announced he was a candidate for Congress, but he lost to Stephen A. Douglas who had been a late entry. Victory that fall sent Douglas into national politics. Carlin threatened to run against him in 1846 but thought better of it. His final political appearance came in 1849 when he served an unexpired term as state representative.

Survived by his widow and seven of 13 children, Carlin died at home February 14, 1852.

8th Governor

Thomas Ford
1800 - 1850

1800 – Born, Dec. 5, Uniontown, Pennsylvania.

1823 – Admitted to the bar.

1841 - 1842 – Served on the Illinois Supreme Court.

1842 – When Democratic gubernatorial nominee Adam W. Snyder dies, Ford becomes the substitute nominee because he is thought to be the candidate least offensive to the large Mormon voting bloc; he wins the election with 53 percent of the vote; Ford realizes that debt must be retired and the economy must grow, so work on the Illinois and Michigan Canal resumes after a hiatus.

1844 – Mormon leader Joseph Smith, being held in a Carthage jail, is shot by a mob. This is the climax of increasing unrest between the Mormons and their neighbors who charge the Mormons with abusing annexation powers, counterfeiting, and polygamy.

1846 – Ford gathers six Illinois regiments for the Mexican War; the Nauvoo Mormons leave the state in the spring.

1848 – Illinois adopts a new state constitution.

1850 – Dies, Nov. 11.

1854 – Ford's history, *Illinois from its Commencement as a State in 1818 to 1847* is published.

Democrat
December 8, 1842 to December 9, 1846

Governor Thomas Ford, a man of unusually sound judgment and integrity, solved frontier Illinois' biggest problem. He saw how the massive internal improvement debt could be paid, and, despite considerable opposition from within his own party, he dominated the legislature and made possible the state's future solvency. Debt management was his great accomplishment, and for it he ranks alongside Edward Coles, the other great governor of the pre-Civil War period.

He was neither an administrator nor a leader of the Democratic party, and on his scrawny shoulders rests part of the blame for the assassination of Joseph Smith, the Mormon prophet. Like Coles, he was not a politician, and he had no talent for negotiation and compromise. At times he was indecisive, vacillating, diffident, stubborn, and opinionated. Nevertheless, his critics conceded that he had been right about three major issues: that a compromise be reached with the unpopular banks; that provision be made for completion of the canal to Chicago; and that, to show its good faith, the state should dedicate a special property tax to the eventual payment of the massive debt incurred during preceding administrations. He was an able jurist, one of the best in Illinois. He reasoned clearly and might have had a long, eminent career on the Supreme Court, if he had not transferred to the executive branch.

Scarcely five and a half feet tall, he was by no means charismatic. Homely features included a sharp nose bent slightly to one side. His voice was squeaky. Charles Ballance, a Whig lawyer who became mayor of Peoria, wrote that at his inauguration Ford had begun to read his speech "when his voice failed and he sank down upon the seat or table upon which he was standing" while another man picked up and read the message clearly.

Ford's second great contribution was authorship of an Illinois history that, based on his personal observation, covers the first three decades of statehood and survives as a remarkable treatise on governmental philosophy.

From Pennsylvania to the Illinois Supreme Court

Ford was born December 5, 1800, near Uniontown, Pennsylvania, and reared by his twice-widowed Irish mother who seems to have had unusual native intelligence, energy, and ambition for her large family. The former Elizabeth Delaney's first husband was killed in a coal mine accident. Little is known about the second husband, Robert Ford, who disappeared, presumably killed by highwaymen, in 1803. Desperately poor, she took her seven children to St. Louis the next year to find that the Louisiana Purchase had spoiled her hope of obtaining free land west of the Mississippi. Then she made a home at New Design in Monroe County. There the future governor, a bright lad, walked three miles to his first school. However, to the impoverished family, the boy's education was less essential than his wages as a farm laborer and a servant in a country tavern.

Ford's half brother George Forquer, who was six years older, acted as Ford's foster father and political sponsor. A successful lawyer and eloquent speaker, Forquer served in both houses of the legislature, held such appointive positions as secretary of state and attorney general, and was defeated by Joseph Duncan when he ran for Congress. In that campaign, Ford entered politics by writing anti-Duncan newspaper articles.

For one term Ford studied law at Transylvania University in Kentucky, until Forquer's business failed. The future governor walked back to Illinois, did farm work, taught school, and studied law under Daniel Pope Cook, a pioneer lawyer who became the state's first attorney general, a member of Congress, and the namesake of Cook County. After admission to the bar in 1823, he worked briefly for a pro-Jackson paper at St. Louis. Thereafter he practiced law at Waterloo and at Edwardsville, where in 1828 he married Frances Hambaugh, a fifteen-year-old. They moved to Galena where he failed to establish a law practice and failed again when he was a candidate for justice of the peace. He held a minor position as a member of a commission to establish the state's northern boundary. Much of his time had been spent at Vandalia, especially when the legislature was in session, and over the years such jobs as committee clerkships had given him a thorough knowledge of the details and background of Illinois government and politics.

Forquer rescued him from Galena in 1830 by getting him appointed and re-appointed state's attorney for the Military Tract district. Ford, who had moved to his father-in-law's farm near Versailles in Brown County, was recognized as a top-grade lawyer when he served as one of three defense counsels in the 1833 impeachment trial of Supreme Court Justice Theophilus W. Smith, who was acquitted. When Forquer became a state senator, Ford was promoted and served two terms as circuit judge and one on the Chicago Municipal Court. In 1841, when the Democratic legislature increased the membership of the Supreme Court from four to nine, one of the openings went to Ford. Assigned to the northern district, he moved to Oregon in Ogle County, where he lived for two years. All his public positions had been in northern or western Illinois. He had never been a candidate for county office, the legislature, or Congress.

The Unruly Puppet

Ford, who had never been involved with litigation or legislation concerning the controversial Mormons, became the Democrats' substitute nominee for governor in 1842. The Mormons had been Whig supporters two years earlier, but Joseph Smith decreed that they should vote for the Democrats, whose nominee for governor was State Senator Adam W. Snyder. A member of the Democratic inner circle, Snyder died in May, 1842, three months before the election. Public sentiment had begun to turn against the Mormons, and the Whigs saw a chance for their candidate, former Governor Joseph Duncan. Ford was given the Snyder vacancy on the theory that any other Democrat probably would lose. His chief asset was that little in his record could be attacked by Duncan. He received 57 percent of the vote, and Democrats won big majorities in both houses of the legislature.

The new governor knew that he was an outsider in his own party. In his *History of Illinois,* he wrote that he was nominated

> because I was believed to have no more than a very ordinary share of ambition, because it was doubtful whether any of the leaders could be elected, and because it was thought that I would stand more in need of support from leaders than an actual leader would. To this cause, and perhaps there were others, I trace the fact that I was never able to command the support of the entire party which elected me....After my election I ascertained that quite a number of such leaders imagined that they, instead of myself, had been elected; and could only be convinced to the contrary on being referred to the returns of the election.

Fiscal Policies

Ford's *History* gives details of the enormity of the financial problems and the legislature's inability to solve them without the guidance of a strong executive. The governor began by rejecting the final recommendation of Thomas Carlin, his predecessor, that the legislature cancel the charters of the state bank and the Bank of Illinois at Shawneetown. Ford wanted to avoid any action that might alarm the far-off financiers from whom additional loans would be needed.

The state couldn't afford to buy postage stamps. Its credit had been exhausted in the accumulation of a debt – Ford itemized it at $15,187,348.81 – for the unfinished Illinois and Michigan Canal to Chicago, the disastrous project for state-owned railroads, and other expenditures. The new governor estimated that not more than $200,000 or $300,000 of good money was circulating in the state. The settlers and business firms were in debt. No one wanted to pay taxes and few could. In that climate, the Democratic party hadn't taken a stand on debt repudiation.

The new governor believed that if he had done nothing, repudiation would have been automatic, with the result that settlers would avoid Illinois and that the state's economic development would be delayed. He was convinced, as he stated in his inaugural message, that somehow principal and interest must be paid in full. He had confidence in the people and the future of Illinois, and he assured creditors that the money could be raised in due time by moderate taxation.

For the 1842-1843 legislative session Ford drafted a compromise bill that allowed the two banks to surrender their charters after exchanging state bonds, auditor's warrants, and scrip (worth 14 cents on the dollar) for depreciated bank stock. The trade, which extinguished $2,306,000 of the state's debt, was introduced as an administration measure and passed with Whig support. The governor and auditor were authorized to sell land and property acquired during the internal canal and railway-building improvements experiment. Reversing a Carlin policy, Illinois accepted from the federal government its share of the proceeds from land sales. Two boards that had been created by the 1837 legislature and which were in large part responsible for the debt were abolished. The governor was empowered to borrow $1.6 million to complete the canal. Negotiations for the loan were started in New York and Europe, but first Ford had additional work for the legislature.

In a letter to an opponent of debt payment through taxation, Ford urged that the state preserve its honor by levying a permanent tax, part of which would be used to reduce and eventually pay off the debt. The plan, which according to Ford was authored by Justin Butterfield, a Chicago attorney, was widely printed in Eastern and Illinois newspapers and commended by canal bondholders and the public. The new legislature approved a mortgage arrangement that had been reached. Eastern financiers loaned the money and controlled both construction and operation of the canal until toll collections retired the debt. Under the agreement the bond holders named two members of a board of trustees, and the governor served as the third.

In a situation that would be repeated many times in Illinois, the reluctant legislature passed the tax bill only because the governor said that the action could not be avoided under the existing circumstances. Looking back, he could point to mammoth results. The new levy on property enabled the state to pay its bills and set aside revenues to pay interest on the debt. Construction of the canal was resumed, and its opening in 1848 helped speed up the growth of northern Illinois. The property tax requirement was written into a new state constitution adopted in 1848. Collection of tolls provided a new revenue source. Other features of the Ford program enabled the state, so long as it operated frugally, to pay its bills. By the time the debt was paid off, a tradition of Spartan government was deeply ingrained in Illinois.

The Mormon Problem

Ford received considerable criticism for his handling of another major problem. It involved law enforcement, especially in Hancock County, where he left Joseph and Hyrum Smith at the mercy of unfriendly militiamen. The climax came on June 27, 1844. Fearing violence, the governor had gone to Carthage, the county seat, where he had been asked to call out the militia to aid in the arrest of Mormon officials who had destroyed an opposition newspaper. Already on hand were 2,500 armed men, western Illinois Democrats and Whigs who were united in their hatred of the bloc-voting Mormons. Ford swore them into the militia, lectured them about the sanctity of the law, and asked for and accepted their pledge that the accused Mormons would not be molested.

Having received the governor's promise of protection, the Smiths and several other Mormon leaders surrendered at Carthage. Ford, who believed that the executive should not interfere in judicial matters, stood by when an anti-Mormon justice of the peace did not follow the letter of the law when new charges were filed against Joseph Smith and his brother Hyrum. When Ford marched to Nauvoo to look for evidence of law violations, the Smiths begged to be taken along. Instead, they were left behind, supposedly guarded by unfriendly militia companies that did not prevent their murder. Since then, all Mormon historians have held the governor responsible for the deaths of the men whose safety he had promised.

Until the Mormons left for Utah two years later, Illinois government could not maintain law and order in the territory around Nauvoo. To his credit, Ford tried, but at the end of his term he reported to the legislature:

> No leading man of either party could be arrested without the aid of an army, as individuals of both parties were justly afraid of surrendering for fear of being murdered; and when arrested, each trial was likely to end in a civil war, and...as a

conviction was impossible, the administration of criminal justice was completely at an end, whilst the Mormons remained in the country.

Murder, arson, and lesser crimes were common where the Mormon and anti-Mormon factions were seemingly equal in armed strength and mutual hatred. Several times the Ford administration sent in militia parties that restored a temporary quiet. Determined that the murderers of the Smiths would be brought to justice, the governor employed lawyers to collect evidence, obtain indictments, and prosecute the ringleaders. Both outside and within the courthouse at Carthage the anti-Mormon sentiment was so rabid that verdicts of acquittal ended trials for murder and press destruction. Because of factional rivalries, some Democratic leaders failed to cooperate in efforts to enforce the law. Twice Ford sent General John J. Hardin, a Whig, into Hancock County with volunteer groups. The first expedition forced cancellation of a "wolf hunt," which obviously would have resulted in casualties among rural Mormons. The second briefly established a truce after a Mormon force was driven from the courthouse at Carthage. After Hardin and other leaders had left for the Mexican War and the evacuation of Nauvoo had been started, a "Mormon War" continued and a force assembled by Ford could not prevent cannon fire. Volunteer negotiators from Quincy managed to arrange a final cease-fire.

Governor Ford was continually under criticism, frequently by both factions in the Nauvoo area as well as by Whig newspapers elsewhere in Illinois. In his *History* he admitted that his power was inadequate but insisted that his efforts were correct and his critics unfair. In his defense, some Whigs volunteered statements that the governor was doing everything possible to keep the Mormon controversy under control. The Mormon custom of bloc voting, usually for Democratic candidates, added to the factionalism. Some militia officers who were Democrats declined to assume commands when Ford found it necessary to recruit volunteers for peace-keeping missions. The governor commended prominent Whigs, especially Hardin, for answering his calls for assistance.

Other Law-and-Order Problems

Lawlessness was not confined to the Mormon settlement. At the close of the frontier period, state government was too weak to enforce the criminal code in other border areas where elected officials could not cope with wide-scale crime. At times, after appeals for help, members of the law-abiding element took the law in their own hands, not always successfully.

In far-off southeastern Illinois, horse thieves, counterfeiters, and robbers long had terrorized the Massac and Pope counties region, where the militia refused to turn out when the governor ordered them to assist the presumably honest faction among local officials. General John T. Davis, who had been ordered to investigate a situation involving rival gangs, supposedly calmed the situation, but trouble broke out again. In 1846, Supreme Court Justice Walter B. Scates was threatened with lynching after several regulators were indicted. At the end of the Ford administration, law enforcement in Massac County was unfinished business.

At the outbreak of the Mexican War in 1846, Ford called for enlistment of three regiments, the Illinois quota. The response was enthusiastic, and eventually three more regiments were formed with the War Department's permission. There were mix-ups, however, for which the governor received some blame. While he was away from Springfield, he accepted companies without notifying his office, with the result that some acceptance orders had to be canceled. In other counties, Ford was blamed because the sheriffs did not enforce the militia law, which was falling into disuse. He vacillated and left the decision to an arbitration board when Colonels Hardin and E. D. Baker both claimed seniority.

The Pauper Historian

Proving his honesty, Ford was financially destitute when his term ended. Refusing to run for other office, he returned to his father-in-law's farm and spent three years writing a history of Illinois in a vain hope that royalties would support his five children. Then he went to Peoria to practice law but again met failure, with poor health a contributing factor. His last illness was diagnosed as tuberculosis.

He died November 11, 1850, at Peoria, a month after his wife had died of cancer. Anonymous acquaintances paid for their last illnesses and burial. He was first buried in the city cemetery but was later removed to Springdale where the state erected a monument in 1895. A brief document described as an autobiography said the governor became a Methodist a few weeks before his death.

Thomas Ford's tragedies continued into the next generation. His five children depended on the charity of friends and neighbors. The governor's two sons, believed to be horse thieves, were hanged by Kansas vigilantes.

Before his death, Ford asked U.S. Senator James Shields to arrange for publication of his masterpiece, *A History of Illinois from its Commencement as a State in 1818 to 1847.* The book was on sale by 1854. Because of its caustic and outspoken criticism of public men, Shields or the publisher reportedly excised more than half of the manuscript, which is regrettable in view of Ford's personal knowledge of the men and events he wrote about. The surviving chapters tell in detail of his troubles during the two legislative sessions he served as governor. Lyman Trumbull and Stephen A. Douglas, future United States Senators of eminence, were among those he criticized with questionable fairness. Be it noted, however, that Ford had reason to dislike many leaders of his party. Other writers and other documents also have exposed many of them, in and out of the legislature, to equally harsh criticism. Errors and misjudgments, if such they be, are more than counterbalanced by the vast amount of information and opinion presented by a scholar who lived in Illinois during the first three decades of statehood and who played a major role in part of the events he wrote about. He has been frequently quoted and cited in this book.

Much of what Ford says about politics and politicians, about government, and private citizens is applicable to other time periods and to other states. The governor wrote compactly, forcibly, and precisely. Even if he wrote with cynicism, his book has been recognized as a superior analysis of American politics and one of the most important volumes printed in Illinois before the Civil War.

9th Governor

Augustus Chaplin French

1808 -1864

1808 – Born August 2, at New Chester (now Hill), New Hampshire.

1831 – Admitted to the bar.

1832 – Teaches at Little Prairie school west of Albion, Illinois.

1837 - 1841 – Serves in the 10th and 11th General Assemblies.

1846 - 1848 – Illinois sends six regiments to the Mexican War.

1846 – Compromise candidate French easily defeats Whig Thomas M. Kilpatrick who didn't attempt a campaign for the office.

1848 – A new state constitution grants greater powers to the governor: sets gubernatorial elections on a schedule coincidental with presidential elections: makes all state and county offices subject to popular election; French wins a four year term when the Whigs fail to run real opposition against him.

1851 – Illinois Central railroad is chartered.

1858 – Loses election for superintendent of public instruction.

1862 – Represents St. Clair County as a delegate to the constitutional convention. Voters fail to ratify this constitution.

1864 – Dies, Sept. 4.

Democrat

December 9, 1846 to January 8, 1849

January 8, 1849 to January 10, 1853

Augustus Chaplin French was a compromise candidate at the Democrat's 1846 state convention, but he became the first two-term governor. As Illinois outgrew its frontier period, French performed a great service by not deviating from Thomas Ford's recipe for slow repayment of the public improvements debt through taxation. Succeeding governors followed his example, and both parties became committed to strict economy and eventual solvency. French himself was a string-saver, a tight-fisted Yankee whose habits of personal economy made it possible for him to educate his orphaned siblings. Stories of his stinginess became legendary, and in his image Illinois government developed a tradition for parsimony.

As for his two consecutive terms as governor, that was a loophole. Like the original Illinois constitution of 1818, the new constitution of 1848 limited governors to single four-year terms. It also decreed that state elections should be synchronized with presidential balloting, beginning in 1848. Since it seemed unfair to dismiss the popular incumbent in midterm, he was elected to four more years, for a total of six. He was the only governor reelected until after the Civil War.

From Lawyer to Lawmaker

Born August 2, 1808, at New Chester (now Hill), New Hampshire, he was the oldest of six children of Joseph and Eunice Dickerson French. In 1827, at his widowed mother's deathbed, he promised to rear and educate his siblings, which presumably he did.

About that time he abandoned his original given name, Aram. If he briefly attended Dartmouth College, which he is reputed to have done, officials there have no record of him under either name. His middle name "Chaplin" is also a small source of controversy. It's spelled "Chaplin" in his daughter's family papers, but there are variant spellings of his middle name.

He did read law in the office of a judge at Gilmanton, New Hampshire. In 1831 he was admitted to the bar and promptly headed westward. The next year as Augustus French he was in Illinois, teaching at the Little Prairie school west of Albion. By 1833 he was at Paris, four counties northward, and active in politics. On his second try, the legislature elected him circuit attorney for the Wabash River district. He served as a colleague of Abraham Lincoln and Stephen A. Douglas in the tenth General Assembly and was reelected to the eleventh. Douglas' friendship might explain French's political advancement thereafter. He began by volunteering to be the Democratic nominee for lieutenant governor, which was unsuccessful but at least gave him some name recognition. Before the end of his second legislative term, President Martin Van Buren appointed him receiver for the land office at Palestine, Crawford County. There he lived and had a fairly good law practice, but he was little known in most of Illinois. Ford's *History* says that French was a member of a group of "regulators," who took law enforcement in their own hands by whipping and expelling a troublesome band of thieves and counterfeiters.

In 1839 French married Clarissa Kitchell of Palestine, who died two years later after giving birth to a son who soon died. The future governor in 1843 married Lucy Southworth at West York. They were parents of three sons and two daughters.

The Compromise Candidate
Becomes a Six-Year Governor

In advance of the 1846 Democratic convention, no one regarded French as a leading gubernatorial possibility. Cautious and rather colorless, French resembled his immediate predecessors, Thomas Carlin and Thomas Ford, in that he was neither a political leader nor an administrator. Among six Democratic candidates, he alone came from eastern Illinois, which had been neglected by Democrats. Lyman Trumbull, whom Governor Ford and numerous other Democrats disliked, led on the first ballot, with French second. After the third ballot, the other four candidates withdrew in a stop-Trumbull movement. One story is that Congressman O. B. Ficklin feared that French would run against him in the Wabash River district and promoted him for the governorship without any idea that he would be nominated.

At their first state convention, the Whigs nominated a superior candidate, Thomas M. Kilpatrick of Scott County, who as state senator had been a leader in a movement for public schools and helped Governor Ford pass the debt reduction legislation. Because of the Mexican War, the Whigs were unpopular and Kilpatrick did not attempt a campaign. For the first time, more than 100,000 people cast votes in a gubernatorial election, with French receiving 58.2 percent. The highest-ranking Whig winner in Illinois was Abraham Lincoln, the new congressman in the Springfield district.

Two years later the Whigs virtually failed to enter state and local tickets, and handicapped the almost-successful campaign to carry Illinois for Zachary Taylor. Names of Whig and Liberty Party candidates were on the ballots, but French polled 86.6 percent. In the legislature, the Whig minority was smaller than usual.

Of medium height and sandy complexion, French wasn't an orator, and in private conversation he combined a New England taciturnity with a penchant for telling preposterous stories in which he often professed to be the hero.

The Governor's Conservative Fiscal Policies

The governor approved enactment of a series of laws that refunded the state's debt, including accrued interest. Thus, he helped establish the state's reputation for fiscal integrity. French corresponded frequently with the state's financial agents in New York and London, and he asked for a constitutional amendment that would allow the state to buy its bonds at a discount with tax revenues. Because the public distrusted the legislature and felt that the state should not profit from under-par transactions, the voters defeated the proposed amendment. In 1851, also at the governor's suggestion, homesteads were exempted from taxation.

The New England-born governor accepted the anti-bank prejudices of Jacksonian Democrats, who wanted business transacted only with gold and silver coins. In 1848, French was reelected on a platform that advocated the outlawing of both banks and paper money. At the 1849 legislative session, the first under the new state constitution, French announced that he would veto any general banking law. Two years later, after election of more bank men from northern districts, the legislature voted to license free or stock banks that could accept deposits and circulate paper money backed by bonds deposited with the state auditor. French did indeed veto the bill, but the legislature passed it over his veto. In the Senate Joel A. Matteson of Joliet, a Democrat who would be the next governor, cast the deciding vote on the paper money bill. In the 1851 referendum, the bank law was approved as a result of strong support from the growing northern districts.

The Governor's Self-Interested Push for Railroads

On French's recommendation, the state sold the Northern Cross railroad at a 90 percent loss. But this was just one facet of the governor's interest in the state's involvement with the railroad industry.

The governor, a land speculator, for several years had actively but unsuccessfully opposed the concept of "state" policy, a provincial belief that Illinois railroads should stay within the state and not serve cities on the other side of the border, especially St. Louis. The governor could not influence the legislature, which repeatedly refused to issue a corporation charter for a cross-state railroad from Cincinnati via Vincennes to St. Louis. French, who reportedly had a financial interest in that road, joined other opponents of state policy at a giant mass meeting at Salem and called a special legislative session at which he recommended enactment of a general law on incorporation of railroads. The legislature insisted on retaining the power to issue charters and fix termini, and the railroad into St. Louis wasn't authorized until French's two terms had ended.

Since Cairo, Galena, and Chicago were within Illinois, there was no state policy objection to the north-south Illinois Central line that opened the east central counties to settlement. After Stephen A. Douglas reached the U.S. Senate in 1846, Congress granted 2,595,000 acres to the state. On the governor's recommendation, the land was turned over to a group of Eastern capitalists who promptly constructed the world's longest railroad. Under the charter, the governor became an *ex officio* member of the Illinois Central board of directors. French did not miss the opportunity to speculate by buying government land, which in some cases was available for 12.5 cents an acre, along the projected lines.

In the developing Western country, most governors had been speculators who bought heavily at government land offices, often at bargain prices, as a result of acquisition of bounty warrants issued to veterans of the 1812 and Mexican wars. New opportunities developed with the railroad era, and French not only acquired land that would increase in value when rail service arrived, but he also had a financial interest in at least one railroad. He presided at a meeting at Charleston of incorporators of a road that would extend from Springfield to Terre Haute, Indiana. Along its right-of-way he owned 3,840 acres near Vandalia. French's two successors also were involved with railroad promotions. Such interests were not unusual and were less obvious than the pressures on the legislature to grant special charters to corporations, a practice begun during the Reynolds administration.

Law and Order and Social Policy

French had little more success than Ford in dealing with lawlessness in Massac and Pope counties, where so called regulators enforced mob rule. The legislature in 1847 created a district court with venue powers intended to produce unbiased jurors. That law proved ineffective, but the situation slowly improved.

Like several of his predecessors, French recommended better common schools, for which public sentiment had been increasing. The legislature responded with authority for local districts by a referendum to levy a tax to build schoolhouses and hire teachers. It did not provide state financial support. In his inaugural message, French also said that the state should provide for its insane. The legislature established an asylum in 1847 and a blind school in 1849, both at Jacksonville. French did not take sides on the slavery issue when the principle of the Wilmot Proviso, which was intended to prohibit human bondage in territory acquired from Mexico, was approved by the legislature in 1849 and disapproved in 1851. He also avoided a controversy when he had an opportunity to appoint a U.S. Senator after the discovery that the Irish-born James A. Shields had not yet met citizenship requirements.

Instead, he called a special session of the legislature that marked time until Shields was eligible.

The Retired Statesman

Upon retirement, Governor Matteson appointed French to state bank commissioner. He moved to Lebanon, where he was a law professor and a member of the board of trustees of McKendree College. Twice more he sought public office. In 1858 Newton Bateman defeated French for superintendent of public instruction. In 1862 he was a St. Clair County delegate to a wartime constitutional convention.

French died September 4, 1864 and was buried in College Hill Cemetery.

10th Governor

Joel Aldrich Matteson
1809-1873

1809 – Born Aug. 2, near Watertown, New York.

1843 - 1853 – Serves in the Illinois Senate.

1847 – State Senator Matteson helps pass a bill that allows citizens to turn in certificates of state indebtedness (such as canal scrip) in exchange for state bonds.

1850 – Organizes Merchants and Drovers Bank at Joliet.

1852 – Wins the governor's chair.

1855 – Lincoln sways the legislature away from electing Matteson U.S. Senator.

1856 – The governor begins redeeming outdated and/or previously redeemed canal scrip for state bonds.

1859 – The scrip scandal begins to unravel.

1863 – Sangamon County Circuit Court rules that Matteson owes the state $253, 723.77.

1873 – Dies, Jan. 31, in Chicago.

Democrat
January 10, 1853 to January 12, 1857

Joel Matteson was a business executive with a great talent for making money legitimately. But his biggest personal accomplishment was avoiding prison after the 1859 exposure of the Great Canal Scrip Fraud, the biggest governmental scandal in Illinois' first century. A never-completed investigation placed a $388,528 price tag on Matteson's fraudulent exchange of 20-year-old scrip for new state bonds. No one believed his alibi, but he had political clout. He avoided prosecution by paying back part of the money he said he hadn't stolen.

Matteson, who was the last Democratic governor for 36 years, was an efficient chief executive whom the public admired and trusted. Unlike his predecessors, he was neither a lawyer nor a farmer. Like most of them, he was a land speculator who invested in unsettled areas out of confidence that valuations would keep pace with the tide of immigrants. Primarily, he was a businessman, the owner of several banks, and the promoter and manager of railroads. He made sizable contributions to the economy of a state that needed banks and railroads. Like a few other prominent businessmen, he also had a successful career in politics. The voters did not regard him as a politician, however, in part because public speaking was not one of his major talents, but also because he skillfully avoided factionalism. He resembled Augustus French, whom he succeeded, in that he advanced few causes and got along well with the legislature.

From Farm Boy to Financier

Joel Aldrich Matteson, the son of Elnathan and Eunice Aldrich Matteson, was born August 2, 1809, on a farm near Watertown, New York. He attended a country school. As a young man, he owned a small store across the Canadian border, attended a seminary, taught school, operated a farm given him by his father, worked on construction of South Carolina's first railroad, and toured as far west as St. Louis. Upon his return home he married Mary Fish. When he was 25, he migrated to Illinois with his wife and their first child. On the way he made money by selling a wagonload of boots and shoes.

Matteson made money easily. In the Chicago land boom, he bought the southwest corner of Clark and Washington streets for $200 and doubled his money in a few days. He bought 869 acres of government land in Kendall County and the following winter lived alone on the lonesome prairie. Just before the Panic of 1837, he sold out at inflated prices and moved to Joliet. Soon he was a town trustee and leading citizen. He became one of the contractors who dug the Illinois and Michigan Canal. Possibly he accepted the canal board's 90-day scrip so that he need not interrupt work on the Aux Sable aqueduct and viaduct project. (When the government could not pay its bills it issued scrip – essentially IOUs – that could be redeemed later.)

When Illinois abandoned its grandiose plans for internal improvements, he bought 700 tons of railroad iron and sold it at a profit to the builders of the first railroad in Michigan. He operated a woolen mill that was Joliet's largest industry. He owned a store, founded the first bank, lived in the biggest house, and was elected as a Democrat to the state senate, where he immediately became finance chairman. Thomas Ford credited the senator with "efficient advocacy" of the debt reduction program. A daughter said Matteson was "independently well off and quite able to give his time to the state."

Matteson had major investments in both railroads and banks. He secretly held, under cover of other names, 1,000 shares of stock in the Illinois Central company. A private letter to Jonathan Sturges, Illinois Central president, spoke of Matteson as "the very ablest man we have in Illinois," adding that "he considers the prosperity of the state to be in no small way identified with the success of your enterprise – and therefore is willing to do all that he can to assist in its consummation."

With Nicholas H. Ridgely as a partner, Senator Matteson in 1847 paid $21,100 for the defunct Springfield and Meredosia railroad, the original Northern Cross that was the only 1837 internal improvements road to be completed. His experience in digging the canal made it logical that by 1851 he would become a grading contractor on the Rock Island and Chicago road. While serving as governor he helped promote and direct the Joliet and Northern. When the line between St. Louis and Springfield failed in 1854, Matteson and W. R. Litchfield of New York acquired it. Matteson served as president several years. He also acquired a half-interest in the St. Louis packet line.

The Matteson Administration

Several Democrats vied for the 1852 the gubernatorial nomination; three of these Democrats were from northern Illinois. Supposedly the strongest was a Chicagoan, Secretary of State David L. Gregg, a Catholic. But, religion crept into the convention, and although Gregg led on the first ballot, Matteson was nominated on the 11th. To signify the importance of the foreign-born, the nomination for lieutenant governor went to Gustave Koerner, the political spokesman for settlers from Germany. Without enthusiasm, the Whigs nominated E. B. Webb of Carmi. The Free Soil party also nominated a candidate, but Matteson avoided controversies and was elected with 52.4 percent of the vote. The Democratic platform said nothing about banks, opposed meddling in the affairs of other states, and recommended Stephen A. Douglas for president. The platform also endorsed the Compromise of 1850, the federal act that: admitted California to the union as a free state; established the Utah and New Mexico Territories with the proviso that they could not make slave laws; prohibited the slave trade in Washington D.C. (but retained slavery); and imposed a Fugitive Slave Law that made federal officials responsible for recovering runaway slaves.

Matteson's election in 1852 was a victory for northern Illinois Democrats – newcomers who were moderates on the slavery issue and had not inherited their party's anti-bank prejudices. He was well qualified to be governor. As a contractor, he had helped dig the Illinois and Michigan Canal. As chairman of the Senate revenue committee during the Ford and French administrations, he had become an authority on state finance. He had cast the deciding Senate vote for legalized banking in Illinois. He had expert knowledge of the details of state government.

The Matteson administration is remembered chiefly for enactment of an effective common school law, support for which had been generated slowly by a series of mass meetings. While Thomas Ford was governor, the secretary of state had been designated *ex officio* superintendent of schools. Laws passed in 1849 and 1851 had permitted an optional local tax for schools, but in practice they were dead letters. Matteson in his inaugural address asked for financial support of a comprehensive school system, but the legislature did nothing until 1855, after two more school conventions and more progress in debt retirement. Then the state levied a tax that was distributed to local districts which levied their own property tax to support schools open six months a year. The state superintendent of schools was made an elective official whose $1,500 salary equaled the governor's. Matteson appointed Ninian W. Edwards to fill the position until the next election.

Ten years after the legislature and the public accepted the Ford austerity program for debt retirement, Governor Matteson found money for construction of a new prison in northern Illinois and had it located in Joliet, his hometown.

The Mattesons were both rich and social. The governor, his attractive wife, and their seven children found that the original governor's house on a small lot at Eighth and Capitol streets in Springfield was inadequate for daily living – to say nothing of their frequent parties. At the governor's request, the legislature spent $52,000 to purchase a square block and to construct and furnish the original Executive Mansion on its present site. An unusually elaborate structure for a Western state, it was the governor's personal project. When more money was needed, he advanced $10,000 so that construction need not stop until the legislature met again. By late 1855 the Mattesons moved and promptly invited the capital's elite to a ball. When the governor decided to make Springfield his permanent home, he spent possibly $100,000 to build an even larger, more palatial home across from the Executive Mansion. The three-story structure with 14 bedrooms was described as the city's finest residence.

Agitation over slavery, which for some time had been a peripheral issue, intruded more and more into partisan matters. Matteson, a moderate, was a consensus Democrat interested both in the success of his party and in the growth of his state. He preferred to stay in the middle ground and, during the uproar that greeted repeal of the Kansas Nebraska law sponsored by Senator Douglas, did not take a public position on the slavery expansion issue.

Without openly being a candidate, Matteson was almost elected United States Senator during the 1855 legislative session. He remained aloof during the prolonged deadlock brought about when a handful of Anti-Nebraska Democrats refused to vote either for Lincoln the Whig or any old-line Democrat. When the anti-slavery group seemed ready to vote for Matteson for senator, Lincoln swung the election to Lyman Trumbull. Lincoln accused Matteson of playing a "double game – and his defeat gives me more pleasure than my own gives me pain."

Lincoln's opinion aside, had the Illinois constitution permitted second terms, Governor Joel A. Matteson would have been a favorite for reelection in 1856. He was popular and, at that time, the electorate did not know that Matteson was a dishonest man.

The Scrip Scandal

Matteson should have known that sooner or later he would be caught.

After his inauguration in 1853, he took custody, in Chicago, of a trunk and a shoebox that contained old records of the state canal board. The governor ordered them shipped to him at Springfield, where no one could recall having seen them. The contents included quantities of 90-day scrip, in denominations of $50 and $100, that in 1839 had been used to pay contractors when the canal board was temporarily broke. The total amount issued was $338,554, and all but $316 had been redeemed at the Chicago branch of the state bank. Bookkeeping being lax, however, no record of names and dates had been kept when the scrip was turned in for redemption. Furthermore, the redeemed scrip had not been canceled. The trunk and box also contained quantities of unissued scrip that had been signed in blank by canal officials. The redeemed and unissued scrip in effect were blank checks, invitations for forgery and embezzlement.

One of the French administration's 1847 refunding bills, which Senator Matteson helped pass, provided that certificates of state indebtedness, including any canal scrip outstanding, could be brought to the Statehouse and exchanged for registered and numbered state bonds at par, plus accrued interest. The governor was the *ex officio* fund commissioner. A clerk he appointed handled the refunding transactions.

In 1856, shortly before his administration ended, Governor Matteson began bringing canal scrip to the clerk for redemption. Many of the bonds thus acquired were deposited with the state auditor as surety for bank note issues of the historic State Bank of Illinois at Shawneetown, one of a half-dozen banks he owned or controlled.

Matteson's redemption of the old scrip went unnoticed until the 1859 legislative session. Jacob Fry, who had been a canal official during the Ford and French administrations, learned that an old certificate was in circulation and warned state officials to beware of counterfeiting. Sensational evidence quickly implicated Matteson, who, after leaving office, had stayed in Springfield as a businessman. The embarrassed Democratic majority of the revenue committee, which Matteson once had chaired, agreed to an investigation. Orville H. Browning, the future United States Senator, helped check the records and quickly concluded that Matteson's guilt was obvious.

Part of the evidence was circumstantial, but it showed that Matteson had received $223,182.66 in state bonds for scrip that had been in the trunk and box. Some of it had been redeemed 20 years earlier, which meant that the state had paid for it twice. Matteson attended the hearings with his lawyers and was allowed to question witnesses. He was not asked to testify and he made no alibi under oath.

In a letter to the revenue committee, the former governor professed innocence, saying he had bought the scrip from strangers whom he could not identify. To preserve his good reputation, he continued, he would not keep the controversial bonds, and he would indemnify the state for its losses. In effect, he was willing to pay back the money he said he hadn't stolen. The public regarded the letter as a confession of guilt, but the committee dropped the investigation with a report that thanked Matteson for saving it "the necessity of determining many embarrassing questions."

The Republican members of the committee were given permission to pursue the inquiry after the legislature adjourned. The secretary of state, state auditor, and state treasurer, all Republicans, kept the controversy alive by demanding that "a great fraud committed upon the people" be investigated by the Sangamon County grand jury. Prosecutor J. B. White, a Matteson partisan, called witnesses who repeated the testimony they had given the Senate committee. Then the jury voted 16-7 to indict the former governor for larceny, reconsidered the action the next day, voted again to indict, reconsidered again, and eventually voted 12-10 not to indict.

The jury then took the unusual step of protesting its own verdict by publishing a 60-page record of its proceedings and summary of the evidence. It hinted at bribery and jury tampering. Contrary to law, Matteson had attended the supposedly secret proceedings. His lawyers were accused of "boldly interfering with the jury to prevent an indictment." The report also criticized the judge, the prosecutor, and the manner in which grand jury vacancies were filled.

An 1861 supplemental report prepared by the revenue committee added $165,346 to the amount embezzled. It found that Matteson had cashed some bonds held in the governor's office for special purposes and that on some he had written the names of fictitious payees. That would add forgery to the list of crimes traced to the former governor. The committee decided that faulty record-keeping made prosecution impossible.

The 1859 legislature passed a special law allowing indemnification, but Matteson stalled the case until 1863 when the Sangamon County Circuit Court decreed that the former governor owed the state $253,723.77. Property owned by Matteson and his wife was sold at auction on the courthouse steps for $238,000. Nothing was done about reimbursing the state for the additional $165,346 reported in 1861.

The Former Governor's Financial Fall

For Matteson, financial misfortunes came in a flood. Back in 1850 Matteson had organized his first bank, the Merchants' and Drovers' at Joliet. After he became governor, he acquired five more – at Peoria, Quincy, Shawneetown, Marion, and Bloomington – in which he owned all or most of the stock. For the successor to the historic State Bank of Illinois at Shawneetown, he paid $15,000. Records of the auditor's office indicate that the state bank had the largest note circulation in Illinois. Until 1857 the law required only that bonds of any state be deposited with the state auditor as surety for note issues. Bankers cashed the bond coupons and could pyramid their capital for added profits. As economic conditions fluctuated, they frequently were called upon to deposit additional bonds. As a result, bank owners frequently needed more bonds, especially if they owned multiple banks. R. E. Goodell, the governor's son-in-law and business partner, claimed before the Senate investigating committee that the Joliet bank especially was profitable and that Matteson's banks earned from $50,000 to $100,000 a year. That testimony is suspect, however, since he was trying to prove that Matteson had no need to steal from the state. Matteson's conversion of scrip into bonds had reached a peak about the time he took over the Shawneetown bank. Soon after the scrip fraud, he lost control of the Chicago, Alton, and St. Louis railroad. By 1861 economic dislocations at the start of the Civil War had forced the suspension of his banks.

In foreclosure proceedings, the Matteson mansion sold for $40,000 – less than half its estimated cost. Title to it was obtained by a son-in-law through a redemption proceeding, and the former governor continued to live there. In 1860 he campaigned in Louisiana and Florida for Stephen A. Douglas. During two of the war years he made a grand tour of Europe.

On January 31, 1873, three days after his Springfield home had burned to the ground, the old governor died in the Chicago home of a daughter.

11th **Governor**

William Henry Bissell
1811-1860

1811 – Born April 25, in Hartwick, New York.

1834 – Earns M.D. degree from Jefferson Medical School, Philadelphia.

1841 - 1843 – Serves with Lincoln as a representative in the 12th General Assembly.

1844 – Earns bachelor of laws degree from Transylvania Law School, Kentucky.

1847 – Serves in the Mexican War, becomes a hero in the battle of Buena Vista, Feb. 22-23.

1848 – Elected to the first of three terms in Congress.

1850 – Accepts a challenge to duel Jefferson Davis.

1856 – Elected governor.

1857 – The newly established 15-member state board of education establishes the state's first tax-supported institution of higher learning in Normal.

1860 – Dies in office, March 18.

Republican
January 12, 1857 to March 18, 1860

William Henry Bissell set several precedents. He was the first Roman Catholic governor of Illinois and the first to die in office. Bissell, who could walk only with crutches, was the only governor inaugurated in the Executive Mansion. He was also the first governor to hold a college degree, and among other distinctions, William Henry Bissell was the only Illinois governor challenged to a duel by Jefferson Davis. They didn't fight the duel, but Bissell's acceptance of the challenge in 1850 made him so popular that six years later, in spite of a constitutional disqualification and physical handicaps, he was elected the state's first Republican governor. A Mexican War colonel and former Democratic congressman, he committed perjury at his inauguration, and as governor he turned out to be a poor administrator. Nevertheless, Abraham Lincoln believed that Bissell was the only antislavery candidate who had a chance of carrying Illinois in the critical year of 1856.

Bissell and Lincoln had never been close associates, but in 1856 Lincoln was certain that the new antislavery coalition would lose its first election if any other man headed its state ticket. In the Republican campaign Lincoln served as behind-the-scenes strategist and made some 40 speeches. After the election, he acted as the new governor's unofficial legal adviser. Bissell's great contribution was that by winning in 1856 he provided Lincoln with a home state power base in 1860. If Illinois had not been a

Republican state, Lincoln would have been a less impressive candidate for the presidential nomination.

The Paralyzed War Hero

The son of Luther and Hannah Shepherd Bissell, the governor was born April 25, 1811, in the obscure town of Hartwick, Otsego County, New York. He taught school, worked on a farm, and studied under a Hartwick physician before entering Jefferson Medical School, Philadelphia, where he received an M.D. degree in 1834. He practiced three years at Painted Post, Steuben County, New York, before he migrated to Illinois. In an unpublished biography, John F. Snyder says that Bissell in 1837 was headed for Galesburg but lost his baggage when a steamboat sank south of St. Louis. He went ashore at Harrisonville, Monroe County, where he found a job teaching school and boarded at the home of a farmer. Bissell married the farmer's daughter, Emily Susan Jones, in 1840, a year after he started the practice of medicine at Waterloo. She died in 1844, leaving two small daughters. The same year he received a bachelor of laws degree from Transylvania Law School in Kentucky.

After coming to Illinois, he discovered that he had talent as an extemporaneous speaker. One contemporary described his style and diction as "elegant" and his use of satire as "cutting and effective." As a Democrat he served one term in the legislature, where he met Lincoln. He practiced law at Belleville, was appointed a bank commissioner by Governor Ford, and became a district prosecutor, all before the Mexican War made him a celebrity.

Bissell, who seemed to have an aptitude for command, was captain of a company of Belleville neighbors he had recruited at the start of the Mexican War. Because Democratic field officers were in demand, he was elected colonel of the second regiment of Illinois volunteers. Attached to General Zachary Taylor's army, he saw action only in the two-day defensive battle of Buena Vista. While under fire his regiment executed a parade ground maneuver that allowed them to change front and help turn back the Mexican army. On his return to Belleville, he was welcomed as a hero and rewarded with election to Congress in 1848 for the first of three terms.

In Washington he came to dislike slave-state congressmen who, in the debate that delayed the admission of California as a free state, boasted of Southern superiority and asserted that

Northerners were trying to drive them out of the Union. Bissell regarded his Southern colleagues as "insolent, overbearing and bullying beyond all belief," but he kept still until James A. Seddon of Virginia (who became the Confederate secretary of war during the Civil War) gave a distorted version of the battle of Buena Vista. Seddon said that Northern troops had retreated under fire and that disaster had been prevented by the Mississippi regiment commanded by Colonel Jefferson Davis.

Bissell replied with a masterful oration. For almost an hour he tongue-lashed Seddon and other Southerners, whom he accused of plotting secession. Concerning the Buena Vista crisis, he said that Davis' regiment was a mile and a half away and that Northern and Kentucky troops, including his own men, had turned back the Mexicans. He credited the Mississippians with heroism elsewhere on the battlefield.

The speech made Bissell a folk hero back in Illinois. Davis, who had been elected senator from Mississippi, claimed that his regiment had been insulted and challenged Bissell to a duel. Northern congressmen customarily refused to settle disputes on the so-called field of honor, but Bissell accepted and stipulated that the two men fight at close range with army muskets loaded with ball and buckshot. Davis backed out of the duel by accepting an explanation for the alleged insult that he had previously rejected. The boastful Southerners lost face.

By 1854 paralysis, caused by an ailment described as rheumatic or neuralgic, prevented Bissell from attending sessions of the House. He had broken with Senator Stephen A. Douglas and the Democratic Party on the slavery extension issue. Douglas was the force behind the pro-slavery Kansas-Nebraska Act that would repeal the Missouri Compromise of 1820 and allow the settlers of Kansas to decide for themselves whether that state would be slave or free. While Douglas was pushing the bill through Congress, Bissell sent word that, if the issue were in doubt, he would have himself carried into the House chamber on a cot to vote against it. The measure passed the Congress with President Pierce's approval.

Bissell's career seemed at its end when his wife brought him back to Belleville in the summer of 1855.

Bissell's Election and Administration

At the start of the 1856 campaign, the politically astute Lincoln believed that the Republican candidate for governor must be a former Democrat. In that category, only Bissell had a chance of winning. Fortunately, he was willing to run in spite of his incapacitated legs and questionable health.

When a group of antislavery editors met at Decatur on February 22, 1856, to arrange for a nominating convention, Lincoln refused to run for governor but said that Bissell would get enough Democratic votes to carry the state. Arrangements for his unopposed nomination were made before the first Republican convention at Bloomington on May 29. In a letter to the editor of the *Alton Courier*, Bissell said he could walk only with "the use of a cane and the aid of a friendly arm" but that his health and mental capacity were good. He said he could make some campaign speeches but couldn't travel extensively. He was nominated by acclamation.

The Democrats ran Senator Douglas' chief lieutenant, William A. Richardson of Quincy against Bissell. Richardson had resigned from Congress earlier that year after he had been defeated for the speakership. In speeches and letters Lincoln argued that votes for the third party Know-Nothing candidates would only help the Democrats. Bissell made at least one speech, possibly one or two more, but there is no record of what he said. At the end of a bitter campaign the Democrats carried Illinois for James Buchanan, but Bissell was elected by 4,787 votes, 46.3 percent of the total in a three-candidate field.

During the campaign and after the election, the Democrats contended that Bissell would perjure himself if he took the oath of office. In an effort to stop an epidemic of duels, the Constitution of 1848 required state officials to swear to a special inauguration oath that they had never fought or accepted a challenge to a duel or acted as a second. Of course, Bissell's acceptance of Jefferson Davis' challenge was part of his popularity. The situation embarrassed the leaders of the Republican Party. There is no record that Lincoln, the dominant Republican in Illinois, spoke or wrote about it before or after the election. However, he did not object to, and presumably he approved of, Bissell's post-election theory that the Illinois Constitution did not apply in his case because the duel acceptance was made in the District of Columbia. That reasoning obviously was faulty since Bissell committed the offense of perjury in Springfield, Illinois, when he took the oath.

For unexplained reasons, the Democrats didn't challenge the governor's right to hold office. They held small majorities in the legislature, however, and heckled Bissell long and caustically. In a two-day speech, Representative John A. Logan, a future Union general and Republican U. S. senator, contended that Bissell knew that he would commit perjury if he took the gubernatorial oath. Secretary of War Jefferson Davis had helped assemble the evidence.

Governor Bissell never entered the state Capitol during the three-plus years of his administration. He transacted state business from a second-floor room of the Executive Mansion, where Lincoln frequently called. When the governor signed an 1859 Democratic reapportionment bill he had intended to veto, Lincoln telegraphed for Joseph Gillespie, a Whig lawyer at Edwardsville and a personal friend, to "come right up" for a conference that was also attended by Norman B. Judd, the Republican state chairman. Bissell then reversed his action and vetoed the bill with a message that is in Lincoln's handwriting. The return of the bill to the legislature was greeted by a scene of what contemporaries called "great confusion." Lincoln argued and won the case when it was appealed to the Illinois Supreme Court.

Anti-Bissell agitation intensified in 1859 with the discovery that the governor had approved the funding at par of 114 thousand-dollar canal bonds on which the legislature had placed a ceiling of 28.64 cents on the dollar. The error was discovered in time to prevent loss to the state, but Democrats questioned the governor's honesty and competence, and Republicans found it difficult to defend his credibility. The governor, who could write as eloquently as he could speak, provided a detailed defense in a letter to the *Illinois State Journal.* Long letters to friendly editors were a favorite public relations medium.

The Governor Dies

As his health deteriorated, Governor Bissell took little part in state affairs and none in the intensified debate over slavery that reached its peak in the Lincoln-Douglas debates. However, in February, 1860, he indicated in a private letter that he preferred Salmon P. Chase of Ohio for the presidency. A month later, on March 17, 1860, Lincoln and other Republican officials called at the Executive Mansion to say farewell the failing governor. The next day, 10 months before his term ended, Bissell died.

After a state funeral, the first Republican governor was buried with Catholic graveside services. While he was ill at Washington, he had become a Roman Catholic in 1854 to please his second wife, the beautiful Elizabeth Kintzing Kane, daughter of Elias Kent Kane, an early U.S. senator from Illinois. His official household as governor included the two daughters of his first marriage and three nieces of his second wife. Religion had not been made an issue in the 1856 campaign. Republicans did not call Bissell's Catholicism to the attention of their predominantly Protestant members, and Democrats likewise did not want to lose the support of Irish immigrants.

The official cause of the governor's death was pneumonia. But according to Dr. John F. Snyder, a personal friend who was both a doctor and a historian, his health battles had a different cause. "He died of the secondary effects of syphilis – he told me so himself – [that] he contracted [the disease] in Mexico."

12th Governor

John Wood
1798 - 1880

1798 – Born, Dec. 20, 1798, in New York.

1822 – Builds the first log cabin on a site that was to become Quincy.

1837 – Begins service as a state senator in the 10th-12th General Assemblies

1856 – Becomes candidate for lieutenant governor after the discovery that the original
Republican nominee can't meet the citizenship requirement to hold the office.

1860 – Governor Bissell dies, March 18; Wood commissioned/qualified as governor,
March 21.

1861 – Becomes state quartermaster general for the Civil War effort.

1863 – Wood, 64, becomes colonel of the 137th Illinois Regiment of volunteers, a
100 day regiment he recruited at Quincy.

1880 – Dies, June 4.

Republican
March 21, 1860 to January 14, 1861

John Wood, the founder of the city of Quincy, completed without incident the last 10 months of Governor William H. Bissell's administration. After he took the oath of office at a quiet ceremony on the day of Bissell's state funeral, he did not bother to move to Springfield but generously allowed his predecessor's widow to continue living in the Executive Mansion. Since he wasn't using the governor's one-room office in the Statehouse, President-elect Abraham Lincoln took it over.

Despite the excitement of the presidential campaign and the turmoil over slavery and its expansion, there wasn't much for Governor Wood to do. Historian John Moses said that under the Constitution of 1848, governors often were lonesome for want of callers when the legislature was not in session. Wood anticipated the Civil War by calling attention to the need to reorganize the state militia, about which nothing had been done since the Mexican War.

Wood's Early Years

Wood was a New Yorker, born December 20, 1798, in Cayuga County, the only son of David and Catherine Krause Wood. His father, of Irish blood, was a Revolutionary War captain and surgeon. He also was a linguist who wrote marginal notes in German and French medical texts. At home the family conversed in "Mohawk Dutch," the only language the mother understood.

The future governor left home when about 20 and wandered through Shawneetown to Pike County, where he farmed for two years. He was credited with recognizing the potential of the bluffs along the Mississippi River where he bought a half section of land. There he founded Quincy, which at one time was the largest city in Illinois. Wood and a companion built the first log cabin there in 1822.

An abolitionist, in 1824 he turned out a large majority in present Hancock and Fulton counties in support of Governor Coles' antislavery campaign. He initiated the organization of Adams County, served uneventfully in the Black Hawk War, helped promote railroads and a bridge over the Mississippi, and was elected mayor of Quincy several times. He resigned his seat in the state Senate to protest having been instructed to vote against Quincy's best interests on a railroad matter. In 1835 he built an imposing Greek Revival house. The German craftsmen he hired out of St. Louis to build his house began a wave of German immigration to the area. Local historians estimate that as many as 80 percent of the families in Quincy today can trace their ancestry to immigrants who followed the craftsmen who built Wood's 1835 house. In 1849, with his two older sons, he joined the California gold rush and was gone nearly a year, returning without having found gold.

In 1826 he married Ann M. Streeter. Of their eight children, one daughter and three sons lived to maturity. His wife died in 1863. Two years later he married Mrs. Mary A. Holmes.

The Second Choice to Second the Ticket Becomes Governor

A rugged man, Wood hadn't been the original Republican nominee for lieutenant governor. Because of the importance of the German vote, the 1856 convention at Bloomington nominated Francis A. Hoffman of Cook County, who hadn't been a citizen for the required 14 years. When his ineligibility was noted, Lincoln and other Republican leaders filled the vacancy by nominating Wood. Of course, the duelist William Henry Bissell was constitutionally unfit to take the oath of office. Thus, the Republican Convention of 1856 led their ticket with two unqualified candidates. (In 1860 the Republicans would again nominate Hoffman for lieutenant governor, but by then he would be eligible to hold office.)

Lincoln went with Wood because the Democratic candidate for governor, William A. Richardson, also came from Quincy. When as lieutenant governor he presided over the Senate during two legislative sessions, Wood worked harmoniously with the majority Democrats. Wood never ran for state office again.

From Governor to Foot Soldier

Wood had an active and varied career during the Civil War. He was one of five conservative Republicans appointed as delegates to a so-called peace convention at Washington that did nothing. The former governor was a successful land speculator but hardly qualified as a businessman, one reason being that he was left-handed and did not like to write. Nevertheless, in May 1861, he volunteered for appointment as state quartermaster general and assumed the enormous job of providing food, shelter, and equipment for the dozens of regiments that Illinois was sending to the federal armies. Wood had to set up a procurement office that included such essentials as an accounting system. The normal duties of a quartermaster department included the purchase, among other items, of uniforms, tents, tools, equipment, means of transportation, and fuel. Since no ordnance officer was on duty at Springfield, Wood had to take over responsibility for supplying arms and ammunition for the first Illinois regiments. When the federal government took over procurement responsibilities, the state quartermaster department was abolished. The adjutant general reported that Wood's department spent $3,714,122 to clothe and equip three-fourths of the first 60,540 soldiers from Illinois.

At the age of 64, Wood went to war as colonel of the 137th Illinois Regiment of volunteers, a 100-day regiment he recruited at Quincy during the manpower shortage of 1863. Stationed at Memphis, the 137th did picket duty on the Hernando Road, where Confederate General Nathan Bedford Forrest's cavalry attacked, causing the loss of seven men, while the colonel was ill at his headquarters.

In his final years, the former governor lost his fortune. In 1873 he told his lawyer, Orville H. Browning, that his extensive property holdings had been mortgaged as security for the debts of his sons. But his financial reversal resulted primarily from the debt on his new home. Finished in 1864, the octogonal stone house was designed by John Murray Von Osdell, the architect who designed the Executive Mansion, and cost $200,000 to build. The Panic of

1873, a severe economic recession, diminished his wealth and by 1875 caused him to sell his properties, including his octogonal house, to pay his debts. He sold the house to English and German College, later named Chaddock College, for $40,000 and moved back to the Greek Revival house, which he had given to one of his sons.

He died broke on June 4, 1880, after an illness of several years. At funeral services held in Quincy's largest church, a eulogist remembered him as "one of the men who planted civilization in the wilderness."

13th
Governor

Richard Yates
1815 -1873

1815 – Born, Jan. 18, Warsaw, Kentucky.
1831 – Ends studies at Miami University at Oxford, Ohio to move to Illinois with his family.
1835 – Graduates from Illinois College.
1843 - 1847 – Serves as a representative in the 13th and 14th General Assemblies.
1849 - 1851 – Serves as a representative in the 16th General Assembly.
1850 – Elected to Congress for the first of two terms.
1860 – Yates is elected governor.
1861 – Abraham Lincoln takes the oath of office to become the nation's 16th president; the Civil War begins on April 12 when Confederate forces fire on Fort Sumter.
1862 – A Democrat-heavy state constitutional convention meets in Springfield, but voters fail to ratify their constitution that would have cut the governor's term in half and created a Democrat-dominated commission to take over the governor's wartime authority.
1865 - 1871 – Serves as U.S. Senator.
1873 – Dies Nov. 27.

Republican
January 14, 1861 to January 16, 1865

During the Civil War Governor Richard Yates was the most popular and most controversial civilian on the divided Illinois homefront. Genial, handsome, and an eloquent orator, he excelled as a recruiter of regiments and his speeches were bugle calls for more men to march southward. Known as the "soldiers' friend," he chartered boats to take doctors, nurses, and hospital supplies to battlefields where the men he had urged to enlist suffered heavy casualties. The role of a war governor is to mobilize his state behind a maximum national effort for victory. That Dick Yates did.

Strongly opposed to slavery, he was a Radical Republican who complained to and about Abraham Lincoln and could not understand why there was any delay in conquering the South. More emotional than intellectual, he never comprehended the complexity of the president's wartime problems, one of which was him.

The governor had his own problems, chiefly with his political opposition: the Peace Democrats and Southern sympathizers who dominated a wartime constitutional convention and the midterm legislature. The governor had no talent for compromise and made no effort to work with them. For example, he could have appointed a Democrat to Stephen A. Douglas' Senate vacancy; he could have been less of an alarmist and more understanding of the president; and, he could have been a saintly character with many virtues that are invaluable in crisis years. Nevertheless, with Yates as governor of a strategic state, the North did win the war. There is no reason to believe that Leonard Swett or Norman B. Judd, who were more qualified for the 1860 Republican nomination, would have done any better. James C. Allen, who lost the election and became a Peace Democrat, probably would not have done as well.

For charismatic and aggressive leadership, Yates' reward, before the war ended, was election to the U.S. Senate. There he was an alcoholic failure who did not deserve, and did not receive, a second term. Nevertheless, the popularity of the wartime governor persisted long after his death. His son, whose chief political asset was that he also was named Richard Yates, was elected governor in 1900.

Yates the Orator, Politician, and Railroad Developer

The first Governor Yates was born in Kentucky, on the Ohio River at Warsaw, Gallatin County, on January 18, 1815, the fourth of 11 children of Henry and Millicent Yates, cousins from Virginia. He was 16 and enrolled in Miami University in Ohio when his father, recently a widower, moved the family to the free state of Illinois in 1831. For a year the boy attended a log cabin school while his father operated a store at Springfield. Henry Yates then moved 20 miles westward and became a substantial landowner.

The son went on to Jacksonville, the next county seat, which was his legal residence the rest of his life. In 1835 he was half of Illinois College's first graduating class. He studied law under John J. Hardin and spent a year at Transylvania Law School in Kentucky. Then he returned to Jacksonville to practice law, make speeches, and as a Henry Clay Whig serve 10 years as state representative and congressman. In 1839 he married Catharine Geers, who was small, dark, and fragile. For nine years they lived with her mother, during which time three of their five children were born. Of the three who lived to maturity, the namesake son, the future governor, was the youngest.

Of medium height and somewhat rotund, Yates had an imposing head, thick auburn hair, bright blue eyes, and a friendly manner. "Nature had fashioned him to be admired by the masses," wrote Alexander Davidson and Bernard Stuve. His strong and flexible voice was adapted to open-air audiences, and Yates, who began as a campus orator, received invitations to speak at Fourth of July celebrations and political meetings. In the great age of Illinois oratory, he was noted for his rhetoric, and he ranked as the equal of William H. Bissell, his predecessor as governor, and Richard J. Oglesby, his successor. Only Robert G. Ingersoll, Owen Lovejoy, and Edward D. Baker were regarded by some contemporaries as the governor's oratorical superiors.

The future governor's law practice was never lucrative, but his son said he made some money as a railroad promoter. Biographers do not credit him with superior intellectual qualities. He is described as convivial, an adjective often applied to heavy drinkers.

A political career was inevitable. At the age of 30, he took an active speaking role in William Henry Harrison's presidential campaign. He was the youngest member of the Illinois House of Representatives, to which he was first elected in 1842, then again in 1844 and 1848. He submitted unfriendly amendments to, but voted for, Governor Thomas Ford's debt management program. At his final session, he was the speakership candidate of the minority Whigs. Gustave Koerner, the German leader who served one term in the House with Yates, said the future governor was "thoroughly anti-slavery" but kept silent about it. Two days before he left the legislature, Yates said that "the earliest impressions of my boyhood were that the institution of slavery was a grievous wrong."

In 1850 Yates was elected to Congress in the old Lincoln district for the first of two terms. Upon the introduction of the Kansas-Nebraska bill — a proslavery bill that would repeal the Missouri Compromise and allow Kansas to become a slave state if the settlers voted for it — he made an early, forceful speech against the spread of slavery. He also advocated homestead legislation and was regarded as something of an oddity because he favored women's suffrage.

Returning to Jacksonville, he became president of the Tonica and Petersburg railroad, which would serve 10 counties in his old congressional district as soon as right-of-way, rails, and rolling stock could be paid for. His job was to raise the money by selling stock to landowners and bonds to counties and townships. To avoid bankruptcy, he discounted mortgages with Eastern capitalists. Train service on the road, which eventually became part of the

Chicago and Alton, had not started when he resigned as its president after being nominated for governor.

During his railroad career, Yates refused to run for Congress again but was available for higher office. In 1855 he promised Lincoln that he would be a candidate for Senator only "in the event you do not succeed." The next year, when the Republican Party held its first convention, Yates was one of 13 vice presidents and made what the official record called a "stirring speech."

The War Governor

Six years after losing his congressional seat and one week before Lincoln won the Republican presidential nomination Yates became the party's compromise nominee for governor. At the Republican state convention at Decatur, his opponents, both of whom had better ratings in the party hierarchy, were Norman B. Judd of Chicago and Leonard Swett of Bloomington. On the fourth ballot, Swett threw the nomination to Yates, who was regarded as the strongest candidate in important central counties. Lincoln, who had close ties to both Judd and Swett, stayed neutral. So the nod went to Yates, who preferred Edward Bates of Missouri for the presidential nomination.

In November Yates won by 12,943 votes over Circuit Judge James C. Allen of Crawford County, who became a member of the Democratic peace wing and was elected congressman-at-large in 1862. Nothing in Allen's record indicates that he would have been a strong war governor.

At the start of his administration, the new governor was too drunk to deliver his inaugural address. Yates kept the president-elect and other dignitaries waiting a half hour before he, aided by an escort, staggered down the aisle and collapsed in a chair while the House clerk read his long speech. The newspapers printed nothing about the new governor's condition. The speech made it clear that Yates was not synchronizing his views with those of Lincoln, who was moving cautiously in an effort to limit the number of seceding states. The Associated Press called it:

> the most decided anti-slavery, anti-compromise and anti-secession document sent to any northern legislature since the beginning of the crisis. Although delivered under the very eye of the president-elect, its tone is so radical as to make it altogether improbable that it has his sanction.

Lincoln had declined when Yates offered to let him read the speech in advance.

Yates, the chief executive of a major state at the start of the nation's greatest crisis, had not borne arms in the Mexican War, had not achieved prominence as a lawyer, had no experience as an administrator, and lacked the full confidence of the president-elect. He did have the backing of several men experienced in state government. After Fort Sumter, Senator Lyman Trumbull, Orville H. Browning, and Gustave Koerner converged on Springfield to help put Illinois on a war footing. They were joined by John A. McClernand, one of the first of the War Democrats. With their help, and with the loyalty of the elected state officials, the Yates administration performed creditably.

When Fort Sumter was surrendered and the White House called on Illinois to contribute six regiments, the governor enthusiastically began a drive that in four years sent 197,360 men into Union armies. He called the legislature into special session and used the occasion to denounce treason and encourage the enlistment of more regiments than the War Department had asked for. The legislature complied with the governor's request for a $3 million appropriation that violated the state constitution's debt limit but was upheld by the state Supreme Court. He ordered drill teams to Cairo when no other troops were available. He secretly sent a steamboat to bring 10,000 muskets from the St. Louis armory.

For a brief time homefront harmony seemed possible. Senator Stephen A. Douglas, on a trip requested by the president, reached Springfield during the special legislative session and convinced Browning, the former Whig he once had defeated for Congress, that bipartisanship was vital. Before the General Assembly and later at Chicago, Douglas eloquently pleaded for Democrats to support the war effort.

Douglas' death less than two months after Fort Sumter was a major tragedy, and Orville H. Browning, his replacement, missed the opportunity to promote homefront unity. Important Republicans had urged Yates to appoint a Democrat to fill the vacancy, but Democrats did not encourage activity that might weaken their party's position in future elections. Again the record is not complete, but the cautious governor ended the matter by appointing Browning. No one knows what would have happened had he named a War Democrat, someone like McClernand. As the war developed, a sizable number of Democratic leaders excused their opposition to the Lincoln and Yates administrations by asserting that their party should not be dismantled and that the Republican governor had given them precedents for partisanship.

In speeches and proclamations, Yates encouraged the belief that drafting Illinois men would be disgraceful. In the summer of 1862, when Washington called for 52,290 more men and refused to allow credit for previous quota excesses, Yates and other officials spread across the state for a series of mass meetings. They filled the quota in 11 days. The governor soon was quarreling with Lincoln, who protested that Illinois had not accepted the service of a federal officer sent to speed up the forwarding of new troops to battle zones. Yates retorted that 50,000 men were ready to go as soon as the War Department supplied guns, tents, and other equipment. Lincoln's last word was that there had been "much trouble between officers sent to Illinois and the state government there."

Because Illinois made a better showing than many states, it was exempt from the first two draft calls. Enrollment under the third call was in progress when the war ended, and a provision for $300 substitutes was never an option for Illinois men. In the fall of 1864, Yates told President Lincoln that a high quota "will not only endanger the peace of the state but will hopelessly defeat us in the coming elections." In his final report to the legislature, Yates boasted that the state had sent into battle 157 regiments, plus miscellaneous units and 13 regiments of 100-day volunteers.

The governor never hesitated to voice his disapproval of the president's war leadership. He wrote to Senator Trumbull that "if I were Lincoln I would lead enough of the Potomac army to take Richmond – and this though Washington could not be saved." Homefront radicals applauded in the discouraging summer of 1862 when he wrote an open letter stating that "the crisis demands sterner measures." He urged the president to "summon to the standard of the republic all men willing to fight for the Union.... Don't waste manpower guarding the property of traitors.... Use Negro troops.... Have invading troops forage off the country.... Mild and conciliatory measures have been used in vain."

Questions of Loyalty

"Old Abe was too slow for me," he told a Brooklyn audience at the end of the 1862 campaign. "I was for the [emancipation] proclamation, for confiscation, for the arrest of rebels and traitors, and for every measure by which we could put down the rebellion."

Yates considered that he was personally responsible for Illinois soldiers, even after they had been mustered into federal service. When heavy casualties had been reported at Fort Donelson and Shiloh, he chartered steamboats and rushed medical aid to the battlefields. During the siege of Vicksburg, the governor socialized with Illinois troops. However, had Illinois drafted replacements for casualties, the original regiments could have been kept at full strength under experienced officers after achieving veteran status. Yates, for whom the appointment of colonels was a patronage opportunity, preferred to recruit new regiments, which meant that inexperienced units were rushed into battle.

The governor took credit for starting Ulysses S. Grant on his Civil War career. A West Pointer who had resigned from the army, Grant came to Springfield hoping for a command. Yates put him to work as a two-dollar-a-day clerk in the adjutant general's office before appointing him colonel of one of the dozens of regiments from Illinois.

Yates himself had to contend with partisan Democrats whom he considered his homefront enemies. A constitutional convention in 1862 unwisely asserted that it had executive and legislative authority, questioned whether Illinois troops were properly equipped, tried to cut in half the governor's term, and proposed that a commission dominated by Democrats take over the governor's wartime authority. A committee that investigated purchases of uniforms reported that no wrongdoing could be traced to Yates and John Wood, his quartermaster general. In 1861, when the Lincoln administration took over military purchasing for Illinois troops, Yates resisted giving the impression that he was profiting politically, if not financially.

He invoked a hitherto unused proroguing power to dismiss the 1863 obstructionist legislature. Because the biennial appropriation bills had not been passed, he and the other state officials were forced to borrow money to pay their office expenses for two years. (The same situation existed in Indiana, where Governor Oliver P. Morton ran his state government for two years without legislative appropriations.)

Yates, who was inclined to be hysterical, believed that the Lincoln administration's arbitrary arrests of civilians were justified but inadequate. "Secession is deeper and stronger here than you have any idea," he wrote to Senator Trumbull. "Its advocates are numerous and powerful, and respectable." In 1862 he asked that a regiment of infantry be sent to Springfield to guard the state government while the constitutional convention was in session. His fears increased amid reports of the organization of pro-Confederate secret societies in areas where there had been a heavy enlistment of loyalists. Yates proposed appointing a U. S. marshal with power to arrest anyone deemed dangerous to the federal government. He called General John M. Palmer back from his command in Tennessee and sent him to ask Lincoln and Secretary of War Edwin M. Stanton that four or five regiments be organized for security service in Illinois. The president's response was to ask, "Who can we trust if we can't trust Illinois?"

As the 1864 election approached, Yates and other Radicals lacked enthusiasm for Lincoln and hoped to nominate someone who had taken a stronger stand on slavery. In September, however, the governor told newspaperman Horace Greeley that Lincoln's election was probable, that he knew of no other man who could carry Illinois, and that it would be disastrous to attempt to substitute candidates. In Illinois, Union victories and Democratic criticism of the war helped the Republican campaign.

The Republican victory included majority control of the 1865 legislature, which elected Yates to the U.S. Senate over Congressman Elihu B. Washburne and General Palmer. In his final message to the legislature, he asked for repeal of the 1849 black laws and, in a long review of how Illinois had supported the war, he included the text of the 1862 letter in which he urged Lincoln to use more decisive measures against the Confederates.

The Senator Drinks a Little

After Lincoln's assassination, Senator Yates helped convince the widow that burial should be in Springfield. Yates wrote a eulogy in which he confessed error in his criticism of the president:

> I thought he was too slow in calling out men, too slow in arming the freemen, too slow in issuing the Proclamation of Emancipation, but in his own time came, in succession, all those important measures, and the whole world now plainly sees and acknowledges that Abraham Lincoln always did the right thing in the right way, and at the right time, and at the right place.

The eulogy was never delivered. Yates included tributes to Lincoln in later speeches.

As governor, Yates had asked that slavery be ended by a constitutional amendment. As a radical senator, determined that the South be punished, he wanted former slaves to have the right to vote, regardless of education. He voted to impeach President Andrew Johnson, but there had been doubt whether Yates would be present for the roll call. Near the end of Johnson's trial in "an address to the people of Illinois," he confessed that he was a periodic drinker who once had been a total abstainer for ten years. "I have never appeared in the Senate except while sober," he wrote to several newspapers. "I have often yielded to temptation and as often have suffered the pangs of unutterable remorse." He apologized, said he had reformed, and swore that he would stay reformed. The *Chicago Tribune* commented that "it would be better taste to reform once without issuing a proclamation than to be continually issuing proclamations and never reforming." To make certain that he did not miss the impeachment roll call, Yates sent to Jacksonville for his wife, who for a month sat in the gallery watching him.

Yates hoped that he might win a second Senate term in 1870 by playing two generals, Richard J. Oglesby and John A. Logan, against each other. Reality closed in, and Yates' farewell to public office was a letter to Governor John Palmer that would not reach Springfield until after his successor had been elected. He regretted his bad habit but wanted credit for his early stands against slavery and for women's suffrage:

> I know not what I can do. I am wedded to politics. I think I will never drink again. I have been a good member of the Senate, done a good deal of work and made a great many speeches, but they are buried because I drank. I have not asked a friend about [reelection to] the Senate because I deserved nothing more from their generous friendship.

General John A. "Black Jack" Logan, who could control his drinking, replaced the one-termer.

Missing the Senate, Yates wanted an appointment to a diplomatic mission or the governorship of one of the Western territories. He hoped that President Grant would remember who had made him colonel of the 21st Illinois Regiment. More likely the president would remember a more recent occasion when Yates had been "uproariously drunk" at a reception given for General and Mrs. Grant by President Johnson. The former senator returned to Jacksonville and waited until the mail brought an appointment as a member of a commission that would disband as soon as it inspected a land grant railroad in Arkansas.

He took the job. On his way back home to an unpromising retirement, he died suddenly in a St. Louis hotel on November 27, 1873. Eulogists at his well-attended funeral recalled only that Yates had been the patriotic homefront leader of Lincoln's state during the difficult years of the Civil War. Fifty years later his statue was erected on the Statehouse grounds.

14**th**
Governor

Richard James Oglesby
1825-1899

1825 – Born, July 25, in Oldham County, Kentucky.

1836 – First comes to Illinois as an orphan.

1847 – Sees action at the Mexican War battles of Vera Cruz, and Cerro Gordo.

1849 – Goes to California during the gold rush; comes home 20 months later with a $5,000 nest egg.

1856 - 1857 – Travels to Europe and the Near East.

1858 – Makes an unsuccessful run for Congress.

1862 – Oglesby is critically wounded at the Battle of Corinth in Mississippi. He recovers and returns to battle, but eventually removes himself from the field. He remains with the army until his first gubernatorial run.

1864 – Wins the Republican gubernatorial nomination for governor and defeats James C. Robinson in the general election.

1869 – John Palmer becomes governor.

1870 – Illinois adopts a new constitution on July 2, among its provisions are that all executive officers of the state run independently and that the governor can succeed himself; Blacks are granted the right to vote, but women are not.

1873 – Oglesby becomes governor on January 13; 10 days later, as part of a campaign deal, Republican legislators send him to the U.S. Senate; Lieutenant Governor John L. Beveridge becomes governor.

1873 - 1879 – Serves in the U.S. Senate.

1877 – Shelby M. Cullom takes office as governor.

1881 – Shelby M. Cullom begins his second term as governor.

1883 – Cullom resigns the governorship to become U.S. Senator; John M. Hamilton becomes governor.

1885 – Oglesby begins his third term as governor.

1886 – On May 4, police move to break up a labor rally in Haymarket Square in Chicago. A bomb explodes, injuring and killing several people, including seven police officers. Oglesby commutes to life imprisonment the death sentences of two of several anarchists convicted in case. Four others are hanged November 11, 1887.

1899 – Dies, April 24.

Republican
January 16, 1865 to January 11, 1869
January 13, 1873 to January 23, 1873
January 30, 1885 to January 14, 1889

Richard James Oglesby, whose speeches "waved the bloody shirt" before Union veterans, was elected governor three times and United States Senator once with a minie ball in his chest and a twinkle in his eye. The wounded general's spread-eagle oratory, which blamed Democrats for the Civil War and its casualties, was a major factor in enabling the Republican Party to extend until 1892 the control of the governor's office that it began in 1856.

One of the most popular politicians of his time, Oglesby was Illinois' first three-term governor. He won nonconsecutive elections in tough political years: in 1864, when Peace Democrats and Copperheads hoped to deny Lincoln a second term; in 1872, when some of Lincoln's associates joined a coalition of Liberal Republicans and Democrats; and in 1884, when Grover Cleveland became the first Democratic president after the Civil War. The second term ended in 10 days, when the legislature elected Oglesby United States Senator. His record of three terms stood until James R. Thompson was elected to his third consecutive term in 1982.

Joseph W. "Private Joe" Fifer, the third man to succeed Oglesby in the governor's chair, praised the affable, portly Oglesby for his "endurance, his bubbling humor, his eloquence, sometimes on the most homely subjects, ...his faculty for remembering names and faces." He also remarked on "the spontaneity of the crowds in their response to his presence." The first Adlai E. Stevenson, who almost never criticized a public man, accused Oglesby of using "imagination" in the oratory that classified all Democrats as unpatriotic Copperheads. He added that in the U.S. Senate Oglesby was over his intellectual depth in debates about revenue and the tariff.

The expanding bullet that struck him down at Corinth ended a promising career as a battlefield commander but enabled Oglesby to campaign for governor before the war was over. After his promotion to major general and before his recuperation was complete, he made his first "bloody shirt" speech at Springfield. Without distinguishing between Copperheads and loyalists, he shouted that Democrats were guilty of treason and hypocrisy and were obstructing the Lincoln and Yates administrations. He called Democratic legislators a "fire in the rear" of patriotic Union soldiers. He encouraged homefront loyalists and prophesied that Copperheadism was forfeiting Democratic chances to win postwar elections. Jeriah Bonham, an agricultural editor who attended many meetings, said he never listened to a more eloquent speech. Oglesby could be vehement, passionate, and scornful. He didn't use notes. He depended on the inspiration of the moment. Consequently, his speeches could be very good or very bad.

A popular perennial, Oglesby was a well-to-do man who could afford and was willing, even in his advanced years, to run for office. Despite his three governorships, however, he had a lower political batting average than his two Republican rivals, General John A. "Black Jack" Logan and Shelby M. Cullom, a noncombatant. Logan was serving his third term as senator when death shortened his career in 1888. Cullom was elected governor twice and senator five times. Together they limited Oglesby to one term in the U.S. Senate. After the 1870 election, Oglesby expected to be elected senator to succeed Richard Yates, but Logan had more votes when Republican legislators caucused. The same thing happened in 1878, when Oglesby's Senate term ended. Oglesby again was a loser in 1883 when Cullom was elected senator the first time.

Oglesby's three nonconsecutive terms have led to two ways of numbering Illinois governors. The *Illinois Blue Book* names him the 14th, 16th and 20th governor, but it assigns only one number to governors like Shelby Moore Cullom who succeed themselves (i.e. the *Blue Book* lists Cullom as the 18th governor, not the 18th and 19th). *Mostly Good and Competent Men* assigns each multiple term governor only one number.

From Orphan to War Hero

Oglesby was born July 25, 1825, in Oldham County, Kentucky, and came to Illinois in 1836 as an orphan. When he was eight years old, a cholera epidemic killed his parents, Jacob and Isabella Watson Oglesby, two brothers, and a sister. His father, a farmer, had been a militia colonel and had served in the legislature. A wandering uncle took the future governor to Decatur where other relatives lived. The uncle and the boy worked a farm for a year, went back to Kentucky and another farm, to Decatur for a month, and then to Terre Haute, Indiana. A year later, the boy walked to Decatur where two aunts soon sent him to Kentucky to learn carpentry. Two years later he returned to Illinois and, for three months, attended school for the first time. That summer he raised hemp and converted it into rope. A friend recalled seeing him "plodding through Decatur's streets with the old ox cart." Nothing had trained him for a leadership career.

In 1844 he abandoned manual labor and took up the study of law in the Springfield office of Silas W. Robbins, where the first volume of *Blackstone's Commentaries* was the first book he had ever read from cover to cover. After 18 months he was admitted to the bar and practiced briefly at Sullivan. "I was never very much of a lawyer," Oglesby wrote a year before his death. "I never studied law."

He did travel extensively. In the Mexican War, as the first lieutenant of the Decatur company, he participated in the siege of Vera Cruz and the battle of Cerro Gordo. He came home in time to make Whig speeches for Zachary Taylor in 1848.

The next journey was to California in the 1849 gold rush. Borrowing $250 for expenses, he joined eight men in driving three six-mule teams from St. Joseph to Sacramento in 95 days. He worked as a miner, teamster, and storekeeper; he repaid the $250, suffered losses in a bank failure and a fire, and was back in Decatur in 20 months with some $5,000 in gold. The California trip, rather than his law practice, was the foundation for Oglesby's wealth.

He doubled his money by speculating in Decatur real estate, but first he went back to Kentucky to keep a boyhood promise and purchase the freedom of Uncle Tim, his father's slave. Oglesby credited his opposition to slavery to his memory of Uncle Tim's sale for $400. Throughout his public career, like Yates, he championed the interests of blacks. At his first inauguration, he said blacks and whites should have the same rights and privileges.

In 1852 Oglesby was a Whig candidate for presidential elector. He formed a law partnership with Sheridan Wait and handled stock subscriptions for the Indiana and Illinois Central railroad. He could afford to make a 20-month trip to Europe and the Near East in 1856 and 1857 that would compensate for his lack of culture and formal education. He traveled far and met important people. As he had done in Mexico and California, he wrote letters to hometown newspapers that told about visiting the English Parliament, hunting boar with the Prussian emperor, witnessing the czar's coronation in Moscow, sailing up the Nile River, crossing the Arabian desert, and reciting the Ten Commandments on Mount Sinai. Back home, his well-attended lectures gave him public speaking practice and a wider acquaintance.

Abraham Lincoln and Oglesby were close associates. In 1854 they corresponded about Richard Yates' drinking problem. Two years later, when Lincoln met with anti-Nebraska editors at Decatur to call the first Republican state convention, Oglesby toasted the Springfield lawyer as "our next candidate for United States Senator." At the 1860 Republican convention at Decatur, Oglesby, with an electrifying speech, was responsible for naming Lincoln the "railsplitter candidate." After the battle of Corinth, the president telegraphed General Grant that he was "very anxious to know the condition of General Oglesby, who is an intimate personal friend." Several hours before the president's assassination, the governor called at the White House and listened to the reading of four chapters of a Petroleum V. Nasby book. He played a prominent role in arranging for Lincoln's burial at Springfield, served as president of the Lincoln Monument Association, and in 1874 made the dedicatory address at the tomb in Springfield's Oak Ridge Cemetery.

Oglesby missed the Republican Party's founding convention at Bloomington in 1856 but returned from Europe in time to run for Congress and lose in 1858. In 1860 he won his first political office. He resigned when President Lincoln called for 300,000 30-day volunteers. Oglesby recruited a Decatur company and went to war as colonel of the 8th Illinois Volunteer Regiment. Until General U. S. Grant replaced him, he was commanding officer at Cairo, the southernmost point then held by Union troops.

As a brigade commander, Oglesby led the attack at Fort Donelson and was promoted to brigadier general. At Corinth he commanded one of the brigades that stopped the Confederates and then was critically wounded while leading a charge. After six months he returned to duty and, as a major general who had performed well in two battles, was given command of the XVI Corps. The wound was troublesome, however, and he soon asked to be relieved. Thereafter, he served in Washington as president of courts martial until it was time to resign from the army and run for governor.

Oglesby's First Term

In the selection of an 1864 candidate for governor, Lincoln did not take sides between Oglesby and State Auditor Jesse K. Dubois, who also had been a close friend. Adjutant General Allen C. Fuller, whose record as a homefront administrator was deserving, also was a candidate, and General John M. Palmer, still in uniform, received some votes. Oglesby led on the first ballot and was nominated on the second. As an ardent supporter of Lincoln, he was elected by 32,000 votes, with the big Republican counties in the north deciding the outcome. His opponent was Congressman James C. Robinson, who had defeated him six years earlier and had consistently voted for compromise and peace.

The country was prosperous, the Republican legislature supportive, and Oglesby's first term as governor was successful. It also was a time of personal tragedy. His inauguration, a quiet ceremony, was delayed a week because of the governor's grief over the death of his five-year-old son Dickie. His first wife, Anna White, whom he had married at Decatur in 1859, died in the Executive Mansion in May, 1868. She was survived by two children.

Before the surrender of Lee's army, at the governor's urging, Illinois became the first state to ratify the Thirteenth Amendment that outlawed slavery. Later the legislature ratified the Fourteenth Amendment that conferred citizenship on Negroes. It also repealed the repressive black laws that in varying forms had existed since statehood. In his official capacity, the governor telegraphed the House of Representatives that "the people of Illinois demand the impeachment of President Johnson and will heartily sustain our Congress."

Despite shortcomings of the legislature, important action was taken by the peacetime session, which the governor asked to give attention to long-neglected problems of education, development of natural resources, the needs of the poor, and encouragement of the arts and sciences. A referendum was ordered on the calling of a constitutional convention. The first appropriation was made for construction of the new state Capitol, which was completed in 1888. Oglesby supported the city of Urbana as the location of the new industrial university (now the University of Illinois) and appointed its first board of trustees. The elective office of attorney general was created, and Robert G. Ingersoll, the agnostic orator who was Oglesby's close friend and appointee, retained the position after the election. To achieve assessment uniformity, a state board of equalization was created, with members elected by districts. A first step was made toward regulation of railroads and warehouses. A law that made eight hours a legal day's work, except for farmers, was enacted at the request of unions but was not enforced. The first voter registration law was enacted.

Oglesby advocated for the reform of the overcrowded prison system under which, since 1837, the penitentiary at Joliet was leased to private parties who could profit from the leased labor of convicts. When the lessees lost money under postwar conditions, the privateers surrendered their lease. In the emergency, a special session of the legislature enacted a law for state control of prison operations and appropriated funds to buy machinery for prison industries. Earlier the logrolling legislature had voted for a southern Illinois penitentiary at Menard and a reformatory at Pontiac.

Masses of special and private bills, sometimes as many as 500 in an omnibus package, were railroaded through without deliberation and with accompanying allegations of bribery. As a result, there was increasing sentiment for a new constitution. Chicago traction ordinances became a legislative issue with passage of a bill extending from 25 to 99 years the franchises of horse-car companies that had refused to issue interline transfers. The governor's veto was quickly overridden, after which he gave up and made no further effort to stop the scandalous flood of special legislation.

Oglesby's Run for a Short Second Term

When his term ended, Oglesby went back to Decatur and cultivated friendships in G.A.R. (Grand Army of the Republic) posts. In 1872 he was available when Lincoln's party faced its greatest crisis, a deep split in its ranks. Scandals marred President Grant's first term; economic conditions had turned sour; some people objected to harsh treatment of Southern leaders; and Governor John M. Palmer, who had succeeded Oglesby, had started to act like a Democrat. The Republicans feared future elections would be lost unless former slaves voted in the South. In Illinois they were alarmed when Democrats and dissenting Republicans held simultaneous conventions on opposite sides of the Statehouse square. For governor, both nominated Gustave Koerner, the German intellectual who had been elected lieutenant governor twenty years earlier by Democrats and then turned Republican on the slavery issue. The two conventions divided the rest of the state offices. In what seemed an emergency, Oglesby got his second nomination by acclamation.

The Liberal Republican movement collapsed in mid-campaign because its presidential candidate, Horace Greeley, was unpopular among Democrats. For second terms, Grant carried Illinois by 57,000 votes and Oglesby by 40,000. It might have been different, at least closer, had Grant been opposed by an Illinois man. Senator Lyman Trumbull, Supreme Court Justice David Davis, and Governor Palmer wanted the nomination. In the future, Trumbull and Palmer would become losing Democratic candidates for governor. Some of the dissident Republicans returned to the mainstream Republican fold, which henceforth had conservative foundations.

At the Republican national convention, Oglesby made an unscheduled speech that focused first on former slaves, who for the first time were voting delegates, and then on the presence in the gallery of Garrett Smith, who before the war had been a prominent abolitionist. Cullom wrote that Oglesby "set the crowd wild."

Oglesby's second term lasted 10 days. During the election he had campaigned for Republican legislators who would elect him to the U.S. Senate. According to plan, the new governor resigned, turned the state over to Lieutenant Governor John L. Beveridge, and replaced Senator Lyman Trumbull in Washington.

Because Oglesby's colleagues did not appreciate his arm-waving speeches, the Senate term was a failure. Like Yates, but unlike Douglas and Trumbull, he contributed little to the discussion of national issues. He dreamed of running for president in 1876, but he found Eastern audiences disinterested in the oratory that was effective at G.A.R. reunions in Illinois. When he sought a second Senate term, the Republican caucus vote was 80 to 26 in favor of John A. Logan, who had been senator from 1871 to 1877.

The Third Term

Twenty years after he first became governor, Oglesby won a third term; this time by 15,000 votes, his closest election. Oglesby's opponent, Carter Harrison, the former and future mayor of Chicago, was Kentucky-born; he didn't understand rural Illinoisans and they didn't understand him. Harrison's political stands drew criticism even in his own party, notably from Congressman William R. Morrison, a downstate Democratic powerhouse.

Because both parties had elected 76 members of the Illinois House of Representatives, Oglesby's 1884 inauguration was delayed more than two weeks until Elijah M. Haines, the lone independent, was elected speaker. Haines, who had become speaker 10 years earlier under similar circumstances, again presided over a disorderly session that accomplished little aside from establishing a soldiers' and sailors' home at Quincy and appropriating money to complete work on the Statehouse.

On May 4, 1886 police moved to break up a labor rally in Haymarket Square in Chicago. A bomb exploded, injuring and killing several people, including seven police officers. For 10 emotional days after the U. S. Supreme Court refused to intervene in the case, Oglesby was deluged with pleas for and against leniency for several convicted anarchists. Like predecessor governors, he had regarded his office as administrative and, hesitating to interfere with judicial findings, he had refused to intervene with many death sentences. But there is evidence that he wanted to commute the Haymarket sentences and hoped for public support from Chicago's business leaders. Finally, a day before the executions were scheduled, he commuted the sentences of Samuel Fielden and Michael Schwab, the only anarchists who might be classified as contrite. Another killed himself in his cell with a bomb. Four others were hanged November 11, 1887.

An economic conservative in public, Oglesby in private criticized corporation heads who called for state protection whenever threatened with violence. When deteriorating economic conditions brought strikes by Joliet and Lemont quarrymen in 1885 and by East St. Louis switchmen and Chicago stockyards employees the next year, he followed precedent and restored order by calling out troops. In Illinois factories, work stoppages were frequent, more than half of them involving long working hours.

Retiring to the Rubber Chicken Circuit

During his first year as senator, Oglesby married Emma Keays, the widowed daughter of John D. Gillett, Logan County's largest landowner and cattle feeder. In Decatur they built in the Italianate style a large and handsome house with seven fireplaces. In it were born the four children of their second marriages. When he left the governorship for the third and last time, Oglesby did not return to Decatur. He and his wife built a house around an old chimney and fireplace remaining from a double log cabin built in 1835 by James Latham, the first settler in Logan County. In 1890 they erected Oglehurst, a more imposing residence on the Elkhart hill.

His final years were active. Republican legislators attempted to return him to the Senate in an 1890 deadlock finally broken when Democrats elected another aging general, John M. Palmer. Oglesby joined four other former Republican governors in a campaign tour in support of John R. Tanner, the 1896 winner. To the end he was in demand as an entertaining and inspirational speaker. One of his best known examples of old-style oratory was his impromptu tribute to Indian corn, delivered September 9, 1894, at the Chicago Fellowship Club's harvest home festival.

He died April 24, 1899, at Oglehurst. Funeral services were conducted by an Episcopal bishop at the Gillett family's private chapel. One of his sons, John G. Oglesby, was elected lieutenant governor in 1908 and 1916.

15th Governor

John McAuley Palmer
1817-1900

1817 – Born, Sept. 13, in Scott County, Kentucky.

1848 – Serves as a delegate to the state constitutional convention

1851 - 1853 – Serves in the Senate as an intermittent member of the 17th and 18th General Assemblies.

1856 – Presides over the Bloomington convention that establishes the Illinois Republican Party.

1859 – Unsuccessfully runs for Congress.

1861 – President Lincoln promotes Palmer to brigadier general; he continues a distinguished Civil War combat career until an 1864 dispute with General William T. Sherman cuts it short.

1864 – Lincoln appoints Palmer military governor of Kentucky.

1868 – Although declaring himself not a candidate, Palmer wins the Republican gubernatorial nomination on the first ballot and easily defeats Democrat Congressman John R. Eden in the general election.

1870 – Illinois adopts a new constitution on July 2, among its provisions are that all executive officers of the state run independently and that the governor can succeed himself; Blacks are granted the right to vote, but women are not.

1871 – An October 8-9 fire destroys three and a half square miles in the heart of Chicago and costs 300 lives.

1872 – Palmer chooses not to seek his party's nomination for a second term as governor because he feels he cannot campaign for the reelection of President Grant.

1888 – After years as a Democratic advocate, Palmer accepts the Democratic nomination for governor; he loses to Joseph Fifer by 1.6 percent of the vote.

1891 - 1897 – Serves as U.S. Senator, unable to support the Democrat's monetary policy, he starts the Gold Democrat faction.

1896 – Runs for president as the nominee of the Gold Democrats.

1900 – Dies, Sept. 24.

Republican
January 11, 1869 to January 13, 1873

During a six-decade career of distinction, John M. Palmer was a Republican governor, a Democratic senator, and an activist in three other parties. Seldom neutral, a man of independence, integrity, and intelligence, he changed political affiliations whenever he was in major disagreement with the party to which he belonged at the time. In an era of political volatility, Palmer was a Democrat, an Anti-Nebraska Democrat, a Republican, a Liberal Republican, a Democrat again, and finally the presidential nominee of the "Gold" Democratic Party.

"I had my own views," Palmer told colleagues in the U.S. Senate near the end of his career. "I was not the slave of any party." He added that, instead of following party doctrine, "I thought for myself and [have] spoken my own words on all occasions."

Much of his life Palmer was a Democrat, but he left Stephen A. Douglas' Democratic party in 1854 on the moral issue of slavery and that of William Jennings Bryan's Democratic Party in 1896 on the economic issue of bi-metallism. He helped Abraham Lincoln found the Republican Party in Illinois. In the Civil War as a major general he rose to the command of an army corps. One of the best lawyers in the state, he accepted a draft to run for governor.

At the age of 79, because he believed that the nation's economy would be ruined by the Bryan-Altgeld silver policy, he ran for president on the National "Gold" Democratic ticket and thereby contributed to the election of Republican William McKinley.

Normally, Palmer was conservative and temperate, but he could be stubborn, as when he asked to be relieved of his army corps command during a quarrel over seniority. He was inconsistent when he called for the impeachment of Andrew Johnson, who was following Lincoln's moderate reconstruction policies, and when he criticized Governor Altgeld for objecting because President McKinley sent federal troops to keep order in Chicago in 1894. Twenty-three years earlier, Governor Palmer had complained to President Grant about the unrequested presence of soldiers in Chicago after the 1871 fire. In 1891, when Palmer as the Democratic candidate was elected United States Senator by the legislature, Altgeld had supported him in public but secretly tried to get the office for himself.

Palmer's Early Legal and Military Career

John McAuley Palmer, a native Kentuckian, was born on September 13, 1817, near Eagle Creek in Scott County. At the age of 14, he was brought to Illinois by his father, Louis D. Palmer, an impoverished Baptist minister who admired Andrew Jackson and hated slavery. A wagon breakdown caused them to settle near Wood River. The death in two years of his mother, Ann Hansford Tutt Palmer, forced the breakup of the family. John, who had little schooling but showed an early aptitude for reading, was 18 when his father "gave him his time," an old-fashioned permission for a minor son to leave home. "I have no money to expend for your education," the father said, "but a healthy boy as you are needs no help; you may go tomorrow morning. I give you your time. Don't disgrace me. May God bless you."

John and an older brother Elihu worked at odd jobs for 18 months while they attended Alton College, which opened under the manual labor system and became Shurtleff College. Then the future governor tried coopering, peddled clocks in the Military Tract, and taught school at Canton, where he began to read law in his spare time.

At 21, Palmer studied law in the Carlinville office of John S. Greathouse and lived with Elihu, a learned and eccentric clergyman. Stephen A. Douglas recommended that he open an office in Carlinville the year he was admitted to the bar because he was too poor to move to a larger town. In time he found clients, and in 1842, while living in a log house, he married Malinda Ann Neely, who became the mother of his ten children. While his law practice slowly developed, he had time to work his way into local political prominence. He was a Democrat by inclination and with Douglas' encouragement, he was elected probate justice of the peace, constitutional convention delegate, county judge, and state senator.

At the 1848 constitutional convention he advocated free common schools in which sectarian education would be prohibited. He established a reputation for independence and fearlessness. He was called an abolitionist when he opposed a proposal to bar free blacks from Illinois.

In the legislature he broke with Douglas by opposing repeal of the Missouri Compromise, a pro-slavery measure that would allow Nebraska settlers to determine the question of slavery for themselves. He resigned his seat and was reelected as an Anti-Nebraska Democrat. He led a five-man antislavery bloc that triumphed when Lyman Trumbull was elected United States Senator, the office Abraham Lincoln wanted. Palmer did not turn Republican until the 1856 Democratic state convention endorsed Douglas for president.

Palmer was the obvious choice to preside at the 1856 Bloomington convention at which the Illinois Republican Party was founded. Robust and ruddy, he was a 200-pounder who stood slightly under six feet. As a speaker, he lacked Oglesby's fluency and Yates' ornate language, but his voice was pleasant, his vocabulary accurate, and his fund of information extensive. He reasoned clearly and his speeches were forcible and convincing. Photographs show him with a beard that covered his cheeks during the Civil War and was spade-shaped most of the time thereafter.

Personal courage was one of his characteristics. On one occasion during a congressional campaign that had been marked by name-calling, he carried a loaded pistol into an opposition meeting and, placing it in cocked position before him, castigated the Democratic Party.

At the 1856 Republican national convention, Palmer placed in nomination for vice president the name of Lincoln, who received 110 votes. At Lincoln's request, he reluctantly and unsuccessfully ran for Congress in 1859. The next year he helped engineer Lincoln's presidential nomination at the Chicago Wigwam convention. He was a Republican elector and in early 1861, in recognition of his political reliability, was an Illinois delegate to a national peace conference that did not make concessions to the South.

During the Civil War, Palmer simultaneously was a loyal supporter of Lincoln and a Radical Republican who protested arbitrary arrests by the military. In Illinois his stature as a volunteer officer was exceeded only by that of General John A. Logan. Without Mexican War experience (he had raised a company that was not needed), he was one of the first politicians to be given a colonel's commission by Governor Yates. Before the end of 1861 he was promoted to brigadier general by Lincoln on recommendation of Republican congressmen. Quickly he demonstrated an aptitude for command, intelligent understanding of the tactical situation, and defensive stubbornness. His 14th Illinois Infantry Regiment began service in Missouri and took part in the capture of Mississippi River Island No. 10. As a major general he stood fast under repeated assaults at Stone's River and Chickamauga. He was promoted to command of an army corps for the Atlanta campaign, but by August 1864, his battlefield career was terminated by a dispute with General William T. Sherman. Palmer had developed a low opinion of West Point officers and protested when General John M. Schofield, whom he considered his junior, was placed over him. Within military channels, he was relieved at his own request. The merits of that dispute are unclear, but Palmer had been hoping that he could resign and return to Carlinville where a son was ailing.

In 1864 Lincoln appointed him military governor of Kentucky, where the population was evenly divided between loyalists and Southern sympathizers. His evenhanded orders, which established the rights of blacks while deferring to Kentucky law whenever possible, involved him in a heated controversy with state authorities. When Palmer was indicted for violating Kentucky's black laws, he announced that if he should be arrested, his second in command was under orders to storm the jail. The sheriff did not serve the warrant on him.

Because a Negro boy had accompanied him home while on sick leave from the army and then became a member of the Palmer household, the general was indicted at Carlinville for violating a black code provision that John A. Logan had introduced in the legislature a decade earlier. Palmer was acquitted when he insisted on being tried by a jury.

On the homefront, Palmer was one of the most popular of the military leaders. While he was still in uniform, 75 delegates to the 1864 Republican state convention in Decatur voted to nominate him for governor. Two years later, when the Grand Army of the Republic spread across the North, Palmer, instead of Logan, was the first state commander.

In September 1866, Palmer moved his family to Springfield and became the partner of Milton Hay, who ran one of the state's most prestigious law firms. In fact, Palmer moved in to replace future governor, Shelby M. Cullom, who was off to Washington to serve as congressman. Palmer's colleagues had great respect for his legal ability. He was an expert on constitutional law who depended more on fundamental principles than the citation of cases. But the former general did not confine himself to the law, and he never avoided politics and public service.

The Reluctant Candidate Becomes Governor

Palmer had personal reasons for not wanting to be governor. As a lawyer, his income in two months was equal to the $1,500 a year salary fixed by the 1848 Constitution. At home in a large and expandable household were his wife, six children, and two dependent sisters-in-law. Tom, the youngest son, was an epileptic who would die near the end of the governor's term. Susie, the youngest daughter, was blind. Mrs. Palmer, an invalid, in a wartime letter had referred to herself as "but a poor, weak woman, not a highly polished wife that likes to cut a dash. But, after all, we have been happy in our own way."

"I am not and do not intend to be a candidate," Palmer insisted in advance of his draft by the 1868 Republican Convention. His repeated declaration of disinterest encouraged Attorney General Robert G. Ingersoll, Congressman-at-large S. W. Moulton, and State Auditor Jesse K. Dubois to run for nomination as governor. At the convention Palmer had a clear majority on the first ballot, accepted the nomination, and won easily over John R. Eden, a Democratic congressman. After the war, Palmer followed the standard Republican practice of "bloody shirt" speeches in which local issues were avoided.

His inauguration speech shocked Republicans and delighted Democrats by taking a strong and unexpected stand for states' rights. The new governor insisted that the United States Constitution recognizes that the states have inherent rights and that the federal government is limited to specifically enumerated powers. Since the wartime emergency had passed, he declared that "the states' just authority must be respected by the federal government." With a general demand for control of corporations and regulation of railroads, he told the legislature that abuses must be corrected and rigid economy practiced. Palmer directly challenged the Republican premise that the simultaneous growth of the federal government and business corporations was beneficial to the country.

He was a reform governor who vetoed more than 100 private and special bills at the start of his administration. His 1869 veto messages complained that floods of corrupt legislation gave special privileges to capitalists and promoters and allowed tax money to be spent for personal or private benefit. Typical vetoes, all over-ridden before adoption of the Constitution of 1870, objected to municipal bond issues that paid for the sites of railroad shops and business firms and to the investment of local tax funds in hotels, coal and insurance companies, and warehouses. The Illinois Supreme Court upheld Palmer's veto of a "tax grab" bill that had wide support in rural communities where tax-supported bonds had been issued to help pay for railroad construction. Counties and other local governments wanted to be relieved of their obligation. Palmer held that taxation should be uniform throughout the state and said that the proposed legislation would be a precedent for unwise bond issues. Vetoed and repassed was the Chicago "lakefront" bill that ceded downtown real estate to the Illinois Central railroad. That law was repealed in 1873 and the controversy settled by federal courts 15 years later.

His barrage of vetoes called attention to legislative excesses that were ended only by the midterm adoption of the Constitution of 1870.

After the 1871 great Chicago fire destroyed three and a half square miles of the city, Palmer showed how nearly $3 million could be appropriated for the city's financial relief. His solution, presented at a special legislative session, was to reimburse the city for money it had spent on deepening the Illinois and Michigan Canal. In the fire emergency, Palmer acted promptly to keep informed about the amount of destruction and looting in the burned area. A diplomatic crisis arose when General Philip H. Sheridan, responding to a direct appeal from a local relief agency, detailed four army companies to Chicago in what seemed to be a long-term, law-and-order mission. In the chaotic situation, the protocol of consulting the governor had been overlooked. Palmer protested that the federal government did not have the power to intrude in a situation in which the state had jurisdiction. President Grant courteously avoided the issue, and neither the legislature nor the public supported the governor.

In the spring of 1872, Palmer announced that he could not campaign for President Grant for reelection. Therefore, although he was eligible under the new state constitution, he would not seek a second term as governor. Whether he could have been renominated is uncertain. Palmer's states' rights advocacy was unpopular with old-line Republicans, and Shelby M. Cullom, who would be the 28th General Assembly's speaker of the House, had lined up high-level endorsements to return Richard J. Oglesby to the governor's office.

Before his term as governor ended, Palmer had ceased to be a Republican. At the 1872 Liberal Republican convention at Cincinnati, David Davis had half the Illinois delegation, with the others split between Palmer and Lyman Trumbull. Palmer ordered his delegates to support Trumbull, but the nomination went to Horace Greeley, who President Grant easily defeated. In the Illinois gubernatorial election, the governor supported the Liberal Republican-Democratic coalition candidate, Gustave Koerner.

A Party-Hopping Ex-Governor

A private citizen again, Palmer resumed a law practice in Springfield and briefly was a mugwump – an independent. He denounced monopolies and called the old parties useless when he spoke at a statewide meeting of farmers. However, by 1876 he was a Democratic activist again – but with reservation. He supported Samuel J. Tilden for the presidency, but at the state level the

Democrats had formed a coalition with the Greenbackers on a platform that opposed specie payment of the government debt. As a result, Palmer, who was a conservative on monetary issues, did not campaign for Lewis Steward, a coalition-supported Greenbacker who lost the governorship to Shelby Cullom by 7,000 votes.

Samuel Tilden beat Rutherford Birchard Hayes in the balloting in the 1876 presidential election, but Republicans challenged the vote totals from Oregon and claimed that blacks had not been allowed to vote in South Carolina, Florida, and Louisiana. With the electoral college votes from these states, the Republicans could put Hayes in the White House. To avoid a legislative deadlock on the issue, the Congress appointed a 15-man Electoral Commission to arbitrate the problem. The national Democratic Party sent Palmer to Louisiana as chairman of a delegation of observers. But the commission itself was stacked with Republicans and the necessary electoral votes went to Hayes.

Palmer stuck with the Democrats a while. For 21 ballots at the start of the 1877 legislative session, Palmer was the Democratic caucus choice for senator. Then he withdrew in a deadlock that eventually saw the election of David Davis as an independent. At the 1884 Democratic state convention, Palmer as keynoter espoused the party's platform planks for an eight-hour day and the right of labor to organize, causes that had gained support since the tumultuous 1877 railroad strikes. In 1888, Democrats proposed that Palmer accept their gubernatorial nomination with an understanding that he need not campaign actively. He insisted that an all-out effort be made to carry the state. He criticized Illinois governors as a class, saying they had used the office "as a stepping-stone to other places."

Aggressively denouncing Republican conservatism and taking an early stand for labor and other liberal causes, the elder statesman spoke in 60 counties and came within 12,547 votes of defeating Republican Joseph W. Fifer in the year that Grover Cleveland lost the presidency to Benjamin Harrison.

Palmer then convinced Democratic leaders that he could be elected senator in 1890, if the party endorsed him in early summer on a liberal and pro-labor platform. A two-month deadlock ended with the election of Palmer. Democratic candidates who campaigned as Palmer supporters were elected to 101 legislative seats, along with 100 Republicans and three members of the Farmers

Mutual Benefit Association.

During the Senate term, which began when he was 75 years old, Palmer opposed the protective tariff and favored the direct election of senators and pensions for Supreme Court justices. He became concerned about inflationist agitation for the unlimited coinage of silver at an arbitrary ratio of 16-to-1 with gold – an idea supported by William Jennings Bryan and Illinois Governor Altgeld. The senator did not object to coinage of silver but believed that gold, being more expensive, would disappear from circulation in the United States and that the national economy could not prosper on a silver basis. He could support the Republican national platform but not McKinley, a high-tariff man. With the quiet encouragement of President Cleveland, Palmer helped organize, wrote the platform for, and became the presidential nominee of the National "Gold" Democratic Party.

At the age of 79, he campaigned in major cities with the vice presidential candidate, Confederate General Simon Bolivar Buckner of Kentucky. Their well-attended speeches denounced bimetallism. While they didn't specifically ask people to vote for McKinley, in an unusually hard-fought campaign they contributed to Bryan's defeat.

After his Senate term, Palmer returned to Springfield. His frail wife had died of tuberculosis in 1885. Three years later he married Mrs. Hannah L. Kimball, the city librarian. In good health and with a clear memory, he completed two valuable books. His memoirs, *Personal Recollections: The Story of an Earnest Life*, in considerable part is an explanation and justification of the positive stands taken during his long career. Also bearing his name is a two-volume collection of biographies, *The Bench and Bar of Illinois*. He was in demand as a speaker. As one of the last survivors, he attended the 44th anniversary reunion of delegates to the 1856 Bloomington convention. He died in his sleep the night of September 24, 1900.

16th
Governor

John Lourie Beveridge
1824 -1910

1824 – Born, July 6, near Greenwich, New York.

1858 – Becomes a delegate to the state Republican convention.

1861 - 1866 – Serves in the Union army, mostly in the 8th and 17th Illinois Cavalry.

1870 – Elected state senator; serves 18 months in the 27th General Assembly

1872 – Beveridge resigns as Illinois congressman-at-large after he is elected lieutenant governor on a ticket headed by Richard James Oglesby.

1873 – Becomes governor on January 23, when, as part of a campaign deal, Republican legislators send Oglesby to the U.S. Senate.

1881 – President Chester Alan Arthur appoints Beveridge assistant United States treasurer.

1910 – Dies, May 3.

Republican
January 23, 1873 to January 8, 1877

John Lourie Beveridge, the third and last Civil War general to become governor of Illinois, served all but the first 10 days of the second term of Richard J. Oglesby, who resigned when he was elected U. S. Senator. Beveridge, the first chief executive from Cook County, lived in Evanston and practiced law in Chicago. He wasn't well known outside Cook and DeKalb counties, but in 1872, when Republicans briefly needed a more liberal image, he was elected lieutenant governor.

Cold and inclined to be unsociable, he was a temperance advocate who had been a hard-riding cavalry commander. More important, at a critical juncture for the GOP in Illinois, the dry, politically conservative Protestant chose not to follow Congressman John F. Farnsworth, his law partner and comrade-in-arms, into the Liberal Republican Party. A decade after the war over slavery, Lincoln's party was in the process of turning conservative, and Beveridge's reputation as something of a reformer was a political asset when he was nominated for lieutenant governor in 1872. But after he advanced to the governorship the next winter, the time for a reformer had already passed.

Beveridge, a dignified man with a venerable beard and silver hair, never tried to be a backslapper. John Moses, who was both a Republican activist and a historian, wrote that the "temperate life of the new governor and the religious tone of his mind were not such as to recommend him to the favor of saloon politicians....He possessed the courage of his convictions and never dreamed of sacrificing principle to popularity."

Tea Totaling Beveridge's Early Years

Born July 6, 1824, on a farm near Greenwich, Washington County, New York, he was the son of George and Ann Hoy Beveridge, who were of Scotch and Scotch-Irish descent. They were seceding Presbyterians so strict that the future governor was 19 before he heard a sermon of another denomination. When he was 18, the family moved to Illinois to a farm near Somonauk in sparsely settled DeKalb County. John, who had received a good common school education in New York, taught school one winter, attended the academy at Granville, and then completed the academic course at Rock River Seminary at Mount Morris.

Rather than burden his parents with the cost of a college education, in 1845 he went to Tennessee with $40 to teach and become a lawyer. Four years later he returned to his father's home with a wife, a son and a daughter, and 25 cents. Due to an associate's mismanagement, a business venture had failed, but Beveridge had stayed in Tennessee until his debts were paid. His wife was Helen Mar Judson, daughter of Philo Judson, pastor of the Clark Street Methodist Church in Chicago. For the next five years Beveridge practiced law in Sycamore, kept books for businessmen, and did some engineering.

In the spring of 1854 Beveridge moved to Evanston, a new suburb north of Chicago platted by Methodists as a site for Northwestern University, for which Judson was financial agent and business manager. Beveridge became a lay leader of the suburb's Methodist church, a member of the drainage commission beginning in 1855, and secretary of the Evanston Pier Company in 1870. In 1855 he opened a law office in Chicago. He became politically active and in 1858, as a delegate to the Republican state convention, heard Lincoln's "House Divided" speech.

The future governor rose quickly through the ranks of the army during the Civil War. When John F. Farnsworth organized and became colonel of the 8th Illinois Cavalry, Beveridge recruited Company F and was elected its captain. The line officers then elected him the second of three majors. Organized at St. Charles, Farnsworth's "Big Abolition Regiment" was sent east as part of the Army of the Potomac. It paraded before the White House and spent the winter of 1861-1862 on the outskirts of Washington. Major Beveridge commanded the regiment during much of the summer of 1863. At Gettysburg two dismounted battalions of the 8th Cavalry fired the first shots of the three-day battle. In 1863 he returned to Illinois and at St. Charles recruited the 17th Illinois Cavalry, which drilled at Alton while guarding Confederate prisoners. As its colonel he spent the rest of the war in Missouri, where he engaged in skirmishes, chased guerrillas, and countered Sterling Price's raid.

Oglesby Opens the Door

When the war ended, Beveridge was given the brevet rank of brigadier general and was sent to St. Louis to preside over military trials. Not until 1866 did he return to his law practice and become involved in the political wars. While his military record was commendable – he had been in several dozen battles and skirmishes – it did not make him conspicuous among the generals and colonels who were volunteering for federal and state offices.

Nevertheless, in seven years Beveridge rose to the governorship. Volunteer officers made good candidates, and he was elected sheriff, a two-year office, in 1866 and state senator four years later for a term that lasted 11 months. When associates of Lincoln, including Farnsworth, began to join the new Liberal Republican movement, Beveridge was rewarded for not following them. Elected to a vacancy as congressman-at-large, he resigned after 11 months when he was elected lieutenant governor in 1872 on a ticket headed by Richard James Oglesby. Oglesby, as part of a deal concocted during the campaign, was elected senator 10 days after he took office, and Beveridge walked into office.

In the pattern of his time, Beveridge was a caretaker governor devoted to economy and a low governmental profile. Steady progress had been made in paying off the public improvements debt of the 1837 era, and the governors were not expected to find new ways to spend public funds. In his 1875 message to the legislature, Beveridge regretted that Illinois did not practice budgeting.

The Beveridge administration coincided with former Governor John M. Palmer's return to the Democratic Party, the prolonged and severe Panic of 1873, and the Granger movement that was a political force in Illinois long enough for the legislature to adopt a workable railroad regulation law. His administration began with a setback when the state senate refused to confirm his nominees for members of the new railroad and warehouse commission. In the 1874 midterm election, for the first time in 12 years,

Illinois went Democratic.

Beveridge's career paralleled that of Governor Ford in that he was criticized for failure to cope with prolonged lawlessness in southern Illinois. A "bloody vendetta" started in Williamson County and extended into Franklin and Jackson counties. Governor Palmer had offered a $1,000 reward for the arrest of night riders responsible for murders and whippings. Beveridge was convinced that the state could do little, and nothing happened when he reminded state's attorneys of their law enforcement responsibilities.

The disastrous and long-lasting Panic of 1873 arrived soon after his inauguration. The next year the governor sent 100 rifles and ammunition to keep order in St. Clair County, where striking white union members, who had been paid four cents a bushel for digging coal, had prevented blacks from working for three cents.

Beveridge was the first governor to occupy the executive suite in the unfinished Capitol building, on which construction continued until 1888. He appointed a black man, John J. Bird of Cairo, as a trustee of the state industrial university that was renamed the University of Illinois.

For three years and 50 weeks, his conservative administration was generally satisfactory, and in 1876 he felt that as a loyal Republican, he deserved election to a full term. The *Chicago Tribune* was persistently hostile, however, and both political parties wanted to steer clear of temperance politics that might close saloons on Sundays, or else close them altogether. Elihu B. Washburne of Galena, the minister to France, announced and then withdrew his candidacy for governor. The only other candidate of consequence was Shelby Cullom. The power of incumbency was not operative, and the Republican state convention voted for Cullom 389 to 87.

Retirement in the Private Sector

Out of office, Beveridge returned to Evanston to live. In Chicago he was a partner in a private banking firm. In 1880 as a Republican national convention delegate, he supported Ulysses S. Grant for a third term. In 1881 President Chester Alan Arthur appointed him assistant United States treasurer at Chicago, an office he held until Grover Cleveland became president. In 1895 the former governor moved to Hollywood, California, where he died May 3, 1910.

17th Governor

Shelby Moore Cullom
1829-1914

1829 – Born, Nov. 22, in Wayne County, Kentucky.

1857 - 1859 – Served in the House in the 20th General Assembly.

1861 - 1863 – Served as speaker of the House for the 22nd General Assembly.

1862 – Loses an election for state senator.

1864 – Begins the first of three terms in Congress.

1870 – Loses a bid for a fourth term in Congress.

1873 - 1877 – Serves in the House in the 28th and 29th General Assemblies; was speaker of the House for the 28th Assembly.

1876 – Survives the "Pekin whisky ring" scandal and rounds up enough delegates prior to the state convention to win the Republican gubernatorial nomination; Defeats Lewis Steward in the closest general election since Edward Coles won in 1822.

1880 – Wins a second term as governor.

1883 – Resigns the governor's office to become U.S. Senator.

1883 - 1913 – Serves as U.S. Senator from Illinois.

1914 – Dies, Jan. 28.

Republican

January 8, 1877 to January 10, 1881

January 10, 1881 to February 16, 1883

Shelby M. Cullom was an able, durable, rather colorless, and generally conservative Republican who sat out the Civil War. But he proved to be a better politician than the generals and colonels who for decades were his competitors for public favor. He was twice elected governor, resigned that office after six years, and then began a five-term, 30-year career in the U.S. Senate. Earlier service as state representative and congressman gave him a total of a half-century in public office, the last 40 years of which were continuous. When he finally retired, unwillingly, he was 83 years old. Of all of Illinois' governors, only Adlai E. Stevenson and Frank O. Lowden were better known nationally.

In the legislature Cullom first established a reputation that stayed with him throughout his career in Washington: He was a conservative who avoided extremes but wasn't always orthodox; he was a dependable Republican on roll-call voting; and he was known for his personal integrity. In the field of government, his greatest achievement was the creation of the Interstate Commerce Commission, the first step toward federal regulation of commerce. As speaker of the Illinois House of Representatives during the

Granger era, he guided to enactment a law for state regulation of railroad rates that survived constitutional attacks. In the Senate, he saw that the problem was national and spent his first term creating the legislative climate for passage of his regulatory bill. He was the first chairman of the Senate Interstate Commerce Committee and later held the Foreign Relations Committee chairmanship longer than any predecessor.

A tall and spare man, Cullom was proud to think that he "looked like Lincoln," who had been a friend of Cullom's father and in whose office the young Cullom had hoped to begin the study of law. Cullom's hair was black, his forehead high and massive, and his clear-cut features expressive. His speeches were convincing rather than oratorical. He was at his persuasive best in face-to-face explanations of his political and legislative plans.

Although Cullom was disappointed three times in his ambition to become president, his political astuteness was exceeded only by Lincoln's. An ego-centered lone wolf, who in his early career had been a well-paid lawyer and later a bank president, he instinctively understood how to get his colleagues to cooperate in solving governmental problems in ways that won public approval. People trusted him, and he had two special talents: He could appear to be favoring both sides of a question, and he could get elected with a minimum of personal effort. Most of the campaigns began with Cullom expecting to lose to generals or colonels who had popular followings at Republican conventions or to Democrats whose optimism increased when economic conditions were unfavorable. And he generally won those elections by narrow margins.

As Republican governor, he distributed state jobs to some Democrats and to spokesmen of Chicago ethnic groups. As senator, he headed a federal patronage organization that loyally and successfully supported him in election after election. Two of its leaders became federal judges. But "Uncle Shelby" seldom tried to influence the nomination of state candidates or to form alliances with other Republicans. The Cullom political machine was unique in that it cared only about Cullom. Between his reelection campaigns, it went into hibernation. Its inactivity encouraged other Republicans to think he could be beaten, but when the senator needed votes, his "federal crowd" efficiently spread the word that the voters should continue to trust the wise and experienced man who was respected and influential in Washington.

From Farm Boy to Congressman

Shelby Moore Cullom was the last of the governors from Kentucky. Born November 22, 1829, in Wayne County, he was the seventh of 12 children of Richard Northcraft Cullom and Elizabeth Coffey, who moved to a Tazewell County farm when Shelby was one year old. The father, an antislavery Whig of some prominence, served eight years in the Illinois legislature. On Abraham Lincoln's advice, young Shelby read law in the Springfield firm of John T. Stuart and Benjamin Edwards. The rest of his life he lived in Springfield or Washington.

In 1855 he was admitted to the bar, married, and entered politics. His first wife, Hannah Fisher, died in six years, leaving Cullom with the care of two small daughters. In 1863 he married her sister, Julia. In his first campaign, he was elected city attorney. In 1856 he was defeated for presidential elector as a Know-Nothing and elected state representative by a local coalition of Republicans and Know-Nothings. A follower of Lincoln, he lost when he ran for reelection in 1858, but two years later, when the legislature for the first time was controlled by Republicans, he was the young speaker of the House at the opening of the Civil War. There he made a reputation as an efficient and harmonious presiding officer. In the Democratic mid-war sweep of 1862, he was defeated for state senator. Lincoln recognized him with an appointment to a commission that investigated claims involving army purchases at Cairo.

He never wore a Union uniform in the Civil War – and hence wasn't later eligible for membership in the politically powerful Grand Army of the Republic (G.A.R.). He never mentioned the reason for his wartime civilian status in his speeches or memoirs. He had been a healthy Tazewell County farm boy. But, as a young man on his way to attend Rock River Seminary at Mount Morris, he became soaked and chilled while leading stagecoach horses through a heavy snowstorm. Thereafter, he was unable to do hard physical work due to a damaged heart. (He nevertheless completed the two-year course at the seminary.) After his death, an associate revealed that the senator – who as speaker of the Illinois House at the start of the Civil War did not retire from public office until Woodrow Wilson entered the White House – was subject to fainting spells that fortunately never occurred in public.

Starting in 1861, he made money as the law partner of Milton Hay in Springfield. Because he wanted a political career most of all, he gave up a lucrative practice to become a congressman. He had accumulated $30,000 and "never saw that much money again." He served three terms in Congress, starting in 1864. There, as chairman of the Committee on Territories, he introduced a bill to outlaw polygamy in Utah. Losing a fourth-term campaign in 1870, he returned to Springfield and briefly was president of the State National Bank. His stature was such that he was chairman of the Illinois delegation to the 1872 Republican National Convention, where he placed President Grant in nomination for a second term with the shortest speech on record, one sentence of 82 words:

> Gentlemen of the convention: On behalf of the great Republican Party of Illinois, and that of the Union – in the name of liberty, of loyalty, of justice, of law – in the interest of economy, of good government, of peace, and of the equal rights of all – remembering with profound gratitude his glorious achievements in the field, and his noble statesmanship as chief magistrate of this great nation – I nominate as President of the United States, for a second term, Ulysses S. Grant.

In the election of 1872, to help block a campaign to move the seat of state government to Peoria, Cullom won a return engagement to the legislature. Again elected speaker, he was primarily responsible for enactment of a law that achieved state regulation of railroad rates. The inflexible Granger laws in other states had failed, and the Illinois Supreme Court had upset rural voters by invalidating an 1871 law that forbade discrimination by passenger carriers. Cullom, who was a reasonable man, persuaded the legislature to provide that railroads charging more than a fair rate were guilty of extortion, but allowed them to prove that their rates were justified.

Cullom was reelected to the House in 1874, but economic setbacks had reduced Republican numbers, and he lost the speakership to Elijah M. Haines, the only independent. He wanted to stay in politics and decided that his best chance was to run for governor.

Governor Cullom

For Cullom, winning was seldom easy. Governor John L. Beveridge, a cavalry general, controlled state patronage and wanted a full term. Two other generals, John I. Rinaker and Green B. Raum, were candidates, as were Thomas S. Ridgeway, the state treasurer, and Elihu B. Washburne, minister to France, who had

Chicago Tribune backing. Before the nominating convention, Cullom's name was involved in a "Pekin whisky ring" scandal. While the other candidates called for his withdrawal, Cullom went before the Republican state committee and angrily denied any wrongdoing, after which the unproved charges were dropped. Cullom's friends contended that the tea-totaling Beveridge had tried to inject the Pekin case into the campaign. It was the only hint of scandal ever raised against Cullom.

In a typical Cullom feat, the master politician solved his immediate troubles in advance of the state convention. In an era of increasing Republican factionalization, some of his opponents withdrew. Cullom rounded up more than a majority of the delegates in advance and achieved a first-ballot nomination on a conservative, hard-money platform. At the opening of the fall campaign, many expected that he would lose if Democrats and independents united against him. In 1876, the Democratic gubernatorial candidate was Lewis Steward, a white-haired farmer, manufacturer, and lawyer who had strong rural and independent backing as a result of the economic depression that began in 1873. In the two-man contest, Cullom won by 6,798 votes in the closest election since Edward Coles won in 1822. The result could have been even closer had former governor-turned-Democrat John M. Palmer, actively supported Steward.

Despite the depression, which Cullom regarded as the inevitable result of a period of inflation and growth, the newly elected governor believed that the productive wealth of Illinois guaranteed an early return of prosperity. Instead of advocating new programs, he warned against legislative excesses. He regarded state government as a business enterprise dealing with the preservation of order, the enforcement of law, the punishment of lawbreakers, the care of the poor and unfortunate, and the education of the young. At the inaugural ceremony, Cullom devoted much of his message to a discussion of state revenues. He asked that the Illinois and Michigan Canal, largely obsolete in the railroad age, be modernized, extended to the Mississippi River, and ceded to the federal government.

Governor Cullom's first problem involved the railroads, which in the depression were having troubles with receiverships and strikes. Fortunately, the legislature had followed his advice and reorganized the state militia, which had fallen into disrepair since the Civil War. Strikes in eastern cities had caused considerable damage in the summer of 1877 before mobs in Chicago shut down several roads. Cullom used contingent funds to buy equipment for the untrained National Guard. He reminded the people of the right to assemble peacefully and then issued an ultimatum to the rioters. He asked for help from President Rutherford B. Hayes, who sent six companies of army regulars to the danger spot at Chicago, and peace was restored promptly. At East St. Louis, another trouble spot, Cullom personally took charge. When strikers disobeyed his orders that they allow trains to run, he called in militia regiments and 300 army regulars. There was little trouble at other rail centers in Illinois. The governor had restored order without loss of life or property damage.

Cullom's Second Term

At the 1880 Republican state convention, the governor remained neutral during a bitter factional fight that ended when Ulysses S. Grant was given the endorsement for a third term. Charles B. Farwell, who had achieved leadership among Chicago Republicans, supported James G. Blaine of Maine. In an anticlimax, six men wanted to replace Cullom, who needed state patronage to win second-term renomination on the fourth roll call. Former Governor Richard J. Oglesby started and finished in second place. In the November campaign, he had two opponents, former Senator Lyman Trumbull, who ran as a Democrat, and Alson J. Streeter, a third party candidate. Cullom was reelected with 50.6 percent of the vote.

Thirty-four years after Thomas Ford retired as governor, Cullom announced at the start of his second term that Illinois was debt-free. Through the frugality of eight governors and 17 legislatures, the state had paid the last cent of, and interest on, the $16 million liability incurred in the visionary era when legislators believed that profits from state banks could pay for state-owned railroads. Governor Ford correctly had predicted that the state's population would expand so rapidly that the debt could be retired by a relatively small tax. A tax on the Illinois Central railroad itself and the post-war currency inflation had helped, but the main factor in debt retirement was the growth of farming and commerce in the post-frontier decades.

Afraid to run for a third term as governor in 1884, Cullom set his sites on the U.S. Senate. The opportunity came when his party won control of the 1883 legislature. A deadlocked legislature had sent independent Supreme Court Justice David A. Davis to the Senate in 1877. But there was no way he would be reelected by the 1883 Republican legislature. Farwell, who wanted a Chicago senator (meaning himself), Oglesby, and two other downstate generals were the 1883 Republican candidates, but the party powerbrokers were unable to agree which one should have their united support. At the Republican caucus, Cullom won on the fifth ballot. In advance, he had submitted a legal brief contending that, regardless of the 1870 Constitution, he had the right to switch offices in midterm.

The Grand Old Senator from Illinois

Before the U.S. Supreme Court in 1886 held that states could not control interstate commerce, the deliberate-minded Cullom concluded that some federal control was essential if railroads were to be regulated. Only the Illinois Granger law, drafted by Cullom when he was in the Illinois House in 1873, established a degree of flexibility that met judicial approval. Given that track record, he accepted the chairmanship of the committee on commerce, an unattractive assignment in the senatorial hierarchy, and presided at a series of regional hearings at which carriers, shippers, and the public were consulted. The bill he introduced included the Illinois theory that the basic evil was unjust discrimination in rail rates but that some discrimination, such as long- and short-haul situations, might be proper.

In the U.S. Senate, Cullom needed all of his negotiating talents to guide to final passage in 1887 a law that created the Interstate Commerce Commission. Experts were provided to deal with transportation problems as they arose. Congress did not give the commission power to fix rates, and the burden of proof rested with the injured shipper, but those defects were gradually corrected.

The first-term senator built his political machine around John R. Tanner, a state senator from Clay County who soon went on the federal payroll as United States marshal for southern Illinois. A genius in political organization, he was Cullom's chief political operator until the end of the century, when their ambitions clashed. Cullom's "federal crowd" included judges, prosecutors, court officials, postmasters, and revenue collectors in every county and district. Sol R. Bethea of Dixon and J. Otis Humphrey of Springfield, influential lawyers, were key figures whose awards were appointments to the federal bench. W. A. Northcott, who became lieutenant governor, also was a key figure in the Cullom machine.

Tanner and the other federal employees soon proved their effectiveness, but they failed three times to get their leader an Illinois favorite-son endorsement for the presidency. In 1888, when first terms ended for Cullom and President Grover Cleveland, Joseph Medill of the *Chicago Tribune* favored Walter Q. Gresham for president. Cullom never announced that he wanted his name presented to the party's national convention, which nominated Benjamin Harrison for president. Cullom settled for a second term in the Senate. For the only time in his long career, he was nominated without opposition. When the legislature met in 1889 with Republican majorities, the senator stayed in Washington knowing that in Springfield Tanner had his reelection well under control.

Early in 1894 he went so far as to say that he wouldn't turn down support for the presidency, but Illinois Republicans wanted James G. Blaine of Maine. With John P. Altgeld in the governor's office, Cleveland in the White House, and the country in an economic collapse, the prospect seemed hopeless; but, out of a sense of duty, Cullom campaigned loyally for his party's legislative candidates. When the election went Republican, several others, including Medill, became interested in going to the U.S. Senate, but Tanner kept the factional confusion under control. Only one other name was presented to the caucus when Cullom won a third term with apparent ease.

Cullom was 66 years old before his presidential ambitions finally died. He hoped that the 1896 boom for William McKinley would collapse, but Charles G. Dawes, newly arrived in Chicago, prevented it. Tanner, who wanted his own political career, was elected governor. In 1900, Tanner could have had a second term with Cullom's support, but he announced his candidacy for Cullom's seat in the U.S. Senate instead. Tanner made maximum use of gubernatorial patronage, but he withdrew just before the Republican state convention. Three congressmen, including Joseph G. Cannon of Danville, also were interested in the Senate but failed to unite. The outlook seemed uncertain when the legislature met, but the Cullom forces had quietly obtained written pledges from a majority of the members. A byproduct of that campaign was an increased interest in replacing nominating boss-controlled nominating conventions with a direct primary system.

In Washington, the senator had accumulated enough seniority to trade the Interstate Commerce Committee chairmanship for that of the Foreign Relations Committee. His experience in that field included the chairmanship of a committee on Cuban relations during the Civil War and the chairmanship of a special committee that drafted the system of government of the Philippine Islands as a United States territory.

In 1906 the Illinois partisan battles were renewed in an effort to send Richard Yates, son of the Civil War governor, to the U.S. Senate. Yates, who had won the governorship in 1900 as a dark horse in a factional war, had lost it in 1904 but believed that he had high-level promises that would allow him to replace Cullom. Again there was a great fracturing of alliances, and the senator had the support in Cook County of Congressman William Lorimer, a Republican wire-puller, and some allies of Governor Charles S. Deneen. Yates, who had lack-luster campaigning talents, conceded defeat before the 1907 legislative session opened. One of Yates' difficulties was that Cullom again was backed by his long-time Republican colleagues.

Cullom, who was the dean of the Senate in years of service and the second oldest senator, vacillated about retirement but finally decided that he would try for a sixth term in 1912. He was concerned about public reaction to his 1911 votes: first to acquit William Lorimer, who had been accused of buying a Senate seat by bribing legislators, and then for a second Senate investigation of the allegations concerning his new colleague. Cullom eventually announced that he would permit his name to be entered for the first time in a U.S. Senate primary election. Under a new law the primary was advisory only, but the senior senator said he would abide by the voters' choice.

Cullom's "federal crowd" found that primary campaigning was both expensive and required new techniques. Cullom's time-tried issue, that he deserved another term because of experience, wasn't enough. He finished second behind Lawrence Y. Sherman, a former speaker of the Illinois House who also looked something like Lincoln. In mid summer, after he cast a soul-wrenching vote to unseat Lorimer, Cullom announced that he was retiring. He did not ask the 1913 legislature to elect him a sixth time, and thus kept his word to abide by the primary's outcome.

Two days before he left the Senate, as a final honor, his colleagues made him special resident commissioner to supervise construction of the Lincoln Memorial at Washington.

Cullom, the last surviving member of the Lincoln funeral party lived another year. He died January 28, 1914, and was brought back to Springfield for burial in Oak Ridge Cemetery.

18th
Governor

John Marshall Hamilton
1847-1905

1847 – Born, May 28, near Richwood, Ohio.

1870 – Admitted to the bar.

1877 - 1881 – Serves as a senator in the 30th and 31st General Assemblies.

1880 – Wins the nomination for lieutenant governor when incumbent Andrew Shuman falls victim to partisan infighting.

1883 – Assumes the governorship on Feb. 16 when Cullom resigns to become U.S. Senator.

1884 – Hamilton is overlooked as a gubernatorial candidate as the troubled Republican Party nominates the tried and true Richard Oglesby for his third term as governor.

1886 – Hamilton is an unsuccessful candidate to fill the slot of deceased U.S. Senator John A. Logan; turns his attention to his Chicago law practice.

1905 – Dies, Sept. 22.

Republican
February 16, 1883 to January 30, 1885

John Marshall Hamilton was nine months past his 35th birthday when he began serving the final two years of Governor Shelby M. Cullom's second term in 1883. Two years earlier he had been elected lieutenant governor because he was a standpat Republican and, as a young state senator, had made a reputation as an able legal draftsman and parliamentarian.

The Learned Politician

The future governor was born May 28, 1847, in a log cabin near Richwood, Union County, Ohio. His father, Samuel Hamilton, was the son and nephew of pioneer Methodist preachers in Ohio. His mother, who had been Mrs. Nancy McMorris, was a Virginian. When John was seven years old, the family loaded two wagons and made a three-week journey to a farm that had been selected in advance in Roberts Township, Marshall County, in north central Illinois. For the son's early education, more credit goes to his mother than to a few months spent in country schools.

His family opposed slavery, and the boy saved money to buy a uniform to march with a company of Lincoln Wide-Awakes – the first association of young Republicans – in parades in 1860. He wanted to go to war with his drill team, which formed the nucleus of a militia company, but because of his youth he was rejected. During the winter of 1863-1864, he attended a Methodist academy at Henry. Accompanied by 13 neighbor lads, he finally escaped from farm work at the age of 17 by going to Elgin, where he was accepted by the 141st Illinois Volunteers, a 100-day regiment that served uneventfully in southwestern Kentucky. As an indication of future leadership, he was promoted to corporal.

Upon his discharge, he taught school for a year then entered Ohio Wesleyan University, where he completed the three-year classical course with honors. In 1871 the university conferred upon him a master's degree. Hamilton thus became the first Illinois governor to hold a graduate degree and was the best educated in the 19th century.

Hamilton came home from college with ambitions to become a lawyer. For a few months he was principal of a Methodist academy. He then moved to Bloomington and studied law in the offices of Weldon, Tipton and Benjamin, whose partners were political activists and future judges. For one year he also taught Latin at Illinois Wesleyan, in Bloomington. In 1870 he was admitted to the bar. The next year he married Helen Williams, daughter of the professor of Greek at Ohio Wesleyan. They became the parents of a son and two daughters.

As the partner of J. H. Rowell, a future congressman, Hamilton rose rapidly in the law and Republican politics. In 1876, at the age of 29, the tall and slender Hamilton, who had clean-cut features and a drooping mustache that partially obscured his youthful appearance, defeated a Democratic-Greenback coalition candidate for state senator.

Hamilton immediately took a prominent role at Springfield and earned the friendship of John A. Logan, a candidate for a second term in the U.S. Senate. In a long deadlock, Hamilton voted for Logan on every ballot. He declined to help Bloomington's most prominent citizen, Supreme Court Justice David Davis, whom Democrats and agrarians finally elected as an independent.

Hamilton had an unusual memory for the statutes and was recognized in the General Assembly for his uncommon talent for writing legislation. He was sponsor of the bar association bill that established the appellate court system as a means of reducing the Supreme Court's workload. He successfully handled controversial legislation that created a state board of health and reorganized the militia. With only two years' experience, he was made president pro tem of the Illinois Senate in 1879. In that capacity he helped

Logan return to the U.S. Senate over the opposition of Richard J. Oglesby.

The Two-Year Governor

At their 1880 state convention, Republicans fought for three days before endorsing Ulysses S. Grant for a third term as president. Governor Cullom won a renomination contest, but most of the other state officials lost out in the factional fighting. One of the casualties was Lieutenant Governor Andrew Shuman, editor and publisher of the *Chicago Journal*, who was replaced by Hamilton. Two years later, when Cullom resigned and was elected senator, Hamilton was quietly inaugurated governor.

In an unusual assertion of executive power, Hamilton reversed official 1884 election returns that showed that by 10 votes Rudolph Brand, a Democrat, had defeated Republican Henry W. Lemen for state senator in a Chicago district. However, statements and affidavits collected by the state board of canvassers showed that Lemen had won by 390 votes. Under those circumstances, the governor assumed a judicial function and issued a certificate of election to Lemen. As a result, the Senate had a Republican majority.

During his quiet two years in office, Hamilton sided with temperance forces and signed the Harper "high license" bill, soon repealed, that allowed municipalities to suppress the number of saloons by requiring $500 licenses. He also signed the first compulsory education law.

A Life Away from Politics

In 1884 Hamilton wanted election to a full four-year term, but the Republican Party obviously was in trouble and again needed "Uncle Dick" Oglesby at the head of the state ticket. Two years later the death of U.S. Senator John A. Logan left Hamilton without high-level sponsorship. When he and seven others became candidates for the Logan vacancy, the Republican caucus selected Charles B. Farwell, who became the first senator from Chicago since Douglas and Trumbull.

Hamilton's future was in the law rather than politics. When his term as governor ended, he went back to Bloomington but soon moved his law practice to Chicago. He died in Chicago on September 22, 1905.

19th
Governor

Joseph Wilson Fifer
1840-1938

1840 – Born, Oct. 28, Staunton Virginia.

1857 – Family moves to McLean County, Illinois.

1863 – Wounded after the fall of Vicksburg.

1868 – Graduates from Illinois Wesleyan.

1869 – Admitted to the bar.

1881 - 1885 – Serves as senator in the 32nd and 33rd General Assemblies.

1888 – Wins the Republican gubernatorial nomination; defeats former governor and Civil War general John Palmer in the general election.

1891 – Illinois women granted the right to vote in school elections; Illinois adopts the Australian, or secret, ballot.

1892 – Fifer renominated for governor by Republicans, but loses to John Altgeld in the general election.

1899 – President McKinley appoints Fifer to the Interstate Commerce Commission.

1900 – Fifer refuses to run for governor.

1903 – President Theodore Roosevelt reappoints Fifer to the Interstate Commerce Commission.

1906 – Fifer leaves the Commerce Commission for health reasons.

1920 – Serves as a delegate to the state constitutional convention. (Voters would reject to convention's proposal in 1922.)

1924 – Fifer's daughter, Florence Fifer Boher, is elected the first female state senator in Illinois.

1938 – Fifer dies, Aug. 6.

Republican
January 14, 1889 to January 10, 1893

A quarter of a century after the Civil War, Joseph Wilson "Private Joe" Fifer acquired his nickname and became governor of Illinois because he had the temerity to argue with a general. The issue was Fifer's $24-a-month pension paid for wounds in the right lung and liver suffered nine days after the fall of Vicksburg. A former state senator from Bloomington, he became an instant celebrity. As spokesman for the common soldier, he defeated six former officers for the Republican nomination for governor. Then he was elected over former governor and Civil War general John M. Palmer, the state's strongest Democrat. Elevated to the governorship, he was less conservative than the Republican leadership.

For his popularity, Fifer was indebted to General John C. Black, a Danville Democrat who was commissioner of pensions in the first Grover Cleveland administration. In testimony before a U.S. Senate committee and in a letter to a Washington newspaper, Black cited Fifer as a typical Republican politician who did not deserve his pension. Fifer defended his personal honor with a sarcastic and incisive letter that was widely circulated by the Republican press and praised at meetings of the Grand Army of the Republic posts. Offering to compare wounds with the general, he said his pension was paid at the standard rate for common soldiers, but that Black, by a special law, received a pension of $100 a month.

A tall and slender man with black hair, "Private Joe" was a moderate Republican who kept state government on an even keel, did not attempt to be a factional leader, avoided partisanship, and worked well with Democrats.

Young Private Joe

He was born at Staunton, Virginia, on October 28, 1840, the third of five children of John and Mary Wilson Fifer. In 1857 they moved to Danvers, McLean County, where his father, a farmer and mason, operated a brickyard. At the start of the war he enlisted. When wounded, he refused a discharge and, upon recovery, was assigned to guard a prison boat. After the war he lived over a downtown store, slept on a straw bed, and did his own cooking and laundry while studying law at Illinois Wesleyan. While still in school, he was elected tax collector of Danvers Township, which paid a welcome $300 a year. In 1870, a year after being admitted to the bar, he married Gertrude Lewis, who became the mother of his two children.

He was elected Bloomington city attorney and then state's attorney for two terms. In 1880 he went to the state Senate as replacement for John M. Hamilton, the new lieutenant governor. After serving in the Illinois Senate, he went back to his Bloomington law practice. He wasn't well-known outside of McLean County until Black attempted to reduce the pension rolls.

Governor Fifer and the "Little Red Schoolhouse" Issue

The publicity over Fifer's celebrated response to Black caused State Treasurer John R. Tanner to recognize Fifer's potential as a candidate. Tanner lined up the support of Chicago factional leaders. At the 1888 Republican state convention, Fifer was nominated on the fourth ballot over three generals, one colonel, one major, and one captain. The best known of his opponents was another Bloomington lawyer, General John McNulta. In the

November election, Fifer won by 12,547 votes over another general, former Governor John M. Palmer.

Fifer conducted the state's business with a staff of three – a private secretary, a stenographer, and a messenger – in the public reception room. He took credit for "enlightened" policies, such as the Australian ballot, which provided that ballots be furnished by the state rather than the political parties. It was a major step toward honest elections and a forerunner of the Progressive Movement.

The most controversial event of his administration was enactment in 1889 of a compulsory education law requiring that children in both public and parochial schools be taught reading, writing, arithmetic, history, and geography, all in English to age 12. There was general dissatisfaction with the state of public education, and Fifer in his inaugural message also had asked for a stronger teacher certification law. Written by Richard Edwards, former normal school president who was state superintendent of public instruction, the compulsory school law was enacted with bipartisan support. Complaints soon were heard from German Lutherans who did not want their children educated in English and from Catholics who did not want truant officers coming into their schools. The "little red schoolhouse" became a political issue in Fifer's bid for a second term.

The legislature permitted women to vote in some school elections, outlawed child labor under 13 years (a statute that was not enforced because it contained loopholes), authorized construction of an asylum for insane criminals at Menard, created the Chicago sanitary district, and approved financing for the 1893 World's Columbian Exposition in Chicago. Bills that would have implemented some campaign promises to working men and farmers were defeated.

On the convention's first ballot, Fifer beat out four candidates for the Republican nomination for a second term as governor. But Private Joe lost the 1892 general election by 22,872 votes to John Peter Altgeld, another Civil War private. The German-born Altgeld had supported the legislation requiring English-only school instruction in 1889. But by the 1892 campaign, he was blaming Fifer for its passage.

Part of Fifer's legacy to Altgeld was a "basketful of documents" relating to pardon petitions for the remaining men convicted in the 1886 Haymarket bombing case. Fifer received these papers late in his administration, and he planned to give their consideration high priority if reelected. But upon losing the election, he left the matter to Altgeld.

The Old Soldier

During Algeld's administration, Fifer's Civil War wounds started to become bothersome, and Fifer never campaigned again. He refused to run for governor in 1900. Like many top-level Republicans in an era of political factionalism, he frequently changed allies. At the start of his administration he appointed Tanner, his original mentor, to the railroad and warehouse commission but soon disagreed with him. He was an enemy of Senator Shelby Cullom in 1891 but his friend the next year. As permanent chairman of the 1900 Republican state convention, he was on Cullom's side against Tanner. One of his closest friends was his predecessor, Richard J. Oglesby, who, when Fifer was in office, had enjoyed a standing invitation to be an overnight guest at the Executive Mansion. Milton Hay, Springfield's leading lawyer, usually joined them in late-night discussions. In his later years, Fifer said nothing about Republican rivalries when he recalled that he enjoyed harmonious relations with other state officers, the legislature, and the public.

He was appointed to the Interstate Commerce Commission by President William McKinley in 1899 and reappointed by Theodore Roosevelt in 1903. Because of his health, he resigned three years later and lived in a tent in his Bloomington yard for several months. In 1918 he took his turn as state Grand Army of the Republic commander. In 1920 his name appeared on the ballots for the last time when he was elected a constitutional convention delegate. His unheeded advice was that the delegates amend the 1870 Constitution but not attempt to replace it.

The badly wounded soldier became an elder statesman who was respected by both parties longer than any other governor. James O'Donnell Bennett, who for four days in 1933 interviewed Fifer for the *Chicago Tribune*, marveled at his memory, lucidity, and knowledge of the classics. He had the respect of later governors, especially Lowden and Horner, who were among frequent callers at the home of the political link connecting two Illinois centuries.

The former governor lived 14 years after his daughter, Florence Fifer Bohrer, was elected the first woman state senator in 1924. When he was 92, both legs were broken when he was hit by an automobile. He was blind, deaf, and crippled before he died on August 6, 1938. He was 97 years old.

20th **Governor**

John Peter Altgeld
1847-1902

1847 – Born, Dec. 30, in Germany.

1875 – Leaves Savannah and moves to Chicago to begin a career as a lawyer and real estate developer.

1884 – Finances his own unsuccessful bid for Congress.

1886 – Elected judge of the Superior Court of Cook County by a coalition of Democrats and members of the United Labor Party; On May 4, police move to break up a labor rally in Haymarket Square in Chicago. A bomb explodes, injuring and killing several people, including seven police officers. Governor Oglesby commutes to life imprisonment the death sentences of two of several anarchists convicted in case. Four others were hanged November 11, 1887.

1890 – Assembles a dozen liberal articles and letters into a book, *Live Questions*.

1892 – Wins the gubernatorial election.

1893 – The governor grants outright pardons to the three surviving anarchist prisoners convicted in the Haymarket bombing.

1894 – A general railway strike from May to July is precipitated by a strike by workers at the Pullman Car Company. President Grover Cleveland sends federal troops to break up the strike, even though Altgeld never requests him to.

1896 – Altgeld helps turn the Democratic National Convention in Chicago against President Cleveland; the party nominates William Jennings Bryan for president; Altgeld loses his reelection bid to John R. Tanner.

1899 – Loses his bid for mayor of Chicago.

1900 – Altgeld is denied delegate credentials to the 1900 Democratic convention at Kansas City.

1902 – Dies March 13, in Joliet.

Democrat
January 10, 1893 to January 11, 1897

John Peter Altgeld was the first liberal governor of Illinois. The German-born son of peasants was undersized and undereducated, but he possessed a superior intellect and massive ambition coupled with compassion for the underprivileged. Also, he was a master politician. He started with as many handicaps as Lincoln and became the first governor from Chicago, the first foreign-born governor, and the first Democratic governor in 36 years.

Since John M. Palmer, Illinois governors had moved slowly from the traditional conservatism that still characterized not only the Republican leadership but also a large sector of Democratic opinion. Altgeld's hopes for the future required caution in dealing with the traditionally conservative lawmakers. For that reason, he was a closet liberal during the first five months of his turbulent administration. But, when all was said and done, Altgeld philosophically turned out to be a markedly different governor than Illinois had seen in a long while.

Altgeld had several careers. In clear and fact-filled prose, he wrote books that were admired by opinion-makers. Overcoming a slight harelip, he became an effective public speaker. Instead of taking time to develop a profitable law practice, he speculated in Chicago real estate, constructed downtown buildings, and achieved the shaky status of paper millionaire. Downstaters admired his business success when he sought the Democratic nomination for governor. In his unusual campaign for governor he refused contributions and spent $100,000 of his own money, which no candidate for governor had done before.

The Rise of a Chicago Liberal

The son of John Peter and Mary Altgeld, the future governor was born December 30, 1847, in the village of Nieder Selters, in the Prussian province of Nassau. Three months later, his wagon-maker father took his family to a farm near Mansfield, Ohio. In his boyhood, "Young Pete" was required to work as hard as a man, without wages but with paternal beatings. For one winter and two summer terms he went to a country school. He escaped from farm work briefly during the Civil War by enlisting in a 100-day regiment and giving his father all but $10 of his $100 bonus. In eastern Virginia, where the regiment served uneventfully, he caught "Chickahominy fever," a malarial-type infection from which he never fully recovered. When he returned home, his father objected but he went to high school for one term and to a select school for three months, long enough to qualify for a teacher's certificate. At 19 he began earning $35 a month as a teacher. All of it went toward paying for his father's farm.

At 21, free from parental domination and rejected by a girl from a prosperous family, he tramped westward. In Kansas, he worked as a railroad section hand until the recurrent fever sent him to a hospital. When partially recovered, he wandered into northwestern Missouri. At Savannah, Andrew County, he found a teaching job and began a white-collar career. He read books, was admitted to the bar, and demonstrated a capacity for getting people to like and help him. Trying his hand at politics, he controlled the local Democratic convention. Endorsed also by the local Grange, he was elected county prosecutor at the peak of the Granger movement.

He stood a half-inch more than five-feet-six. He had uneven features and unruly hair, but he grew a Vandyke beard, brown and neatly trimmed, and bought comparatively expensive clothing, signs that he was ambitious to advance in the world. For Altgeld, one year as county prosecutor was enough. In 1875, four years after arrival in Savannah, he resigned. With the $100 he earned from the sales of his law books, he took a train to Chicago, a city of strangers.

Altgeld opened a law office and slept in it until he became solvent. Lacking time to practice liberalism, he cultivated the acquaintance of important men who helped him find clients. As soon as he saved $500, he began buying and selling real estate. Two years after his arrival in Chicago, he went back to Mansfield, Ohio and married Emma Ford, a school teacher. He was a lawyer with corporate clients, but chiefly he was a businessman who erected commercial and office buildings needed by the growing city. His big ambition was to own a tall building that would be one of Chicago's show places. (But not until the early 1890s did he erect the Unity Block, 12 stories high, at what is now 127 North Dearborn Street.)

In English and German, Altgeld made liberal speeches to available audiences. By 1884 he had collected enough important friends to run for congressman in a heavily Republican district. Minority parties in such situations do not discourage volunteer candidates, especially if they finance their own campaigns. In defeat he was impressive: he polled more votes than a more prominent Democrat had two years earlier. While he campaigned, he wrote and published, apparently at his own expense, his first book, *Our Penal Machinery and its Victims*. It blamed crime on urban conditions and denounced the judicial system that was more concerned with learned precedents than with justice for the young defendants who were filling jails. The book established Altgeld's credentials as a liberal and widened his acquaintance. One of the lawyers to whom he sent autographed copies was young Clarence Darrow, thereafter his admirer and friend.

Altgeld continued his part-time career as a writer of essays that he submitted to editors and of letters mailed to officials and opinion-makers. One of the first, printed by the *Chicago Evening Mail* in

1886, urged that strikes be settled by arbitration. It marked his first public stand on the side of labor and appeared a week before the bombing in Haymarket Square that broke up a meeting called to protest police brutality. In 1890 he assembled a dozen articles and letters into the first edition of a new book, *Live Questions,* of which *Our Penal Machinery and its Victims* took up the final 174 pages.

"The Little Dutchman" had friends in a short-lived United Labor Party that in a coalition with Democrats elected him a judge of the Superior Court of Cook County in 1886. Meanwhile, he did not join 60,000 Chicagoans who signed clemency petitions for the professed anarchists who were hanged for the Haymarket bombing.

Altgeld's service as a judge was marked not so much by liberal stands as by instances of questionable personal ethics. In 1891 he sent Darrow to Springfield when the legislature again deadlocked in a Senate election. He tried to sway votes away from the eventual winner, John M. Palmer, the Democratic Party's endorsed candidate and thereafter Altgeld's enemy. The judge sued the city of Chicago on a claim that one of his properties had been damaged by a change in the street grade. He was fined $100 for writing a contemptuous letter to three appellate court judges. In a spirit of revenge, he spent $5,000 to help defeat Mayor John Roche.

The Progressive Administration

After five years as a judge, he resigned and ran for governor with support that ranged from upper-crust liberals to the ranks of Germans and labor. Downstate Democrats who hadn't been enthusiastic when Chicago Mayor Carter Harrison ran for governor in 1884 did not object to "the man with a barrel," who paid for his own campaign.

His downstate opposition was divided, and Altgeld, running as a law-and-order candidate, was nominated on the first ballot at the Democratic state convention. In early summer, far in advance of the traditional campaign season, he began an energetic tour during which he charged that Republicans had mismanaged state government. Repeatedly, he displayed unusual finesse in putting his opposition on the defensive. He blamed his opponent, Governor Joseph W. Fifer, for the 1889 compulsory education law that Altgeld himself had helped pass but which turned out to be unpopular among Lutherans and Catholics. Altgeld's campaign style was to work hard and to answer every opposition charge with a counter charge of his own.

Spending his own money helped him take on the protective coloration of apparent conservatism. In the past both parties had been equally conservative. There had been some variation at the leadership level, however, and the governors tended to be less conservative than other party leaders. For example, Palmer, who had been a conservative governor, had turned pro-labor and anti-corporation after he returned to the Democratic Party. Among Republicans, Beveridge was something of a progressive, although hardly a liberal, and Fifer had been elected as a friend of the working man and common soldier. While Altgeld sought to broaden his base of support, he did not rush espousal of liberal causes.

With Democrats leading the state and national tickets, Altgeld defeated Fifer by just under 23,000 votes. On his coattails the Democrats elected legislative majorities.

However, instead of taking a vacation, the governor-elect overtaxed his strength by accepting invitations to establishment dinners and receptions. Exhausted physically and suffering from a bad cold, against his doctor's wishes he went to Springfield for an overcrowded swearing-in ceremony that resembled Andrew Jackson's presidential inauguration in 1828.

Obviously ill, Altgeld arrived at his inauguration on Fifer's arm and could read only the opening paragraphs of his inaugural speech. The long and rather innocuous inaugural message contained good advice in vague terms that would not alarm members of the establishment. The new governor mentioned the possibility of inheritance and corporation taxes but hardly endorsed them. He also referred vaguely to municipal ownership of utilities. He also pointed out the need for a constitutional convention. (The Senate, but not the House, agreed with him.) The message also lamented that an "ever increasing proliferation of boards and commissions, each dealing with an isolated problem" added to governmental complications. Since there was no centralized supervision of state funds, the governor called it "a notorious fact" that custodians of public funds, state treasurers among them, pocketed the interest on bank balances. (Both of those situations would not receive corrective action until the next century.)

That evening he attended part of a reception at which the crowd was so large that Adlai E. Stevenson, the vice president-elect, could not squeeze into the room. Then Mrs.

Altgeld insisted that he go to Asheville, North Carolina, to rest, and Altgeld missed more than a month of the legislative session. Speaker Clayton E. Crafts, a Chicagoan, ran the House of Representatives without too much attention to the absent governor's wishes.

As a candidate for governor in 1892, Altgeld followed Democratic custom and complained about high taxes under Republican administrations. Once in office, however, he abandoned the emphasis on economy, and he did not hesitate to spend treasury surpluses and raise the state levy on property. As part of his progressive administration, he increased appropriations for the University of Illinois and encouraged its expansion in graduate, medicine, and science fields. He was responsible for the opening of normal schools at DeKalb and Charleston, for insane hospitals at East Moline and near Peoria, and for the soldiers' widows' home at Wilmington. One of his appointees, Florence Kelley, a protégé of Jane Addams, rigidly enforced a labor law requiring inspection of factories. The law also limited employment of women to eight hours a day and strengthened an earlier child-labor statute. Regulation of insurance companies was strengthened.

However, common school education took a step backward under Altgeld. Four years earlier he had supported the Fifer administration's compulsory education law. In his campaign of 1892, Altgeld switched sides and made opposition to the legislation his chief issue among Germans and Catholics. In office, he made good on an unwise pledge to the voters and signed the repealer. The Altgeld administration did nothing to increase school financing.

Altgeld's Financial and Physical Woes

Financial scandals in his administration embarrassed the governor. Harry Barnard's biography, *Eagle Forgotten: The Life of John Peter Altgeld*, says that an audit – brought about by the 1894 discovery that Treasurer Rufus N. Ramsey was some $300,000 short in his accounts – uncovered $50,000 worth of Altgeld's promissory notes were part of the state treasury. Altgeld apparently borrowed the money to help with his Unity Block development project in Chicago. The governor's friends were reported to have covered up the transaction and repaid the $50,000.

Altgeld's physical and financial condition deteriorated during his governorship. Hard work and mental stress were punctuated by occasional illnesses. During his second year in office, he was diagnosed as having multiple sclerosis. The Unity Block, a financial albatross, had suffered from absentee management, and the governor lost his status as a paper millionaire. (Unable to meet bond payments, he would lose the building in an 1899 foreclosure.)

To attest to Altgeld's personal honesty, there is evidence that he rejected a bribe that would have ended his personal financial troubles and saved the Unity Block. Author Harry Barnard is convinced that Charles T. Yerkes, the key figure in the Chicago traction industry, offered the governor from $100,000 to $1 million if he would sign legislation to extend maximum streetcar franchises from 20 to 50 years. (Edward F. Dunne, who became the next Democratic governor, told of congratulating Altgeld, then out of office, for turning down $1 million. He says that Altgeld replied that the amount was a half-million.)

The Haymarket Pardons and the Pullman Strike

The turning point in Altgeld's career came as a result of the fallout of the 1886 Haymarket bombing case. In the early months of his administration, Altgeld ignored requests that he free the three anarchists who had not been hanged for the Haymarket bombing. Many prominent men favored clemency, and many thought that public opinion would accept their release on grounds of mercy. The governor studied the trial record and collected *ex parte* information about police brutality at the Haymarket labor rally. On June 23, 1893, without advanced notice, he granted outright pardons to the prisoners.

His courageous but belligerent 18,000-word justification of the decision made him the most hated man in Illinois. In complete detail, he criticized the judge, jury, prosecution, and police, especially Judge Joseph E. Gary and Police Inspector John Bonfield. Later generations have believed that Altgeld acted properly when he held that the trial six years earlier was unfair, the jury packed, and the judge prejudiced. In 1893, however, the pardon was a public relations disaster. The public, which hysterically feared a reign of terror by bomb-throwing foreigners, believed that criticism of the judge and police was the equivalent of attacking law and order. The newspapers, with the *Chicago Tribune* in the lead, began an incessant vilification of the governor. Outside of liberal and labor circles, John "Pardon" Altgeld's reservoir of goodwill dried up.

Altgeld, who had told friends that he would do justice to the anarchists whatever the consequences, had the option of releasing them on compassionate grounds without passing on guilt or innocence. Instead, with a display of venom he shortened his own career and handicapped the Democratic Party in future elections. An explanation might be that Judge Gary had just written for *Century* magazine an article that belittled the anarchists and their defenders.

The governor's unpopularity increased as a result of his 1894 quarrel with President Grover Cleveland over the unrequested use of federal troops in the American Railway Union's strike. Like the governor, socialist union organizer Eugene V. Debs, who called the strike, sympathized with the starving residents of the company town owned by George M. Pullman, the sleeping car manufacturer. Like predecessor governors, Altgeld had called out state troops to maintain order during strikes at Lemont and elsewhere. He insisted, however, that they must not be used as strikebreakers. The president sent army units to Chicago, although Altgeld, at the request of Mayor John P. Hopkins, had dispatched two brigades of National Guardsmen. Altgeld protested the action as well as the Justice Department's use of injunctions to break the rail strike. He was accused of siding with strikers who were acting in open violation of the law, triggering a new wave of vilification that was not limited to Illinois newspapers.

The Politically Undone Altgeld Flexes His Muscles

Nationally, the 1894 midterm election showed a Republican trend that in Illinois was increased by anti-Altgeld sentiment. By margins of 130,000, Republicans were elected state treasurer and superintendent of public instruction. Both houses of the new legislature had strong Republican majorities, and Shelby Moore Cullom was elected to a third term in the U.S. Senate. The minority Democrats did not offer Altgeld as their choice for senator.

His personnel record was mixed. More than his predecessors, Altgeld closely supervised administrative agencies. Believing that good government required frequent turnovers, he arbitrarily fired a number of top-level officials, including the eminent Frederick H. Wines, who for years had been secretary of the State Board of Public Charities. One downstate editor called Altgeld a poor judge of men who was inclined to consider party loyalty more important than personal integrity. On the other hand, he signed a bill, a fore-runner of the Progressive Movement, that permitted some municipalities to adopt civil service.

Though it destroyed his electability, the Haymarket pardon did not terminate Altgeld's political influence, and the 1896 Democratic National Convention at Chicago was the setting of his greatest triumph. A populist whose political career began as a Grangerite prosecutor in rural Missouri, he was a bimetallist who wanted to increase the supply of money by coining silver at a ratio of 16-to-1 with gold. Unlike John Palmer, Grover Cleveland, and prominent Chicago Democrats, he believed that the gold standard was a chief cause for widespread poverty. He opened the convention with an eloquent attack on the gold standard. In firm control, he wrote the platform that repudiated Cleveland by taking stands for free coinage of silver, a tariff for revenue only, and a federal income tax, and against government by injunction. In an obvious reference to Altgeld's quarrel with Cleveland, the platform denounced federal interference in local affairs. No longer would Democratic and Republican conventions support duplicate economic policies.

For the Democratic presidential nomination, Altgeld reluctantly backed William Jennings Bryan, whom he had rebuffed a year earlier. As chairman of the Illinois delegation, he cast its vote four times for Richard P. Bland of Missouri, a veteran congressional worker for free silver. On the fifth ballot, he yielded to home-state pressure and voted for Bryan, who at 36 had a silver tongue but had not matured as a politician. If he had not been foreign-born – and thus constitutionally ineligible – the governor may have been a strong candidate for the nomination. Altgeld had declined to support Vice President and Illinois resident Adlai E. Stevenson for the presidency.

Altgeld neglected his own reelection campaign, which he realized was hopeless, and worked valiantly for Bryan, who in Illinois received 9,733 fewer votes than the unpopular governor. With 43.7 percent of the gubernatorial vote, Altgeld lost by 113,381 to John R. Tanner, a conservative Republican.

In private life, he joined Clarence Darrow's law firm. Still head of the Democratic Party in 1897, he dictated that the second Carter H. Harrison be the candidate for mayor of Chicago. It was an error, for after the election Harrison joined the party's gold wing. Two years later, outcast from the leadership, Altgeld ran for mayor as an independent. Sizable crowds turned out for his speeches, but he finished third. He was denied delegate credentials to the 1900 Democratic convention at Kansas City, which endorsed Altgeld policy by renominating Bryan on a liberal platform. In Illinois he made speeches for the Democratic ticket.

"The Little Dutchman" never stopped being spokesman for the underdog. He died March 13, 1902, at Joliet of a cerebral hemorrhage several hours after a speech advocating Boer independence from the British in South Africa.

Inauguration of Shadrach Bond, as depicted by Robert A. Thom. Sitting, left, Ninian Edwards. Standing, next right, Elias Kent Kane. Standing to the right of Bond, Jesse Thomas, Nathaniel Pope, Daniel Pope Cook.

Artist's depiction of Edward Coles freeing his slaves on the Ohio River.

Shelby and Julia Cullom.

Joseph Fifer and his brother George in Civil War uniforms.

John Peter Altgeld with Illinois National Guard officers.

Governor Richard J. Oglesby in retirement at Oglehurst, near Elkhart.

Shelby M. Cullom in his first automobile.

"Flying Squadron" campaign for Tanner in 1896. Sitting, from left, John L. Beveridge, Richard J. Oglesby, Shelby M. Cullom, John M. Hamilton. Standing, from left, John C. Smith, John R. Tanner, James Van Cleve, Joseph W. Fifer, Lyman R. Ray.

Tanner Cadets at Executive Mansion in 1898.

Governor Tanner lying in state in the rotunda of State Capitol, May 26, 1901.

Governor Richard Yates and his private secretary, John Oglesby, both sons of former governors, in the Capitol.

Governor and Mrs. Yates ready for a Christmas party in the Executive Mansion, 1902.

From left, Governor Yates, Mrs. J.W. Strong, Mrs. Charles Sumner, Vice President Theodore Roosevelt, unidentified guardsmen. Seated Mrs. Delia Ann Wadsworth, mother of Mrs. Yates, and Mrs. Richard Yates.

Charles S. Deneen and Richard Yates II.

Charles S. Deneen making an address at Lawrenceville, Illinois.

From left, Vice President James S. Sherman, Speaker Joseph Cannon, Lieutenant Governor John Oglesby in background, President Taft, and Governor Deneen at a deep waterway convention, East St. Louis, 1909.

Governor Dunne signing the Illinois Women's Suffrage Bill in 1913.

Campaign poster for Len Small.

The Visions d'Art show at the Illinois State Fair displays its "endorsement" by Governor Horner.

Governor Horner with his Lincoln collection.

Governor Dwight H. Green with a Volk bust of Lincoln, 1938.

John Stelle rides a mule presented by Sam Plant, Murphysboro, who allegedly stole a mule from Stelle in France in first world war. Plant is holding the mule.

Governor William Stratton with Senator Everett Dirksen and President Dwight D. Eisenhower.

Governor and Mrs. Dwight Green with Adlai and Ellen Stevenson.

The Stratton family decorating the Christmas tree at the Executive Mansion.

Governor Otto Kerner and family dressed for inauguration.

Governor and Mrs. Richard Ogilvie with Miss Illinois County Fair.

Governors Stratton, Ogilvie, Walker, Shapiro, and Kerner.

Governor James Thompson with newborn daughter Samantha Jayne, 1978.

Governor Edgar's retirement plans were to become a fellow at the University of Illinois' Institute of Government and Public Affairs.

Secretary of State and future Governor George Ryan discusses state politics during an interview for Illinois Issues *magazine.*

Governor Edgar and two of his best friends.

21st Governor

John Riley Tanner
1844-1901

1844 – Born, April 4, Booneville, Indiana.

1863 – Enlists in the union army.

1881 - 1885 – Serves as senator in the 32nd and 33rd General Assemblies.

1886 – Elected state treasurer; serves 1887 to 1889

1894 – Manages the midterm election campaign that elects Republicans by unprecedented majorities.

1896 – Defeats Altgeld for governor.

1898 – A special session of the legislature makes more than 12,000 Illinoisans available for the war with Spain.

1900 – Tanner covets Cullom's U.S. Senate seat; he is denied it, and the Republicans run Richard Yates in the gubernatorial election.

1901 – Dies May 23.

Republican
January 11, 1897 to January 14, 1901

Tall, virile, and amiable, John R. Tanner was a six-foot, two-inch 200-pounder with a dark complexion and long hair. He was a master of the complexities of organizing political factions, and got great practice by organizing Shelby M. Cullom's political machine. He parlayed his connections into a term as the governor. And then he committed political suicide by challenging, Cullom, his patron for his seat in the U.S. Senate.

The Young Organizer

The fourth generation John Tanner was a country boy from southern Illinois, where he had been taken soon after his birth in a log house near Booneville, Indiana, on April 4, 1844. He grew up on a farm near Carbondale, with an education limited to country schools. His mother, Eliza V. Downs, was the daughter of a Baptist preacher. His great-grandfather John Tanner was killed in the Revolutionary War and his grandfather was killed by Indians in Kentucky. His father died in a Confederate prison camp. The future governor enlisted with the Union in 1863 and served in Sherman's army from Kentucky to Georgia.

After the war he bought 60 acres in Clay County, where he farmed, sold fruit trees and real estate, ran a sawmill, and took up Republican politics at the age of 26. In a Democratic county, he was elected sheriff and circuit clerk. At 30, he began long service as a member of the Republican state central committee. He was elected state senator in 1880 at the start of Cullom's second term as governor. When Cullom became U. S. Senator, the invaluable Tanner went on the federal payroll as marshal for southern Illinois. At the start of Grover Cleveland's Democratic administration, he kept in politics by being elected state treasurer. When Tanner disagreed with Governor Joseph W. Fifer, who had appointed him to the state railroad and warehouse commission, Cullom arranged for his appointment as assistant United States treasurer at Chicago.

As Republican state chairman, Tanner managed the midterm campaign that, in the wake of Altgeld's Haymarket pardons, elected Republican candidates by unprecedented majorities. In 1896 he was the Republican's best hope to limit Altgeld to one term. The five living former Republican governors – Oglesby, Beveridge, Cullom, Hamilton, and Fifer – formed a "flying squadron" that campaigned for Tanner. Oglesby did it reluctantly, but party tradition required that rivalries be forgotten during campaigns. Tanner's winning majority was sensational, 113,381 votes.

The Ornate Administration

Republicans who wanted to replace the Democrats that Altgeld had appointed immediately flooded the governor-elect with job applications. The governor's office received more than 3,000 letters in two weeks, and swarms of patronage seekers stood in line all day to see him.

Tanner's first wife, Lauretta Ingraham, died in 1887, leaving two children. The celebration of election to the governorship included the announcement of his engagement to Cora Edith English, a Springfield socialite who was 20 years his junior. The wedding, eleven days before the inauguration, was Illinois officialdom's brightest and possibly most expensive social event. Some of the invited guests were unable to crowd into St. Paul's Episcopal Church. Wedding presents, many of them accompanied by job applications, included a trunk of solid silver tableware (348 pieces) and a Landau carriage and team of matching horses. For the first time, festoons of electric lights were part of the state Capitol's lavish decorations. The Tanners lived in a hotel for several months while the Executive Mansion was remodeled and redecorated.

The governor, addicted to pomp and circumstance, reviewed a long parade before the elaborate inauguration ceremony, which was followed by a dinner and a ball. At formal events during the next four years, he was accompanied by his personal staff, one man from each congressional district. They were known as "sunburst colonels" because of the elaborate gold braid on their tailor-made uniforms. The governor rode with his staff in President McKinley's inauguration parade.

Soon after his inauguration, Tanner signed a controversial bill, similar to one that Altgeld had vetoed, that permitted the Chicago City Council to grant 50-year franchises to street-car companies. Chicago newspapers and assorted reformers then turned public sentiment against the governor, who found that no one listened to his explanation that financing of some corporations, including utilities, required long-term bond issues for which 20-year franchises were inadequate. The utility companies, which were essential to the growth of cities but not yet under governmental regulation, were forced to pay tribute to venal politicians. In the uproar, the unused 5-year franchise law was repealed in two years. There is no record that Tanner profited personally when he signed the bill. (Altgeld was rumored to have turned down a bribe to sign the legislation.)

Like Altgeld, Governor Tanner refused to allow state troops to be used as strikebreakers. Governor Shelby Cullom in 1877 had called out the militia when mine owners asked for protection during strikes. Twenty-one years later, Cullom's protégé sided with union members who were striking at Virden and Pana. He blamed mine owners for violence and said that the laboring man's right to strike "is as dear to him as the capitalist's millions." When twelve men were killed and forty wounded at Virden, Tanner sent troops to the railroad station there to prevent the unloading of Alabama blacks – presumably potential strike breakers – who were guarded by private detectives hired at St. Louis. He said that the train would have been stopped at the state line had he known that a private army was on board. He earned the gratitude of labor at the expense of rural support.

As a conservative Republican, Tanner stood for economy. He borrowed money to retire the treasury deficit and reduced the state's property tax rate. In the wake of the Haymarket controversy, he sponsored creation of a pardon board of three members to review clemency applications. He approved a bill that outlawed the hiring of out-of-state strikebreakers. Like most postwar Republican governors, he wanted but didn't get Chicago police placed under a state board. His solution for local tax troubles was to have property assessed quadrennially at one-fifth value. A judicial reorganization abolished the Ottawa and Mount Vernon divisions of the Supreme Court, which thereafter met only at Springfield.

The legislature, which was in special session at the outbreak of the Spanish-American War in 1898, by resolution gave the governor full power to raise men, munitions, and money as needed. The governor's call for troops produced more regiments than could be used; one of them was black.

Political Suicide

Governor Tanner's dual positions as a key member of Cullom's organization and as the head of his own faction turned out to be incompatible. When harassed by heavy criticism, he needed someone to blame for his troubles. Republicans were shocked when he severely criticized the senator and then ran against him. The state payrollers and the "federal crowd" fought over the nomination of legislators and the election of delegates to the 1900 Republican state convention. Before it was over, the great campaign manager conceded defeat without consulting William E. Lorimer, the only congressman who supported him. Cullom, who had no objection to his lieutenant's gubernatorial ambitions, said that Tanner could have been reelected in 1900 had he remained loyal. Why the governor split with the senator is one of the mysteries of Illinois political history. Lorimer, the British-born son of a minister, was frequently blamed, often with apparent justification, for whatever went wrong. The frequent shifting of alliances encouraged multiple candidacies and deadlocks that helped give Illinois politics a bad name.

When Tanner left office, he was broken politically and physically. He had been handicapped in his last campaign by an illness that was diagnosed successively as gastritis, neuralgia of the stomach, and gallstones. Four months after he returned to private life, he died in his Springfield hotel suite on May 23, 1901. His funeral was as impressive as his inauguration. An estimated 30,000 passed before his casket in the Statehouse rotunda. His grand mausoleum is in Springfield's Oak Ridge Cemetery, where Abraham Lincoln's is also.

22nd Governor

Richard Yates
1860-1936

1860 – Born, Dec. 12, a month after his father's election to the governor's office.

1892 – Loses his bid to be congressman-at-large.

1894 – Elected Morgan County judge.

1900 – Emerges from the Republican convention as its dark horse nominee, wins the general election by over 60,000 votes.

1904 – Is not renominated for governor.

1908 – Runs in the gubernatorial primary and loses to incumbent Governor Deneen.

1912 – Runs in the gubernatorial primary, finishes fourth in a field of seven.

1919 - 1933 – Serves as congressman-at-large.

1936 – Dies, April 11.

Republican
January 14, 1901 to January 9, 1905

The second Richard Yates, the first governor of the 20th century, lived in the past in the stirring times of the Civil War when his father, the patriotic orator for whom he was named, was Republican governor and then a U.S. Senator. Father and son had the same assets – charisma and the ability to electrify an audience. Unfortunately for the son, who was the first Illinois-born governor, he was a peacetime chief executive without a martial stage on which to perform. He had no interest in the developing Progressive Movement that sought to disturb the status quo with governmental reforms, regulation of business, and improvements in the lot of the common man. Generally, the postwar governors were less conservative than the legislatures and the Republican leadership, but the second Yates was an exception.

As governor, he had no program of his own and left no imprint on Illinois government. Four times a candidate for governor, he won only his first campaign in 1900. His participation in a series of deadlocked conventions led to one of the major reforms of the Progressive era, the direct primary law, the enactment of which was the first order of business when Yates was replaced by a stronger governor. He failed when he tried to unseat Senator Shelby M. Cullom. Later, he found his political niche and had a 14-year career as congressman-at-large, an office for which name recognition was a chief qualification. Harold L. Ickes, who at that time was a Progressive worker and seldom was charitable toward conservative Republicans, described Yates as a "weak, easy going nonentity with few ideas, no real purpose and little character."

The Governor's Son

Yates was born in Jacksonville on December 12, 1860, a month after his father's election to the governor's office. He grew up with vague memories of soldiers marching outside the Executive Mansion. As a boy, he sat with his mother in the state Senate gallery while his father mingled with famous men on the floor below. In the genteel poverty of his widowed mother's home, his dream of a military career vanished when President Grant did not appoint him to West Point. When he reached Whipple Academy, the preparatory school for Illinois College, he made a friend of classmate William Jennings Bryan, the son of an important downstate Democrat. "Oh, dear," Yates' mother once said of Bryan, "I wish you had the energy and iron will of that boy. He will go far." At one time they considered forming a Bryan and Yates law partnership.

While at Illinois College, Yates won second honors in an interstate oratorical contest. Of slight build, with a pale face and dark eyes, he was a University of Michigan Law School graduate, but he never practiced outside Jacksonville. Before and for two years after law school, with the title of city editor, he was most of the editorial staff of the Jacksonville *Daily Journal*. At every opportunity he made speeches reminding Civil War veterans and other Republicans that he bore a famous name. He was active in local politics, but his hometown law practice was never important. He was city attorney when he married Ellen Wadsworth, who became the mother of his two daughters.

In 1892, a Democratic year, Yates was the losing nominee for congressman-at-large, a statewide congressional office tied to no geographic district. Two years later he was elected Morgan County judge. In four more years, he was congressional district leader for the McKinley campaign and made speeches in seven midwestern states.

He lacked administrative experience, but he could make friends in high places and get patronage jobs from them. Over objections from Senator Cullom, President William McKinley appointed him collector of internal revenue for the central Illinois district. At Republican conventions his downstate followers loyally supported him during long deadlocks.

The Son Becomes Governor

Not yet 40 years old, he was elected governor in 1900. Better known men were among the Republican candidates, but Yates began campaigning as a neutral dark horse and picked up support from Senator Cullom's "federal crowd." When his original candidate seemed to be a loser, Congressman William Lorimer grabbed a Yates banner and stampeded the convention. The result of the third ballot was never announced and Yates won on the fourth. Since he at least was presentable, he was accepted as being preferable to a split in Republican ranks.

For a gubernatorial candidate, the Democrats compromised on an Altgeld follower, Samuel Alschuler of Aurora, who lost to Yates by 61,233 votes but nevertheless ran over 15,000 votes better than the Bryan-Stevenson presidential ticket.

Yates, a spoils politician, had no trouble with the standpat legislature, and they would have no trouble with him. He opened his inaugural address with an unprecedented confession of ignorance and inexperience: "At this time my knowledge of state affairs is so limited that it would be discourteous to attempt to convey that limited knowledge to the legislature." After 1902 he was for civil service reform, which had been endorsed by both parties, but he avoided a leadership role on this and other issues. He did nothing about paving roads, which would increase rural taxes and mean that more autos would kill chickens and scare horses. In his autobiography, Yates said his administration was "a prosaic affair" that "could really be summed up in one word – economy." He signed bills that permitted municipal ownership of street railways and restricted prison industries. A new child-labor law made Illinois the first state with a 48-hour week for children. He vetoed a bill for centralized auditing of state agencies.

The governor complained to downstate followers that he was being unfairly criticized by the Chicago newspapers. They complained that the governor made state employees do campaign work and contribute to a slush fund. Like Tanner, he had a personal staff of "sunburst colonels" who rode behind him in parades. One of his proudest moments occurred during the McKinley inauguration parade. As Yates, in top hat and frock coat, rode past the reviewing stand, his trick horse saluted by lowering one knee to the ground.

Wrangling for Patronage and Power

In 1904, Yates attained some prominence by being the first Western Republican to declare for the nomination of Theodore Roosevelt at the national convention in Chicago. But, by that time, the governor knew he had no hopes of a second consecutive term as governor. At the Republican state convention, downstate backing gave him the lead over six rivals for 58 ballots between May 13 and June 3. He had lost his only Chicago power base when Congressman Lorimer defected to another candidate. When Yates convinced himself that he couldn't get the votes to win, he decided throw his support to State's Attorney Charles S. Deneen of Cook County. He thus denied the nomination to Frank O. Lowden, who had finished second on the earlier ballots.

Deneen handily won the 1904 general election. But the two soon became political enemies. Deneen remained neutral when Senator Cullom came up for a fifth term in 1906. Yates, who thought that Deneen had promised to support him, unsuccessfully challenged Cullom in one of the bitter campaigns for which Republicans were notorious in that era. Two years later Yates failed to prevent Deneen's second-term nomination. When Yates ran for governor again in 1912, Deneen was first and Yates fourth in a primary field of seven.

After he moved out of the Executive Mansion, Yates lived in a large house in Springfield and divided his time between the chautauqua lecture circuit and patronage jobs, which he found to be scarce during the Deneen and Lowden administrations. Briefly, he was an assistant attorney general. Edward F. Dunne, a Democratic governor, appointed him a minority member of the state utility commission, in charge of telephone companies. Then, in 1919 he became a conservative congressman-at-large. He lost in the 1928 primary but was given the nomination when the man who defeated him died before the election. Finally defeated in the 1932 Franklin Delano Roosevelt landslide, he nevertheless polled more votes than any other Illinois Republican. He ran and lost one more time. In 1933, after voting against repeal of Prohibition during the lame duck session of Congress, he was an unsuccessful candidate for delegate to the convention that ratified the Twenty-first Amendment.

He retired to Harbor Springs, Michigan, where he died April 11, 1936, while writing his memoirs.

23rd Governor

Charles Samuel Deneen
1863-1940

1863 – Born, May 4 at Edwardsville.

1893 - 1895 – Serves in the House of Representatives in the 38th General Assembly.

1897 – Begins a two-term stint as a state's attorney, convicts a state treasurer, several bankers, and prominent people.

1904 – Deneen wins the gubernatorial nomination as a compromise candidate on the 58th ballot; He easily beats Democrat Lawrence B. Stringer in the general election; One of his legislative triumphs is to bring about legislation that establishes primary races that determine party slates for the general election.

1908 – Deneen defeats Democrat Adlai E. Stevenson I to win a second term as governor.

1909 – General Assembly passes the "ten hour" law for women, limiting their legal work day to 10 hours.

1910 – After several attempts, the General Assembly passes the direct primary law that is upheld by the courts.

1911 – The "mother's aid" law provides funds for dependent and neglected children; Illinois gets its first "Workmen's Compensation Act" (the forerunner of the state's modern workers' compensation laws.)

1912 – Deneen gets the Republican nod for a third term and remains loyal to the Republican Party even though a progressive faction of it breaks away. The Progressive Party nominates its own gubernatorial candidate and splits the general election vote so that Democrat Edward F. Dunne wins with a little more than 38 percent of the vote.

1925 - 1931 – Serves in the U.S. Senate.

1940 – Dies in Chicago on Feb. 5.

Republican

January 9, 1905 to January 18, 1909

January 18, 1909 to February 3, 1913

Charles S. Deneen was one of the state's strongest governors. A mildly liberal reformer who headed the respectable faction among Chicago Republicans, he championed much of the Progressive Movement's legislative program but would not be its candidate when he sought a third term in 1912. In number and importance, the legislation and administrative advances for which he gets credit exceed those of Governor John P. Altgeld, the Democratic hero of the 1890s.

Deneen, who had been a vigorous state's attorney in Cook County, rose to the governorship on the groundswell of complaints about municipal corruption and corporate domination of government that culminated in formation of the Progressive Party and Theodore Roosevelt's unsuccessful presidential campaign of

1912. The first two-term governor since Cullom, Deneen was the first of three reform governors who overlapped the Progressive Movement and remade the face of Illinois government between 1905 and 1921. He was succeeded by Edward F. Dunne, a former Democratic mayor of Chicago, and Frank O. Lowden, a civic-minded Republican. In a period of intense factionalism in both parties, these men had the same goal – better government. But they acted independently of each other. Deneen and Lowden cooperated at times but were political rivals for two decades.

A cold, cautious man, Deneen didn't know how to engage in political small talk with the Democrats and the conservative Republicans who made his leadership difficult. Effective, unpopular, and durable, Deneen could, nevertheless, count considerable accomplishments. His honesty was never questioned, and the "jackpotters" who sold their votes in the legislature detested him.

The Republican Prosecutor

The future governor was the son of a Latin professor at McKendree College, grandson of a Methodist minister, and the great-grandson of a territorial legislator who opposed slavery. He was born May 4, 1863, at Edwardsville where his mother, the former Mary Ashley, lived with a sister-in-law until Adjutant Samuel H. Deneen returned from the Civil War to his home at Lebanon. Young Deneen graduated from McKendree and taught in downstate and Chicago schools before getting a degree from Union College of Law. He was married in 1891 to Bina Day Maloney of Mount Carroll. One of their four children was born in the Executive Mansion.

In Chicago he lived within the congressional district of William Lorimer, the "blond boss" of West Side Republicans. With Lorimer's backing he became a state representative, attorney for the sanitary board, and a member of the Republican state central committee. Starting in 1897, during two terms as state's attorney, he convicted a state treasurer, several bankers, and others of prominence. By 1900, Lorimer and Deneen were dominant powers in Cook County Republican politics. Deneen terminated their alliance before he ran for governor.

The Progressive Governor's Accomplishments

In 1904, Chicago Republicans, who wanted the next governor to come from the city, had two strong candidates, Deneen and

Frank O. Lowden, who helped create an unusually long deadlock at the state convention. Because Governor Yates and others who opposed Lowden couldn't agree on anyone else, Deneen won nomination on the 58th ballot. He named his personal friend Roy O. West, a Chicago lawyer who later became President Coolidge's secretary of the interior, to be Republican state chairman. Running with the popular Theodore Roosevelt, Deneen was elected by a 2-to-1 margin over Democrat Lawrence B. Stringer of Lincoln.

Deneen appealed chiefly to middle-class and professional voters. Charles E. Merriam, a Progressive who might have been elected Chicago's mayor in 1911 had the governor supported him, wrote that Deneen's standards of integrity and competence were "quite superior" to those of competing politicians. He was a straight-laced Methodist who rode a day coach to his inauguration, served nothing stronger than lemonade in the Executive Mansion, and invited popular evangelist Billy Sunday to hold a prayer meeting there. He abolished the personal staff of "sunburst colonels" who had paraded behind Governors Tanner and Yates.

The new governor, who owed his nomination to boss-controlled convention politics, endorsed primary elections and civil service, both high items on the Progressive agenda. "Our state needs a compulsory primary law," he said at the opening of his inaugural address. Four years later he won his longest fight when the Illinois Supreme Court finally approved a law, the fourth enacted at his insistence, that gave the nomination of candidates to the voters at primary elections.

Espousing another Progressive crusade, Deneen at his first legislative session used the power of his office to place employees of the seventeen welfare institutions under civil service. When the perverse legislature omitted an appropriation for the new civil service commission, the governor allocated $14,000 from contingency funds.

The unusual success of his extensive legislative program reflected the governor's campaigning ability and persistent refusal to accept conservative rebuffs. He did not hesitate to call special legislative sessions, and time after time he stumped downstate counties and Chicago wards, appealing for public support and eventually getting his bills passed. Excluding old-line conservatives, he had a sizable segment of public opinion on his side. The Municipal Voters League had elected a majority of the Chicago City Council, and at a 1904 referendum the statewide vote was 4 to 1 for selection of candidates by the voters instead of by convention delegates.

Dunne, his Democratic successor, in his autobiography commended Deneen for supporting legislation needed by Chicago. He gave special mention to replacement of the justice of peace system with a Municipal Court, abolition of township government in the metropolis, construction of the municipal harbor and pier, and authorization for the council to fix electric and gas rates.

The Deneen administration made major changes in state government. Management of the welfare institutions was centered in a five-member state board of administration. It replaced seventeen local boards that had been a major source of political patronage. Inmates of county homes and local almshouses were transferred to state institutions. A state highway commission with a salaried engineer began propaganda for paved roads. Motorists were required to register their cars and pay two dollars for identification plates, with the money going into a road fund. The nation's first "mother's aid" law provided funds for dependent and neglected children. Workmen's compensation and occupational diseases laws were enacted, women were limited to a 10-hour workday, and mining laws were modernized. The board of health was authorized to distribute diphtheria antitoxin. Suburban and downstate municipalities received permission to adopt commission government. A local option law was passed with Anti-Saloon League support. State school appropriations, which had been $1 million a biennium since 1872, were doubled. More money was provided for the University of Illinois.

The governor was a hard-nosed administrator. During a race riot at Springfield, he called out the National Guard and ordered the state's attorney to convene a grand jury. At Deneen's request, Attorney General William H. Stead forced the Illinois Central railroad to pay additional taxes on its gross receipts. State agencies were required to deposit all collected funds into the state treasury.

The reformer governor had enemies in both parties. When the 1904 deadlock was broken, Yates believed that Deneen had given at least an implied promise to support him in the future for the U.S. Senate. Two years later, however, the governor remained neutral when Yates ran against Cullom and lost. In the 1908 primary, held under a primary election law that was later invalidated by the courts, Yates lost again when he sought revenge by running against the governor. In the 1908 election, William Howard Taft carried Illinois handily for president, but the popular Adlai E. Stevenson, the former vice president, came within 23,164 votes of defeating Deneen for governor. Democrats claimed that the election had been stolen in Chicago wards controlled by Mayor Fred A. Busse, leader of another Republican faction. Win or lose, Illinois governors traditionally run poorly in second-term campaigns.

A Second Term Troubled by Partisan Politics

The unstable factionalism in both parties made Deneen's second term especially complex. He faced diplomatic problems involving his legislative program, and Old Guard elements considered it improper for a political leader to support the reform program of the puritanical Progressives and to attempt to drive standpat elements from Republican leadership. He controlled the Senate, but House Speaker Edward D. Shurtleff was reelected by a conservative Democratic coalition. U.S. Senator Albert J. Hopkins of Aurora won an advisory primary but had few supporters in the legislature the last time it elected a senator. After months of maneuvering, during which Deneen refused to be "kicked upstairs" to the U.S. Senate, another bipartisan coalition elected Lorimer to succeed outgoing Senator Albert J. Hopkins. (In two years Lorimer was expelled from the Senate after investigations at Washington and Springfield turned up evidence of graft and payoffs in the legislature.)

Progressive sentiment was at high tide in 1912. Deneen had six opponents in the Republican primary but was nominated for a third term by 152,997 to 64,168 votes over Len Small, a future governor who ran second. Deneen willingly voted for Theodore Roosevelt at the Republican's national convention. When President Taft was renominated and the Roosevelt forces bolted to form the progressive Bull Moose Party, Deneen, out of party loyalty, refused to be the Progressive candidate for governor. He had endorsed the federal income tax amendment and had been primarily responsible for enactment of much of the Progressive program. However, after considerable debate, the new Progressive Party split the general election vote by running Frank Funk of Bloomington for governor. Funk was a virtual unknown in Chicago. As a result, Democrat Edward F. Dunne won the crowded general election with a little more than 38 percent of the vote. Deneen finished second and Funk third. Whether Deneen could have been elected as a Progressive is doubtful. In that case the conservative Republicans no doubt would have entered their own candidate, again giving Dunne the advantage.

Senator Deneen

After he returned to his Chicago law practice, Deneen remained a political force, but his leadership was handicapped by Governor Lowden's greater popularity. On occasion they cooperated, but they never attempted a political partnership of non-machine Republicans. In 1916 Deneen cautiously supported Morton D. Hull, a wealthy Chicagoan, for governor but Lowden was nominated. During the Lowden administration, Deneen and Roy O. West kept their faction alive and won a few Cook County and Chicago offices.

In 1924 the former governor was elected U. S. Senator with the help of William Hale Thompson, who especially hated the incumbent, Medill McCormick, a former Progressive leader. In the Senate, where his legal ability and integrity were respected, Deneen supported President Calvin Coolidge on the World Court and other issues. As the Republican Party declined in influence during the 1920s, Deneen was accused of dealing with Roger Sullivan, the rising Democratic leader, in some campaigns. In 1930, with 38 percent of the vote in a three-man field, he was defeated for renomination by Ruth Hanna McCormick in a campaign scandalous for its heavy spending.

Deneen was practicing law when he died in Chicago on February 5, 1940.

24th Governor

Edward Fitzsimmons Dunne
1853-1937

1853 – Born, Oct. 12, in Waterville, Connecticut.

1895 – Dunne is elected to a vacant circuit judgeship.

1905 - 1907 – Serves as mayor of Chicago, after being elected on an immediate municipal ownership (IMO) of public transportation and utilities platform.

1907 – Turns the mayor's office over to Republican Fred A. Busse after losing the general election by 12,000 votes.

1912 – A progressive faction splits from the main-line Republican Party and nominates its own candidate, dividing Republican votes in a multi-candidate race; Dunne wins election to the governor's office with a little more than 38 percent of the vote.

1913 - 1917 – Dunne's administration sets in motion infrastructure improvements, such as the push for paved roads, and governmental restructuring recommendations from the governor's commission on efficiency and economy.

1916 – Frank O. Lowden, with the help of a reunified Republican Party, defeats Dunne in the gubernatorial general election; Dunne never again runs for public office.

1937 – Dies of heart disease, May 24, in Chicago.

Democrat

February 3, 1913 to January 8, 1917

The only mayor of Chicago who became governor of Illinois was Edward F. Dunne, a personable and idealistic Irishman who led the Democratic Party's reform wing when Republicans were split by the Progressive Movement. A disciple of John Peter Altgeld and supporter of William Jennings Bryan, he was a progressive at heart, the second Democratic governor since the Civil War, and the second Catholic governor (Bissell was the first). His four productive years as governor coincided with and complemented the first term of Woodrow Wilson's presidency.

As mayor from 1905 to 1907 and governor from 1913 to 1917, Dunne failed to achieve his major ambition to provide immediate municipal ownership (IMO) of street railway and utility companies. His campaigning under an IMO slogan did pay dividends with creation of a state utility commission that regulated privately owned companies.

He was the connecting link between Charles S. Deneen and Frank O. Lowden, Republican reform governors, both of whom were his superiors as public administrators and leaders of the legislature. One of his accomplishments was creation of a legislative commission on efficiency and economy, whose wide-ranging recommendations he backed. However, only a few of them were approved by the foot-dragging Republican legislature during the Dunne administration. Lowden continued the drive for governmental reorganization with triumphant success.

An Irish Boy Becomes His Honor

Edward Fitzsimmons Dunne was born in Waterville, Connecticut on October 12, 1853, the son of P. W. and Delia M. Lawler Dunne. Before he was two years old, the family moved to Peoria. He went to Peoria grammar and high schools and then to Trinity College in Dublin, Ireland, for three years, but he did not graduate because of his father's business reverses. Back in Peoria, he worked in his father's mill and began the study of law. In 1876 he went to Chicago and graduated the next year from Union College of Law. Five years later he married Elizabeth J. Kelly. Intelligent, friendly, and good-looking, he entered law partnerships that were successful. Active in political and legal circles, he came under the influence of Governor Altgeld. In 1895 he was elected to a vacant circuit judgeship.

While the Hearst newspapers beat their drum, Dunne rode the traction [streetcar] issue into the mayor's office. Drawing on information obtained during a European trip in 1900, he argued that gas and electric rates were lower in cases where foreign and American cities owned their own plants. When Mayor Carter Harrison equivocated, Judge Murray F. Tuley, a senior member of the bench, proposed that public ownership forces unite and agree on Dunne as their candidate. With Hearst's help, Dunne was endorsed by most wards, nominated when Harrison stepped aside, and elected by 25,000 votes over a Republican who favored franchise-operated utilities.

Although referenda showed that he had public backing, the "hopelessly hostile" city council ignored his IMO messages and, after considerable stalling, adopted ordinances that he vetoed. "The so-called bosses of my own party were decidedly opposed to municipal ownership and quietly helped the utility corporations beat me," he remembered. When the traction companies finally agreed to sell, the mayor asserted that the settlement did not protect Chicago's interests. The council overrode his vetoes. Meanwhile, a Deneen administration law allowed the city to reduce gas, electric, and water rates. The mayor took satisfaction that he had erased the city's treasury deficit, added 1,000 police-men, doubled saloon license fees, and enforced building ordi-nances. High quality appointments included Walter L. Fisher as special traction attorney, Jane Addams as a member of the school board, and James Hamilton Lewis for corporation counsel. "Honest service had been rendered to the city," he said. "Graft and crookedness had been driven from the city hall."

In 1907 traction again was the issue that frustrated Dunne. He was renominated by Democrats after defeating Carter Harrison in an advisory primary, but he lost by 12,000 votes to Republican Fred A. Busse. Dunne believed that he could have been reelected had he made deals with river ward leaders. He said that Democratic leaders cooperated in raising a $600,000 slush fund that was used against him and that he had been offered bribes to change his stand on municipal ownership and to let brothels stay open another year.

Some contemporaries said he had tendencies toward "star-ry-eyed" idealism. But in his history/autobiography Dunne admit-ted that he simply lacked "political finesse" and had made some mistakes in the mayor's office. He also discovered some mundane features of the job he didn't like: His signature was needed to get dogs released from the city pound and common drunks from the house of correction. Five years later, he found out that being gov-ernor was more enjoyable.

The Roads and Public Utilities Governor

Split opposition enabled Dunne to win both the 1912 guber-natorial primary and election. He saw signs that the Republicans were weaker, one of them being Adlai E. Stevenson I's strong race for governor in 1908. Chicago votes helped his nomination over two downstaters, Samuel Alschuler of Aurora, who was backed by former Mayor Harrison, and Congressman B. F. Caldwell of Springfield, the choice of Roger Sullivan, who within a few years would be the dominant Democrat in Illinois. Party ranks closed in the fall campaign, in contrast to the Bull Moose split among Republicans. Against Deneen he used a "jackpot government must go" slogan — jackpotism being the popular lingo referring to the sale of public office. Dunne charged that the Republican governor was part of a corrupt conspiracy at Springfield. Deneen protested that the charge was "shameless and untruthful." Dunne was elect-ed with 38.1 percent of the vote.

Dunne and his wife, the former Elizabeth J. Kelly, were the parents of 13 children. Nine lived to help overcrowd the Executive Mansion, into which Mrs. Dunne moved extra beds.

In his inaugural message, which was delayed three weeks by a speakership fight, the former mayor emphasized his views on municipal ownership. He was successful in the creation of a public utilities commission with power to control the financing, service, and rates of privately owned companies. (In a case of questionable judgment, he appointed former Governor Yates a minority member.) One feature of the reform law outlawed granting of railroad passes to politicians and other prominent men. Another Dunne law authorized cities to operate their own utility plants.

The drive for paved roads moved forward under Dunne, who had made a downstate campaign with a hired car and chauffeur. He proclaimed April 15, 1913, as "road day" and asked able-bodied men to contribute their labor to the elimination of mudholes. Surrounded by state officials in overalls, the governor used a silver-plated shovel at Mooseheart to start the improvement of the Aurora-Elgin highway. Checks for one cent each went to 1,300 volunteers who showed up. As part of a prison reform movement, he offered to commute one-fourth of the sentences of honor prisoners who worked on roads. At Grand Detour, Ogle County, 51 convicts spent the winter cutting through a hill and grading one mile. Responsibility for work on major routes was shifted from townships to counties by a law that gave increased powers to a bipartisan state commission that supervised the work of highway superintendents in each county. The state was to assume half of the cost and take over maintenance. Only Vermilion and Cook counties made extensive use of new bonding powers.

Dunne started the state reorganization drive that Governor Lowden would finish. Since statehood, the state's problems had been met by the creation of myriad agencies, which were usually inadequate and, at times, conflicting. Except that they appointed the governing officials and received reports from them, the governors had little control over the agencies. Some progress had been made in the last half-century, especially by Deneen in the welfare field, but, in general, centralized accounting did not exist. The decentralized system provided autonomous patronage polls and kept governors from becoming too powerful. The system was not unique in Illinois, and many other states had their own versions of governmental inefficiency.

On Dunne's strong recommendation, the legislature created an eight-member commission on efficiency and economy, which engaged Professor John A. Fairlie of the University of Illinois as chief of staff. The governor endorsed its report, which called for consolidation of state agencies, including those under other state officials, into 10 departments. Intensive lobbying was not his style, however, and the legislature was more attentive to fears of many state employees who believed that their jobs would be eliminated. At the end of the Dunne administration, the only reorganization bills of consequence that had passed created a superintendent of printing, provided for uniform reports, and set up a legislative reference bureau with responsibility for preparing a biennial budget.

By a one-vote margin in the House of Representatives, Dunne failed to win enactment of legislation by initiative and referendum, which was one of the top items on the Progressive agenda. Abolition of the controversial state board of equalization was killed in the Senate. The governor also wanted to consolidate the Chicago park districts, which didn't happen until Henry Horner became governor. Dunne wanted action on the long-delayed plan to open the Illinois waterway to barge traffic, but federal officials and Henry T. Rainey, a downstate congressman, refused to approve a channel of only eight feet. Dunne also unsuccessfully urged the abolition of capital punishment.

Dunne applauded major steps forward for women's suffrage. Illinois became the first state east of the Mississippi River to allow women to vote for presidential electors and some local officials, those whose jobs were created by statute but not by the state constitution.

Retirement

Most Progressives had closed ranks with the Republicans by 1914, when Republican Lawrence Y. Sherman defeated Harrison in the first popular election of a United States Senator. The next year the controversial William Hale Thompson became mayor of Chicago. Dunne worked hard in a dull campaign for a second term as governor but lost to Frank O. Lowden.

Dunne never ran for public office again. Roger Sullivan took over Democratic leadership in Chicago and started building the party organization that under Anton J. Cermak in the next decade led to the debilitation of the faction-ridden Republicans. The former governor remained an elder statesman. Frequently, he spoke

211

in major cities on the municipal ownership issue. Irish ethnic groups sent him and Frank Walsh of Montana to the Paris peace conference to plead for independence for Ireland. With Clarence Darrow, Dunne convinced Cook County Democrats that they should oppose ratification of the 1922 state constitution. At the 1932 Democratic National Convention, he was an early supporter of Franklin D. Roosevelt. After a long illness, he died May 24, 1937, of heart disease in Chicago.

25th **Governor**

Frank Orren Lowden
1861-1943

1861 – Born, Jan. 26, Sunrise City, Minnesota.

1896 – Marries Florence Pullman, daughter of George M. Pullman, the sleeping car millionaire.

1904 – At the Republican state convention, backed by Congressman William Lorimer, Lowden makes a strong showing for the gubernatorial nomination; he loses the bid when, after 58 ballots, Governor Yates throws his support to Charles S. Deneen.

1906 - 1911 – Serves in the U.S. House of Representatives.

1916 – Lowden defeats Dunne in the governor's race.

1917 – Lowden's Civil Administration Code reforms Illinois government.

1917 - 1918 – Illinois sends more than 350,000 people to fight in World War I.

1918 – Lowden pushes a $60 million bond issue, to be paid off by increased automobile license fees, to pave Illinois' roads.

1920 – An Illinois constitutional convention convenes in Springfield; voters would reject its recommendations in 1922; Lowden, who refuses to consider a second term as governor, loses an Illinois preferential primary for president; the Republican national convention held in Chicago nominates Warren G. Harding.

1924 – Lowden refuses to be a favorite-son candidate for president.

1928 – Lowden is an unenthusiastic presidential candidate who barely challenges Herbert Hoover for the Republican nomination.

1943 – Dies of cancer on March 20, in Tucson, Arizona.

Republican
January 8, 1917 to January 10, 1921

Governor Frank O. Lowden, a farm boy turned millionaire, deserves major credit for enacting the Civil Administrative Code of 1917, which reorganized Illinois government in the interest of efficiency and economy and was one of the two most important laws ever put forth by the state legislature. In long-term effect, it was equaled only by Governor Thomas Ford's 1843-1845 debt retirement program that saved frontier Illinois from bankruptcy.

The governor didn't make all the changes he wanted in state government, but his biographer, William H. Hutchinson of the University of Chicago, concluded that the Lowden reforms exceeded those of any other state to that time. Credit goes to the governor for vigorous and persistent backing of his program and for skillful handling of the legislature and patronage. Before or after, no Illinois governor has had more success in getting legislative support at critical times.

An activist, Lowden was both a conservative Republican who believed that government should operate on business principles and an administrative reformer who backed many of the Progressive Movement's goals. He launched Illinois on the bond issue financing of paved roads, obtained referendum approval for a constitutional convention, and during World War I rallied the Illinois homefront in full support of the Wilson administration. He actively supported suffrage for women but was neutral on the constitutional amendment for national Prohibition.

In addition to the governorship, Lowden had several careers. His interest in government and politics developed while he was a brilliant young Chicago lawyer. He was financially successful before he married Florence Pullman, the daughter of George M. Pullman, the sleeping car millionaire. He left his law practice and moved from the "silk stocking" Second Ward to downstate Illinois. As the "Squire of Sinnissippi," owner of a model farm on the Rock River, he demonstrated ways to increase the productivity and income of American farmers. In his final years he was a major advocate of governmental assistance to depressed agriculture.

From Iowa Farm Boy to Millionaire Farmer

Frank Orren Lowden was born in the obscure town of Sunrise City, Minnesota, on January 26, 1861, the son of Lorenzo O. and Nancy Elizabeth Bregg Lowden. He was seven when his farmer-blacksmith father, who had been a Granger, Greenbacker, and Democrat, moved to a farm in Hardin County, Iowa, and in time became a lawyer. The boy did farm work and attended a Quaker academy at New Providence. For five years, with little hope for advancement, he taught in rural and small town schools. Money loaned by a Quaker enabled him to attend the University of Iowa. There his brains, energy, good looks, and personality forecast future success. He graduated as class valedictorian and taught one year at Burlington, Iowa. Then Writ Dexter, general counsel of the Burlington railroad, gave him a clerkship in his Chicago law office. He became valedictorian of his class at Union College of Law and was admitted to law practice in 1887.

Within a few years after Dexter's death, Lowden headed a law firm with corporate clients. In addition to a general practice, he helped arrange the merger of corporations of which he became a stockholder and director. He was one of the financiers of the

Coliseum, which was donated to the city as a permanent convention hall. Lowden probably was the wealthiest Illinois governor. In 1896 he married Florence Pullman, whom he had met on an ocean liner two years earlier. Endowed with tact as well as her father's intellect and firmness, she fully supported Lowden's political career. Their marriage produced four children. Lowden managed or was a director of some of his father-in-law's enterprises after Pullman's death in 1897.

The young lawyer, as a member of the Civic Federation's political action committee, worked for primary elections. He resigned as president of the Second Ward Republican Club when it resisted his anti-patronage proposals. During the Tanner administration, he backed a futile effort to abolish and combine local governments within Chicago. The title of colonel, by which he was deferentially addressed in later years, traces to the Spanish-American War. Lowden was lieutenant colonel of a National Guard regiment that was not called into federal service.

An active role in the McKinley campaign of 1900 gave the congenial Lowden a statewide acquaintance among Republican leaders. One who recognized him as an attractive candidate was William Lorimer, the Westside Chicago boss, who offered to run him for U.S. Senator in 1902. Lorimer's support for years put Lowden in the midst of Republican factional entanglements. And, Lowden's public image was not helped much when he bought and developed his farm on the Rock River near Oregon in Ogle County. The "squire's" manorial style of living did little to guarantee his popularity among farmers, just as the Pullman millions could be a liability among city dwellers.

In 1904 as a Lorimer-backed candidate for nomination as governor, he opposed Governor Richard Yates, State's Attorney Charles S. Deneen, and three other candidates. In a deadlocked convention, Deneen, who was his rival for the support of the more respectable element among Chicago Republicans, finally won. As a consolation prize, Lowden became Republican national committeeman. Two years later, he was elected to a congressional vacancy. At Washington he was interested in agriculture, the tariff, and natural resources. He led a successful fight to upgrade the State Department's consular service. After slightly more than two terms he retired from Congress.

In the Bull Moose Party split of 1912, Lowden proposed the compromise under which Republican convention delegates were elected by congressional districts. As a district delegate he voted for his friend Theodore Roosevelt, but in the campaign, as a traditional Republican, he supported President Taft. Later, he was influential in getting the Progressives to return to the Republican Party.

The Governor Who Reformed the Government

In the role of a harmony candidate who could unite Chicago and downstate, Lowden finally won the governorship in 1916. In the primary he was endorsed by, among others, William Hale "Big Bill" Thompson and Fred Lundin, who called himself the "Poor Swede" and had succeeded Lorimer as the "Great Manipulator" of Chicago politics. Lowden had the impossible task of not affronting the Chicagoans while simultaneously showing downstaters that he was not a City Hall puppet. In the primary, he polled 54 percent of the total vote over two other millionaires, Morton D. Hull of Chicago, who was Charles Deneen's man, and Frank L. Smith of Dwight.

In the fall campaign, Governor Dunne pointed at Lowden when he charged that corporations controlled the Republican Party. (Four years earlier Dunne had won by making the same charges against Deneen.) Lowden, who had pledged to introduce business methods in government, asserted that Dunne had raised taxes and administrative costs alarmingly. With the party reunited, Illinois again was a Republican state and Lowden carried 79 counties.

Before the legislature convened, Lowden announced that he would not run for a second term and that his top priorities were administrative reorganization and the calling of a constitutional convention. His inaugural address stressed that Illinois had entered an industrial age and that political reforms must follow economic and social changes. The reorganization bill, drafted under the new governor's supervision, abolished some of the 125 controversial state agencies and reorganized the others into nine departments, each headed by a director responsible to the governor, whose power to make appointments was greatly increased. Centralized budgeting and accounting were provided. Unlike Dunne, Lowden avoided political complications by not interfering with the lesser state officials, each of whom was an ambitious and jealous political power who would fight to protect his patronage and prerogatives.

In the first weeks of his administration, Lowden was applauded nationally for putting Illinois into the front rank of modern states with the passage of the Civil Administrative Code. For several decades a few hesitant steps had been taken toward modernizing state government, and Edward F. Dunne, the preceding governor, had sponsored a centralization bill that the legislature ignored. Lowden's program was passed by both houses in 12 days with only two negative votes. Fourteen other states copied the Lowden blueprint, and, in some features, so did Congress when it created the Bureau of the Budget.

Only after the code passed did Lowden give attention to the requests of Republican legislators who wanted the right to name some of the men who would fill the reduced number of patronage positions. He went outside Republican ranks when the directors of the new code departments were appointed. The nonpolitical head of the new public welfare department was Charles H. Thorne, retired president of Montgomery Ward and Company.

Lowden wanted a new constitution with a flexible revenue article that would centralize the state's tax structure, permit an income tax, and abolish township assessors. The legislature at the 1917 session and the voters in 1918 approved the calling of a convention that met in futility for two years, beginning in 1920. The controversial constitution it drafted was approved of by Lowden and Deneen; opposed by Dunne, Thompson, and Len Small, the man who succeeded Lowden; and rejected in 1922 by the voters.

The Deneen and Dunne administrations had laid the foundation for a hard-road system, but cement was being poured too slowly to suit Lowden. His solution was to finance 4,800 miles of pavement with a $60 million bond issue, to be paid off by increased automobile license fees rather than by real estate taxes. The bond issue, first advocated by the Illinois Highway Improvement Association, was approved at a 1918 referendum. In order to have a backlog of public works jobs for returning veterans, Lowden did not sell bonds during the war, but he ordered the public works department to go ahead with surveying, grading, and bridge construction. As a result, the Small administration was able to make an early start at cement pouring.

Where Governors Deneen and Dunne had failed, Lowden negotiated an agreement with federal officials that allowed construction to start on the Illinois waterway between Lockport and Utica. Support for the waterway, a major public works project, began soon after opening of the Panama Canal. Barge navigation was the main objective, but some hydroelectric power was produced.

In 1919 Lowden openly supported ratification of the Nineteenth Amendment that gave women the right to vote. In another reform, the 1919 legislative session created a three-member tax commission, appointed by the governor, to replace the elected state board of tax equalization, which since 1869 had met once a year to adjust corporate assessments. William H. Malone, the retiring board chairman, thereafter carried on an anti-Lowden vendetta during which he contended that the Pullman companies had been underassessed. The governor also prevailed upon the legislature to abolish more than 500 private banks that had never been under state supervision.

Before his term ended, Lowden had the support of John H. Walker, president of the state labor federation, and Frank Farrington, president of the miners union. He successfully sponsored a workmens' compensation law that required employers to report accidents in hazardous occupations. Twice the legislature failed to reduce from ten to eight hours the maximum working day for women in industry. The legislature did not approve an administration request for a commission to study economic and industrial aspects of the racial problem.

To increase state pride, on the 100th anniversary of Illinois statehood the Lowden administration constructed the Centennial Building to house expanding departments and provided for the publication of a scholarly six-volume set of Illinois histories.

In World War I, Lowden's patriotic leadership was as wholehearted, if less emotional, than that of Governor Richard Yates in the Civil War. Because Copperhead influences had been troublesome six decades earlier, there was some concern about the loyalty of the large German and Austrian populations. When five Illinois congressmen voted against the declaration of war, the General Assembly, at Lowden's request, called upon Illinois to forget partisanship and to give the Democratic administration in Washington shoulder-to-shoulder support. Samuel Insull, the utility executive, was appointed chairman of a council of defense whose 14 members represented business, labor, agriculture, the professions, civic groups, and social agencies. "Gentlemen, you have got to work together," the governor told them. He called for public support of such activities as bond sales, food conservation, thrift measures, and Red Cross drives.

He had some difficulties. When a strike tied up coal production in the upper Mississippi valley, Lowden considered taking over the mines, but his legal authority was questioned. He used troops to prevent strike violence and restore order when mobs at East St. Louis and Chicago attacked blacks who had come from the South to meet manpower demands. Mayor Thompson had permitted the Chicago situation to get out of control before he asked the governor to send in the National Guard. Lowden tried to prevent a meeting at Chicago of pacifists and socialists who criticized the war effort and wanted peace terms set. Except for one lynching, the homefront record was otherwise harmonious.

Thompson, like Lowden, had opposed the declaration of war, but was less than fervent in his patriotism after the war was actually declared. The mayor complied with manpower conscription laws but opposed the draft in speeches that sought the ballot box support of the foreign-born, especially those of German extraction.

Lowden found it impossible to work with Mayor "Big Bill" Thompson who persistently belittled the governor's programs. No wonder the ever-ambitious Thompson was turned down in 1918 when Chicago for the first time asked for financial aid from the state treasury. The final break came at the 1920 Republican state convention, where the mayor wanted downstate delegates to approve an isolationist Cook County platform. Lowden called it radical, socialistic, and demagogic and declared that the mayor was unworthy of being Republican national committeeman. On a vote to table Thompson's platform, Lowden won 1,110 to 631.

Frustrated Presidential Ambition

Lowden refused to reconsider his decision to be a one-term governor. He ran for president, but in the 1920 Illinois preferential primary, as a result of Thompson's opposition, he lost Chicago by 30,000 votes. In other farm states his campaign for delegates was disappointing, in part because of political ineptness of his manager, Secretary of State Louis L. Emmerson. At the opening of the national convention in Chicago, Lowden was embarrassed when opponents claimed that Emmerson had bribed two Missouri delegates. For nine ballots the convention was deadlocked by Lowden, U.S. Senator Hiram Johnson of California and another cadidate. Then the nomination went to Warren G. Harding. Had he been supported by Thompson's Chicago delegates, Lowden might have been the presidential nominee in a landslide year.

In the 1920 primary, Lowden's candidate for governor was John G. Oglesby, who had served two terms as lieutenant governor but lacked the campaigning ability of his father, the Civil War general and three-term governor. Lowden's other candidates were nominated, but Oglesby lost to Thompson's candidate, Len Small, the winner of the general election. In 1924 Lowden refused to be a favorite-son candidate for president since he would be required to support Small for a second term as governor. When he was offered the vice presidential nomination, Lowden refused in a message read to the Republican convention.

In 1928 he was the popular choice of Midwestern farmers who objected to President Calvin Coolidge's vetoes of farm policy bills. Without enthusiasm, Lowden was a candidate for the presidential nomination but had no chance of winning over Commerce Secretary Herbert Hoover. Thereafter, as the rural depression of the 1920s spread to urban America, from Sinnissippi Farm, Lowden's national role was to raise a respected voice in advocacy of governmental assistance for farmers.

In his final years he was distressed that Illinois had violated the spirit of the Lowden code by creating some autonomous boards and commissions. Lowden died of cancer on March 20, 1943, in Tucson, Arizona.

26th **Governor**

Lennington Small

1862-1936

1862 – Born, June 16, Kankakee.

1901 - 1905 – Serves in the Senate in the 42nd and 43rd General Assemblies.

1905 - 1907 – Serves as state treasurer.

1912 – Loses the Republican gubernatorial primary to Governor Charles Deneen.

1917 - 1919 – Serves as state treasurer.

1920 – Small narrowly defeats Lieutenant Governor John G. Oglesby (son of three-time Governor Richard J. Oglesby) in the Republican gubernatorial primary; Defeats Democrat James Hamilton Lewis in the general election.

1921 – Attorney General Edward J. Brundage indicts Small on charges that he ran a money laundering scheme during his days as treasurer; Small is acquitted in the case, but may have tampered with the jury.

1922 – Voters fail to ratify a new state constitution that many feel would give too little representation to Cook County and that would provide for the imposition of a state income tax.

1924 – Small wins a second term as governor; Oscar E. Carlstrom, his candidate for attorney general, also wins as part of a Republican sweep.

1927 – Brundage's civil suit against Small's money laundering scheme results in a judgment of over $1 million against Small.

1928 – Small loses the Republican gubernatorial nomination to Louis Emmerson.

1932 – Small wins the Republican nomination for governor, but loses the general election to Democrat Henry Horner.

1936 – Dies May 17.

Republican
January 10, 1921 to January 12, 1925
January 12, 1925 to January 14, 1929

The inauguration of Governor Len Small in 1921 abruptly ended the 16-year Deneen-Dunne-Lowden reform era in Illinois government. A farmer from Kankakee, Small was one of the great American road builders. He also was the downstate Republican partner of William Hale "Big Bill" Thompson, the notorious Republican mayor of Chicago. Small's election gave the ambitious Thompson a share of political spoils at Springfield as well as major control of those in Chicago. During the next eight scandalous years, machine politics triumphed over the cause of good government. Small, who scoffed at the complaints of reformers and metropolitan newspapers, never deviated from Thompsonism.

Early in the automobile age, Small pulled Illinois out of the mud and gave it one of the nation's best hard road systems. The 7,000 miles of 18-foot wide pavement he constructed in eight years were badly needed, well engineered, economically built, and highly political. Each county got its share of the pavement if it voted for Small and his legislative candidates. In Small's second term, LaSalle County ran short of paved roads; not coincidentally its state senator, Thurlow G. Essington of Streator, had opposed the governor in the 1924 Republican primary.

From Farm Boy to State Treasurer

All his life Small's home was at the edge of Kankakee. He was born on the farm of his parents, Dr. Abram Lennington and Calista Currier Small, on June 16, 1862. How long he attended Northern Indiana Normal School and a business college official biographies do not say, but he didn't need a formal education in his chosen fields of politics and agriculture. He taught school briefly, and he boasted that his first wages were invested in Kankakee County farmland. At 21, he was secretary of the State Board of Agriculture; later he became its president. Soon he was a county supervisor, which led to long service as secretary of the Kankakee Interstate Fair. He became clerk of the circuit court and a member of the Republican state committee. The Kankakee State Hospital was his political ficfdom as a result of appointments by Tanner and Yates to its board of trustees. (In fact, his name was first tied to scandal when, in 1902, Small's patronage employees were allegedly coerced into making political contributions to the Yates campaign.)

In 1883 he married Ida Moore, a schoolteacher and the daughter of a neighboring farmer. (Stricken by apoplexy, she would die the day the jury acquitted Small in a misappropriation of funds trial in 1921.) Their two sons and son-in law would be prominent appointees in his gubernatorial administration.

Small's given name was Lennington, but after his election as state senator in 1900, he shortened it to Len. At the end of his first term as treasurer, President William Howard Taft appointed him assistant U.S. treasurer at Chicago. He was a Republican county chairman who didn't mind making political deals with the Democrats, if he had to, and he also played the patronage game well. In the 1912 primary, as Senator William Lorimer's candidate for governor, he finished second to Governor Deneen in a field of eight. He was a conservative Republican who never supported Progressive causes and whom farmers especially regarded as a kindred spirit.

In 1916 he was again elected state treasurer, and apparently used the office for personal gain. In fact, after each of Small's terms as treasurer, laws were passed to tighten the regulation of treasury funds. In 1907 the Deneen administration required that all public money received by the treasury be deposited in state banks. When Small left the treasury in 1919, the Lowden administration ordered that banks bid for state treasury deposits.

Small had prospered during a long political career, and at the time of his gubernatorial inauguration, he owned a model farm, a bank, and Kankakee's daily newspaper.

The Pavement, Patronage, and Political Corruption Governor

Small was lucky when he ran for governor again in 1920. Frank O. Lowden, who had presidential ambitions, was popular and undoubtedly could have been renominated over any opposition. Small's campaign manager was Fred Lundin, a one-time congressman who called himself the "Poor Swede" and was credited for masterminding Thompson's two elections as mayor of Chicago. Governor Lowden supported the uninspiring lieutenant governor, John G. Oglesby, the son of the Civil War general and three-time governor. In a four-man primary field, Small won, but only by 7,902 votes. Lowden men were nominated for the other state offices. In November, the Harding landslide gave Small a big margin over Democrat James Hamilton Lewis.

Lewis was a hard campaigner who took issue with Small's questionable record as state treasurer and his close affiliation to Chicago Mayor Thompson, who specialized in patronage and political favors and who fostered the environment in which "Scarface Al" Capone thrived. But Small's political machine carried him to victory: Downstaters wanted the road projects he promised, and Thompson paved his way in Chicago.

Small's inaugural address emphasized the economic value of hard roads but otherwise largely echoed the platform that Thompson used in Cook County.

The Small administration effected several popular measures during his eight-year term in office. A state bonus for war veterans was financed by a $55 million bond issue. State aid to schools was placed on an equalization formula designed to help weaker districts. The state conservation department was created, and pari-mutuel betting on horse races was legalized. Also, electrocution replaced hanging for capital punishment.

But Small's lasting contribution to Illinois' infrastructure was more concrete. The Lowden administration's $60 million road bond issue, advance engineering work, and right-of-way purchases enabled Small to start road building quickly. He rejected the first bids, which averaged nearly $40,000 a mile for 18-foot cement pavement, and announced that under normal conditions costs could not exceed $30,000 a mile, including grading, culverts, and some bridge work. By 1924 his administration had reduced the cost to $27,000. Year after year he set new national records as a road builder. When he ran for a third term in 1928, Small could boast that "Illinois leads the world. . .and its 7,000 miles of completed concrete pavement exceed the mileage of any other state in the Union." To fund the roads, he won a 1924 referendum approval of a new issue of $100 million in bonds. The 1927 legislature enacted a two cent-a-gallon tax on gasoline, to be divided between the state and counties. (But after $200,000 was collected in five months, the tax was held unconstitutional.)

Using a $20 million bond authorization that also had been inherited from Lowden, Small pushed construction of locks and dams on the waterway between Utica and Starved Rock. Designed to bring to the Midwest some of the benefits of the Panama Canal, the waterway project was part of Mayor Thompson's efforts to get national attention. The mayor, who in 1918 had lost a race for nomination as senator, seems to have considered himself presidential material.

But the good the governor did couldn't erase his penchant for graft and nepotism.

Given the skeletons in his closet, Governor Small made a huge political error at the end of the 1921 legislative session when he made deep cuts in Lowden-backed Republican Attorney General Edward J. Brundage's appropriation bill. The attorney general, who was one of the mayor's factional rivals in Chicago, retaliated by indicting Small for conspiracy and embezzlement of interest money during his second term as treasurer. Small had deposited state funds in the Grant Park Bank, a long-dormant private bank in suburban Kankakee, and then loaned the laundered money to

Chicago meatpackers. From them he collected interest at standard commercial rates as high as six percent. He reimbursed the state at call money rates of two or three percent. He did not account for the difference. Brundage brought the governor up on charges in Sangamon County in July of 1921. Tried at Waukegan in 1922 under a change of venue, Small denied wrongdoing and testified that he had paid the state more interest than all preceding treasurers. The criminal trial ended with an acquittal verdict. Historian Donald Tingley reports that the verdict may have been the result of jury tampering. (After the trial four jurors received state jobs.)

Brundage then charged Small in a civil suit. When the evidence about the interest money was resubmitted in that trial, the judgment went against the governor. The Illinois Supreme Court upheld a master-in-chancery ruling that he owed the state $1,025,434. In 1927 a friendlier attorney general, Oscar E. Carlstrom, cut the figure to $650,000 and stipulated that Small had not received any interest illegally. Small had been instrumental in electing Carlstrom in 1924.

Patronage, which got Small where he was, also played its part in bringing him down. He appointed his son, Leslie Small, to head the Department of Purchases and Construction, which controlled highway construction for the state. A.E. Inglesh, the new administrative auditor of the Department of Finance, was the governor's son-in-law. Before Small's administration was over, Leslie had a trial date to answer charges related to rigging state highway contracts.

When the state public utilities commission would not ratify Mayor Thompson's streetcar program for Chicago, Small replaced it with a commerce commission with duplicate powers but a compliant membership. When Will Cloven, superintendent of paroles and pardons, resigned after he was accused by two grand juries of selling paroles, he was promptly placed on the commerce commission payroll. In 1926, Small appointed commerce commission chairman, Frank L. Smith of Dwight, to a short-term Senate vacancy caused by the death of Senator William McKinley. Smith had already won his own Senate seat in 1926 election. But the Senate refused to seat Smith for either the elected or appointed position after an investigation revealed that Smith had received a $125,000 campaign contribution from Samuel Insull, a utility magnate. The Senate saw the conflict of interest in the commerce commission chair accepting contributions from a utility owner, even if the governor did not.

The Machine Goes Bust

Small found it difficult to hold his power base together when his cronies started to lose influence and fight amongst themselves. A succession of scandals in Chicago soon made "Big Bill" an embarrassing partner. Fred Lundin, who wanted credit for the mayor's election-day majorities, broke off relations when Thompson appointed his private secretary as chief of police. Small retained Lundin for his own machine by giving him control of patronage of Chicago's west and north side parks. Faced with graft charges and lawsuits, Thompson retired from the mayor's office in 1923, but he continued to hold public attention by making statements belittling Great Britain's King George and the League of Nations.

William Lorimer, a political harmonizer who had been in an eclipse since the U.S. Senate unseated him in 1912 when it declared he had won an illegal election, returned from South America and patched up relations between Small and Thompson. By this time, Thompson had won another term and returned to the City Hall in 1927. The mayor, who had planned to back Carlstrom for governor in 1928, instead supported Small for a third term. Chicagoans, traditionally tolerant about letting politicians have a free hand, became fed up with Capone-style gangsterism and Big Bill's loose talk. In the Republican primary, in both Cook County and downstate, Small ran behind Secretary of State Louis L. Emmerson, who in the November election won the difficult job of dealing with the city's accumulating financial problems.

Between 1912 and 1936, the optimistic Small was a candidate for governor six times. In 1932 he led a field of eight Republican primary candidates but was the big loser in the first Franklin Delano Roosevelt-led Democratic landslide. In that campaign Thompson and Small made a flamboyant barge cruise, stopping at Illinois cities along the Illinois and Mississippi rivers.

Small died May 17, 1936, a month after Thompson had backed him as the Union Progressive candidate for governor.

27th Governor

Louis Lincoln Emmerson
1863-1941

1863 – Born, Dec. 27, in Albion.

1912 – Loses a bid for the Republican nomination for state treasurer.

1917 - 1929 – Serves as secretary of state, winning elections in 1916, 1920, and 1924.

1924 – Republican caucus leaders discourage Emmerson's bid for the gubernatorial nomination.

1928 – Defeats Governor Small in the Republican gubernatorial primary and wins the general election.

1929 – The Oct. 29 stock market crash marks the beginning of the Depression; the governor calls four special sessions of the General Assembly to help in the economic crisis and establishes relief commissions and a state income tax that is later declared unconstitutional.

1932 – The governor chooses not to run for reelection.

1941 – Dies, Feb. 4, in Mount Vernon.

Republican
January 14, 1929 to January 9, 1933

L ouis L. Emmerson was elected governor a year before the arrival of the Great Depression. A conservative Republican from southern Illinois, he defeated Governor Len Small in the 1928 primary and was an easy winner in the landslide election that put Herbert Hoover in the White House.

Emmerson had made a good record as secretary of state, an office of high exposure to which he had been twice reelected. His loyalties were to the Lowden, rather than the Small-Thompson, branch of his party, and his private honors included the top Illinois office in the Masonic Lodge. He was a courageous executive who tried to cure the financial hangovers of the almost bankrupt Cook County government. But he couldn't foresee the Depression, which became his biggest burden, as it was Hoover's. To cope with the crisis, Emmerson appointed special relief commissions, summoned the legislature into multiple special sessions, and advocated a state income tax, which the Supreme Court ruled unconstitutional.

From Store Clerk to Secretary of State

Tall and angular, with protuberant ears, Emmerson was a small town boy from the Wabash valley. At Albion in Edwards County, he was born to Presbyterian and Republican parents, Jesse and Fannie Saurdet Emmerson, on December 27, 1863. His father was a farmer and village official. His grandfather, Alan, was a cobbler from Virginia who arrived in Albion in 1818 with the Beckwith-Flower colony of English settlers. He served with Lincoln in the legislature.

Young Lou, whose formal education ended with graduation from high school, played the tenor horn. After a concert at nearby Grayville, he met Anna Mathews, whom he married in 1887. (There is some disagreement over the exact name of his bride, however. Her name is given as Anna in *Who's Who in America,* on information presumably provided by her husband. Obituaries and other documents have variations, such as Ann Eliza, Eliza Ann, Ann, and Annie.)

Also in 1887 he moved to Mount Vernon to take a job as a furniture store clerk. Previously, he had clerked in stores at Albion and Sullivan, Indiana. At Mount Vernon, his home for the rest of his life, he became a partner in the furniture store and later founded the Boston Store. An undated clipping from the *Mount Vernon Register-News* says that in 1898 he "graduated in embalming under Prof. Sullivan of St. Louis." (Small city furniture retailers frequently doubled as undertakers.) As time passed, he became one of the county seat's leading citizens, active in the Presbyterian church, and several lodges. He was an alderman and school board president. He helped organize the Third National Bank, was its treasurer, and its president for 28 years.

As a Republican, he was county chairman, briefly a member of the state board of equalization, and a trustee of the Menard penitentiary by appointment of Governor Deneen. In 1912 he made a losing race for nomination as state treasurer but was a delegate to the first of 10 Republican national conventions he attended. For the first of three times he was elected secretary of state in 1916, defeating Lewis G. Stevenson, the son of a vice president and father of a future governor, who had been appointed to the office by Governor Dunne. As secretary of state, he reduced administrative expenses and sponsored new securities and corporation laws. He assigned automobile license plates 3 and 23 to his own cars.

Despite inexperience in national politics, Emmerson in 1928 was manager of Lowden's presidential campaign. In that capacity he gave $2,500 checks to two St. Louis politicians who later became convention delegates. That situation enabled Lowden's opponents to claim improper use of campaign funds. But, the governor never lost confidence in Emmerson.

The Governor of a State in Economic Crisis

In 1924 Emmerson wanted to run against Governor Small but was turned down at an elimination caucus of Republican leaders. That November he polled the highest vote among state candidates when he was elected secretary of state for the third time. Four years later his chief competition was Attorney General Oscar Carlstrom, who finally withdrew. In the primary, backed by Lowden and former Governor Charles S. Deneen, he carried Cook County as well as downstate and finished 539,793 votes ahead of Governor Len Small. His Democratic opponent in the general election was Floyd E. Thompson of Rock Island, the young chief justice of the state Supreme Court, who had no chance, while Secretary of Commerce Herbert Hoover won the presidency over Governor Al Smith of New York.

The new governor, facing a Republican legislative majority that included Small holdovers, postponed patronage appointments until the 1929 session ended. In a departure from the preceding administration, he disregarded many patronage requests and recalled some officials who had served under Lowden. Emmerson set a precedent when he appointed a woman as assistant director of public welfare. A woman and a black were named to the parole board. His wife, meanwhile, replenished the supply of silverware and china in the Executive Mansion. He constructed 2,000 miles of pavement to complete the Lowden-Small program and sponsored a three-cent-a-gallon gasoline tax, one-third of which went to the counties. This time it was upheld by the Supreme Court. In his first year in office, he launched a $2.5 million building program at welfare institutions.

In the largely sectional split over Prohibition, Emmerson was a downstate supporter of the Anti-Saloon League. In spite of a 1930 public policy referendum, he vetoed a bill to repeal the Illinois law that prohibited the sale of intoxicants and gave search and seizure powers to enforcement officials.

Emmerson tackled the streetcar problem that had been a Chicago issue for a third of a century. Under his leadership, the legislature adopted a franchise law that the metropolitan newspapers had opposed when it had Small-Thompson sponsorship. Former Governor Dunne testified in opposition, but the ordinance was approved by the Chicago City Council and by a large majority at a 1930 referendum. The basic difficulty remained, however, as the surface and elevated lines still were unprofitable.

Even before the Depression, the Chicago government was on the verge of bankruptcy. At Mayor Thompson's request, the state tax commission had ordered a reassessment of Cook County real estate that delayed tax collections. They were two years behind schedule and a $40 million loan on tax anticipation warrants was necessary. Emmerson insisted that reckless extravagance by city officials was responsible for the trouble and complained that Cook County had not paid its share of the state property tax for two years.

Massive unemployment was Emmerson's biggest problem. In October 1930, he called a conference of influential Chicagoans and proposed that governmental activity be limited to providing institutional building and road construction jobs. To coordinate private funds and distribute them through charitable organizations, he appointed the Governor's Commission on Unemployment and Relief. In Chicago, money raised by the Association of Commerce and the Council of Social Agencies was gone before spring. The 1931 legislature, dominated by downstaters, limited itself to making townships rather than counties responsible for poor relief. When for the fourth time the governor summoned a special session, he asked it to reorganize the metropolitan assessment machinery and to provide state funds for the impoverished. He accepted administrative responsibility by appointing an Illinois Emergency Relief Commission. Backed by Lowden, he proposed a state income tax and increased tobacco and motor vehicle levies. The legislature provided the necessary two-thirds majorities, but the graduated income tax was held unconstitutional because it violated uniformity requirements. For Cook County a $17 million relief bond issue was enacted without a requirement that it have referendum approval.

As a stockholder, Emmerson personally suffered in the Depression's wave of bank failures. He had given up the presidency of the Third National Bank at Mount Vernon but was a stockholder in the Ridgely-Farmers State Bank at Springfield. He attended a directors' meeting that, without advance notice, asked State Auditor Oscar Nelson to liquidate the bank. Despite double indemnity liabilities that reportedly were heavy, he was comparatively well-to-do in retirement.

The Governor Retires

Emmerson was inaugurated 18 days after his 65th birthday, older than any of the other governors had been while in office. He had suffered a minor stroke and, a year in advance, Emmerson announced that he would not seek a second term. Age and health would have been reasons enough, but there were additional factors. The Depression had made Republicans unpopular in Illinois, and party factionalism had intensified during the Emmerson administration. Attorney General Carlstrom, who had "wet" leanings, believed that in 1928 he had been promised Emmerson's support four years later. However, the retiring governor favored Omer N. Custer of Galesburg, newspaper publisher, businessman, and believer in Prohibition, for the gubernatorial nomination. When Small won the primary, the retiring governor, who had been grand master of the Masonic Lodge in Illinois, quietly passed word that he favored Henry Horner, the Democratic candidate who also was a 32nd degree Mason.

His final message expressed pride in the state employees who, at his suggestion, had contributed a day's pay a month to the relief of the needy during two winters. "Probably in no similar period since the Civil War has there been so much financial distress," he commented. Urging rigid economy and revision of the tax laws, he condemned "profligate" borrowing to meet current needs and government encroachment on private business. A conservative to the end, he said he was "unalterably opposed to the dole system."

Most of his retirement was spent in his Mount Vernon home. He died there on February 4, 1941.

28th
Governor

Henry Horner

1878-1940

1878 – Born, Nov. 30, in Cook County.

1897 – Receives law degree from Kent College of Law.

1899 – Passes the bar; begins practice with Frank Whitney.

1914 – Elected judge of Probate Court.

1932 – Wins the Democratic gubernatorial nomination and defeats former Governor Len Small in the general election.

1933 – After a 3 percent sales tax is declared unconstitutional, the General Assembly passes a 2 percent sales tax that has no exemptions for farm products.

1935 – Horner asks that the sales tax be raised to 3 percent and that utility bills also be taxed; the General Assembly passes the Old Age Security Act to give state aid to the elderly.

1936 – Defeats Chicago Democratic machine candidate, Dr. Herman N. Bundesen, in a costly and bitter primary; Defeats Republican C. Wayland Brooks in the general election.

1940 – Dies in office on Oct. 6.

Democrat

January 9, 1933 to January 4, 1937

January 4, 1937 to October 6, 1940

No chief executive of Illinois had a more difficult administration than Henry Horner, the Depression governor. With a humanitarian's compassion, an extrovert's personality, and a marathoner's determination, he prevailed upon the reluctant legislature in repeated emergencies to vote taxes and bond issues for unemployment relief. The first Jewish governor, he was a former Chicago judge, an administrator in the Progressive tradition, and a proud man who, as governor, decided he would not be pushed around by the mayor of Chicago. Somewhat out of character, the first two-term Democratic governor since before the Civil War fought the Chicago political machine by becoming himself a successful, vindictive political boss. Between Depression responsibilities and political victories, he literally worked himself to death. He was the second Illinois governor to die in office.

Horner's long-term legacy to Illinois government was a major revision of its revenue system – substitution of the retail sales tax for the inadequate property levy that had been the state's chief support since the frontier era. His predecessor's income tax had been invalidated by the Supreme Court and only with a sales tax could the state pay its share of unemployment relief costs. After Horner twice forced the legislature to enact sales tax laws, the people grumbled about the extra pennies they paid. Chicago Mayor Edward J. Kelly believed that "High Tax Henry" was a loser. However, Horner's triumph in the 1936 primary, followed by election to a second term, established the governor's political independence.

Judge Horner, the "Professional Honest Man" of the Ticket

Horner, who never married, was the first governor who was a native of Cook County. He was born into an established German-Jewish family on November 30, 1878. When Horner was five years old, his mother divorced his father, Solomon A. Levy, a businessman, because he had physically and emotionally abused her. She resumed her maiden name, Dilah Horner, and insisted that her son's name also be changed to Henry Horner II, after his grandfather. With a degree from Kent College of Law (which would later be Chicago-Kent College of Law), Horner began practicing in 1899 with Frank A. Whitney, the son of Henry Clay Whitney, a friend of Lincoln's and collector of Lincoln memorabilia. Horner moved into a bachelor apartment in the Hyde Park vicinity of Chicago, where he too collected Lincoln material. He assembled a 5,000-volume Lincoln library that he willed to the State Historical Library.

As an attractive young candidate for underdog Democrats, he was elected judge of the Probate Court of Cook County in 1914. For 18 years Horner vigilantly made certain that widows and orphans got a square deal in the settlement of estates. At the same time he broadened his acquaintance among important families as inherited wealth passed from generation to generation. For Cook County Democrats, he was what ethnic politics expert John M. Allswang calls a "professional honest man," a candidate of impeccable reputation whose name made ballotmates more acceptable.

The Taxing Concerns of Governor Horner's Administration

Throughout his judicial career, Horner was politically subservient to Roger C. Sullivan, George E. Brennan, and Anton J. Cermak, who in succession dominated Democratic politics in

Chicago. Chicago Mayor Cermak, who also was county chairman, wanted to run for governor in 1932 but estimated that his election was unlikely since he had been defeated for senator four years earlier. Because Jews were a major element in Cermak's political coalition and prominent campaign contributors favored Horner, the mayor backed Horner in the primary. Horner defeated Michael L. Igoe, the hero of the Chicago Irish, and State Democratic Chairman Bruce A. Campbell of Belleville. Horner captured 50.4 percent of the total, with 397,499 votes, while Igoe and Campbell received 255,527 and 134,972, respectively. Then in the first Roosevelt landslide, Horner was elected easily over Len Small, the former Republican governor.

At his inauguration, the bald, stout, and affable Horner asked for nonpartisanship in facing the financial and social problems of the Depression. His immediate troubles were mostly caused by Cermak, who objected when the governor appointed personal friends, men he trusted, to sensitive positions. One was Ernest Lieberman, who was given charge of awarding highway contracts. Among steps to placate Cermak was appointment of his son-in-law, Dr. Frank J. Jirka, as state health director. However, Horner filled positions with people best suited to do the job, including some Republicans. That not only upset Cermak, but also downstate patronage chiefs like John Stelle.

Less than two months after the inauguration, Horner gave the eulogy at the funeral of Cermak, who had been assassinated in Florida. Horner helped with legislation that enabled the city council to fill the vacancy. The Irish returned to power when Edward Joseph Kelly got the job and shared leadership with Patrick A. Nash, the Democratic county chairman.

Horner's troubles continued as the new mayor, like Cermak, tried to control the governor's office. Kelly established a close relationship with President Roosevelt, who preferred to deal directly with big city mayors and came to admire the election night majorities in Chicago. Horner soon found that he was being bypassed by Harry L. Hopkins, director of the Emergency Relief Administration, when decisions were made about the distribution of federal funds. The governor preferred to deal with Harold L. Ickes, the Chicago Progressive who had become Roosevelt's interior secretary and public works administrator.

Repeatedly, the legislature, which only met from January to June every other year, was reconvened for emergency action.

After the regular session of 1933, there were four special sessions. Nevertheless, complaints came from Washington that Illinois was contributing less to relief financing than other high-unemployment states. In the year ending August 1, 1933, the federal government contributed 99 percent of the $68 million spent for relief in Illinois. A $20 million bond issue floated with difficulty by the Emmerson administration had been exhausted. Horner raised $30 million with another issue, but the money was gone in a year.

Horner, who considered Depression victims his personal as well as his official responsibility, fathered the Illinois sales tax out of necessity. During his first legislative session in which Democrats were in the majority but downstate Republicans were especially balky, he drove a three percent tax through the legislature. The Supreme Court promptly invalidated it because motor fuel and sales of farm produce were exempted. With corrections made and the rate reduced to two percent, Horner tried again. After another series of cliffhanger roll calls, the bill passed a week before the end of June, after which two-thirds majorities would have been required. This time the Supreme Court concurred.

In 1935 he asked that the sales tax be raised to three percent and that utility bills also be taxed. The legislature grudgingly complied only after state funds had been exhausted, Hopkins had shut off federal funds, and the governor had pleaded that the jobless and their families faced starvation. With increasing rates and a broadened base, the tax became the foundation of the state's revenue system for a third of a century, until it was coupled with a state income tax.

Horner gave tax relief to homeowners and farmers by canceling the annual meeting of the *ex officio* board that traditionally levied the state property tax, effectively suspending the tax and lowering bills. The board was later abolished.

The idealistic Horner was loyal to the Democratic Party and its social philosophy, but like many others he had reservations about Roosevelt's court-packing proposal that would permit the executive by appointment of additional justices to control the judiciary. In spending programs for the unemployed, he was closer to Progressive Harold L. Ickes than to Hopkins. He also held back from embracing the "blue eagle" of the short-lived National Recovery Administration, which was invalidated on the ground that it would put private business under governmental dictation.

In an administrative reform, he agreed to consolidation of

Chicago parks. Those on the city's north and west sides had been controlled by boards appointed by the governor, with patronage abuses frequently arising. Synchronizing with New Deal innovations, Illinois adopted old-age pension and unemployment insurance legislation. He tried but failed to settle mine union warfare. The gaining national prominence of United Mine Workers leader John L. Lewis worked to nullify any negotiating power of the governor. Horner had somewhat more success in helping the state's teachers. Chicago teachers had been paid only in scrip and tax anticipation warrants for a year. The special legislative session Horner called in early 1934 passed a bill to temporarily divert one-third of the state motor fuel tax to the school fund, with half going to Chicago.

The Fight for Reelection

A political "wet," Horner signed a repealer of the Illinois prohibition law and presided at the state convention that ratified repeal of the Eighteenth Amendment in December 1933. He wanted legal liquor sales to be regulated by a state law that would keep political influences out of saloons. Kelly caused a deadlock in the legislature by insisting upon local control. Eventually, they compromised but other conflicts between the governor and the mayor kept arising. Because of rivalry between City Hall and the governor's office, the legislature awarded enforcement of the new driver's license law to the secretary of state.

The final break with the Kelly-Nash Democrats came late in 1935. Without advance notice, Horner on public policy grounds vetoed a bill that would have given Chicago a new revenue source by permitting the city council to license off-track betting. In the mayor's view, the veto proved that the governor was a bluenose. On December 9, in the presence of President Roosevelt, who was in Chicago for a farm speech, Kelly called Horner a "one-termer." Roosevelt offered Horner an appointment to some federal judgeship if he would step aside.

The mayor's candidate for governor in 1936 was the city health commissioner, Dr. Herman N. Bundesen, whose subservience to the Chicago organization was undoubted. Bundesen wore spats and had written a book on baby care, characteristics that downstaters did not regard as qualifications for the governorship.

On the other hand, in the 1936 primary race Horner made a

spectacular transformation from the unpopular sponsor of the sales tax into a hero. Thoroughly angry, Horner announced his second-term candidacy with organized support in only three Chicago wards. Making political bossism his chief issue, he scathingly denounced Mayor Kelly and Cook County Democratic Chairman Nash. Charging wholesale vote frauds in Chicago, he befriended Cook County Judge Edmund K. Jarecki, who also had been dropped from the Democratic ticket. In Illinois political history, the 1936 Democratic primary rates as one of the most bitter and most expensive. Thomas B. Littlewood, Horner's biographer, estimates that $3 million, an enormous sum in pre-television campaigning, was spent for the two candidates in a mudslinging campaign. As a byproduct, Horner's primary strategy gave Republicans a precedent for future campaigning against "Kelly-Nash bossism."

Thus, Horner cast himself as a popular underdog who wouldn't take orders from the party bosses, a message that played especially well with downstaters. His unexpected talent as an organizer and propagandist blossomed and, with Republicans helping, Horner carried every downstate county and eight Chicago wards, beating Bundesen 820,313 to 659,221. The victory was personal, for the other statewide nominations went to incumbents who ran on the Kelly-Nash slate. Horner had tried to defeat all but Secretary of State Edward J. Hughes and Attorney General Otto Kerner, who had personal followings as well as Kelly-Nash support.

After the primary, Horner remained angry. At the request of the League of Women Voters, he changed his position and called a special session, which, over City Hall protests, enacted permanent registration of voters in Cook County. He vetoed a bill to allow Chicago to use sales tax money to pay part of the local costs of relief. The continuing feud alarmed the White House, but surface harmony was restored, and in November the Democrats carried Illinois again. Horner got his second term by defeating Republican C. Wayland Brooks by a little more 385,000 votes. Democrats Roosevelt and Senator James Hamilton Lewis won their races by lager margins than Horner did, and some observers suspected that Kelly had trimmed the governor's vote totals.

Determined to purge his enemies from party leadership, Horner resumed the Democratic warfare in 1938 by running Scott W. Lucas, his tax commission chairman, for U. S. senator. The downstate incumbent, William H. Dieterich, stepped aside and the Chicagoans countered with Michael L. Igoe, a former leader in the legislature. Lucas won the primary and the general election.

A Crusade Cut Short

Horner's next political steps might have been a third-term campaign for governor in 1940 and/or an effort to turn Mayor Kelly out of office in 1943. Had he succeeded, the political history of Illinois would have some different chapters. But two days before Lucas's election, the overworked governor suffered a coronary thrombosis. Thereafter, his office (when he was not wintering in Florida) was his bedroom in the Executive Mansion, reached by a one-man elevator. He conducted state business through a "regency" of administration officials, although under the Illinois Constitution, Lieutenant Governor John H. Stelle was acting governor when Horner was out of the state. At one point, he returned from Florida just in time to appoint James M. Slattery, his commerce commission chairman and campaign manager, to succeed Senator James Lewis, who died (conveniently) just as Horner was about to cross into Illinois. Lieutenant Governor Stelle might easily have appointed Patrick Nash.

The incapacitated governor gave up his third-term ambitions. Because he hated Stelle almost as much as he hated Kelly, he refused to resign and turn the state over to the lieutenant governor. Nevertheless, so that Democrats could have a united front in the 1940 campaign, he consented to a harmony ticket. Kelly and Nash came to Springfield but never rode the elevator upstairs. They allowed Horner to dictate the important decisions. He blackballed Stelle (who ran in the primary anyway) and named Harry B. Hershey of Taylorville, his insurance director, to be the candidate for governor.

In order to retain his official powers, Horner refused to leave the state again. The last months of his life were spent in a rented mansion on the lakefront. At the age of 61, the man who had guided Illinois through the Depression died on October 6, 1940. He had lived long enough to see Hershey defeat his lieutenant governor for the 1940 Democratic gubernatorial nomination.

29th
Governor

John H. Stelle
1891-1962

1891 – Born, Aug., 10, in McLeansboro.
1916 – Graduates from Washington University Law School.
1917 - 1919 – Serves in the army; Sees combat action in World War I.
1934 – Wins election to the state treasurer's office.
1936 – Wins the lieutenant governor's race on the Nash-Kelly Democratic slate.
1940 – After Governor Horner refuses to let Stelle be slated for governor on the
       Democratic ticket, Stelle runs in the primary anyway and loses.
1946 – Serves as national commander of the American Legion.
1962 – Dies July 7.

Democrat
October 6, 1940 to January 13, 1941

John H. Stelle was the downstate chum of the Chicago political machine headed by Mayor Edward Joseph Kelly and Democratic Cook County Chairman Patrick A. Nash. The alliance with the Nash-Kelly Democrats helped him in the divisive political warfare of 1936. That year, Stelle advanced from state treasurer to lieutenant governor.

But the alliance also drew the wrath of Governor Henry Horner, who did everything he could to make sure Stelle would never be governor, including seeing to it that Stelle would not win the 1940 gubernatorial nomination. In the end, however, it wasn't enough. Horner worked himself to death, and Stelle served out the remaining 99 days of Horner's second term.

The Doughboy Who Entered Politics

Stelle was born at McLeansboro August 10, 1891, the last of seven children of Thompson B. and Laura Blades Stelle. His great-grandfather had been an early settler and his grandfather a farmer and Civil War soldier. His father owned 2,000 acres of farmland, operated a department store, and practiced law. The future governor attended high school and Western Military Academy before he played professional baseball for several seasons without reaching the major leagues. In 1913 Stelle married Wilma Wisehart of Shawneetown. Together they would have two sons.

He graduated from law school at Washington University and was admitted to the bar in 1916. The next year he enlisted and attended the first officers training school at Fort Sheridan. After 17 months in the army, during which he was gassed and wounded, he returned home with the rank of captain.

Stelle was a fourth-generation resident of Hamilton County. There he was a lawyer who operated a 769-acre farm but gave major attention to successful business ventures, which included oil and racing horses. He helped organize and was president of the Cahokia Downs racetrack across the Mississippi River from St. Louis, and became the most influential downstater in the horse racing circles of his day. At McLeansboro, he owned a creamery and manufactured brick and drain tile. He owned a coal company at Evansville, Indiana and a glazed structural tile plant at Brazil, Indiana.

He was a member of the Methodist church and several lodges. He was very active in the American Legion. From the end of World War I until a few years after the second war, the Legion was a major political organization, much like the Grand Army of the Republic had been after the Civil War. He attended the Legion's organizing conference at St. Louis. Broad-shouldered and virile but an indifferent speaker, he became one of the group's king-makers, helping shape its policy and select the top officers.

Ambitious for a political career, he cultivated friendships among Legion leaders in Chicago. In the 1930 campaign, he headed a committee that helped veterans on the Democratic ticket. One of the candidates he worked to elect was Edward J. Barrett, a political unknown. When Barrett was elected state treasurer, Stelle went to Springfield as assistant treasurer. After the next election, Barrett was state auditor and Stelle his right-hand man. In 1934 Stelle was nominated and elected state treasurer.

The Ninety Nine Days

In the 1936 primary, Kelly and Nash slated Stelle for lieutenant governor. Kelly and Nash were feuding with Governor Horner, who had a slate of his own. In the Democratic primary, the Kelly-Nash gubernatorial candidate, Dr. Herman N. Bundesen, lost every downstate county; Stelle carried only his home county, but votes in Chicago nominated him over Horner's candidate, Attorney General John E. Cassidy of Peoria. Horner and his lieutenant governor rarely saw eye-to-eye on political matters, and two years later, Stelle did not support Scott W. Lucas, who was Horner's winning entry for United States senator.

The ailing Horner might easily have resigned during the long illness that haunted his second term. But he refused because he did not want Stelle as his successor. When it became obvious that Horner could not himself seek another term as governor, he conferred with Kelly and Nash on a Democratic "harmony" ticket. Horner insisted that Stelle not appear on the slate, and so named Harry B. Hershey of Taylorville, his insurance director, to be the candidate for governor.

But Stelle ran for governor in the 1940 Democratic primary anyway. He and Benjamin S. Adamowski and Edward J. Barrett challenged the harmony ticket, with Adamowski running for U.S. Senator and Barrett for auditor.

During his illness, Horner began running state business through a "regency" of administration officials, even when wintering in Florida. Stelle made this practice a primary issue. He called it "Nudelmanism" after regency member Samuel Nudelman, Horner's finance director. He felt government by regency was improper. The lieutenant governor should assume leadership when the governor is unavailable or incapacitated, he felt. He also felt administration officials were making decisions that only the governor or acting governor could make. If there was a constitutional issue of executive disability, it received little support because Horner was a popular hero. No one on the rogue Democratic ticket won the primary.

Stelle was working in a wheat field on his farm when he learned of Horner's death on October 6, 1940. He was inaugurated in a brief ceremony in his old office; then he proclaimed a 10-day period of official mourning and gave Nudelman time to resign. Later, a large number of Horner partisans were discharged.

Those who thought Horner a hero automatically thought Stelle a villain. Critics whispered scandal when the Executive Mansion, dingy after eight years as the residence of bachelor Governor Horner, was redecorated and the new first family sent dinner invitations to McLeansboro neighbors and Springfield friends. The *St. Louis Post-Dispatch*, which watched the Stelle administration closely, would report on March 16, 1953 that a "tremendous amount of equipment, coal and other merchandise" was bought. Rumors of irregularities were never documented. Milburn P. Akers, who had been part of the Horner regency, blamed the men around Stelle and wrote, "If John Stelle was ever off base, he was never tagged."

War clouds were growing more ominous as the new governor denounced appeasement, appointed draft boards, set up an emergency defense council, and created a reserve militia to take the place of the National Guard, which had been called into federal service. As he went out of office, he told the legislature that the state police and the parole board should be taken out of politics. He asked his friends to cooperate with Dwight H. Green, the incoming Republican governor who had defeated Hershey in the general election.

The Legionnaire

At the end of World War II, Stelle was one of the American Legion leaders who drafted the GI Bill of Rights and lobbied it through Congress. His turn to be national commander came in 1946. From that position he criticized General Omar N. Bradley, who headed the Veterans Administration after the war. Bradley, who had refused to build a veterans hospital at Decatur, charged that Stelle "deliberately obstructed" his office.

Out of office and back at McLeansboro, he frequently raised his voice as a southern Illinois Democrat who had Republican friends in high places. In 1952 he turned his back on Adlai E. Stevenson's bid for the presidency and made speeches for Dwight D. Eisenhower. In Illinois and Indiana, he supported the winning Republican candidates for governor.

The governor died on July 7, 1962, at Barnes Hospital, St. Louis, of acute leukemia.

30th Governor

Dwight Herbert Green
1897-1958

1897 – Born, Jan. 9, at Ligonier, Indiana.

1917 – Leaves Wabash College to serve in the Army Air Force; As a second lieutenant, spends the war in California teaching others to fly.

1920 – Finishes his undergraduate degree at the University of Chicago.

1922 – Earns his law degree from the University of Chicago.

1925 – Takes a job in Washington as an attorney for the IRS.

1931 – Green plays an instrumental part in building and presenting the tax evasion case against Al Capone.

1939 – Defeats former mayor William Hale "Big Bill" Thompson in the Republican Chicago mayoral primary, but loses the general election to Mayor Edward J. Kelly.

1940 – Defeats Democrat Harry B. Hershey to win the governor's race.

1941 – The U.S. declares war on Japan, Dec. 8.; On Dec. 18, the General Assembly convenes a special session to prepare Illinois for war; 670,000 Illinoisans would serve in World War II.

1944 – Green squeaks by Democrat Thomas J. Courtney to win a second term.

1945 – World War II ends.

1947 – A coal dust explosion kills 111 miners in Centralia. Green aides had solicited campaign contributions from mine owners while ignoring the coal miner's warnings about unsafe conditions.

1948 – Fails to get the vice presidential nomination and gets badly beaten by Democratic challenger Adlai Stevenson in the governor's race.

1958 – Dies Feb. 20.

Republican
January 13, 1941 to January 8, 1945
January 8, 1945 to January 10, 1949

Governor Dwight H. Green made his reputation as the prosecutor who sent "Scarface Al" Capone to prison. As for politics, his early specialty, the denunciation of Chicago Democratic leaders on the "Kelly-Nash bossism" issue, enabled the conservative Green to win reelection during World War II. While he was governor, Republicans extended their control to all state offices, the legislature, the Supreme Court, and half of the Cook County offices. But then Green's ambitions for either a third term – or maybe the vice presidency – fell flat.

An amiable blond with classic features and compact frame, Green was perhaps the most handsome of Illinois governors. He tried to be noncontroversial as he shared Republican leadership with U.S. Senator C. Wayland "Curly" Brooks, a golden-voiced World War I marine, who also was first elected in 1940 and roundly defeated eight years later. Brooks was an isolationist favorite of Colonel Robert R. McCormick of the *Chicago Tribune*. In anti-Roosevelt campaigning, Green balanced the public's patriotism against its dislike of regimentation. While patriotically supporting the two-ocean war effort, he criticized the federal agencies that during the Depression and the war regulated homefront activities.

Green established the precedent that Republican governors cooperate with Democratic mayors for the good of Chicago. Once in office, he stopped denouncing Mayor Edward J. Kelly by name. Early in his second term he invited the mayor, to whom he had talked only at public gatherings, to lunch at the Executive Mansion. Together they solved a problem that had perplexed non-cooperating governors and mayors for a half-century. To the surprise of those downstaters who believed his warnings about Democratic bossism, he and the mayor jointly sponsored legislation that created the Chicago Transit Authority and put streetcar, elevated lines, and the new subway under public ownership, which had been Edward F. Dunne's recurring dream. Thus ended five decades of agitation about traction franchises. As part of the bipartisan program, the mayor appointed four members of the Chicago Transit Authority and the governor appointed three. At the same time, the Republican administration enacted housing and terminal authority bills that City Hall wanted. Green's example of state-metropolitan cooperation became a model for the Stratton, Ogilvie, and Thompson administrations.

The Law-and-Order Prosecutor
Who Brought Down Scarface Al

The future governor was born on January 9, 1897, at Ligonier, Indiana. He was the son of Harry and Minnie Gerber Green. A 1948 campaign biography said that his grandfather came from Germany and that his father had been a farmer. For two years "Pete" Green went to Wabash College in Crawfordsville, Indiana, where he played quarterback and third base before he enlisted at the age of 20 and applied for assignment in the Army Air Force. As a second lieutenant, he spent the war in California teaching others to fly at Mather Field, Sacramento.

After the armistice, Green resumed his college education, for one quarter at nearby Stanford and then at the University of

Chicago, where he finished his undergraduate work in 1920 and obtained a law degree in 1922. While studying, he did apprentice work in the office of Roy D. Keehn, a family friend who was the Hearst counsel in Chicago. Green's wages came from the Chicago papers, where he was a reporter for the *Examiner* and wrote a legal column.

In 1925, U.S. Senator Charles S. Deneen got him a job in Washington as an attorney for the Internal Revenue Service. The next year he married Mabel Victoria Kingston and in a few months took her to Chicago, where their two daughters were born. He was the only tax specialist on a staff assembled by District Attorney George E. Q. Johnson to investigate Prohibition era hoodlums. He prepared the income tax case on which Capone was indicted and did most of the work of presenting the evidence to the jury in 1931.

When Capone went to Atlanta penitentiary, Green's reward was appointment by President Herbert Hoover as the United States attorney in the Chicago district. The Senate's Democratic majority failed to confirm him, but he held the office for three years during the Roosevelt administration until the faction-split Illinois Democrats agreed upon a successor. Meanwhile, orders came from Washington to prosecute Samuel Insull and his brother Martin, whose expansive utility and transportation empire had failed. (Samuel Insull had at one time controlled Commonwealth Edison, Peoples Gas Company, the Public Service Company of Northern Illinois, the elevated railways in Chicago and utilities in St. Louis and Indiana.) Although the Insulls were unpopular, Green regarded the mail fraud case as weak and requested the help of special prosecutors. His judgment was vindicated when the jury quickly acquitted the Insulls.

In the 1939 mayoral primary, Chicago Republicans needed an attractive candidate to run against former mayor William Hale "Big Bill" Thompson, who was trying for a comeback. Barney Goodspeed, treasurer of the Republican National Committee, raised a $100,000 fund and recruited the young former prosecutor, who had a law office in the Chicago Loop. Green won easily and then, with only $50,000 for campaign expenses, faced Mayor Edward J. Kelly. The Capone prosecutor ran as a reformer, and his speeches promising clean government were patterned after Governor Henry Horner's 1936 and 1938 denunciations of Chicago politicians. Kelly was reelected, but Green carried 14 wards and polled 43 percent of the vote, an unusual showing for a Republican in Chicago.

Governor Green

In 1940 Green was the bright hope of Republicans who wanted to extend gains made two years earlier. As a candidate for nomination as governor, he opposed Richard J. Lyons, a Lake County legislator who was backed by the *Tribune.* Green won the primary without difficulty, 618,025 to 457,643. Running against Harry B. Hershey of Taylorville, whom Democrats had nominated at Horner's request, Green promised to reduce taxes and work to reform state welfare institutions. He accused Kelly-Nash Democrats of tolerating crime and gangsters, and he charged there had been corruption in the way Horner's campaigns had been financed. Green was the strongest Republican vote getter in the strong Republican race of 1940. The only winner on the Democratic state ticket was Edward J. Hughes, the veteran secretary of state.

In advance of his inauguration, Green's appointment of Leslie P. "Ike" Volz as his executive secretary signaled that he did not plan a reform administration. The official explanation was that the governor, a political newcomer, needed someone who understood the background of Republican factionalism. Volz, who in 1915 was Fred Lundin's secretary, had been an insider in the "Big Bill" Thompson-Len Small era.

The war in Europe stimulated the economy, and the Green administration opened with a tax cut, reducing Horner's sales tax from three to two percent. Part of the revenue loss was recouped by the state's first tax on cigarettes – two cents a pack – and increases in beer and liquor taxes. Although the Depression had wound down, relief was still a major expense. At Green's request, the 1941 legislature created a permanent public aid commission to replace the emergency relief commission that since 1932 had allocated state and federal funds to local agencies.

With the approach of Pearl Harbor, Green steered a middle course between Senator C. Wayland Brooks, who opposed the draft, and Congressman Everett M. Dirksen, who in 1941 changed positions and announced support of President Roosevelt's policies. When hostilities began, the governor followed the example Governor Lowden set in the previous war by appointing a state council of defense and calling the legislature into special session to put Illinois on a war footing. He worked hard, traveled the state tirelessly, and spoke to innumerable groups concerned with war bond sales, victory gardens, and civil defense.

Green generally had the cooperation of the legislature, which had Republican majorities. In the House, if there was trouble in passing an administration bill, he could usually rustle up some votes from a handful of downstate Democratic members who were grateful for patronage favors. After tackling the Chicago transit problems, he turned his attention to downstate roads. Hundreds of miles of all-weather farm-to-highways roads that were previously impassible for weeks at a time were constructed in 1946 and 1947. Nevertheless, the Republican legislature showed its independence several times. At the opening of the 1945 session, Green demonstrated his political ineptness when he announced, without consulting the leadership, a preference for T. Mac Downing of Macomb for president pro tem of the state Senate and Hugh Green of Jacksonville for House speaker. House Republicans fumed but complied. The senators figuratively thumbed their noses by putting Edward E. Laughlin of Freeport in the leadership post. Green, who had been elected on a pledge to remove the sales tax from food, could not get the required two-thirds approval of a constitutional amendment. The legislature also denied his request for a "gateway" change that would make the amending process easier.

When the first bill for a fair employment practice commission (FEPC) appeared in 1943, the governor avoided a stand by appointing an interracial commission, without power to act against discrimination. Two years later, all labor groups supported FEPC bills, but for nearly 20 years the legislature refused to pass them.

As is traditional for Illinois governors, Green ran poorly in his 1944 second-term campaign. He and his Democratic opponent, State's Attorney Thomas J. Courtney, lived in the Edgewater Beach apartments on the lakefront. Courtney, an early riser, went to bed thinking he had been elected. Green, who stayed up until southern Illinois reported its vote, knew differently. His winning margin was 72,271.

A year after World War II victory celebrations, demobilization had not been completed and meat shortages caused griping. In 1946 Republicans won half of the Cook County offices and increased their majorities in the legislature and the Congressional delegation. Green and his advisors assumed it was a personal endorsement and expected to keep on winning. To them Illinois no longer was a doubtful state, and any of the governor's shortcomings as an administrator did not seem important.

Unfulfilled Veep and/or Third-Term Ambitions

Green's reputation took a ding, however, when a coal dust explosion killed 111 men in a Centralia mine in 1947. Green's aides had solicited the mine owners for campaign contributions and had ignored repeated warnings from the coal miners that the mine was unsafe. The state belatedly accepted federal rules on mine ventilation, and the mine company was fined $1,000 for negligence.

Green in 1948 dreamed of becoming the vice presidential nominee in what promised to be a Republican year. To ensure the solid support of the Illinois delegation to the national convention, he announced his third-term candidacy for the governorship. Lieutenant Governor Hugh W. Cross, who thought it was his turn to run, upset the surface harmony by announcing that he would oppose Green. The *Tribune* then reported that Warren Wright, a perennial candidate, also would run. Since he would have no chance in a three-man race, Cross withdrew. So did Wright, leaving Green unopposed for the nomination.

Through Old Guard contacts, Green was appointed temporary chairman of the convention. That provided an opportunity to stampede the convention with a rousing keynote oration. The governor, though never a spellbinder, could speak convincingly from a ghostwritten text he hadn't seen before. Close friends passed the hat and paid an Easterner to write a latter-day imitation of William Jennings Bryan's 1896 "Cross of Gold" speech. Each of the contributors was allowed to see the speech in advance. Each took the liberty of revising some of the ghostwriter's rhetoric. As delivered by Green in a sweltering hall, it was a typical anti-New Deal speech. The delegates didn't listen closely, and the vice presidential nomination went to Governor Earl Warren of California.

Truman wasn't a strong top of the Democratic ticket (indeed he barely won the 1948 presidential election), and Green expected election to a third term. He campaigned as an experienced executive who merited appreciation by the voters, and he derided Democratic challenger Adlai Stevenson as a striped-pants diplomat. Republicans were overconfident because of their 1946 victory and because Mayor Kelly had been forced to retire as mayor.

They didn't count on how effective the "egghead" Stevenson would be in attacking the governor's record. Stevenson was as persistent and effective as Green had been eight years earlier in his disapproval of Kelly-Nash Democrats. He kept talking about the Centralia mine disaster, accused the Republicans of a permissive attitude toward gambling and slot machines, pointed out that scores of newspaper reporters were on the state payroll without doing any work, and disapproved of Attorney General George F. Barrett's indictment of a St. Louis reporter who was investigating evidence that the Shelton gang was expanding its activities from southern Illinois into the Peoria area. Green lost the general election by a half-million votes.

Away from public office, Green opened a law practice in the Loop and became a Republican elder statesman. He died painfully of lung cancer on February 20, 1958.

31st **Governor**

Adlai Ewing Stevenson
1900-1965

1900 – Born, Feb. 5, in Los Angeles.

1916 – While at Choate prep school, Adlai learns that his father has lost the election for secretary of state.

1918 – Enters Princeton as a freshman and an apprentice seaman.

1919 – Discharged from the Navy.

1922 – Receives B.A. from Princeton.

1926 – Earns law degree from Northwestern.

1928 – Marries Ellen Borden, the couple will have three sons, including Adlai Stevenson III, who will run for governor in 1982 and 1986.

1933 – Works on the legal staff of the Agricultural Adjustment Agency, one of Franklin Delano Roosevelt's New Deal agencies.

1935 – Elected president of the Chicago Council on Foreign Relations.

1941 - 1944 – Serves as special assistant to the secretary of the Navy.

1945 - 1946 – Stevenson takes a position at the state department and participates in conferences leading to the foundation of the United Nations.

1947 – Serves as an alternate U.S. delegate to the United Nations.

1948 – Defeats Governor Green by over 570,000 votes.

1949 – Divorces Ellen Borden; secures passage of a bill that puts the Illinois state police under civil service.

1951 – Orders police raids against illegal gambling; Gets a highway construction program through the legislature.

1952 – Although he prefers to run for reelection as governor, Stevenson finally accepts a draft to run against Dwight D. Eisenhower in the presidential race; Stevenson carries only nine states in the presidential election.

1956 – Again runs against Eisenhower for president but fares even worse than he did in 1952.

1960 – Loses the Democratic nomination for president to John F. Kennedy.

1961 – Passed over as President Kennedy's secretary of state.

1961 - 1965 – Serves as U.S. ambassador to the U.N.; Advises Kennedy during the Cuban missile crisis and publicly supports President Lyndon Baines Johnson's Vietnam policies.

1965 – Dies of a heart attack in London, England on July 14.

Democrat
January 10, 1949 to January 12, 1953

Adlai E. Stevenson was the most nationally prominent of all modern Illinois governors, and it's certainly impossible to give his career its proper due in just a few pages. However, a look at his work in Illinois shows why four years as governor propelled him to two presidential nominations. His landslide election in 1948, followed by reform efforts in Illinois government, brought invitations to appear before influential out-of-state audiences. There, his witty, articulate speeches coincided with the Democratic Party's search to replace Harry Truman in the White House.

At Springfield, in a demonstration that executive experience is not necessarily a requisite for the governorship, he was fairly successful with his ambitious legislative program. He practiced fiscal as well as personal economy, preferring to spend more on schools and the unfortunate; and, when his term was over, his presidential supporters could claim that he had improved the moral climate of state government. His failures could be blamed, in part, on Republican legislators to whom the nonorganization Democrat was a political threat they did not understand.

The Rise of an "Egghead"

Adlai Ewing Stevenson II was born February 5, 1900, in Los Angeles, California, where his father was assistant manager of William Randolph Hearst's *Examiner*. His mother was Helen Louise Davis, whose family owned the *Bloomington Pantagraph*. Important Bloomington names were in his pedigree. On the Republican side was a maternal great-grandfather, Jesse W. Fell. Fell was a Quaker who had been Bloomington's first lawyer and was the friend who suggested and pressed Lincoln into the Douglas debates.

The Democratic Stevensons came from Kentucky. The first Adlai E. Stevenson, the governor's grandfather, supported Lincoln's opponents in 1864. Later, he was elected to Congress as a Greenbacker and Democrat. A gregarious man, he became Grover Cleveland's assistant postmaster general assigned to getting rid of some 40,000 Republican postmasters. He was elected vice president on the Cleveland ticket in 1892 and was defeated as William Jennings Bryan's running mate in 1900. In 1908 he came close to beating Charles S. Deneen for governor. Lewis G. Stevenson, the governor's father, also had political experience but at a lower level. He was the vice president's secretary and, in the Dunne administration, parole board chairman and secretary of state by appointment. In 1916, as a candidate for a full term as secretary of state, he led the losing Democratic ticket. At other times, he managed 49 midwestern farms owned by his family and Arizona copper mines owned by the Hearst estate.

After attending Choate prep school, earning his undergraduate degree from Princeton, studying law at Harvard, and earning his law degree at Northwestern, Adlai Stevenson II began a public service career that often took him to the nation's capital. In 1933 he was brought onto the legal staff of the Agricultural Adjustment Agency, a New Deal agency formed by President Franklin Delano Roosevelt. His work grew in responsibility and included a trouble-shooting post with Navy Secretary Frank Knox, the publisher of the *Chicago Daily News* and Alf Landon's running mate in 1936. He also participated in economic missions abroad for President Roosevelt and assisted two U.S. secretaries of state – Edward R. Stettinius, Jr. and James F. Byrnes – during the time the United Nations was being organized. He served as an alternate U.S. delegate to the United Nations in 1947.

Stevenson Becomes a Candidate

Every few years Stevenson returned to an intermittent law practice and local leadership of the Chicago Council of Foreign Relations. Thus he had the status of a public-spirited Chicagoan, rather than that of a career man in Washington. At a time when both parties were in disrepute in Illinois, he aspired to a seat in the U. S. Senate. On his behalf a group of friends started to explore the possibility of an independent campaign in the 1948 Democratic primary.

Former U.S. Secretary of State Byrnes provided a break-through when he told Jacob M. Arvey, the new mastermind of Illinois Democrats, that Stevenson was qualified to be senator or ambassador. Arvey was a practitioner of the Democratic theory that it is better to win an election with a reform candidate than to lose with an organization man. He had maneuvered Mayor Edward J. Kelly out of Chicago City Hall and replaced him with Martin H. Kennelly, a businessman with a good government image who had never been aggressive in politics. The Democrats needed two more clean faces to run against Governor Dwight H. Green and U.S. Senator C. Wayland "Curley" Brooks. Already campaigning for governor was Paul H. Douglas, a University of Chicago economics professor and an ex-Marine with a Purple Heart for wounds received in combat in the Pacific. But, he had been an independent Chicago alderman, and the Democrats didn't want him in Springfield. Arvey made an offer: If Stevenson would run for governor and Douglas for senator, both would have the party's support. Stevenson accepted after a period of private agonizing.

Despite his Washington career, the candidate was a stranger to the electorate. Republicans derided him as an "egghead." Nevertheless, Stevenson campaigned before small audiences, accusing Green of eight years of mismanagement. The result was a landslide repudiation of the incumbent. President Harry Truman carried Illinois by a little more than 33,000 votes, Douglas by a little less than 408,000, and Stevenson by 527,067 votes, a record at the time.

Governor Stevenson

With a plea for nonpartisanship, contending that party differences at the national level had nothing to do with state and local issues, Adlai Stevenson was inaugurated before a conservative legislature. With Paul Powell as speaker, Democrats had a small majority in the 1949 House. Otherwise, Republicans controlled both legislative branches during the Stevenson administration.

Green and Stevenson were the last Illinois governors until the late 1990s without severe budgetary problems. The Democrat inherited a wartime treasury surplus and spent it, following gubernatorial custom, on education, welfare, and other pressing governmental needs. To modernize Len Small's hard roads, in 1951 he proposed highway use taxes to support a $100 million, 10-year program. The legislature allowed a two-cent gasoline tax increase, to five cents a gallon, and a $28 million increase in truck license fees. The next legislature cancelled part of the truck fees.

Stevenson wanted a new constitution, with or without an income tax. The Senate, always happy to be uncooperative, refused to vote for a convention. To the Republican contention that changes should be made piecemeal by individual amendments, the governor responded with a challenge to join him in supporting a gateway amendment and a "blue ballot" procedure that increased prospects for ratification. Opposition then ceased and the gateway, adopted in 1950, rated as a major achievement and helped pave the way for a successful constitutional convention 20 years later.

The legislature accepted the governor's proposal to reorganize the state police, which Green had used as a political agency. He enlarged the force, giving Democrats half the positions, and installed a merit system. But Stevenson failed to put the conservation department under a commission.

Stevenson asked that Illinois follow the example of President Truman, who had appointed Herbert Hoover to survey the organization and procedures of the federal government. Again the legislature agreed, and Walter V. Schaefer, a Northwestern University law professor who had been the governor's chief legal advisor, was appointed chairman of a "Little Hoover" commission. In the first survey of state government since enactment of the Lowden code in 1917, Schaefer's group did not attempt a top-level reshuffling but submitted several core recommendations, many of which were adopted by the legislature. Under the governor's sponsorship, Schaefer was elected to the Illinois Supreme Court. There his career was as distinguished as those of better known staff members who later went to Washington.

Other appointees included J. Edward Day, future postmaster general, Carl McGowan, who became judge of the U.S. Court of Appeals in Washington, and William McCormick Blair, later ambassador to Denmark and the Philippines. Among cabinet posts, Democratic politicians were interspersed with professionals. Richard J. Daley, later mayor of Chicago, was the first revenue director. Fred K. Hoehler, who had headed the Chicago Community Fund, took over the public welfare department when promised that he could disregard patronage demands of politicians.

Stevenson was the first governor to ask for a fair employment practice law and to place his prestige behind the Chicago Crime Commission's effort to improve law enforcement. Both failed. Taking an unpopular stand, he vetoed an American Legion-backed bill requiring that persons on public payrolls swear a noncommunist oath. Earlier he was accused of being "soft on communism" for giving a deposition that Alger Hiss had a good reputation for integrity, loyalty, and veracity when Stevenson knew him in 1933 and later in 1949.

His own administration's scandals embarrassed the governor. James W. Mulroy, his campaign manager and executive secretary, resigned by request when it was discovered that as an insider he had bought Chicago Downs racing stock at five cents a share. Charles W. Wray, superintendent of foods and dairies, was fined for taking a $3,500 bribe to allow the sale of horsemeat as beef.

During his eighth month as governor, Stevenson announced with regret that on grounds of incompatibility, he and his socialite wife of 20 years, the former Ellen Borden, were separating. "I do not believe in divorce but I will not contest it," he announced.

With Republicans out of power and Kennelly an inactive mayor, Stevenson had no problems with the Chicago City Hall. A lucid writer and engaging speaker, he depended upon rhetoric to sway public opinion and seldom became involved in Democratic problems.

The Presidential Campaigns and the U.N.

Given Stevenson's convincing victory in 1948, some in the Democratic Party had early in his term pegged him as a presidential candidate. Not only did Stevenson appear to be a vote getter, he had extensive interest and experience in foreign policy. But by January 1952, Stevenson had already announced that he wanted another four years as governor. That month, President Truman met Stevenson in Washington and asked him to be the Democratic nominee for president. Stevenson balked; he refused to have his name entered into primaries even though by February Stevenson for President committees had already formed without him. The media was persistent. In March, Stevenson was interviewed on "Meet the Press," and again confirmed that he was not a candidate for president, but for governor of Illinois. In a written statement in April, Stevenson said there was "unfinished work in Illinois" and that that he "could not accept the nomination for any other office this summer." But Stevenson supporters at July's Democratic national convention in Chicago refused to let this be the final word. Indiana Governor Henry F. Schricker placed Stevenson's name in nomination saying, "There are times when a man is not permitted to say no." The delegates agreed, and Stevenson could not say no. After accepting the presidential nomination, Stevenson intervened with the Democratic state committee to insure that his successor nominee for governor was Lieutenant Governor Sherwood Dixon, rather than Secretary of State Edward J. Barrett.

The Republicans nominated Dwight D. Eisenhower as their presidential candidate in 1952, and the "egghead" ran a distant second to the war hero in the election. He was decidedly less reluctant to run against Eisenhower again in 1956. Still his image could not match Ike's. At one 1956 campaign event a woman is reported to have called out, "You have the vote of every thinking person," to which Stevenson replied: "That's not enough, madam. We need a majority." In the general election, Stevenson faired worse than he had in 1952. Stevenson sought the Democratic nomination in 1960, but this time the nod went to John F. Kennedy.

Stevenson wanted Kennedy to name him secretary of state, but Kennedy chose Dean Rusk instead. Stevenson served as U.S. ambassador to the United Nations for the Kennedy administration and continued into the Johnson administration. The former governor died of a heart attack July 14, 1965, on a London street.

32nd Governor

William Grant Stratton
1914 -

1914 – Born Feb. 26.

1934 – Graduates from the University of Arizona with a degree in Political Science.

1941 - 1943 – Serves as Illinois congressman-at-large.

1943 - 1945 – Serves as state treasurer.

1945 - 1946 – Becomes a lieutenant in the U.S. Navy and serves in the South Pacific.

1947 - 1949 – Serves a second term as Illinois congressman-at-large.

1948 – Loses the general election race for secretary of state.

1951 - 1953 – Serves a second term as state treasurer.

1952 – Defeats Lieutenant Governor Sherwood Dixon to win his first term as governor.

1955 – Illinois adopts the first new legislative reapportionment act since 1901.

1956 – Stratton asks for Auditor Orville E. Hodge's resignation after he learns that Hodge has been embezzling state money; Wins his second term as governor.

1960 – Loses the gubernatorial election to Otto Kerner.

1965 – Stratton is acquitted of income tax evasion charges stemming from the way he spent some of his campaign funds.

1968 – Receives only seven percent of the vote in the Republican gubernatorial primary.

1997 – Co-chairs a campaign finance task force that recommends, among other things, that the state "define inappropriate expenditures and prohibit personal use" of campaign contribution money.

Republican
January 12, 1953 to January 14, 1957
January 14, 1957 to January 9, 1961

William G. Stratton was a hands-on administrator who, more than any other governor before him, was an authority on Illinois and its governments, state and local. During the 1940s and 1950s he held statewide office 16 years – two terms each as governor, state treasurer and congressman-at-large. He called himself a progressive Republican, and he combined a political scientist's concept of what Illinois needed with a politician's understanding of what the legislature and the people would accept. Before 1952, when he was elected governor, he had expert knowledge of the power structures at Springfield, Chicago, and Washington. He had driven the roads and visited the cities and villages, and he knew the people and their problems. He hadn't taken time to go to law school or earn a doctorate, which handicapped his employment possibilities when he was out of office.

Elected before his 39th birthday, he didn't look like a typical governor. Almost boyish in build, he lacked the fluency of a platform orator, and his voice was pitched a little too high. Nevertheless, he was a strong governor. Important bills cleared the legislature rather easily, some with bipartisan support. Few administrations accomplished more.

Stratton was personally responsible for the Illinois toll highway system and for the first legislative reapportionment since 1901. Among other initiatives, his cooperation with metropolitan officials made possible the expressways inside Chicago. He persuaded the legislature to let large and small municipalities bolster their finances with a sales tax. Stratton bond issues financed major building programs for universities and mental hospitals. He advocated judicial reform and civil rights.

Politics as a Family Business

The governor came from a politically active Republican family in Lake County. William Grant Stratton was born February 26, 1914 at Ingleside, and was taught to read and write by his mother, Zula Van Wormer Stratton, who had been a schoolteacher. His father, William J. Stratton had made his way upward as supervisor, county chairman, and deputy warden during the future governor's formative years. In the Small administration, he was chief game warden and the first state director of conservation. In 1928 he took Louis L. Emmerson's place as secretary of state. The Depression and Franklin D. Roosevelt ended his office-holding career.

As a schoolboy, young Bill learned basic campaign techniques when he shook hands with leading citizens while touring the state with his father. Young Bill was eight years old when, during a trip to the Capitol, he sat in Governor Len Small's chair for a half-hour. He attended public schools only five years before entering high school at age 12. He was a political science major at the University of Arizona, graduating at the precocious age of 20.

After graduation, he married Marion Hook of Gurnee and landed a trainee job with Northern Illinois Public Service Company. He bought a ten-room Victorian house in Morris that had been built in 1869 by Lieutenant Governor Lyman B. Ray. Thereafter, it was his legal residence.

In 1940, at age 26, his chief political asset was his late father's name. (William J. Stratton had died two years earlier.) Without campaign funds, he was one of 14 candidates for two Republican nominations as congressman-at-large. Hitchhiking from town to town, often hungry, he polled the highest vote in the June primary and November election. When the new Congress met, he was the youngest member of the House of Representatives. Being more interested in state government, at the end of his term he returned to Illinois. In 1942, at only 28, he was elected state treasurer.

Stratton wanted to be secretary of state, the office his father had held. But in 1944 Governor Dwight H. Green blackballed his candidacy for that office. According to Stratton biographer David Kenney, Green apparently was afraid that Stratton would defer to his friend Senator Waylon "Curly" Brooks on patronage choices and shift party power away from the governor. Stratton ran anyway, but lost in the primary to the slated candidate, Arnold Benson, by nearly 100,000 votes. Then he volunteered for service as a navy officer in the South Pacific, which gave him the politically valuable status of being a war veteran. He was back from service in 1946 when he shocked liberals by defeating Emily Taft Douglas, the new congresswoman-at-large. In 1948 Green Republicans did not oppose him for secretary of state, but it was a Democratic Party year. President Truman defeated Thomas Dewey; Adlai Stevenson beat Governor Green; and Paul Douglas replaced Curly Brooks in the U.S. senate. Stratton lost to Edward J. Barrett, another veteran. In two more years, as a candidate for state treasurer Stratton defeated six Republicans in the primary and Michael J. Howlett in the election.

In 1949, while out of office, Stratton, on grounds of desertion, divorced his wife. The next year, after election as state treasurer, he married Shirley Breckenridge of Chicago, who was nine years younger and had been divorced three years earlier. Two daughters of this first marriage lived with them. A second-marriage daughter was born in 1962.

Stratton's First Term as Governor

In early 1952, Stratton was convinced that he could unseat Governor Adlai E. Stevenson. Many Republicans, however, did not believe he would be their party's candidate. Only one ward committeeman in Chicago supported him. Most of the others lined up behind William N. Erickson of Evanston, chairman of the Cook County Board, who in mid-campaign withdrew because he was indicted in a ghost payrolling scandal. The race then seemed to be between Park Livingston of Hinsdale, president of the University of Illinois Board of Trustees, and Richard Yates Rowe of Jacksonville, who had been secretary of state by appointment. A fourth candidate was James Simpson, former Lake County congressman. To their surprise, Stratton was nominated with 57 percent of the vote. By July, Stevenson had dropped out of the governor's race to accept his party's draft to run against Dwight D. Eisenhower in the presidential election. In November, Stratton carried 92 counties and was elected by 227,642 votes over Stevenson's stand-in, Lieutenant Governor Sherwood Dixon.

At his inauguration, Stratton announced that he would give major attention to highway and building construction projects. The first step in rebuilding Governor Len Small's hard roads was to widen U.S. 66, the diagonal route connecting Springfield with Chicago and St. Louis, to four lanes. Funds for the project came from the Stevenson administration's increases in the gas tax and auto licenses. Stratton also used bond issue financing for multilane construction in northern Illinois where traffic volume and land values were beginning to rise. Before his second term ended, he took credit for 7,057 miles of new roadways and 638 bridges, many of which received financial help under the federal interstate highway program.

At his request, the legislature created the Toll Highway Commission, which issued bonds to buy right-of-way and build 187 miles of expressways in northeastern Illinois. To speed up construction, which was finished in 1958, contractors were limited to ten miles of work each. Stratton also made possible the early completion of the expressway system radiating from the Chicago Loop. Cook County had voted a $70 million bond issue in 1950, but work didn't start because funding was incomplete. As soon as the 1952 election returns were in, Dan Ryan, president of the Cook County Board, asked for help with an expressway program that Governor Stevenson had vetoed. Stratton cooperated and, with the legislature's approval, the city, county, and park districts used their distributive shares of the gas tax to service a $245 million bond issue. In dollars spent, if not in miles of pavement, Stratton built more roads than Len Small. Forecasting a future bond issue, in 1959 he said that financial troubles of mass transit systems were Illinois' greatest weakness.

In his first term, Stratton accomplished the first reapportionment of the legislature since 1901. Using the full prestige of his office, he won approval of a constitutional amendment that made population the basis for districts from which House members were elected. The House districts would be redrawn every ten years after the census. The act gave downstate permanent control of the Senate, whose 58 districts were geographically based – a feature of the proposed constitution rejected in 1922. In the next decade, geographically-based districts were held unconstitutional in one of the U.S. Supreme Court's one-man, one-vote decisions.

With determination, Stratton sponsored bond issues that won referendum approval on a second try and financed major construction projects at state universities and welfare institutions. The bonds were important to the development of the new Chicago Circle and Edwardsville campuses and to the existing universities at DeKalb, Macomb, and Charleston. Defeated in a 1958 referendum, the bonds were approved two years later. With funds from the mental health bond issue, Governor Otto Kerner would build a series of zone centers.

The Green administration had given municipalities permission to levy a half-cent sales tax, but it was meaningless because local approval had to be obtained at a referendum, which never happened. Republican legislators, not wanting the Chicago City Hall to be too prosperous, routinely refused to broaden the sales tax to cover road repair services. Chicago Mayor Richard J. Daley did not help in 1959 when budgetary problems arose after the legislature refused to broaden the tax again while public aid costs were rising. Downstate followers of Paul Powell, the Democratic speaker of the House of Representatives, provided the added votes needed to increase the sales tax by a half-cent. It was the only major tax increase during Stratton's two terms. Determined that Illinois should remain a low-tax state, the governor opposed a state income tax. At the start of his second term he asked, without success, that the legislature approve a constitutional amendment for more flexible taxing authority.

In early June of 1956, the media began printing rumors about the spending habits of Orville Hodge, the Republican state auditor of public accounts, who was quickly going through his budgeted appropriation. Investigation revealed that Hodge was embezzling the state's money – to the tune of $1.5 million. On July 17, the governor asked for, and received Hodge's resignation.

The Second Term

Illinois governors usually have trouble with second term candidacies, and, in the wake of the Hodge scandal, things shouldn't have been so easy for Stratton. But the political fallout from the Hodge case took an odd political turn. The 1956 Democratic candidate for governor was Cook County Treasurer Herbert C. Paschen. The Hodge investigation led to Paschen's organization: He had deposited county funds in banks connected to the Hodge embezzlement. The kicker, however, was the revelation that Paschen kept an "employees' welfare fund," supposedly for flowers for funerals and such, sustained by banks in which county funds were deposited. The fund's books showed that most of the payouts went to Democratic Party people and affairs. The Democrats replaced Paschen with Richard B. Austin, a judge of the Superior Court whose handicap was that he had never campaigned in downstate Illinois. In the second Eisenhower landslide, Stratton was reelected by 36,877 votes, and with stronger Democratic candidates available, cynics wondered whether Richard J. Daley, the new Chicago mayor and Cook County chairman, didn't prefer to work with Republican governors.

In his second term, Stratton pushed for judicial reform, as he had in his first term. When the legislature, following orders by Daley, blocked a proposal to take selection of judges out of politics, the Stratton administration achieved partial reform by establishing a new office of court administrator, authorizing the Supreme Court to reassign judges, and putting justices of the peace on salaries.

During the centennial of the Lincoln-Douglas debates, Stratton broke with conservative Republican opinion downstate and with much of the business community by speaking out against racial segregation. At Quincy, he said that "legal discrimination is the stepchild of slavery." Speaking at Charleston, he said that a "divided set of social attitudes cannot survive." His bill to create a fair employment practices commission was killed by the Republican Senate in 1959.

The governor, who believed that prosperity required a harmonious business-labor climate, displeased conservative Republicans by supporting part of the legislation sought by union leaders. "This man is a friend of ours," Joseph Germano, district chairman of the steelworkers union, told the United Steelworkers Political Action Committee in 1959. Stratton gained nothing politically. He was booed while addressing the 1960 AFL-CIO state convention, which endorsed only Democratic candidates.

Life Out of Office

Certainly during the gubernatorial phase of his public career, Stratton's political successes were personal rather than organizational. At times he was resented by county chairmen, most of whom he had placed on state payrolls. He did not hesitate to dominate party affairs, especially if his own future was involved, but he seemed disinterested in developing a Republican organization. At times Stratton allowed Republicans to have an "open primary," meaning Stratton did not endorse any candidates. In 1954 he did not interfere with the nomination of Joseph T. Meek, a conservative who was no match for U.S. Senator Paul H. Douglas. In 1958 his candidate for state treasurer, Louis E. Beckman of Kankakee, was defeated in the primary by Warren E. Wright, a perennial who lost the general election.

Like Deneen, Small, and Green, Stratton ran and lost for a third term. He won the Republican primary. But then his political good fortune ran dry. Unlike 1952 and 1956, the Democrats' chosen candidate did not leave the race. In the fall election the voters didn't care whether he had done a good job for eight years. Overwhelmed by Democrat Otto Kerner, Stratton was the biggest Republican loser of that year.

The governor's political philosophy was that Illinois was a swing state that could be carried by Republican candidates if they had good issues but that the issues could change during a campaign. He also believed that a candidate couldn't win if his name wasn't on the ballot. In 1968, the year Richard B. Ogilvie was elected governor, Stratton made his last campaign. As the third candidate in the Republican gubernatorial primary, he received seven percent of the vote.

Four years after he left office, Stratton was indicted on charges of violating income tax laws. At the end of an expensive trial, he was acquitted on tax evasion charges that centered on political contributions. The government did not claim that state funds had been mishandled. Senator Everett M. Dirksen, the climactic defense witness, testified that a governor, unlike legislators, has ceremonial duties that are official in part and for which use of unrestricted campaign fund contributions is justified. In the Stratton case the U.S. Tax Court later ruled that the Internal

Revenue Service should not assess a tax on outright unrestricted gifts.

In 1968 Stratton abandoned campaigning, sold the Morris house and moved to a Lake Shore Drive apartment, and started a successful career as a Chicago businessman. Starting as a vice president of Canteen Corporation in 1968, he became a director in 1981. Retired when he turned 70, he took up banking, eventually becoming a vice president of the Associated Bank of Chicago. From the sidelines, in an advisory, capacity he continued his interest in the Republican Party. Meanwhile, he was actively involved in business, charitable, and educational causes, including the presidency of the Mental Health Association of Greater Chicago, the Rotary Club of Chicago, and several other organizations. He served as board chairman of the Chicago and Illinois Restaurant Association and Chicago Temple First Methodist Church. He also has made his expertise available to the study of public policy and politics. In 1987 he served as a co-chairman for Governor Jim Thompson's "Committee of 800," to help seek a tax increase. Ten years later he and former U.S. Senator Paul Simon chaired the Illinois Campaign Finance Task Force, a nongovernmental body. One of the recommendations of the task force's final report was for state law to "define inappropriate expenditures and prohibit personal use" of campaign contribution money.

33rd Governor

Otto Kerner
1908-1976

1908 – Born, Aug. 15 in Chicago.
1930 – Graduates from Brown University.
1934 – Takes a law degree from Northwestern University.
1934 – Joins the Black Horse Troop of the Illinois National Guard.
1942 - 1946 – Transfers from the guard to serve in a mobile artillery unit in World War II. After the war, he rejoins the Illinois National Guard and remains active for several more years.
1947 - 1954 – Serves as U.S. attorney.
1954 - 1961 – Serves as Cook County judge.
1960 – Defeats Governor Stratton in the general election.
1963 – Kerner vetoes a Republican redistricting bill, when a bipartisan commission fails to effect an acceptable plan, all Illinois House candidates appear on the yard-long 1964 state ballot as at-large candidates.
1964 Kerner defeats Charles Percy to win a second term as governor.
1967 – President Johnson appoints Kerner chairman of the National Advisory Commission on Civil Disorders.
1968 – Kerner resigns the governor's seat to become a judge in the Chicago U.S. Court of Appeals; Lieutenant Governor Samuel H. Shapiro becomes governor.
1973 – Kerner is convicted of bribery, conspiracy, income tax evasion, mail fraud and perjury in relation to Illinois race track corporation stock deals; One of Kerner's chief prosecutors is U.S. attorney for the Northern District of Illinois, James R. Thompson.
1974 – Kerner enters the Federal Correctional Institution at Lexington, Kentucky.
1975 – Suffering from lung cancer, Kerner is released from prison.
1976 – Dies, May 9.

Democrat
January 9, 1961 to January 11, 1965
January 11, 1965 to May 20, 1968

Otto Kerner, a popular but indecisive governor, would have been a strong candidate for a third term in 1968 if he had not resigned to accept an appointment to the U.S. Court of Appeals, the nation's second highest tribunal. Six years later he was in a federal prison, convicted on all counts in a conflict of interest case involving state supervision of race tracks.

Proud, handsome, and naive, Kerner never could admit that he had made a mistake. Perhaps his biggest error in judgment was his trust and confidence in Theodore J. Isaacs, his friend, financial adviser, campaign manager, revenue director, and prisonmate. He never repudiated Isaacs, who also corrupted the state division of printing, the financial institutions department, and the Illinois Supreme Court.

A Judge Goes to the Governor's Office

Of Bohemian parentage, Kerner had ties to one of Chicago's East European ethnic groups. Born in Chicago on August 15, 1908, he was the son of Otto and Rose Barbara Chmelik Kerner. The father, a close associate of Mayor Anton J. Cermak, had been alderman of Cermak's ward, attorney general, and, on Governor Henry Horner's recommendation, a member of the State Court of Appeals, where his record was commendable. Like Horner, both father and son played for the Democrats the role of "professional honest men" – candidates of impeccable reputation whose names made ballotmates more acceptable. They were attractive candidates the public regarded as being at least a cut above the party's precinct captains and ward committeemen.

Kerner had an Ivy League education, a degree from Brown University followed by a year at Trinity College, Cambridge University, in Cambridge, England. He was admitted to the bar after graduating in law from Northwestern University in Evanston in 1934, the year after Cermak was assassinated in Florida. He married the mayor's daughter Helena. Later, when Helena developed a drinking problem, the public sympathetically approved his solicitous care of her.

While getting a start in a law practice, he joined the Black Horse Troop of the Illinois National Guard and was promoted to captain before the guard was federalized at the start of World War II. Most of his overseas service was with artillery regiments in Africa and Sicily. At the end of the war he was a lieutenant colonel. He returned to Chicago but stayed in uniform while he reorganized the 33d Division. His final National Guard rank was major general.

Near the close of the Truman administration, the post of U.S. attorney for the Northern Illinois district was open to some Democrat who didn't seem too close to City Hall. Kerner, who hadn't yet settled into a law practice, caught the eye of Cook County Chairman J. M. Avery, who recommended him for the job. During seven years as federal prosecutor Kerner didn't prosecute anyone of political consequence.

Having proved his reliability, in 1954 Kerner was the Democratic nominee for county judge, a politically sensitive post in which his duties included supervision of elections in Chicago and part of the suburbs. He appointed Isaacs, whom he had met in the army, attorney for the Chicago Election Commission. Meanwhile, the public approved his sympathetic handling of child welfare and mental health cases. He had the largest Cook County vote when he was reelected in 1958.

The Governor's Job:
Finances, Civil Rights, and the Yard-Long Ballot

The urbane and courteous Kerner in 1960 again was the Democratic man of the hour. Stephen A. Mitchell, who had been Adlai E. Stevenson's choice for Democratic national chairman in 1952, criticized City Hall slatemaking, saying it discouraged Democratic voting, and announced that he was an anti-organization candidate for nomination as governor. So did State Treasurer Joseph D. Lohman, who had been a University of Chicago criminologist and parole board chairman. Kerner opposed them and easily won what Mayor Richard J. Daley called an "open primary." No endorsements were made, but the ward organizations backed Kerner who was nominated overwhelmingly.

In the fall campaign Kerner did not resign the county judgeship. Among downstaters, he pretended to be a political independent to whom Daley was unimportant. The mayor went along with the act to the extent that their joint appearances were limited. Supported by independents and some Republicans, Kerner ran well in the suburbs and downstate. A short man with a military bearing, he had a sincere manner and an ironclad memory. As governor he would show that he didn't know how to compromise with the legislature, and he never fully understood the complexities of state government, but the people loved him. When the final tallies were in, Kerner had beaten Governor Stratton by well over 500,000 votes. (John F. Kennedy carried Illinois by less than 9,000 votes.)

The governor remained "independent" in the sense that he never tried to be a Democratic leader; but after his inauguration he deviated on only a few Chicago City Hall policies. He insisted that a constitutional amendment to reorganize the judiciary must continue the system under which judges were nominated at party conventions and elected on partisan ballots. During the 1961 legislative session, bar leaders who had wanted selection of judges taken out of politics gave in and let Daley have his way when the constitution was amended.

The Kerner administration was not immune from the budgetary squeezes that arose partly because of the money drain caused by increasing public aid costs. At Kerner's inauguration he said increased revenues were essential. In 1961 he got the state sales tax raised a half-cent and a new tax was levied on hotel and motel rooms. But often his fiscal planning decisions were postponed, and his policy objectives muddy.

Kerner saw the need for a more flexible revenue article in the state constitution and appointed a commission to make recommendations, but he let months pass before giving it funds and appointing legislative leaders to its membership. Observers were baffled about what he wanted. The governor omitted the revenue article matter from an early winter special session call. It could be done in the spring, he said. As time passed he denounced Republican legislators as being incompetent, irresponsible, and politically motivated. Stratton, the two-term Republican he had defeated in 1960, criticized the indecision saying that governors should accept final responsibility for budgeting and devote full time to improving official relations with the legislature.

Kerner's position on an income tax frequently shifted until his 1964 campaign for a second term. When hard pressed by Charles H. Percy, the Republican nominee, Kerner announced flatly that Illinois didn't need an income tax. He kept asking for increases in existing taxes, some of which the legislature voted. He was turned down when he wanted part of a gas tax increase diverted to general revenues. In 1967 he got higher sales, cigarette, utility, and corporation taxes and a one-cent gas tax increase for highways.

Perhaps his biggest flip-flop was on the public aid financing issue in 1962. Under budgetary pressures, without consulting the public aid commission, he had arbitrarily cut $91 million from its biennial appropriations request for $613 million, half of which came from the federal government. To avoid a special session, in May he ordered a 10 percent cut in individual grants. The commissioners, including Auditor Michael J. Howlett and Finance Director James A. Ronan, refused. After a crisis month, Kerner caved in, presumably due to pressure from Daley. Instead of administrative cuts, the governor agreed that the commission should have more caseworkers. The legislature provided added money in controlled amounts and insisted that Illinois, like 31 other states, put ceilings on individual grants.

During the controversy, C. Virgule Martin, a Chicago State Street merchant, resigned in protest as commission chairman and was replaced by Arnold H. Maremont, an industrialist friend of Kerner. When Maremont said that Republican senators were anti-Negro, he was refused confirmation by the majority. The commission soon was replaced by a public aid department, created in 1963.

On the positive side, to maintain Illinois' standing as the leading export state, Kerner led trade missions to Europe in 1963 and to Japan in 1965. In 1967, he succeeded in a drive to locate at Weston, DuPage County, the Atomic Energy Commission's high-energy accelerator. The state appropriated $30 million for the 6,800-acre site. With bipartisan support, the board of higher education and the junior college board were created and land acquisition authorized for Governors State University and Sangamon State University, which later became the University of Illinois at Springfield.

In response to the feminist movement, Kerner arranged for birth control services to be dispensed to married women living with their husbands. That compromise cleared the legislature as a resolution that did not need to be signed by the governor. Attorney General William G. Clark then ruled that birth control services were illegal.

During his first year in office he achieved creation of a fair employment practices commission, legislation for which had been routinely killed by the state Senate since 1945, but even in victory, three of his appointees to the commission were turned down by the Senate. When the legislature refused to pass an open occupancy law, he achieved the same goal by an executive order prohibiting discrimination in the sale and rental of real estate. An earlier order prohibited discrimination by persons licensed by the state.

The governor had a strong record on civil rights. In 1967, Kerner was appointed by President Lyndon Baines Johnson to the chairmanship of the National Advisory Commission on Civil Disorders. Its report denounced racial discrimination declaring that America had become "two societies, one black, one white – separate but unequal."

Census data from 1960 triggered the process of redistricting. But things didn't go smoothly. In 1963, House Republican leadership passed a redistricting bill strictly along party lines. After the legislature adjourned, Kerner vetoed the bill, and then, in accordance with the constitution, appointed a 10-member bipartisan commission to draw new districts for the Illinois House. When the commission failed, the next step was to have a statewide at-large election for the Illinois House. Thus, in 1964, every ballot in the state contained the 236 names of all the candidates for the legislature (118 names from each party): the nearly yard-long ballot of that year came to be known as the "bedsheet ballot." Democrats won a two-thirds majority, but it did Kerner little good. The Senate in the 1960s was dominated by Republicans.

Despite problems and setbacks, the governor had planned to run for a third term, but in February 1968 decided not to seek reelection. One month later, President Johnson nominated Kerner to the Seventh Circuit U.S. Court of Appeals. Kerner took the oath for that office on May 20, 1968. Lieutenant Governor Samuel H. Shapiro succeeded him as governor.

The Judge Goes to Jail

However, Kerner's ultimate fate was set in motion during his second-term campaign, in which he defeated Charles H. Percy by over 175,000 votes. The campaign was endangered by a scandal involving Theodore J. Isaacs, who quickly resigned as its manager. Percy was ineffective in exploiting Isaacs' role as counsel of the Cook Envelope Company, which sold large quantities of envelopes to the state. (Isaacs stonewalled an investigation until after the 1964 election.) Later it was stipulated in Sangamon County Circuit Court that he had organized the company after the 1960 election and owned a half-interest in it. Indictments for conspiracy, collusion in bid-rigging, and defrauding the state were dismissed on technical grounds.

Meanwhile, Isaacs had resigned as revenue director, although he maintained backdoor contacts that embarrassed his successor. He became counsel for the Civic Center Bank in the Chicago Loop, which previously had been unable to obtain a charter from Joseph E. Knight, Kerner's director of financial institutions. Isaacs secretly controlled a bloc of bank stock, which influential people, including Knight, could buy at cut-rate prices and sell at a profit.

In 1969 after Kerner left office to be a judge, a special commission headed by Frank Greenberg, president of the Chicago Bar Association began looking into bank stock transactions. Its report forced the resignation of two Illinois Supreme Court Justices. Nothing happened to Isaacs as a result of the bank stock investigation.

Marjorie Lindheimer Everett, the dominant figure in Illinois racing, had secretly dispensed her race track stock in the same manner as Isaacs did the bank stock. Judge Kerner's troubles began when Internal Revenue Service agents wondered why Mrs. Everett in her 1966 income tax return claimed a capital loss on a stock sale. U.S. Attorney James R. Thompson, a future governor, investigated the complicated case and found that Mrs. Everett had secretly issued track stock to then-Governor Kerner and Isaacs at bargain-basement prices and that both men profited when they sold the stock back to her. In return, she received special treatment from the state. Kerner had appointed her friends to racing boards, given her tracks the racing dates she requested, signed legislation she desired, and fired a harness racing chairman who insisted that a competing track deserved consideration.

On February 12, 1973, Kerner and Isaacs were convicted of conspiracy, income tax evasion, mail fraud, and making false statements in income tax returns. Kerner also was found guilty of perjury and making false statements to revenue agents. A special panel of the Court of Appeals called the transactions bribery and found that Kerner and Isaacs each gained nearly $150,000 from dividend earnings and the sale of stocks for which they had paid only around $15,000. The opinion told of "devious and complicated devices" used to conceal the governor's role in the bribery. Checks had been laundered – the opinion twice used that term – and Isaacs had arranged that Kerner did not have to endorse the check received in the final payoff.

On the witness stand Kerner projected an aura of untouchability that did not impress the jury. After the trial he insisted that, while he might have been indiscreet, criminal intent was not involved. He said his troubles with the Republican prosecutor were in retaliation for President Nixon's failure to carry Illinois in 1960. Kerner appealed his conviction with only partial success. He resigned from the federal bench in July 1974 and entered the Federal Correctional Institution at Lexington, Kentucky. In May 1975, he was released when he was diagnosed with lung cancer. He had been a pack-a-day smoker.

Kerner's last public appearances were at a series of testimonial dinners given by his admirers. He died May 9, 1976, in a Chicago hospital, two months after removal of a cancerous tumor from his right lung.

34th Governor

Samuel Harvey Shapiro
1907-1987

1907 – Born, April 25, in Estonia.

1908 – Shapiro family moves to Kankakee.

1929 – Graduates from the University of Illinois Law School.

1933 – Appointed city attorney for Kankakee.

1936 – Wins election as state's attorney.

1940 – Narrowly loses his bid for reelection to state's attorney.

1947 - 1949 – After a World War II navy stint, Shapiro serves in the Illinois House in the 65th General Assembly.

1951 - 1961 – Serves in the Illinois House in the 67th - 71st General Assemblies.

1960 – Wins election as lieutenant governor.

1964 – Shapiro is reelected lieutenant governor.

1968 – In May, Shapiro takes the oath of office on the heels of Kerner's resignation; Vietnam War protesters clash with police in Chicago during the Democratic national convention in August; Shapiro loses the gubernatorial race to Richard B. Ogilvie in November.

1976 – In the gubernatorial Democratic primary, Shapiro endorses Secretary of State Michael J. Howlett instead of incumbent Governor Dan Walker.

1981 – Shapiro is the Democratic tie-breaking vote on the commission that redraws the legislative district map that helps gives Democrats control of both houses of the General Assembly for a decade.

1987 – Dies, March 16.

Democrat
May 21, 1968 to January 13, 1969

Samuel H. Shapiro, a smiling specialist in soft-sell politics, knew how to work with Republican legislators and was a successful governor during the last eight months of Otto Kerner's second term. With a background of 14 years in the House of Representatives and more than seven as lieutenant governor, he quietly obtained the cooperation of Republican legislators in solving temporarily the financial problems Kerner left behind when he resigned to become a judge of the U.S. Court of Appeals.

From the Baltic to Illinois State Government

Shapiro was the second foreign-born and the second Jewish governor. He was born April 25, 1907, in Estonia near the Baltic Sea, but he could not remember the name of the village. Tillie Bloom Shapiro brought her first son to Kankakee when he was one year old. Her husband, Joseph Shapiro, a Polish bootmaker, had established a shoe repair shop there.

A violinist, young Sam paid for most of his education by playing with dance orchestras, starting in his high school years. The job paid four dollars an hour and led to the presidency of the local musicians' union. After high school he enrolled at St. Victor College in Kankakee and then transferred to the University of Illinois, where he got good grades and was president of his fraternity while working as a shoe salesman and soliciting business for a photographic studio. He graduated in law in 1929.

For a legal and political career, the young Democrat went back to Republican Kankakee, the home of former Governor Len Small. At the approach of the Depression, he became the junior partner of J. Bert Miller, a leader of the local anti-Small Republican faction, and helped Democrats take over half of the county offices. In 1933, Shapiro was appointed city attorney. Three years later he was elected state's attorney with a higher vote than Franklin D. Roosevelt received for president. Shapiro married Gertrude Adelman in 1930. She met Shapiro at a dance in Kankakee when he was state's attorney. Her parents came from Latvia and Lithuania. In 1940, a Republican year in downstate Illinois, he came within 176 votes of a second term.

During his reelection campaign, Shapiro convened a special grand jury that indicted Archie L. Bowen, director of public welfare in Governor Horner's cabinet, for malfeasance in connection with a typhoid epidemic at Manteno State Hospital. Bowen, a tight-fisted and unpopular administrator, under Horner's orders had enforced economy and stopped political appointments at state institutions. Shapiro accused him of "palpable omission of duty." After the first trial ended with a hung jury, Bowen was convicted in a bench trial, fined $1,000, and removed from office. The Supreme Court reversed the conviction on the ground that the prosecution had not shown that the epidemic was caused by polluted drinking water.

Shapiro, who was overweight and a fraction under the five-foot, six-inch requirement, became a World War II navy officer by dieting severely and taking back-stretching exercises before his physical. Assigned to anti-submarine warfare intelligence and then to a court-martial staff, he finished the war as a lieutenant.

In the legislature, to which he was elected in 1946, he cosponsored legislation to raise standards of mental health institutions.

The Research Foundation for the Mentally Ill named him "Mr. Mental Health," and a Republican administration renamed the Kankakee State Hospital for him. In Democratic factionalism, Shapiro sided with his party's Chicago leadership against downstate followers of Paul Powell. He had been secretary and state treasurer of the Young Democrats of Illinois and had been prominent in Jewish organizations. In 1960 slatemaking he became the party's candidate for lieutenant governor and twice was elected on the ticket headed by Kerner. He represented the administration at numerous occasions at which the governor could not appear. By Kerner's appointment, he was chairman of the state mental health commission and headed a commission on mental retardation.

Taking the Governor's Seat

When he was inaugurated governor, with Kerner presiding, Shapiro called for mutual cooperation with the legislature and said he would not retreat from Kennedy, Johnson, and Kerner policies. Although the new governor did use the larger executive office on the second floor of the Statehouse, he didn't much change his lifestyle. On a busy day, legislators could easily find him eating a hot dog while standing at a lunch counter near the legislative halls.

Kerner had left the state in a financial bind. Faced with a flood of major and minor bills during the fiscal emergency, the legislature needed Shapiro's calming influence. At the start of his abbreviated administration, he told House and Senate leaders that fund transfers and belt-tightening would make additional taxes unnecessary for a year. In July he got their agreement to borrow $60 million from gasoline tax funds, enough to keep state government operating until the next General Assembly met in January. The emergency bill came up for Senate passage when Shapiro was in Cincinnati attending a governors' conference. W. Russell Arrington, the Republican president pro tem who was acting governor, "worked the floor" to get the necessary votes. Kerner had never worked closely with Arrington and other Republican leaders.

In an era of protest, the rights of citizens' free speech versus the tactics police could use to keep order often clashed. When the legislature insisted on passing a stop-and-frisk bill designed to clarify police authority to question suspects, Shapiro worked out a compromise he could sign. Kerner had vetoed the first stop-and-frisk legislation.

The Election of 1968

The announcement that Kerner would become a federal judge came in time for Shapiro to take his place on the Democratic slate in the 1968 primary. To give him campaign exposure at the Democratic national convention at Chicago, he had a spotlight role as chairman of the rules committee, and he opened the nominating process to minorities. Before the convention, which was plagued with dissent over the Vietnam War, he mobilized 5,649 National Guardsmen to join Chicago police in keeping order in the streets.

Kerner's delayed resignation and Hubert Humphrey's controversial presidential nomination hurt Shapiro's campaign for a full term as governor. The 1968 Republican ticket was strong, headed by Richard M. Nixon for president and Senator Everett M. Dirksen, who would win his fourth term. But, Shapiro, a comparative stranger in much of downstate Illinois, carried 14 counties and came within 127,794 votes of defeating Republican Richard B. Ogilvie. Paul Simon, Shapiro's running mate, was elected lieutenant governor by 96,421 votes.

Two days before his term ended, Shapiro complied with Mayor Richard J. Daley's wishes by appointing 10 Democrats and one Republican to judicial vacancies. The unexpected action was invalidated by the Supreme Court.

Although he did not hold a major elective office again, Shapiro, as an elder statesman, did occasionally have a role in state politics. He did not comment when the Ogilvie administration sponsored a state income tax. But later he said that, had he been elected to a full term, he would have tried to meet appropriation increases by broadening the sales tax. In the 1976 Democratic primary, he endorsed Secretary of State Michael J. Howlett instead of incumbent Governor Dan Walker. After the 1980 census, when the legislature deadlocked on the reapportionment issue, Shapiro was named the ninth – and tie-breaking – member of a bipartisan commission to remap legislative districts. As a result of the map he drew, Democrats had control of both houses of the General Assembly throughout the 1980s, starting with the 1982 election.

The former governor for several years was a senior partner in the Chicago law firm of Friedman, Koven, Shapiro, Salzman, Koenigsberg, Specks, and Homer. Meanwhile, he kept his Kankakee home and three-man law office there. When the 79-year-old former governor failed to appear in court on March 16,

1987, police went to his home and found that he had died of natural causes during the night. Gertrude, his wife of 47 years, had died four years earlier. They were childless.

35th **Governor**

Richard Buell Ogilvie
1923-1988

1923 – Born Feb. 22, Kansas City, Missouri.

1944 – Ogilvie, who has dropped out of Yale to join the army, is wounded in France.

1947 – Graduates from Yale.

1949 – Graduates from Chicago-Kent College of Law.

1954 - 1955 – Becomes an assistant to the U.S. attorney.

1958 – Becomes a special assistant to the U.S. attorney general in charge of a new Midwest office to combat organized crime; his work helps lead to the income tax evasion conviction of mobster Tony "Big Tuna" Accardo (which was later reversed by the Court of Appeals in a split decision).

1962 – Wins election as Cook County sheriff.

1966 – Wins election as Cook County board president.

1968 – Republican Ogilvie defeats Democratic Governor Shapiro to become the state's 35th governor; the successful candidate for lieutenant governor is Democrat Paul Simon.

1969 – Ogilvie pushes through a bill creating the state's first income tax; creates the Bureau of the Budget and the Department of Corrections.

1970 – In June, Illinois passes an environmental protection act and establishes the state's Environmental Protection Agency.

1970 – The constitutional convention adopts a new state constitution in September; voters ratify it in December, the new constitution shifts elections of statewide officers to nonpresidential election years; requires that the governor and the lieutenant governor be elected as running mates; gives the governor the power to reorganize state agencies; gives the governor the power to amend portions of bills passed by the legislature.

1972 – Ogilvie creates the Illinois Department of Transportation; loses the governor's seat to Dan Walker.

1988 – Dies on May 10.

Republican
January 13, 1969 to January 8, 1973

Short on charisma but long on executive ability, Richard B. Ogilvie made major administrative and fiscal reforms in Illinois and Cook County governments. A hard-working, tough-minded Republican, Ogilvie insisted that the legislature enact an income tax. It was an issue most governors would have avoided, but the state needed it. He was defeated when he ran for a second term, which proves that the public cannot always be trusted to make the right decisions. Among Illinois governors, he rates as one of the statesmen.

One of Ogilvie's political handicaps was his stern look, the result of a war wound to his face and jaw. Others were that he had limited acting talent and did not excel as an extemporaneous speaker. Pragmatic rather than philosophical, he ran for office not out of public demand but with a conviction that he could do a better job in Cook County as sheriff and president of the county board of commissioners, and in Springfield as governor. His executive capacity was better appreciated later when he became managing partner of a major law firm in Chicago.

War Hero, Sheriff, Board President

Richard Ogilvie was born February 22, 1923, at Kansas City, the first of two sons of Kenneth S. and Edna Mae Buell Ogilvie. He credited his mother, whom he described as a strong-minded woman who believed that hard work and determination could overcome obstacles, for his public career. Kenneth Ogilvie, a casualty insurance executive, moved the family to Evanston, where the future governor lived seven years starting in 1930, and then to Rockville Center and Port Chester, New York, where he graduated from high school in 1940. He attended Yale, where for two years he was active in politics and played junior varsity football.

Because of bad eyesight, at the start of World War II he was rejected by the army, navy, marines, and air corps, but the Army Enlisted Reserve Corps accepted him. Two years later Sergeant Ogilvie, a tank commander near the French Swiss-German border, was hit on the head by an exploding shell. Months of hospitalization and plastic surgery preceded his discharge in July 1945, with a Purple Heart, two battle stars, and a permanent facial scar.

He returned to Yale as an American history major and planned a teaching and coaching career. Instead, he went to Chicago-Kent College of Law under the GI Bill of Rights and helped Charles H. Percy and William J. Scott, fellow students, revive the Young Republican organization in Cook County before he graduated in 1949. In January 1950 he was admitted to the Illinois Bar, and in February he married Dorothy Shriver of Oak Park. They had one daughter, Elizabeth, and lived in Northfield.

He intermittently interrupted a Chicago legal career to become involved with law enforcement. After five years with Lord, Bissell and Brook, he became an assistant U. S. attorney. Back in a year, he became a partner in the firm. In 1958 he left his law practice to become a special assistant to the attorney general in charge of a new Midwest office to combat organized crime. He won the conviction of Tony "Big Tuna" Accardo, syndicate chief and one-time associate of Al Capone, in a complex income tax case that was reversed by the Court of Appeals in a split decision. At the end of the Eisenhower administration he became a partner in Hackbert, Rooks and Pitts.

In 1962, for the first time, Ogilvie was a candidate for election. Running for sheriff of Cook County, asserting that the office needed upgrading, he was the only Republican elected in the county-wide race. In the sheriff's office he replaced patronage with civil service and initiated professional training for his police force. Gaining the public's attention, Ogilvie sent his new force on 1,800 raids to dens of illegal activities, which had heretofore been safe from bother from the sheriff's office. The Chicago Crime Commission said the office had never been more effective in suppressing organized crime and rackets. During a racial disturbance in Dixmoor and a civil rights march in Cicero in 1966, Ogilvie took personal command in tense situations and prevented full-scale rioting.

In 1966, Ogilvie was elected president of the Cook County board by 172,320 votes, the biggest margin among several Republican winners of local office. By putting civil service regulations into effect, he increased merit system coverage in the county from 33 to 85 percent. For economy, he left 2,000 jobs vacant. He increased competitive bidding on highway projects and supported election reforms. Improved billing procedures were credited with a $7 million increase in Cook County Hospital revenues.

Ogilvie's only legislative experience came when as county board president he had to deal with its Democratic majority. Nevertheless he believed his Cook County experience was the best possible training for the governorship.

The Governor Makes a Tough Stand For Taxes

Midway in his term as county board president, Ogilvie announced that he would be a candidate for governor in 1968. Chicago Republicans protested that 600 patronage positions would be forfeited because his successor would come from the board's Democratic majority. In the Republican primary he finished 46,823 votes ahead of John Henry Altorfer, a Peoria businessman, with former Governor William G. Stratton far behind.

In the general election he polled 127,794 more votes than Shapiro, only slightly less than Richard M. Nixon's Illinois margin over Hubert Humphrey. When Paul Simon, a Democrat, was elected lieutenant governor, it was the first time that the two top offices had gone to men from opposing parties. In the interest of governmental harmony, Ogilvie and Simon agreed to forgo partisanship. When Ogilvie was out of the state, Simon, who was then acting governor under the 1870 constitution, did not attempt to take partisan advantage of Ogilvie's absences.

During the campaign he and Samuel H. Shapiro, who was completing Otto Kerner's second term, both avoided the subject of possible tax increases. Ogilvie, contending that the state's executive machinery was outmoded, warned that the state's financial situation was critical, but he talked hopefully about an easy solution in which the federal government would share its revenues with the states.

After his inauguration, he surveyed the treasury's income prospects and the increasing demands for money. As he had feared, the revenue gap had become critical during the eight years of the Kerner and Shapiro administrations. He decided it could be closed only if Illinois supplemented the retail sales tax, which had been the chief revenue source since the Depression, with a tax on corporate and personal incomes. Other industrial states had income taxes, but the Illinois Supreme Court in 1932 had ruled that the 1870 Illinois Constitution prohibited them. Rather than drastically curtail state expenditures, Ogilvie decided to stake his prestige as an incoming governor on enactment of an income tax law. He hoped that constitutional problems would be solved by taxing individuals and corporations at a flat rate, rather than the graduated rate used by the federal income tax system. He proposed a 4 percent tax on corporate and individual incomes to finance increases in school, welfare, and other appropriations as well as to bring under control the costs of public aid that had been troublesome since the second Stratton term.

Most governors would have broken the bad news gently and started a public relations campaign, but during his first weeks in office Ogilvie proved that he was not a politician. In speeches, interviews, and meetings with opinion-makers, the new governor never mentioned the possibility of an income tax, which had been recommended by a revenue study commission appointed by Shapiro the year before. The day before his biennial budget message was scheduled, Ogilvie told legislative leaders, metropolitan newspaper editors, and others of his plans on an off-the-record basis. Not until noon on April 1 did the public learn that he wanted an income tax coupled with large increases in spending. The word spread quickly, and that day Republicans lost some local elections.

Because of Ogilvie's determination and willingness to compromise, the administration bill was enacted three months later in the closing hours of the 1969 legislative session. There were revolts in both houses in both parties. Downstate Democrats insisted that personal incomes be taxed at a lower rate than corporations. Mayor Richard J. Daley, who liked an Ogilvie income-sharing provision that local governments be given one-twelfth of the revenue on a no-strings-attached basis, won additional concessions. The final compromise taxed corporations at 4 percent and individuals at 2.5 percent. On the final roll calls, Democrats made certain that the tax bills passed and that the Republicans would be held responsible. Earlier in the session, new or increased levies on beer, cigarettes, and hotel receipts had also been passed. Local governments were given an additional quarter-cent of the sales tax.

Of course, the constitutionality of the income tax was immediately challenged. But, the state Supreme Court unanimously upheld its constitutionality. Thus, it reversed its 1932 position on the tax, an opinion obviously informed by 40 years of social changes. As a result of the increased revenue, Illinois was spared a near-shutdown of government such as Pennsylvania and some other states underwent. The income tax, and the favorable ruling on its legality, removed what could have been an insurmountable issue from the agenda of the constitutional convention that met midway through the Ogilvie administration. The convention prepared a new constitution that was ratified by the voters in 1970. The new constitution became effective the following year and replaced the state's third constitution that had been the law of Illinois for 100 years.

Reshaping State Government

Ogilvie's reforms extended into the state's executive and legislative branches. He asked that annual budgeting replace the increasingly unsatisfactory traditional system of having the General Assembly appropriate funds for two-year periods. The legislature, which for several decades had frequently met in special sessions to consider requests for deficiency appropriations, followed his advice and shifted to an annual-session basis before the constitution of 1970 mandated the change.

Another Ogilvie law established a Bureau of the Budget within the governor's office and gave the executive direct control of the budgetary process. As a result, a legislative commission that traditionally had made final budgetary decisions went out of business, and the director of the budget bureau, responsible only to the governor, became the second most powerful official in the executive department. Its first director was John McCarter, who was conspicuous among the young and bright staff members brought into state government. One of his assistants was Robert Mandeville, who became budget director for Governor James R. Thompson.

From the governor's office Ogilvie continued to make administrative reforms in Cook County government. He prevailed upon the legislature to consolidate the Cook County and Chicago jails, put them under a merit system, and modernize the county's budgetary and administrative systems. Other Ogilvie proposals, to which City Hall Democrats had stronger objections, were blocked in the House of Representatives. They would have reorganized the city health department, required state licensing of building inspectors, and consolidated Chicago and suburban elections. Downstate Republicans blocked an administration effort to provide a state subsidy for the Chicago Transit Authority.

To improve the state highway system, the governor sponsored a 1.5 cent increase in the gasoline tax and the creation of a highway trust authority with bonding power. Under Ogilvie the state's Department of Transportation was created. William F. Cellini, Jr. was its first director. The state's twenty-four adult and youth correctional facilities were put under a newly created Department of Corrections. The state's law enforcement machinery was reorganized. In education the state school aid formula was changed from $400 to $520 per pupil. The governor also signed a bill to permit silent prayer in public schools. In June 1970, six months before the federal government, Illinois became the first state to pass an environmental protection act and establish an environmental protection agency. He won approval of a $750 million antipollution bond issue to enable local governments to improve sewage facilities.

Even with the infusion of more income, revenue problems persisted. Because tax rates had been shared with local governments and because of compromises dictated by the legislature, revenues were less than Ogilvie had expected. Costs of government kept increasing, and the budget bureau soon had to order cuts in spending requests. Meanwhile, the legislature could not resist the temptation to appropriate more than the treasury could afford. That problem grew worse in following administrations.

Income Tax as Political Suicide

Politically, the governor wanted the Republican Party to be competitive in Chicago as well as downstate and believed that he should be its leader. But the backlash of the income tax hurt the party. Democrats carried the 1970 off-year election, including state treasurer and superintendent of public instruction.

Naturally, the income tax was the chief issue in Ogilvie's campaign for a second term in 1972. In the general election, many thought that the governor would face his lieutenant governor, Paul Simon. Simon had Democratic organization backing for the governorship, but an aggressive maverick named Dan Walker took the nomination away from him. Ogilvie, who in midsummer was several points behind in the polls, focused on the nonrevenue changes he had made in Chicago as well as downstate. He had additional handicaps, including an unpopular ban against leaf burning ordered by the state Environmental Protection Agency. The governor had given free rein to the EPA and its Pollution Control Board and paid for it when voters took their anger out on him. On election day he lost by 77,494 votes.

After an absence of 12 years, Ogilvie returned to the practice of law in Chicago and, like William G. Stratton, demonstrated that a former governor can have a future in private life. He became managing partner of the venerable firm of Isham, Lincoln and Beale, of which Robert Todd Lincoln had been a co-founder. As the court-appointed receiver of the bankrupt Chicago, Milwaukee, St. Paul, and Pacific Railroad Company, he restored it to solvency by drastically cutting its mileage. His executive ability also was recognized with an appointment to take charge of an incomplete addition to McCormick Place. In the role of an elder statesman, he sought to strengthen Republican tickets in Cook County, but he declined opportunities to run for mayor of Chicago. In the 1976 presidential primary, he took a public stand for President Gerald Ford's reelection when Ronald Reagan, who was born in downstate Illinois, was also a candidate. Ford carried Illinois that year.

He earned millions of dollars as a trustee of the Chicago, Milwaukee, St. Paul and Pacific Railroad Company, reorganizing the bankrupt line and saving more than a thousand jobs. He also was appointed trustee for the Chicago, Missouri, and Western railroad. In the 1980s, an era known for consolidations, Ogilvie surprised the legal profession by arranging the merger of Isham, Lincoln and Beale with the larger, younger, and more aggressive firm of Reuben and Proctor. When conflicts arose, Isham, Lincoln and Beale dissolved and the former governor became a partner with the firm of Wildman, Harrold, Allen and Dixon. On May 9, 1988, while working in his downtown Chicago office, Ogilvie suffered a heart attack. He died the next day, after undergoing quadruple coronary bypass surgery. His body was cremated, and his ashes were placed at Rosehill Cemetery in Chicago.

36th Governor

Daniel Walker
1922-

1922 – Born, Aug. 6, in Washington, D.C.

1940 – Graduates valedictorian in his San Diego High School class.

1940 - 1942 – Serves in the U.S. Navy.

1945 – Graduates from the Naval Academy, serves two more years in the navy.

1950 – Graduates from Northwestern Law School; works on the staff of Illinois Commission to Study State Government, then becomes law clerk for U.S. Supreme Court Chief Justice Fred Vinson.

1951 – Recalled to the navy to serve in the Korean conflict, but soon is released from service to take the civilian post of deputy chief commissioner of the U. S. Court of Military Appeals in Washington.

1952 – Joins Governor Adlai Stevenson's staff.

1953 - 1966 – Works for a law firm that would come to be known as Hopkins and Sutter.

1960 – Democratic Party slatemakers reject his bid for the Illinois attorney general's office.

1968 – Walker is chosen by the National Commission on the Causes and Prevention of Violence to investigate the confrontations between Chicago police and Vietnam War protesters during the 1968 Democratic National Convention in Chicago. His findings in "The Walker Report" are critical of the police force and Mayor Richard J. Daley.

1971 – Begins to walk the state of Illinois as part of his campaign to win the Democratic primary for governor.

1972 – Defeats Lieutenant Governor Paul Simon for the Democratic gubernatorial nomination; defeats Governor Richard Ogilvie in the general election.

1973 – Walker signs a bill in August that creates the Illinois Department on Aging, and one in December that creates the Illinois State Lottery.

1976 – Loses the Democratic gubernatorial primary to Secretary of State Michael J. Howlett, who loses the general election to Jim Thompson.

1981 – Flirts with a run for the governorship, but withdraws from the primary when Adlai Stevenson III enters the race.

1988 – Goes to prison to begin serving a seven-year sentence in connection with misusing funds from his failed First American Savings and Loan Association of Oak Brook.

1989 – Walker is released from prison and begins working for the homeless.

Democrat
January 8, 1973 to January 10, 1977

Daniel Walker, who liked to be called Dan, was confrontational, brilliant, ambitious, and tragic. He left a $120,000-a-year post as a corporation lawyer, and, as an underdog, was elected governor in 1972.

Walker played the role of a big-city populist turned giant killer to win the governorship, first by upsetting Lieutenant Governor

Paul Simon in the primary and then by beating Governor Richard B. Ogilvie in the general election. Unique in Illinois, Walker was an adversarial governor. Scornful of compromising, he publicly downgraded the importance of the legislature and managed by using the "me-versus-you" tactics that had brought him courtroom success. For the four years of the Walker administration, hostility and dispute were the orders of the day. Walker and Chicago Mayor Richard J. Daley were constant adversaries, especially when Walker tried to wrest control of the state Democratic Party from "His Honor" the mayor. For his part, Daley, early in the Walker administration, expressed regret that Republican Ogilvie wasn't serving a second term. Had Walker not challenged Daley's leadership, he could have had a long political career. Instead, he squandered his opportunity by waging a power struggle that had more to do with personality than ideology.

Young Walker

Dan Walker was born August 6, 1922, in Washington, D.C., the son of a U.S. Navy chief petty officer who soon retired and moved to a truck farm outside San Diego, California. Dan Walker left farming after his graduation from San Diego High School as class valedictorian. It did not matter that he had academic weaknesses in mathematics and science and that he lacked money for a college education. He enlisted in the naval reserve, went to sea on a destroyer, finished third in a competitive examination open to all seamen, and in a year was attending classes at the Naval Academy at Annapolis. Graduating in 1945, he spent two years on fleet duty and then became a resident of Illinois by resigning his commission and entering Northwestern University Law School. In the class of 1950, he was editor in chief of the *Law Review*. Thereafter, he had his pick of legal jobs as he demonstrated a capacity to move on quickly to something better.

In 1947 while he was a law student, Walker, a Methodist, married Roberta Dowse, a Catholic whose grandfather had been a state representative from Lake County and whose great-uncle had been an early president of the Chicago Board of Education. In Deerfield they reared seven children before divorcing in 1977. In 1978 Walker married Roberta Nelson, executive director of the Illinois Epilepsy Association. She divorced him in 1988.

After law school, Walker showed up in Springfield as a staff member of Governor Adlai E. Stevenson's "Little Hoover" commission on governmental reorganization. Soon he was in Washington with a prestigious appointment as law clerk to U.S. Supreme Court Chief Justice Fred M. Vinson, but before his year was over the navy recalled him for Korean War fleet duty. Then he returned to Washington released from active duty to serve as deputy to the chief commissioner of the U.S. Court of Military Appeals, a civilian review body. In 1952 he resigned to join Stevenson's staff in Springfield. Instead of working in the political headquarters – Stevenson had been drafted to run for president against Dwight D. Eisenhower – he learned the routine of state government by going to the Statehouse as an administrative aide.

Next, Walker became a Chicago lawyer, a litigation specialist who became partner in the firm of Hopkins, Sutter, Owen, Mulroy, Wentz and Davis. Walker had Democratic political ambitions but no desire for apprenticeship with the City Hall organization. In the role of an outsider who was concerned about the quality of government in Springfield during the Stratton administration, he founded and was chairman of the Committee on Illinois Government. When it went out of business in two years, he organized and was president of the Democratic Federation of Illinois, which hoped to mobilize young, college-educated, and idealistic amateurs as a reform element. Mayor Richard J. Daley, who saw it as a potential challenge, smothered the group.

In 1960, Walker appeared before Democratic slatemakers and asked that they nominate him for attorney general. Walker believed he would get the endorsement, but William G. Clark, a legislator who later became chief justice of the Illinois Supreme Court, had more influence with Democratic powers, and so Walker was not slated.

After his rejection, he played a minor role as the secretary of Businessmen for Kennedy. That year he became vice president and general counsel of Marcor, Inc., the holding company for Montgomery Ward and Company, which put him in the $100,000-plus salary bracket. The corporation had no objection to his civic and political activities, and he served as president of the Chicago Crime Commission and, by Governor Kerner's appointment, as the last chairman of the Illinois Public Aid Commission.

Any possibility of career help from Mayor Daley ended when he accused the Chicago police of violence and rioting instead of keeping order during the 1968 Democratic National Convention. "Rights in Conflict," a report he compiled for the National

Commission on the Causes and Prevention of Violence, gave Walker coast-to-coast attention.

Walking Into the Executive Mansion

A year before the 1972 primary he gambled his nestegg and became an anti-organization candidate for governor. In a low-budget, off-season campaign, he acquired name recognition and a downstate education by walking the length of the state, 1,197 zigzag miles from Brookport to South Beloit and into Chicago in 116 days. To show that he was a man of the people, he slept in farmhouses. Speeches struck populist themes – "government is out of touch with the people" and "patronage has got to go." He promised to hold the line on taxes and spend more on education.

Walker, who 12 years earlier had asked Democratic slatemakers to endorse him for attorney general, berated Simon for running against him with their support. As a major issue, the argumentative Walker insisted that Simon, who had commented about future school financing possibilities, planned to increase the income tax.

For his nomination by 40,293 votes, the independent candidate also was indebted to meddlesome Republicans. The Supreme Court recently had legalized crossover voting, and Republicans had no contests in their own primary. Without realizing how many others had the same idea, Republicans who didn't want Simon to be nominated by too large a majority couldn't resist casting their ballots for his opponent.

Being against big government, Walker boycotted his party's national convention and never during his race for the governor's seat did he mention George McGovern, the controversial Democratic presidential nominee. To get support in Chicago, he made obligatory appearances at Democratic ward rallies. Continually, he reminded the voters that Ogilvie was responsible for the income tax. He won the general election by 77,494 votes.

The Governor Without a Party

Executive combativeness marked the next four years. To distance himself from the legislature, he took the oath of office in bitter weather outside the Statehouse. In a brief speech he posed as the only honest man in town and proclaimed that the lesser men should go elsewhere. When he said, "the free ride is over," Republicans interpreted it as an unwarranted insult to Ogilvie, the retiring governor. He neglected the face-to-face conferences that could develop friendly relations and roll call support, and the Walker administration soon ostracized Lieutenant Governor Neil Hartigan, one of Daley's ward committeemen. This, of course, further distanced the powerful Chicago Democrats. One Democratic faction, mostly downstaters, was loyal but others in ad hoc alliances with Republicans overrode vetoes and refused to confirm several appointments. Thus his legislative power base was small. In fact, the legislature treated him as a minority governor.

Walker's executive ability was such that he could clear his desk in an hour, which left the rest of the day for politicking. In campaigns and in running the state, his right-hand man was Victor de Grazia, who was rated as a political genius. They were better at collecting enemies, however, than in rallying supporters. After his involuntary retirement from the governor's office, Walker said he should have spent more time with legislators and other establishment members instead of trying to build up a grassroots following, but he still blamed Daley for their confrontations.

One of the Walker-Daley battles delayed creation of the five-county Regional Transit Authority that took over bus, elevated train, and subway service in the Chicago area. Chicago leaders and Republican legislators wanted something done about the servicing and financial problems of the old Chicago Transit Authority, but during the 1973 regular session the governor failed to submit his own program and enter into negotiations. Walker finally participated during a special session that met in October. He contended that Daley wanted state financial grants set at an unreasonably high level that would be a precedent for later state aid requests for other programs.

Walker kept firm control of executive departments and made final decisions for the Bureau of the Budget. Since he had campaigned against Simon and Ogilvie on the income tax issue, he had no choice but to cut spending drastically during a period of tight economic conditions nationally. Some help came with enactment of a state lottery that was a secondary but nevertheless important revenue source. Another landmark was creation of a Department on Aging.

The administration seemed to be dollar honest, but critics accused the governor of having a double standard of ethics. In the 1972 campaign Walker had challenged Ogilvie to issue an executive order requiring businesses that contracted with the state to reveal their campaign contributions. In office, he found legal excuses for not following his own preaching. Under media heckling, he finally issued the executive order, which a court invalidated. He took credit for enactment of a financial disclosure law that covered state officials. His own campaign finances were confused by the formation of two committees and by long delays in making incomplete reports. In his last campaign, state employees were solicited for contributions, something Walker had promised never to do.

Loss, Tragedy, and Hope

The Democratic fight for the 1976 gubernatorial nomination was the roughest since the Henry Horner-Herman N. Bundesen Democratic primary of 1936. Full of national ambition, Walker entered a full slate of candidates for district delegates to the Democratic national convention. In this way Walker aspired to replace Daley as leader of the Illinois delegation. If he could take his own delegates to the convention, he would be on equal terms with Jerry Brown of California and Jimmy Carter of Georgia as presidential possibilities. The primary, however, focused more on Walker's bid for a second term. Daley's candidate for the job was Secretary of State Michael J. Howlett, who in addition to support from the mayor had a large downstate following as a result of long service as auditor and secretary of state. The City Hall organization, which hadn't realized that Simon was in trouble in the 1972 primary, fired up its precinct workers on behalf of Howlett. Near physical and financial exhaustion, Walker concentrated on the suburbs and downstate. This time liberals and independents in Chicago did not endorse him. Howlett was nominated by 115,341 votes. As for the Walker slate, only two of his candidates won.

Involuntarily retired before his 55th birthday and hopeful that he again could hold high office, Walker formed a multi-city law firm based at Oak Brook with branches at Chicago, Springfield, Moline, Peoria, Kankakee, and Mount Vernon. That ambitious project soon failed. Before he entered politics he had shown business ability – Marcor had wanted the head of its law department to switch to an executive office – and he saw moneymaking opportunities outside the law. For the former governor, however, nothing seemed to work out. Among other investments, he bought into banks in Illinois, Arkansas, and Florida.

Promising to "cut Jim Thompson down to size," in the late summer of 1981 he announced that he was a candidate for governor. Two months later he withdrew after Adlai E. Stevenson III received the Democratic endorsement.

He became chairman and chief executive officer of the First American Savings and Loan Association of Oak Brook, which he and his second wife acquired in 1983. Four years later it was declared insolvent by the Federal Home Loan Bank Board. A federal grand jury had determined that Walker, contrary to conservative practices, had engaged in a rapid-growth program that included insider trading and high-risk commercial lending. Prosecutors said he had received $1.4 million in fraudulent loans.

The former governor elected not to stand trial. On the eve of his 65th birthday, he pleaded guilty to bank fraud, misapplication of bank funds, and perjury. "I have deep regrets and no excuses," he announced. He had hoped to avoid a prison term, but on November 19, 1987, U.S. District Court Judge Ann Williams said he had "placed himself above the law" and had used First American as "a personal piggy bank, a personal kitty" to keep his businesses afloat and to finance a lifestyle that included ownership of a yacht. Walker was sentenced to seven years in prison to be followed by five years probation and ordered to pay $231,609 restitution to First American. On January 4, 1988, the former governor surrendered to authorities at the Federal Prison Camp in Duluth, Minnesota, a minimum-security facility. He was released in June 1989, after serving a year and a half of his sentence. After he left prison, he completed his community service by helping the homeless in Virginia Beach, Virginia. He then moved to San Diego and continued to work with the homeless. By the time Dan Walker turned 70, he had written a cookbook and drafted a manuscript on the life of Jesus.

37th
Governor

James Robert Thompson
1936 -

1936 – Born, May 8, DeKalb County.

1956 – After finishing his undergraduate degree at Washington University, Thompson begins Northwestern University Law School.

1959 – Begins work at the Cook County state's attorney's office.

1964 – Becomes an assistant professor at Northwestern University Law School.

1971 – Becomes U.S. attorney for the Northern District.

1971 - 1975 – Thompson's office wins convictions against many political figures including: former Governor and the U.S. Court of Appeals Judge Otto Kerner; Chicago Alderman Thomas E. Keane, Cook County Clerk and former State Treasurer, Auditor, and Secretary of State Edward J. Barrett.

1976 – Thompson wins his first term as governor. He will serve a special two-year term to enable future gubernatorial elections to fall on years that do not coincide with the presidential election.

1977 – The legislature stands still for the first five weeks of the session while 187 roll call votes are taken before a senate president is selected; in June Thompson signs a bill that allows the death penalty for people convicted in any of 16 categories of murder.

1979 – Thompson signs a bill, to take effect in 1980, that makes the minimum drinking age 21.

1980 – The cutback amendment, a ballot proposition passed by the voters, eliminates the system of electing three representatives from each Illinois House district. The new amendment, which goes into effect in the 1982 elections, divides each district in two and voters are to elect one member per district, rather than three members from each district as had been the custom. Thus the House is reduced by one-third.

1983 – Thompson proposes and the legislature passes a temporary increase in the income tax.

1984 – Thompson creates the Department of Alcoholism and Substance Abuse and the Department of Employment Security.

1985 – A flooding Illinois River turns 22 downstate counties into disaster areas.

1986 – Candidates for the right-wing Lyndon LaRouche party win upset victories in the Democratic lieutenant governor's race and the secretary of state's race; Democratic gubernatorial candidate Adlai Stevenson III runs in the general election on the Solidarity Party ticket to avoid having to run on the same ticket with the LaRouche-backed candidates; Thompson wins his fourth campaign for governor.

1989 – The legislature approves a temporary, two-year increase in the state income tax.

1990 – Illinois legalizes riverboat gambling; the first boat goes into operation in 1991.

1991 – Leaves the Executive Mansion after having decided not to run for reelection or seek another elected office.

Republican
January 10, 1977 to January 8, 1979
January 8, 1979 to January 10, 1983
January 10, 1983 to January 12, 1987
January 12, 1987 to January 14, 1991

James R. Thompson was Illinois' longest-serving governor. After 14 years in executive office, including one two-year term, he accepted a lucrative partnership in Winston & Strawn, one of Chicago's most prominent law firms.

A tall man at six feet, six inches, "Big Jim" was spectacular on the political stump. With no prior electoral experience, he made his first run for governor at the age of 40 and managed to poll 64.7 percent of the vote, an Illinois record at the time for a contested election. Though Thompson had had little contact with much of Illinois before that campaign, he built name recognition and a solid reputation as U.S. attorney for the Northern District by successfully prosecuting several dozen Chicago politicians, including a former governor.

In early 1990, the last year of his fourth term, he surpassed the tenure of Ninian Edwards, who was appointed territorial governor for nine years before he was elected to a four-year term.

Unlike his predecessor, the confrontational Dan Walker, the pragmatic Thompson was a master of the negotiated compromise and a specialist in getting along with most Democrats. A spontaneous speaker, he was gregarious, media-savvy and informal.

A flamboyant politician, Thompson clearly enjoyed being with people and being governor. He was an avid parader, and he often showed up at the Illinois State Fair in a T-shirt to skid down the giant slide – with his dog on one occasion. He also once rode a horse in the Capitol.

And he was durable. When he took office in 1977, Gerald Ford was president and Chicago Mayor Richard J. Daley had been dead only three weeks. When he left office, George Bush was president and Mayor Richard M. Daley was about to run for his second term as mayor of Chicago. His greatest obstacle throughout four terms was a lethargic economy.

A Corruption Buster

Jim Thompson came from Chicago's unglamorous West Side. Born during the Depression, on May 8, 1936, he was the oldest of four children. His parents, J. Robert Thompson and the former Agnes Josephine Swanson, had never gotten involved in politics. DeKalb County natives, they lived in a middle-class neighborhood near Garfield Park. The hard-working father, who had been a farm boy, qualified for the University of Illinois College of Medicine by going to night school for nine years at Lewis Institute and working days as a laboratory technician. During an accelerated medical course, he supported his family as a morgue attendant. Thompson was eight when his father graduated and became a pathologist at Municipal Tuberculosis Sanitarium, where he practiced medicine at night by making house calls and giving insurance examinations. Eventually the family moved to Oak Park.

The precocious oldest son, who skipped two years of elementary school, became addicted to reading magazines for political news. And in grade school he decided he would become a politician.

Because the West Side was changing, Thompson's parents decided that he would spend his high school years at North Park Academy, a private school on the Northwest Side. Aiming for a law degree as a prelude to a career in politics, he enrolled at the University of Illinois branch on Navy Pier and specialized in history and government. Later, while his father was on army duty in St. Louis, Thompson transferred to Washington University. After the family moved to Oak Park, he was a deacon in a Presbyterian church and taught a Sunday school class. Two of his siblings became lawyers and the other a geology professor.

At Northwestern University's law school, which he entered in 1956, Thompson came under the influence of Professor Fred E. Inbau and was the first student to address a prosecutors' workshop. At the time, most law students were pro-defendant activists, but Thompson, a hard worker and a good speaker, gained a reputation by taking the side of law enforcement. After graduation, though he had no political sponsor, Cook County State's Attorney Benjamin S. Adamowski, a Democrat turned Republican, made Thompson head of his appellate division. In 1964, Thompson would make his mark by arguing for the state before the U.S. Supreme Court – and losing on a 5-4 decision – in *Escobedo v. Illinois*. The case was the first to test the constitutional limits of the police in obtaining confessions. Speaking before police groups in other cities, Thompson predicted that additional decisions would extend the legal protections of defendants in police custody.

Thompson did not lose his job when Democrat Daniel P. Ward became state's attorney. However, he left the state's attorney's office to become an assistant professor of law at Northwestern University. While there, he co-authored three casebooks on criminal law. He returned to Republican politics in 1969 as chief of Attorney General William J. Scott's criminal division, but he did not stay long. Before his 35th birthday, Thompson became assistant U.S. attorney for the Northern District of Illinois, and on November 29, 1971, the U.S. attorney for the Northern District. He was sponsored for the post by U.S. Sen. Charles H. Percy, a moderate Illinois Republican. In the 18 months Thompson worked as assistant U.S. attorney, staff in the prosecutor's office doubled, thanks to President Richard Nixon's Omnibus Crime Bill of 1970.

Thompson knew Chicago politics well, and he promptly convened a series of grand juries that ignored whatever unspoken agreements had protected the city's top-level political figures. And he began winning convictions. Judge Otto Kerner, who had left the governor's office to take a post in the U.S. Court of Appeals, went to prison, as did Thomas E. Keane, Chicago's most powerful alderman. County Clerk Edward J. Barrett, who had been state treasurer, state auditor, and secretary of state, was permitted to serve his bribery sentence at home due to poor health. Mayor Richard J. Daley's former press secretary, half a dozen aldermen, several legislators, suburban politicians, policemen, and employees of the politically sensitive election commission and assessor's office also were convicted. Some were Republicans, but most were part of the Democratic organization headed by Daley.

Thompson made the final call on the Kerner prosecution. The grand jury indicted the judge on 19 counts. Thompson appeared in the courtroom as chief prosecutor. When he cross-examined Kerner and made the final argument to the jury, Thompson's future was at stake, for an acquittal would have brought a backlash of sympathy for the urbane former governor. Indeed, the defense criticized Thompson's methods. He was one of the first federal prosecutors to obtain convictions by grants of immunity to reluctant witnesses. Nevertheless, a special panel of Court of Appeals judges from outside Illinois upheld the conviction of Judge Kerner for income tax fraud, conspiracy, perjury, and mail fraud.

By 1975 Thompson was the best-known Illinois Republican. Under pressure to be a candidate for major office, he astutely declined to run against Richard J. Daley for mayor of Chicago. Soon he announced his candidacy for governor and began hand-shaking among downstaters and assembling a campaign staff. He spent six months as a part-time attorney on the payroll of Winston & Strawn, where he engaged in the private practice of law for the first time.

Thompson's weakness during that first campaign was that, having begun at the top, he knew little about the machinery and problems of state government. And he had never seen most of downstate. Nevertheless, the young prosecutor easily triumphed over a conservative businessman in the 1976 Republican primary. In the fall election his opponent was Secretary of State Michael J. Howlett, a popular, experienced state official who had eliminated Governor Dan Walker in the Democratic primary. Howlett tried to exploit Thompson's lack of experience, but the tactic wasn't successful. The Republican conceded that he needed on-the-job training, but he was a quick study. He had an excellent memory for names and faces, and he was a better speaker than Howlett. Further, the Democrat had been slated for governor by Richard J. Daley – he even looked somewhat like the Chicago mayor – enhancing Thompson's image as a fresh face and enabling him to capitalize on his reputation as a corruption-buster. The Republican candidate repeatedly asked whether voters wanted a governor who was close to the mayor. With the support of independents and some Democrats, "Big Jim" polled nearly two-thirds of the vote and won by 1,390,137 votes.

Cracking Down on Crime and Boosting the Economy

Two issues remained in the forefront throughout Jim Thompson's 14-year tenure: public safety and the economy.

Early in his first term, the former prosecutor focused his attention on the state's criminal justice system. In particular, he called for stiffer mandatory sentences for certain crimes. Indeed, during his administration, the emphasis in criminal justice policy throughout the country shifted from rehabilitation to punishment. Thompson won a new Class X category of felony for such serious crimes as attempted murder, rape, and armed robbery, which carried the penalty of minimum sentences and, for third-time offenders, imprisonment without possibility of parole. And during his first year in office, he signed legislation to reinstate the death penalty. Shortly before he left the Executive Mansion, the state carried out the first Illinois execution in 28 years.

The get-tough-on-crime policies carried a stiff price tag. Thompson's administration built more prisons than at any time in state history. Yet, there still weren't enough. In the first decade of Thompson's tenure alone, 24,000 offenders were convicted under Class X. When he left office, 120 offenders were sitting on death row. Illinois' prisons were bursting at the seams, and even some of the most ardent law-and-order proponents began to reassess the impact of Class X and mandatory minimum sentencing.

Nevertheless, Thompson's stance on criminal justice was popular and he was well-positioned for his second campaign. His first term had lasted only two years because the state shifted statewide elections to non-presidential years. Perhaps for that reason, voters were especially disposed to renew the young governor's lease on the Executive Mansion. He also may have been helped by the attention-getting, but non-binding Thompson Proposition, which asked voters whether they thought property tax rates should be controlled. And possibly they were drawn to images of the second baby born to a state's first family and the first in 72 years. Samantha Jayne was born in the midst of that second campaign. Thompson had courted and married lawyer Jayne Carr of Oak Park during his first campaign. Whatever the reasons, he scored his second landslide. He beat his Democratic opponent, state comptroller and former state schools chief Michael Bakalis, by 596, 550 votes, or 59 percent of the total.

Thompson's second term was marked by a deep recession and structural shifts in the economy. Older industrial plants were shuttered, and jobs were forever lost in the so-called "Rust Belt" of the Midwest. Illinois' overall jobless rate soared from 6.2 percent in 1977 to a high of 11.2 percent in 1984. Between 1979 and 1983, the state lost a quarter of its manufacturing jobs. Throughout the '80s, the Thompson administration energetically implemented strategies to lure and keep businesses in order expand the state's job base. Striving to improve the export economy by promoting Illinois products abroad, he opened overseas trade missions. His frequent trips to Japan and Europe also promoted Illinois as a site for industrial investments. The best-known and most controversial success in luring such investment was an agreement to locate Diamond-Star Motors in the central Illinois community of Bloomington-Normal. Meanwhile, he convinced homegrown companies such as Sears, the state's largest private-sector employer, to stay in Illinois. It was an era when businesses were driving hard bargains with many governors, often demanding tax breaks and infrastructure development, even cash incentives. Thompson was determined to be a player in the competition for jobs and revenue. A high-profile case involved the Chicago White Sox. The team threatened to leave the state unless it received a publicly financed stadium. On June 30, 1988, in the last hours of the legislative session, the governor wrangled votes out of Republican legislators to pave the way for the new Comiskey Park. Nevertheless, critics argued such deals weren't always as advantageous for the state as advertised. By the '90s, incentives and so-called smokestack chasing had bottomed out. Yet Thompson was prescient in positioning Illinois for the coming global economy.

Thompson was forward-thinking, as well, in envisioning history, art, and culture as a way to boost the economy. He launched the Art-in-Architecture Program, which set aside one-half of one percent of all public building construction costs for art to be displayed in public buildings. He established the state's artisan shops, where artists could sell their work. And he pumped dollars into historic preservation.

But in the mid-'80s, he devised his boldest, certainly his biggest, economic development plan and dubbed it Build Illinois. The program provided $2 billion in new bonding authority for capital improvements throughout the state, including construction of the new State Library. Build Illinois enhanced Thompson's reputation as a governor who loved larger-than-life schemes. Certainly no one could dispute his love of anything involving bricks and mortar, especially if it could be sold as a jobs program, but critics charged taxpayers would bear the debt for such wholesale renovations for decades.

Running as the Taxpayer's Friend

In his final two campaigns, good luck helped Jim Thompson defeat the strongest Illinois Democrat, Adlai E. Stevenson III, who had left the U.S. Senate after 10 years because he believed the governorship was more challenging. In 1982 and 1986, Thompson was fortunate that Stevenson, unlike his father, was a dull speaker with negative charisma. And the governor chose to run as a friend of the taxpayer, a man who had enforced economy and made tax increases unnecessary.

Still, the traditional reelection campaign troubles of incumbent governors were recalled in the summer of 1982, Thompson's third bid for office, as polls showed he was running a poor second. By October, the situation had reversed and the governor looked like an easy winner. The pollsters, however, had not realized that Chicago blacks, overwhelmingly Democratic, were in revolt against their party's white leadership and would turn out en masse as a warm-up for the mayoral election of Harold Washington the next winter. Thompson, who had expected to win easily, had to wait several days before official returns showed he had won by 5,074 votes. Two landslides had been followed by the closest gubernatorial election in Illinois history.

In 1986, Secretary of State Jim Edgar and Lieutenant Governor George Ryan were both available to run for governor, but Thompson did not retire. Stevenson, whom Democratic leaders still considered their best candidate, was given a clear track in the primary. Whether under normal circumstances he might have been elected on his second try will never be known. With Illinois House Speaker Michael J. Madigan as his manager, the former governor's son began an aggressive campaign that ran into unexpected trouble in the primary. The post-Daley Democratic leadership had concentrated on renominating their Cook County candidates and ignored a slate entered by Lyndon H. LaRouche Jr., an extremist. When the nominees for lieutenant governor and secretary of state turned out to be disciples of LaRouche, Stevenson refused to run with them. During a difficult summer he resigned the Democratic nomination for governor and became a futile candidate of an ad hoc Solidarity Party.

Thompson worked hard and was elected to his fourth term, not by a landslide but with a respectable plurality of almost 400,000 votes. He carried 13 Chicago wards, two more than he had four years earlier. In four elections, he had polled 57 percent of the vote and won by an average plurality of 597,742 votes.

Costs Climb and So Do Taxes

Thompson won his last two elections by claiming that state finances were sound. But after each of those campaigns, the governor decided the state treasury was tapped out.

Shortly after the 1982 election, a lame-duck legislature gave Thompson unprecedented authority to cut appropriations by 2 percent for the rest of the fiscal year. Then when the new General

Assembly was seated, Thompson asked for $1.9 billion in new revenue in the form of higher income, liquor, gasoline, and highway user taxes. The legislature agreed to some of those increases. Then in 1983, the state faced an immediate $300 million budget gap because the recession-plagued economy played havoc with the initial state budget revenue estimates. Thompson proposed a temporary increase in the income tax rate; the legislature agreed to it. Likewise, booming maintenance costs for the extensive highway system had depleted the fund designated for the state's roads. That problem was solved by a deal that increased the gasoline tax and tied downstate road improvements to a state subsidy for Chicago-area transit. Thompson had taken the initiative in urging two Chicago mayors to recognize that economic health depended on workforce mobility. At the same time, the governor's advocacy of a special sales tax for the collar counties jeopardized his popularity in that Republican stronghold. The governor also found extra dollars for elementary and secondary schools and for colleges and universities, though not enough to satisfy the educational community.

After his 1986 reelection, Thompson again asked for new taxes in quantity. His requests totaled $1.6 billion, which was more than he had any chance of getting. The Democratic response in the House, dictated by Speaker Michael Madigan, was negative. Traditionally, the legislature plays a spendthrift role by passing appropriations that have to be vetoed. But under Madigan the House for the first time took charge of the budgetary process and dictated that taxes would not be raised. After the stalemated session adjourned, the governor responded with a 4 percent cut in spending and vetoes totaling $363 million. Reminiscent of Governor Deneen 80 years earlier, Thompson in speeches and interviews appealed to the public and warned that the state faced a lowered bond credit rating and possible bankruptcy. He triumphed in the fall session of the legislature when Madigan tried to override vetoes of $62.5 million in school spending. In the final showdown in the Senate, Thompson won with the support of Philip Rock, the Democratic Senate president. Then, in 1989 in a surprising turnabout, Madigan, with Rock's help, rammed another temporary income tax hike through the General Assembly. Thompson signed the measure, which earmarked new revenue for education and local governments. That surcharge was made permanent during the administration of Thompson's successor, Jim

Edgar.

Political Summitry

Through most of his tenure, Thompson faced a Democrat-controlled legislature. In fact, Republicans controlled only one chamber, the House, in only one two-year span, 1981 to 1983. From the start, Thompson had a Democratic Senate to work with, but from 1978 Senate President Phil Rock was generally helpful with the administration's major legislation.

However, partisan control of the legislature became particularly pointed in light of the "cutback amendment" and the redistricting precipitated by the 1980 census. The cutback amendment was triggered, in part, because the 1978 lame-duck legislature voted itself, the governor, and other officials pay raises. Thompson vetoed the measure, but the General Assembly immediately overrode the veto. Angry voters in 1980 passed a ballot proposition that changed the way representatives were elected to the Illinois House. Traditionally, each district sent three members to the House, two from the majority party and one from the minority party. The amendment doubled the number of House districts, but dictated that only one member would represent each district. Thus, starting with the 1982 election, the House was reduced by a third and the minority party could not automatically be assured of having a third of the House seats. Compounding the reforms necessitated by the cutback amendment, the 1980 census spurred redistricting on the grounds of shifting demographics. Partisan control of the House and Senate was very much up for grabs. The situation was settled only when the luck of the draw in a lottery gave Democrats a majority on a deadlocked redistricting commission.

Thompson's style meshed well with the challenges brought forth in the early years of the legislative reorganization. In and out of the legislature, the governor specialized in summit conferences when faced with critical problems. And they were generally effective. Key agreements, for example, were hammered out pertaining to Chicago schools and unemployment insurance. When, in 1980, Chicago schools faced a financial crisis, Thompson called board members, bond experts, and other officials to the Executive Mansion, not letting them leave until an agreement had been reached. And, from his middle-ground stance, the gregarious Thompson maintained contacts that helped him bring labor and business together for a five-year agreement on insurance for unemployed workers.

Like other recent governors, Thompson was in Chicago much of the time. But he was the first to move into the modernistic State of Illinois Center, which was designed to his wishes. Traditionally, Republican governors have worked well with Chicago's Democratic mayors, but Mayor Harold Washington, who sat out a 1987 deadlock between the governor and the General Assembly on taxes, was less cooperative than his two predecessors, Michael Bilandic and Jane Byrne, had been. The governor considered Washington partly responsible for his administration's failure to bring a 1993 World's Fair to the lakefront.

The Changing Rules of the Game

Throughout the era encompassing Thompson's public career, reform movements and court decrees had chipped away at political parties' abilities to reward loyalty through jobs. Earlier, in a case involving the city of Chicago, public workers were protected from political firings. Then, in the last months of his tenure in the governor's office, the U.S. Supreme Court extended the principle to political hiring. The high court ruled in 1990 in *Rutan v. Illinois* that government hiring based on political affiliation is an unconstitutional abridgment of free speech. Thompson said he would comply with the court's decision, but he argued that a governor could not function without some party patronage.

Yet, modern era officeholders were already turning to no-bid contracts as a way to reward friends, and the term "pinstripe patronage" was coined during the Thompson administration. Thompson argued that he took personal responsibility for approving some no-bid contracts to ensure that state business was rotated among capable companies and bond houses. And he argued that only a small fraction of those contracts went to friends.

While Thompson struggled with changing rules on patronage, he supported legislation in 1983 granting government employees and teachers collective bargaining rights.

National Ambitions

As a former prosecutor, Thompson knew that his ethics would be closely scrutinized. And his administration remained scandal-free. Prompt and public apologies were effective in nullifying such mistakes as the questionable acceptance of four Kruggerrands from a labor leader, a midnight veto of a legislative pay raise bill on the understanding that it would be quickly overridden, and a foredoomed attempt to elect a Republican president of a Democratic Senate. He was also embarrassed by his wife's application for appointment to a federal judgeship, which he endorsed. It was withdrawn when bar leaders indicated disapproval.

This impressive durability in a big and diverse state attracted national attention, but his career was intrastate. Thompson made several out-of-state speeches, but he was a pragmatic moderate who didn't impress the conservatives who had put Ronald Reagan in the White House. In advance of the 1988 nominating convention, Thompson ignored the impending caucuses and primaries on the ground that he couldn't spare time to solicit delegates and contributions. That year, the presidential nomination went to George Bush.

Several times, there was speculation that he might be appointed a cabinet officer, but it didn't happen. So in 1990, after serving four terms and more years than any other Illinois governor, Thompson decided not to run for a fifth term. Instead, he put an end to his political career and returned to Winston & Strawn in Chicago.

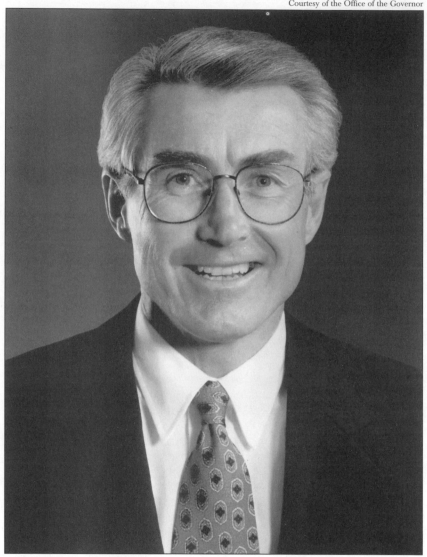

38th Governor

Jim Edgar
1946-

1946 – Born, July 22, in Oklahoma.

1968 – Receives bachelor's degree in history from Eastern Illinois University in his hometown of Charleston.

1968 – Accepts a legislative internship sponsored by the University of Illinois; Works for Senate Republican leader W. Russell Arrington.

1968 - 1974 – Serves on the staffs of Senator W. Russell Arrington and House Speaker W. Robert Blair.

1974 – Makes an unsuccessful bid for the Illinois House.

1974 - 1976 – Works for the National Conference of State Legislatures in Denver and as an aide to legislative leaders.

1977 - 1979 – Serves in the 80th and 81st General Assemblies.

1979 – Leaves the General Assembly to work on Governor Thompson's staff.

1981 – Governor Thompson appoints Edgar secretary of state to fill out the term of Democrat Alan J. Dixon, who was elected to the U.S. Senate.

1983 - 1987 – Serves his first full term as secretary of state.

1987 - 1991 – Serves his second full term as secretary of state; George Ryan succeeds Edgar as secretary of state.

1990 – Defeats Democrat Neil Hartigan to become governor.

1993 – A rainy summer floods 500,000 acres of Illinois land causing $1.5 billion in property and crop damage.

1994 – Handily defeats Democrat Dawn Clark Netsch to win a second term as governor.

1995 – Edgar and lawmakers vest authority in Chicago's schools in Mayor Richard M. Daley in hopes he will be able to reform them.

1997 – The new Department of Human Services is created. It absorbs three major state agencies – the departments of Mental Health and Developmental Disabilities, Alcoholism and Substance Abuse, and Rehabilitation Services – along with programs from the departments of Public Aid, Public Health, and Children and Family Services; lawmakers agree to some school reforms favored by the governor: They guarantee a foundation level for school spending over three years, increasing taxes on cigarettes, telephones, and riverboats to cover the cost; Edgar decides not to run for reelection.

Republican
January 14, 1991 - January 9, 1995
January 9, 1995 - January 11, 1999

Jim Edgar was the right governor at the right time. Cautious and credible, he moved into the state's Executive Mansion in the after-shock of the high-spending '80s, and in the wake of an administration given to grand gestures. After 14 years of "Big Jim"

Thompson, Illinoisans were content with a governor who was comparatively dull, and Edgar remained popular throughout his two terms. Though he risked raising the subject of taxes during his first campaign, voters believed his promise of fiscal discipline. And after delivering on his pledge not to surprise them, they reelected him by the second-widest gubernatorial margin in state history. Only Governor Thompson's 1976 campaign netted a greater margin of victory.

Throughout much of his career, the downstate Republican had shown a knack for good timing. He was appointed to his first statewide office and moved up the political ladder to Illinois' top elected post, where he was instinctively suited to solving the state's growing financial crisis. The national economy had weakened and Illinois was living beyond its means when Edgar, a moderate with a modest approach to governing, was elected Illinois' 38th chief executive. He immediately moved to trim spending and reduce a stack of unpaid bills. He won the first permanent increase in the state's income tax and pushed successfully to cap the growth in local property taxes. Edgar's decisions to cut social entitlements, beef up jobs programs, and overhaul the state's welfare agency were in tune with Washington's move to limit social supports. And his emphasis on smaller government pilot projects and expanded citizen and corporate involvement reflected the tenor of the downsized '90s.

Though he quickly earned a reputation as "Governor No," Edgar increased funding for higher education throughout his eight years, pumped money into early childhood programs and steadily boosted state spending for primary and secondary schools. And, as a capstone on his career, he negotiated with lawmakers a guaranteed level of funding for each elementary and secondary student, meaning the state's poorest schools would be assured of additional dollars at least through the turn of the century.

But this governor's greatest strength was also his greatest weakness. A born administrator, he was naturally suited to managing the state's day-to-day affairs, but less comfortable with the give-and-take of an increasingly partisan legislature and less successful when it came to mobilizing public support and cajoling lawmakers into taking political risks. As a result, Edgar failed in an 11th-hour bid to convince lawmakers to find a politically palatable way to shift the locus of school funding away from property wealth. Lawmakers did agree, for the first time, to set and then provide the dollars to fund a minimum foundation level of spending on each elementary and secondary student and allow that foundation level to increase over three years. They also agreed to guarantee funding for those increases. To cover the costs, they cobbled together a package of minor tax hikes. Yet, faced with another election, they would not risk fundamental property tax reform aimed at solving for the long term the inequities in education finance. So Edgar was forced to settle for half a loaf, though, as his supporters argued, a fairly substantial one.

As befitting his temperament, Edgar's tenure was marked by incremental programmatic changes. Nevertheless, he balanced the books and restored the state's credit rating without a general tax increase. And that, as he had promised it would be, was his legacy.

But as the national economy boomed and the state's bank account grew, Edgar decided to step down. His health was a likely concern. He had suffered heart trouble for several years. And family was almost certainly a consideration. So, at 52, Edgar accepted a two-year renewable appointment with the University of Illinois' Institute of Government and Public Affairs, where he planned to lecture and conduct seminars, and he accepted a three-month fellowship at the John F. Kennedy School of Government.

Edgar faced a $1 billion debt on his first day as governor. Heading into his final month, he expected to leave a $1 billion cash balance for his successor. True to form, his timing was good. He had, he said, always wanted to go out on top.

At the Center of Attention

Jim Edgar showed an early aptitude for politics, an early preference for the Republican Party and an early streak of stubborn independence.

While in grade school, he helped Dwight David Eisenhower win a 1952 mock presidential election. Though he and other boys in his class were drawn to the Republican's military standing, his parents were surprised by the choice. Cecil and Betty Edgar were not active partisans in their small east-central Illinois community of Charleston, but at the least they considered themselves Democrats. And no one in the immediate family showed the slightest interest in becoming a politician. Edgar's mother, he often said, hoped her son would grow out of it and become something prestigious, like a doctor or a lawyer, though she later decided being governor was okay.

If Edgar's nascent political ambitions received little encouragement at home, they were nurtured in the school library, where he competed with classmates to be the first to read the latest issue from the Landmark Series on American and world history, books filled with tales of military heroes, pirates, and explorers. He was a class officer throughout grade school and high school, where he was elected class president in his sophomore and junior years, and student council president in his senior year. He always liked, he said, to be at the center of attention. And he liked running the show. So it was no surprise that in his 20s he considered a career in government.

Edgar's interest in public service might have seemed unusual to his rural Illinois neighbors, but not to his cohorts. He was born in Oklahoma on July 22, 1946, during the post-World War II baby boom. His parents had moved there shortly after the war so that Cecil could find work with Betty's family. But his parents had moved back to Coles County by the time Edgar was a toddler. He came of age during John F. Kennedy's presidency, a time when public service became a calling to many in his generation. By the late 1960s, though, young people were pushing the boundaries of social norms and marching for civil rights and against the Vietnam War. Once again, Edgar chose his own path. He was a political moderate and a devout Baptist. He didn't smoke or drink. And before he graduated from Eastern Illinois University in his hometown, he became a husband and a father. And student body president.

Years later, even his toughest critics would call this governor tenacious. He shared with other politicians the requisite ambition and drive, certainly. But if, as was also suggested, Jim Edgar took everything too seriously, that pattern was cut from early experience.

The Family's Fortunes Change

Jim Edgar was the youngest of three boys, raised by a single mother at a time when that was still unusual. The family's fortunes had changed the year Edgar turned 7. Cecil was killed in a head-on automobile crash, and, while his office supply business had just begun to take off, there wasn't much equity yet. The insurance payout didn't go far. So Betty, who had always planned to be a stay-at-home mom and housewife, sent the kids to relatives while she took typing classes. She found work in town, first with the federal agriculture department, later at Eastern Illinois University. They didn't seem poor, Edgar recalled, but they didn't have much either. And he learned early to be frugal. Edgar said he usually had enough to get into the movies, and sometimes the extra 10 cents for popcorn. Yet because he never seemed to have enough change left for Cokes, his classmates called him "Scrooge."

Nevertheless, Edgar said his mother had more impact on him than anybody. She was advised to sue the driver of the tractor-trailer who had killed her husband, but she refused to do so, though the driver was apparently operating without a valid license. When she lost her federal job, she refused to sign up for disability payments, though with a bad back she might have been eligible. Yet she always paid the family's bills. At the same time, Edgar said, Betty and her boys could count on help from an extended family and from the church.

While he attended Eastern, working toward a degree in history, he met a fellow student, Brenda Smith, from the southern Illinois town of Anna. They married and had two children, Brad and Elizabeth.

After receiving his bachelor's degree in 1968, Edgar considered law school, but decided to accept a legislative internship sponsored by the University of Illinois. Interns worked for legislators in Springfield. The position paid a small salary, but it also promised an invaluable practical education in politics.

A Ringside Seat on History

Jim Edgar picked out a dark green suit on his first day at the Capitol, believing it looked "very governmental," put on a conservative print tie, and reported for duty. He was assigned to work with Senate Republican Leader W. Russell Arrington, and nothing could have prepared him for the experience of the next few months. Arrington hailed from suburban Evanston, and Edgar recalled some 30 years later that he was "a moving force, the likes of which we have never seen around here." Edgar added that he was a little scared of Arrington every day he worked for him: "I think some of the members were scared of Senator Arrington." Even so, the future governor found his first political mentor. And he got a ringside seat on history at what he later called the legislative "session of all sessions."

Edgar's job that year was to sit next to Arrington on the chamber floor with the bill analysis book and keep the senator posted on staff recommendations. As it happened, during the closing days of that spring session lawmakers created the state's first income tax. While they were at it, they passed an increase in the gasoline tax and a license plate fee. Republican Governor Richard Ogilvie had asked Arrington to sponsor the bill, knowing it would be politically risky. And because the package was negotiated off the floor by the governor, Chicago Mayor Richard J. Daley, and legislative leaders, the actual vote took little more than half an hour, belying the revolution that had taken place and the revolution yet to come. Indeed, Ogilvie, a force all his own, used his one term to bring the structure and financing of state government into the modern era. But he paid a political price. He lost reelection, at least in part because of the income tax. And Illinois politics would never be the same. Every governor since, every General Assembly, has stepped carefully around the subject of taxes. And every campaign strategist has looked for ways to hammer an opponent on the issue.

Edgar's own career would be affected by that vote. But at the time, he remembered, he was simply impressed. "I thought that was the way government was always supposed to act. It all happened quickly." By the end of his internship, he was "an Illinois Republican, locked in." And committed to state government. Most important, Ogilvie and Arrington were both moderate Republicans. Edgar had worried about taking that assignment with Arrington, fearing the leader would be too conservative. But Arrington turned out to be the most "progressive guy in the legislature," Edgar said. "He really believed that if there was a problem, the General Assembly stayed until they got it solved."

He remained on Arrington's staff for two years. But when the Senate leader got sick and left the legislature, Edgar went to work for House Speaker W. Robert Blair. The Park Forest Republican turned out to be another party powerhouse. During Edgar's time on his staff, Blair handled legislation creating the Regional Transportation Authority to oversee mass transit in Chicago and the surrounding suburbs. That effort involved balancing the conflicting needs within the metropolitan region.

Edgar would later recall that battle and describe his tenure with Blair as "interesting."

He could have said culture shock. In the 1970s, before the membership was cut by one-third, the Illinois House had 177 members. Because they were chosen from three-member districts, including one member from the minority party, many of the representatives were independent-minded and outspoken. Some were outright eccentric. Edgar recalled the difference between the two chambers: "One day I left the House, and it was in its usual chaos. Somebody had a bill up, and nobody was paying any attention, and there were 45 different conversations going on. And it was just genuine bedlam in the House. A pretty normal day. I went to the Senate. I hadn't been over there for a few months. I thought they were adjourned. But they were in the midst of a major debate. And actually a pretty hostile debate."

In 1974, Edgar decided it was time to strike out on his own, and he made an unsuccessful run for state representative from Charleston – his only electoral loss. Edgar faced two opponents in the primary: one the incumbent and the other favored by the Coles County Republican Central Committee. Edgar came in a close third. What stuck in his mind, and likely his craw, was that he was beaten by a florist who had never spent time in Springfield. Nevertheless, he considered that race the best thing that ever happened to him. He said he learned two important lessons. "One is that you can always lose. And two, I never wanted to lose again."

Edgar subsequently went to work for the National Conference of State Legislatures in Denver, giving him an opportunity to visit other states. But in 1976, he ran again for a seat in the Illinois House. The 1974 campaign had given him a chance to build name recognition and party support. This time he won.

The Frustrations of a Back-Bencher

At age 30, Jim Edgar took a seat in the legislature, representing the 53rd House District, including his hometown of Charleston. The experience turned out to be an eye-opener. After serving on the staffs of Republican leaders in both legislative chambers, Edgar was suddenly a freshman back-bencher in the minority party. He cut a low profile throughout his two and a half years in the legislature, though he garnered attention for an unsuccessful proposal allowing school districts to opt for a local income tax. He would trot out that bit of history, briefly, during his first run for governor.

While he served in the House, Edgar backed another proposal that would have a significant impact on policy during his years in the Executive Mansion. He voted for one of Governor James R. Thompson's first initiatives to toughen criminal sentencing. Dubbed Class X, the law established longer sentences for certain crimes. As Edgar noted years later, "We've been building prisons ever since."

Among the more politically controversial proposals Edgar supported while in the House was a pay raise for lawmakers and other state officials. In fact, Edgar supported the hike during his 1978 campaign for reelection, and he was one of the few downstate legislators to vote for it in the post-election veto session before the new General Assembly was seated. Thompson vetoed the measure by auto pen while on vacation, in plenty of time for lawmakers to overturn the veto. And, as Edgar remembered it, "The whole world blew up." Thompson apologized to the public, and he and lawmakers renegotiated the raises. But the damage was done. That vote would spark public anger and, as a result, a citizen initiative was approved in 1980 that eliminated multimember districts and reduced the membership in the House, beginning in 1983.

Because Edgar was mad at Thompson for backing off on the raises, he hesitated to return a phone call from the governor some five months later. When he did, Thompson offered a job as his legislative liaison. So, near the beginning of his second term, he left the legislature to go to work in the executive branch of state government.

As Thompson's top lobbyist, Edgar helped negotiate temporary relief for the financially troubled Chicago schools. The state provided a bridge loan and created a panel to monitor finances. But the problems of that school system, the state's largest, were far from over. Edgar would face them again during his own administration.

In late 1980, Democrat Alan Dixon was poised to leave the secretary of state's office to take a seat in the U.S. Senate. According to the constitution, Thompson was in a position to name a replacement until the next election. Handed such a boon for the Republican Party, this was not a decision the governor would take lightly.

George Ryan, considered the top contender, had the most experience. He came from the powerful Kankakee Republican organization and was minority leader in the Illinois House. But there were other considerations. Because the Republicans had regained the House that year, Ryan was in line to become speaker. His skills would be needed by his party while legislative districts were redrawn for a smaller House. Edgar got the call instead.

The official line, according to reports of the time, was that

Thompson offered the post to Ryan but he declined because he wanted to be speaker. Pundits believe Thompson encouraged Ryan to make that choice. Indeed, Ryan was naturally suited to the give-and-take of the legislative arena. Much like Thompson, Ryan was a pragmatist who loved rolling up his sleeves and negotiating deals in back rooms. He was a likable bridge-builder. He kept his word. He was loyal to his party and to his party's leader. And he would be beneficial to the governor in the General Assembly.

With Ryan staying in the House, Thompson considered Edgar, and the governor may have seen something he admired. Good looking, a straight arrow, and conscientious, Edgar had an instinct for administrative detail. In many ways he was unlike his flamboyant boss. Thompson was a quick study who loved to party. He was fond of wearing T-shirts, even in the Capitol. Edgar was just as likely to march in a parade in a suit and tie. He was compulsive and disciplined. And he preferred a quiet evening at home. While the outgoing Thompson was at his best when moving through crowds, Edgar was stiff in public. Thompson was an orator. Edgar was not. But Edgar was unlikely to turn out to be an embarrassing pick for Thompson. "Throughout his public career," Thompson said in announcing Edgar's appointment, "his actions and his work have been in the best tradition of public service."

Edgar maintained the choice came as a surprise, though he had weighed the possibilities. At first glance, the office wouldn't appear to have much appeal for an ambitious politician. The secretary of state's most significant responsibility is to issue driver's licenses, though the office has accrued a hodgepodge of administrative and service-oriented duties over the years. But the secretary of state post has also become the second-most powerful political job in Illinois. Only the governor has more employees. And it can be argued that even the governor can't command as much day-to-day visibility as the official who administers the rules of the road. Certainly the office has been a patronage cornerstone for political parties and a potential stepping-stone for officeholders.

An Activist Secretary of State

At age 34, Jim Edgar became the youngest secretary of state in the 20th century.

In his first statewide executive office, Edgar had the chance to call the shots again. He led the fight to close loopholes in Illinois' drunk driving law, won the long-running battle to require insurance for all Illinois drivers, launched literacy and organ donor programs, modernized the state's securities laws, and oversaw construction of a new state library. And he wasted no time making a name for himself.

But Edgar's first few weeks on the job may have been his toughest. He discovered he had inherited a license-selling scandal in his Chicago office, as well as an army of Democratic activists, some of them county chairmen, some of them guilty of doing political work on state time. Edgar created an inspector general's office, then quickly settled on a public cause: traffic safety.

The issue was personal as well as political. Though there was never any indication alcohol had been involved in his father's death, Edgar said the accident made him realize the seriousness of traffic fatalities. He began by pushing to strengthen the state's 1972 drunk driving law. Edgar had been on Blair's staff when lawmakers approved the law, which he called a compromise so the state would qualify for federal funding. Edgar argued arrests and convictions were actually declining while that law was in effect. He championed provisions to abolish the waiting period for the Breathalyzer test, eliminate a second test, and double the penalty for driving drunk. After those provisions took effect in 1982, Edgar began to promote quick suspension of driver's licenses with judicial review for drunk drivers. Those provisions also were signed into law.

Edgar won an even tougher fight for mandatory insurance. In the early 1980s, nearly a quarter of all registered motorists in Illinois had no insurance, according to the state insurance agency. The insurance industry, however, argued such a law would be unenforceable. Political opponents, including a few Chicago Democrats, argued it would impose undue hardship on poor people. But 31 states already had some form of mandatory auto insurance. And Illinois got in line with a temporary program that was later made permanent.

His other major accomplishment was completion of a new state library. Thanks to Thompson's Build Illinois program and Edgar's willingness to support and administer a new tax on the sale of used cars, the $30 million library was built on his watch.

Edgar was elected to the office on his own in 1982, winning big during a tough Republican year, and he was reelected in 1986 by what was at that time the largest plurality of any statewide candidate in Illinois history. That year *U.S. News and World Report* named him one of 30 "rising stars of American politics."

"The secretary of state's office was – it is – probably one of the greatest offices in the United States," Edgar recalled. "From the point of view that you can get something done. You don't have all that many problems. You don't get all that attention from the news media. And for the most part, you don't make people mad." Yet Edgar said he hadn't wanted the job when he and Thompson discussed it, preferring instead the idea of lieutenant governor, "Which shows how naive I was." He quickly learned to use the office to build goodwill throughout the state, including among blacks and Hispanics, two potential constituencies his party had ignored, if not alienated. And he positioned himself to grab a higher rung on the political ladder.

Edgar was sitting in the St. Louis airport in the summer of 1989 when he had a third telephone conversation with Jim Thompson that would change his life. Aides reached Edgar and told him to call the governor. It was urgent. When he did, Thompson said, "It's yours." Thompson had called to say he was going to announce in half an hour that he was not running for a fifth term. "And it's your turn. The governorship is yours. If you can get elected."

A No-Surprises Governor

Jim Edgar was the second secretary of state to move up to the governorship, and the first governor elected to succeed a member of his own party in 62 years.

Yet, while he and Thompson were moderate Republicans, they couldn't have been more different. And, no doubt calculating that his mentor's popularity had lost some of its edge after 14 years, Edgar set about early to highlight those differences. He was ready and willing to enforce spending limits. And he wouldn't mislead before election day. Voters would know exactly what they were getting. "I don't want the people of Illinois to be surprised by anything I do after the election, and they won't be," he said on Governor's Day at the Illinois State Fair in the summer of 1990.

In fact, Edgar established an agenda for his entire two-term administration during that first 15-month campaign and his first six months in office. And he remained strikingly consistent on the key points throughout his eight years as governor, the major exception being apparent shifts over the years on proposals to reform school finance by swapping higher state taxes for lower property taxes.

Edgar's agenda, established in that first campaign, included restoring the state's fiscal integrity while providing additional financial support for education and early childhood programs. And it included capping rising property taxes in the high-growth suburban counties surrounding Chicago and making permanent a temporary income tax surcharge. On election night, Edgar would say that his victory proved a candidate can be honest about taxes and still win.

Taxes quickly became the central issue in that first race for governor. On the day he launched the campaign, he told reporters the two-year state income tax surcharge should be made permanent for schools. "If that tax ended in 1991, that would mean we would pull $350 million away from schools. And I really don't want to be part of any attempt to pull the financial rug out from under our schools."

The state's income tax had not been permanently increased since 1969, when Edgar watched the creation of the tax while working as an intern for W. Russell Arrington. But in 1989, a temporary surcharge had been instituted by the Democrat-controlled legislature. It increased the individual rate from 2.5 percent to 3 percent. The corporate rate was increased from 4 percent to 4.8 percent. The $756 million raised by the increase was split, roughly, between the state's schools and local governments, though some of those dollars were used to cover the cost of doubling homeowners' property tax deductions on individual returns.

The surcharge was set to expire six months after the new governor was sworn in, but calling for an extension during the campaign was politically risky. Nevertheless, Edgar's assessment was that most antitax sentiment was aimed at the local property tax, which covered roughly 60 percent of the costs of elementary and secondary schools. His stance on the income tax secured him the backing of educators and organizations, including some representing minorities, that believed the extra dollars benefited their constituencies. But it also earned him stiff primary opposition from conservatives, who labeled him a tax-and-spender. It is fair to say that pressure from the right during the early phase of the campaign, along with the general public's sensitivity to any taxes, had some impact on Edgar's thinking. Though he remained consistent on the surcharge, his tax policy did evolve.

Early in the campaign, he was prone to thinking out loud, and openly discussed possible shifts in the state's tax mix in order to reduce the burden on property taxes for funding schools. "When I was in the General Assembly 12 years ago," he mused at virtually every stop on that first flyaround, "I introduced legislation which some people thought was political suicide – to allow school districts at the local level by referendum to adopt an income tax. I wanted to see if there's a way we could get off the real estate tax to fund our schools. Now that didn't cause my political demise because I think people recognize they need that kind of option." Edgar argued taxpayers ought to be given another way to pay for schools. "There's no correlation, I believe, between real estate and education. Now there may be for fire protection and police protection. But, if you look at most property tax bills, what has driven those up is education." In the same vein, he toyed with the idea of raising the income tax beyond the surcharge to offset possible reductions in the property tax.

But Edgar dropped any public pronouncements on tax shifts after one journalist suggested that his position could open the door to an increase in the income tax without offsetting property tax reductions. Edgar settled for saying the debate on a tax swap should continue, though he was making no promises. Discussion of tax or school spending reform proved difficult in the context of a campaign.

As that campaign progressed, Edgar leaned more heavily on property tax relief. Shortly before the primary, he told the Arlington Heights Chamber of Commerce he would push for legislation limiting property tax increases to 5 percent or the rate of inflation, whichever is lower, unless local voters approved a greater increase. Most dramatically, though, Edgar also pledged not to raise state taxes beyond the surcharge level. Throughout the campaign, he argued he did not believe a permanent extension of the surcharge constituted an increase. Nor did he include so-called user fees, including levies on cigarettes and telephones, in his definition of higher taxes.

Whether or not the "no-new-taxes" pledge was the result of the surprisingly strong primary challenge from the right in his party, Edgar also pledged in the general election campaign to support the principles of the conservatives' proposal to require an extraordinary vote in the General Assembly for any legislation aimed at generating new revenue. Edgar believed the 60 percent vote requirement would give Republicans in the legislature a greater say on taxes. And, presumably, a stronger voice in negotiating any extension of the surcharge. At any rate, he faced Democrat Neil Hartigan in the fall in what he called a "classic campaign." Both were about equally well known and both had about the same money to spend. Hartigan appeared to run a more conservative campaign on the issue of the surcharge. At the same time, though, he would not promise not to raise taxes. The narrow vote margin in Edgar's favor was credited, to some extent, to his believability on the issue of taxes. Though, to his benefit, Edgar also had built good relations with blacks and Hispanics while he served as secretary of state. Hartigan, meanwhile, did poorly among Chicago blacks.

Beyond the surcharge, Edgar believed he would need to concentrate his energies on the spending side of state finance. The day after the election, he began to calculate how many millions would need to be cut. "We are not in a position where we're going to have a lot of new dollars for new programs," he later told his transition team. "If we're going to have new programs, we're going to have to eliminate old programs."

Edgar had talked economy throughout the campaign. He promised, for example, to de-emphasize so-called smokestack chasing, an economic development strategy employed throughout the country in the 1980s. In the competition for job producers during that decade, governors offered incentives to corporations to stay or relocate in their states, including tax breaks and infrastructure development. Thompson used incentives in negotiating controversial, and costly, arrangements with Diamond-Star Motors and with Sears. Yet economic circumstances were different in Thompson's era. Corporations played hardball, and no state wanted to be the first to blink. By the time Edgar took office, smokestack chasing was becoming passé anyway, and he shifted his focus to education and to improvements in the state's infrastructure as a way to attract businesses and keep jobs. Indeed, Edgar's approach to economic development, which looked unfavorably on subsidies for sports stadiums or gambling, was at the heart of a long-running feud between the Republican governor and Chicago's Democratic mayor, Richard M. Daley. Throughout Edgar's tenure, the two would spat over airports, sports stadiums, and land-based casinos.

But at the center of Edgar's economic program was his belief in preventive social services. He argued, for example, that health care prevention programs for poor people would save money in the long run. In fact, spending on entitlement programs was the fastest-growing portion of the budget. The state had become a $1 billion deadbeat, and Edgar faced a mountain of overdue bills from doctors and others who had provided services for low-income Medicaid recipients. While the new governor said he expected to see spending increases in the departments of Corrections and Children and Family Services, he would not rule out cuts in social welfare programs.

Make Them Sit Up and Take Notice

Edgar said the first six months of any administration are always the most important. It was especially critical to make lawmakers understand that this administration meant business on the budget. He believed the legislature had grabbed the spending initiative during Thompson's last two years, so it would be necessary to make them sit up and take notice.

On his first full day on the job, Edgar called for cuts in spending to close a projected $300 million budgetary gap. Due to declining sales tax revenues, the actual deficit turned out to be double that amount in his first fiscal year. The recession would last into the next two years. And it would take much of Edgar's first term for the state to pull itself out of the fiscal hole. But the governor, with the support of his party's leaders in the General Assembly, made a good start that first legislative session.

Against the wishes of Democratic lawmakers, Edgar did away with General Assistance for welfare recipients in his first budget and replaced it with Earnfare, a program that required people to work. And, despite Democratic opposition, Republicans won the day on property tax caps for the collar counties in the Chicago metropolitan region. Cook County got caps later. And later still, downstate counties got the option to impose caps through referendum. More important, Edgar won an immediate permanent boost in the education portion of the income tax surcharge, and formula changes for distributing the rest of the surcharge revenue that were designed to benefit the state's coffers in the short run and local governments' in the long run. The higher individual and corporate rates were ultimately made permanent.

That first legislative session, complicated by the effort to remap legislative districts, ran into overtime. But after the dust had cleared, Edgar was declared a winner. And even Democratic House Speaker Michael Madigan called the new governor "tenacious."

Nevertheless, a number of problems lay ahead. Social service costs continued to rise, the result of a combination of the slowing economy, expanding federal mandates in Medicaid spending, a move by the Edgar administration to recalculate Medicaid payments, and court decisions affecting child welfare and mental health programs. Edgar and lawmakers executed such maneuvers as short-term borrowing to solve an immediate cash flow problem and new taxes on hospitals and nursing homes to close a budgetary gap.

Yet throughout, Edgar never deviated from an overarching approach to governing: a downsized role for the public sector. Further, Edgar, like many moderate Republicans in the '90s, was disposed to look to citizens to solve some social problems. He launched Project Success, for example, a program to use schools to link existing social services with the people who need them. Such an effort, he argued, could be started by government, then picked up and expanded by communities. He began during his second year with pilot programs in six districts. In his final year, Edgar's office said 800 schools throughout the state were involved in the program or were slated to be. Another example was Edgar's successful effort to get the legislature to authorize community-based charter schools that could operate out from under the rules and regulations of the education bureaucracy. When critics charged that he lacked vision, Edgar responded that he didn't define vision by spending money. To this governor, smaller government was better government anyway. And private initiatives would have the advantage of holding down costs. He believed, for instance, that better prenatal care for poor mothers and preschool programs for their children could save millions in health care, education, welfare, and prison programs. During his two terms, he pumped hundreds of millions of new dollars into those programs, nearly doubling funding for preschool education.

Prepared for Disaster

Jim Edgar faced two unforeseen crises that first term. The first came in the form of a flood, one of the worst in state history. In the spring and summer of 1993, the Mississippi and Illinois rivers jumped their banks and inundated the western section of the state, putting 16,000 residents out of their homes and 10,000 workers out of their jobs.

Edgar, who said he had been told at a new governor's conference that disasters are the worst thing that can happen to an administration, mobilized as if for war. Which, in a sense, it was. From a makeshift command center in Springfield, and in his element as a manager, Edgar put the resources of the state to work fighting the flood waters. When critics asked why he couldn't muscle his agenda through the legislature in the same way, the governor responded that with a flood he could make decisions and simply send the bill to lawmakers. And they would pay it. Political controversies proved more difficult to manage.

Edgar's second crisis was personal. In the summer of 1994, he underwent emergency quadruple heart bypass surgery. It wasn't the first time he had been hospitalized for heart trouble; he had already had an angioplasty. And it wouldn't be the last. In 1998, he was hospitalized after experiencing chest pains while working out. But Edgar's response to his health problems were characteristic. He threw himself into a heart-healthy diet and exercise regime. After bypass surgery, he signed the fiscal 1995 budget in his hospital room and hit the campaign trail in less than a month.

Using Taxes as a Political Hammer

In fact, Jim Edgar wiped out his Democratic opponent in his second campaign for governor. He faced Chicago liberal Dawn Clark Netsch, the state's comptroller and a former state senator who won only one county in the fall election. Edgar maintained, probably accurately, that Netsch lost the race when he began running ads that summer reminding voters the Democrat was against the death penalty and portraying her as unwilling to talk about her stance on crime and taxes. But the lingering perception is that Netsch lost that race because she had called for a large increase in the income tax. And it is clear that Edgar's forces helped spread a message that Netsch was for such an increase. His stance on the subject of education spending during that campaign constitutes the starkest inconsistency in his career, and helped poison the political well against reform during his second term.

Netsch did propose an increase in the income tax to provide $1 billion for schools and another $1 billion in property tax relief. She called for an additional $500 million for a graduated personal income tax exemption. But her point was to suggest a way to end inequities in school spending, something Edgar had debated throughout his entire career. Yet in the context of this campaign, he hammered Netsch for calling for a 42 percent increase in the income tax rate. At the same time, he refused to endorse a proposed constitutional amendment requiring the state to bear half the cost of funding schools, arguing the measure would not accomplish what it intended.

Once his second term was secured, though, Edgar established a high-profile commission, chaired by former University of Illinois President Stanley Ikenberry, to examine the subject of education finance reforms. The commission served a political purpose as well. It gave the governor cover on the subject of taxes. Citing the panel's report, Edgar called for reforms that bore some resemblance to Netsch's plan.

Reflecting during his final weeks in office, Edgar said he did not see an inconsistency. Rather, he argued, a tax swap wasn't politically feasible at the time of his reelection. The suburban Republican legislative leadership, most particularly Senate President James "Pate" Philip, wouldn't support reforms in school finance until changes had been made in Chicago schools. That was likely true. Suburban lawmakers saw nothing to gain from sending state dollars to poor schools in other parts of the state. And Philip, who tended toward colorful rhetoric, had long argued, in essence, that giving more school money to Chicago amounted to sending good money after bad. Still, Edgar failed at using the substantial persuasive powers of his office.

Edgar and lawmakers did manage to put the capper on Chicago school reform in 1995 by vesting authority over Chicago's schools in Mayor Daley. In short order, Daley restructured the bureaucracy in that school district, put the budget in the black, and established peace with the teachers' union for the first time in years. Edgar also called for a plan of action to revamp what he termed the "unfair and uneven" way in which the state funded schools. When the commission established to study the question issued its report, Edgar endorsed its recommendations, which called for generating $1.9 billion through increases in taxes or spending cuts. Those dollars would have provided $1.5 billion in property tax relief and left an extra $400 million to spend on schools. The report further recommended that $4,225 per year was the minimum level that could be spent to achieve a quality education for each child. Edgar hit the airwaves, using his own campaign funds, to promote the plan. Still, it went nowhere in a General Assembly whose members were skittish about hitting the campaign trail after approving any legislation with the word tax in it. They may have had in mind the campaign strategy used against Netsch.

So Edgar changed his approach. He suggested reforms without offering specifics that might box lawmakers in. He had something else going for him. Lawmakers in some districts were beginning to get heat for doing nothing to support education. And, late in 1997, lawmakers agreed to some of the reforms suggested by the Ikenberry Commission. They committed to fund a foundation level for school spending, and they hiked taxes on cigarettes, telephones, and riverboats to come up with extra cash. Overall, more than $500 million would go to the state's poorest schools through the year 2001, even if projected revenues were to fall through – a seismic shift in school finance in Illinois. Another $1.5 billion was designated for school construction and repairs.

Social Welfare Spending

Even before the federal government set limits on welfare, Edgar had begun in his first term to trim the rolls. In his second term, he established a new Department of Human Services, an effort to streamline the social services delivery system. His critics argued the state was more concerned about moving folks off the rolls than keeping them in jobs. Nevertheless, Edgar was no hard-edged conservative. Early in his tenure, he supported moves to end penalties against families when fathers stay in the home and when recipients take part-time or temporary jobs. He also backed a successful measure that required teen-age welfare mothers to finish their education and to live at home.

In his final year in office, Edgar launched KidCare, an insurance program for minors from low-income families. That spring, lawmakers appropriated dollars to expand the program.

Scandals and Fights

Edgar's administration was not free of scandal. One of his friends and fundraisers, Robert Hickman, was convicted in connection with a lucrative tollway land deal while he served as executive director of the Illinois State Toll Highway Authority. And in 1997, Edgar was called to testify in an unrelated federal trial involving improper payments in a $12.9 million state computer services contract with Management Services of Illinois Inc. The founders of the company, hired to ferret out Medicaid overpayments, were among his biggest campaign contributors. Prosecutors won convictions against the contractors and two administrators in Edgar's Public Aid department by arguing the state employees had accepted cash and gifts in exchange for giving the contractors favorable treatment. Edgar was not accused of wrongdoing, but he ended up being the first sitting governor in Illinois to testify in a criminal trial in 75 years. He argued that his aides turned evidence over to authorities as soon as it was discovered. That same summer, Edgar issued an executive order banning most gifts to state employees under his command and requiring more state contracts to be competitively bid.

Edgar's relationships with some of the state's most important public officials were strained throughout his eight years in the Mansion. He got off on the wrong foot with Chicago Mayor Richard M. Daley almost immediately. The decision, shortly after he took office, to abrogate a pact providing state money for Chicago's mass transportation system left Daley and his aides believing this governor could not be trusted. City officials argued the dollars had been promised by the state; Legislative Democrats overrode the governor's cuts, but Edgar's response that the agreement wasn't binding because it had been negotiated by his predecessor likely caused lasting political damage. Further, the governor entered into a political tiff with the state's Supreme Court, in particular Justice James Heiple, over a decision in the so-called Baby Richard case, a matter involving the question of parental rights versus the best interests of the child. But Edgar also had a difficult relationship with leaders of his own party in the legislature, Lee A. Daniels and James "Pate" Philip. As Senate president, Philip thwarted Edgar at virtually every turn. He refused to advance the governor's plan to shift the tax mix to fund schools. And, a final humiliation, Philip and other Republican senators made a public show of voting down more than 100 of Edgar's appointments to boards and commissions in the last weeks of the governor's tenure. Nevertheless, Edgar made more than 2,000 such appointments during his two terms. Many of those appointments went to political friends.

Despite the challenges and controversies, Edgar judged his second term to be easier and more fun. The economy was going great guns, the state was building a surplus, and the frugal governor was able to loosen the state's purse strings. Edgar and legislators agreed to double the individual exemption on income taxes, and the governor decided to put a few dollars into bricks and mortar, including $10.4 million in planning money for a Lincoln presidential library in Springfield and $30 million for a new Department of Natural Resources building.

Three Decades of Change

Illinois state government moved into the modern era during Edgar's 30 years in public service.

The Ogilvie administration had helped to reform state finance by creating an executive budget process, establishing annual budgets, and enacting the income tax. And, on paper, Illinois' governor had more power when Edgar moved into the Executive Mansion than when Ogilvie moved out. The state's new constitution, implemented in 1970, definitively separated the legislative and executive branches and broadened the governor's authority to veto initiatives from the General Assembly. But it also gave lawmakers more power to override vetos.

For the most part, though, Edgar was not as successful as some others at using the formidable powers of this bully pulpit. Certainly, tough economic times made it more difficult for Edgar to offer local projects in exchange for legislative approval of his own agenda. Court decisions diminished his power to hand out jobs. And the policy differences between the moderate downstate governor and the more conservative suburban Republican leadership in the legislature served to weaken his hand. Further, Edgar argued that in an arena where lawmakers' self-interest extends only as far as the next election, it is frustratingly difficult to get them to do something they don't want to do. If Ogilvie and Richard J. Daley were here today, Edgar reflected during the last weeks of his tenure, they wouldn't have gotten the income tax.

Yet, there were also marked stylistic differences in the way Edgar played the game. Ogilvie took a hands-on approach to getting the income tax. Thompson did the same for his pet projects, bargaining right on the House floor in the last hour of a legislative session to help the White Sox build a new stadium. While Thompson thought nothing of showing up in one chamber or the other, Edgar kept an arm's length in public and was not much given to camaraderie behind the scenes. Thompson was spectacular on the stump, and used it regularly. It could be fairly argued that Edgar rarely ventured beyond the forum provided by an annual State of the State and budget message.

Of course, the legislature had strengthened its position since the Ogilvie era, too. As the state moved into annual budget-making, lawmakers met more often. And more often they chose to make lawmaking a full-time career. With the help of a professional staff, created in the late '60s, legislative leaders were better able to organize and control the content of policy decisions and political decisions. As legislative districts became more competitive, and more expensive in some sections of the state, legislative leaders used their campaign cash to tighten their control by contributing to members in tight races. During the Thompson administration, policy was more often hammered out in summits between the legislative leadership and the governor. The four leaders had truly become a co-equal partner at the table.

Indeed, the first governor of the 21st century faces a far different political dynamic than Jim Edgar did in 1968 when he decided to wear that dark green suit on his first day at the state Capitol.

39th
Governor

George Ryan
1934 -

1934 – Born February 24 at Maquoketa, Iowa.

1954 - 1956 – Serves in the U.S. Army, including 13 months in Korea.

1961 – Receives bachelor's of science degree in pharmacy from Ferris State College in Big Rapids, Michigan.

1968 - 1973 – Serves on Kankakee County Board of Supervisors.

1973 - 1983 – Serves in the Illinois House of Representatives, including two terms as House Republican leader and one term as speaker of the House (1981-1983).

1983 - 1991 – Serves as lieutenant governor under Governor James R. Thompson.

1991 - 1999 – Serves as Illinois secretary of state, taking a leading role in cracking down on drunk drivers, streamlining the efficiency of driver's license facilities around the state, receiving national attention for his efforts at promoting organ donation, quadrupling funding for workplace literacy grants, and using his position as state librarian to develop a comprehensive network of library services.

1994 – Elected to a second term as secretary of state by winning 100 of Illinois' 102 counties.

1998 – Runs virtually unopposed for the Republican Party nomination for governor and outdistances Democrat Glenn Poshard to get elected Illinois' thirty-ninth governor. Makes Illinois history by having State Representative Corinne Wood as his running mate, which makes her the first female lieutenant governor in Illinois.

1999 – Takes oath of office as Illinois governor.

Republican
January 11, 1999 -

Georgge Homer Ryan, Sr. reached the pinnacle of a long career in public service when he was elected Illinois' thirty-ninth governor in November 1998. "I believe in the Republican philosophy of low taxes and growth and opportunity for the families of Illinois," he said the day before the election. He campaigned on the premise that tax increases were not needed to keep Illinois prospering and with a pledge to devote 51 cents of every new state dollar to education. He received the endorsement of the Illinois Education Association, the state's largest teachers' union.

Post-election pundits predicted Ryan would become a governor more like James R. Thompson than Jim Edgar in working with the legislature. Ryan spent 10 years in the Illinois House of Representatives, serving two as speaker, before moving to the executive branch of government.

Before becoming governor early in 1999, Ryan had spent the previous sixteen years in two other constitutional offices – eight years as Governor James R. Thompson's lieutenant governor and then eight years as Illinois' secretary of state.

The Druggist Turns to Politics

George H. Ryan was born in 1934 in Maquoketa, Iowa, but soon enough was in Kankakee, Illinois, where he spent his entire childhood. After his father, Thomas Ryan, earned a degree from the University of Iowa, he took a job with Walgreen's and was sent briefly to Chicago and then to Kankakee. Thomas Ryan opened his own independent pharmacy in Kankakee in 1948, when George was in high school.

George worked in the family pharmacy and then went to Ferris State College (now Ferris State University) in Big Rapids, Michigan, where he received his degree in pharmacy. With several family members working in the family pharmacy business, George's brother Tom was the first to enter politics. He became Kankakee's mayor in 1965 and stayed in the position for 20 years.

George won a position on the Kankakee County Board of Supervisors and served as the board chairman before getting elected as a Republican member of the Illinois House of Representatives in 1972. He began to distinguish himself there and was chosen by his peers to serve two terms as House Republican leader, from 1977 to 1980, and then speaker of the House in 1981 and 1982.

Speaker Ryan

Ryan presided over the House during politically perilous days when Illinois was a national focal point for ratification of the Equal Rights Amendment (ERA). But Ryan opposed the amendment, and blocked a procedural change that would have allowed the amendment to be ratified with a simple majority rather than a three-fifths vote in the legislature. Militants from around the nation staged some dramatic demonstrations that received nationwide attention, and some wrote Ryan's name in blood on the Capitol floor as part of their protest. The Illinois legislature never did cast enough votes for approval of the ERA, and the ERA failed to become an amendment to the U.S. Constitution.

Although remembered most prominently for those ERA battles, Ryan likes to point to other significant issues during his time as House speaker. He was involved in a bipartisan agreement to reform unemployment insurance and in a successful effort to repeal the state inheritance tax, which was making it difficult for farmers and some business owners to retain their family farms and businesses when their forebears died.

Ryan in the Executive Branch

In 1982, when Governor Jim Thompson was running for the third time after having won in 1976 and 1978, Speaker Ryan became Thompson's running mate and was elected lieutenant governor, a position he held for eight years before getting elected secretary of state in 1990. That year, the current two-term secretary of state, Jim Edgar, was elected governor for the first time, and history would repeat itself eight years later, in 1998, when Ryan won the governor's position after serving two terms as secretary of state.

Ryan used his position as secretary of state to increase his statewide visibility and focus on some innovative programs and legislation. He worked with traffic safety groups to promote passage of a law to reduce the legal intoxication limit from a blood-alcohol content of .10 to .08. While running for governor, he touted this as the top legislative accomplishment of his career. For his anti-drunk driving efforts, he received major awards from the National Commission Against Drunk Driving in 1994 and from Mothers Against Drunk Driving in 1995.

It was during the 1990s that the Internet was transformed from an obscure network known only to a scant number of government officials and academics to an essential source of information and networking for millions of computer users throughout the world. As state librarian, Ryan promoted the use of new technologies, developing a comprehensive network of library services that included sharing of resources by 3,200 school, public, academic, and special libraries. He also raised additional money for library construction, and quadrupled funding for literacy grants used in businesses.

Ryan also used his position to promote organ donation. His office's organ donor awareness program became a model for other states and was a finalist in the John F. Kennedy School of Government's "Innovations in American Government" award Ryan used many television ads to promote this program and built the state's organ donor registry to 3.5 million people.

Governor Ryan

So Ryan entered the governor's office in 1999 with years of experience as a legislator and statewide leader. He carried with him the reputation as a pragmatic dealmaker capable of working with both parties in both chambers of the legislature.

He campaigned in an era when making education a top priority was popular among politicians. The economy was strong and the state was enjoying a surplus in its budget. He promised to allocate 51 cents of every new available dollar to educational programs, and he hoped that would amount to $2 billion in four years. He also pledged to reduce gun violence in Illinois, and said many times that guns were one of the defining issues in the campaign. His ads labeled Democratic opponent Glenn Poshard, a congressman from southern Illinois, as an extremist on guns and other issues such as the environment. Ryan also promised to address people's concerns about health care by promoting a Patients' Bill of Rights that would provide certain guarantees to patients and their doctors, and check the influence of insurance companies. Ryan raised an estimated $14.5 million for his 1998 gubernatorial campaign, about three times as much as the $4.5 million raised by Poshard, who accepted no funding from political action committees but who had some "soft money" support from labor unions and the Democratic Party of Illinois.

Ryan made Illinois history by choosing State Representative Corinne G. Wood as his running mate. She was not the first woman candidate for governor or lieutenant governor in Illinois, but she became the first woman *elected* to one of those positions in 1998. An attorney from Lake Forest, she was serving her first term as a state representative when Ryan selected her.

As Ryan entered the governor's office in 1999, Republicans controlled the Senate and Democrats controlled the House. Ryan's ability to lead the state would be determined to some degree by how well he could work with both parties and their longtime leaders, Senate President James "Pate" Philip, a DuPage County Republican, and House Speaker Michael Madigan, a Chicago Democrat.

The Changing Means of Good Governance: Reflections on the Last 30 Years

by Mike Lawrence

Virtually all governors of Illinois have come to the Executive Mansion with a policy agenda. But the means for advancing it have changed tremendously over the last 30 years because the sphere in which a governor operates has undergone a drastic metamorphosis. To succeed, a governor must map a relevant, far reaching agenda and, even more important, advance it by garnering the necessary support from legislators and the people of Illinois. The foremost challenge of a modern governor, then, is not having an agenda, but discovering the means by which it can get implemented.

In 1969, Governor Richard Ogilvie served up an indigestion-inducing piece of news at an Executive Mansion breakfast meeting with his party's legislative leaders. He told Senate Republican Leader W. Russell Arrington and House Speaker Ralph Smith that he was primed to push for enactment of the state's first viable income tax. As Ogilvie later recalled, "Arrington's face got red and his neck swelled. I remember his words exactly. He said, 'Who is the crazy son of a bitch who is going to sponsor this thing?' I looked at him and said, 'Russ, you are.'" Arrington, a self-made multi-millionaire, was both philosophically and viscerally antagonistic to an income tax. But he took his role as a leader seriously. So he and Smith became key supporters of Ogilvie's tax. "I had two really competent legislative leaders in Ralph Smith ... and Russ.... they took the lead, and when they needed help, they would ask me to step in," Ogilvie recalled in a 1982 interview. Moreover, the governor had another key ally: Chicago Democratic Mayor Richard J. Daley. The two had plenty of power, and they knew how to use it. Daley could abruptly abbreviate the political career of almost any Chicago Democratic legislator. He and Ogilvie also could hire and fire city and state workers almost at will — a patronage potency that did not escape Republican county chairmen when they were enlisted to bring hesitant GOP lawmakers into the income tax fold. Though it may have cost Ogilvie his political career, he cultivated the right alliances and wielded his power effectively to get the income tax measure passed.

Nearly 30 years later, more than a year before Governor Jim Edgar decided not to run for reelection to a third term, the tight-fisted and essentially peace-loving chief executive parted with $375,000 from his campaign stockpile to bankroll a television air war. For weeks during the spring of 1997, Edgar spoke directly to the people of the state through provocative television commercials he had helped purchase. His message was unfiltered, and his target unmistakable: Tell your legislators that you want them to over-haul the fundamentally unfair way we fund our schools. His tactic did not give him instant or total victory. But it helped him and his allies achieve a major reform that had proven elusive for decades. Just months after those unprecedented aerial strikes, the General Assembly approved landmark legislation guaranteeing adequate funding for each and every school child in the state.

Ogilvie's initiative succeeded without the World War II tank commander having to mount a major air war – let alone finance it out of his campaign treasury. Edgar was forced to adopt a more innovative strategy because the political environment of the '90s had remarkably transformed since the '60s, when Ogilvie embarked on his monumental mission.

The Rise of the Career State Legislator

The 1970 constitution, enacted during the Ogilvie reign, provided sweeping veto authority and strengthened the governorship in other ways, thereby increasing the horsepower the state's chief executive could muster. But the new constitution also – even if far more subtly – seeded atmospheric changes that could blow up headwinds strong enough to knock a gubernatorial initiative dead in its tracks. By permitting – indeed dictating – annual state budgets and annual sessions of the General Assembly, the document led to changes in the legislature itself and, more important, in the attitudes of legislators.

From the time Illinois became a state in 1818 and well past the midpoint of the next century, no more than 2 percent of the Illinois Senate and the Illinois House were full-time legislators. Almost every lawmaker had another job, which provided another, typically greater source of income. This was true when Ogilvie entered office in January 1969 and when he exited in January 1973. But three decades after the constitution decreed more frequent legislative sessions, at least 36 percent of legislators considered themselves full-time and many others depended primarily on their General Assembly pay to provide for their families. Even more important, many astute state government watchers will argue, the legislature had steadily and often stealthily improved pension benefits for retiring members. During the 1960s, a retiring legislator could receive as much as 60 percent of his or her annual pay as an annuity as early as age 60. At the twilight of the 20th century, legislators can focus – and the vast majority of them are focused – on a potential annuity equaling 85 percent of their salary if they can cobble together 20 years of government service. Moreover, they can retire as early as 55 and begin collecting their full retirement stipend. Some legislators courageously have placed conscience over continuity. But most legislators stand for reelection and, when it comes right down to it, almost nothing else.

Thus, a governor's plea to cast a vote that might even remotely invite rebuke from any significant segment of the electorate often is construed as a seduction into suicide. Contributing mightily to the paranoia is the prospect that the opposing party will not only use sensitive roll calls but also abuse incumbent members of the General Assembly through distortions in attack ads and negative mailers. In fact, many skittish legislators are not paranoid and deluded; the opposition truly is out to get them. Making matters worse, campaign operatives and consultants from both parties are constantly developing new, more effective mechanisms for trashing incumbents. Until the final quarter of this century, there was customarily a season for campaigning and a season for government. Those seasons have merged – and governing is not the dominant element. The next legislative campaign begins the moment the current one ends. Partisanship persists and too often prevails. Politics too often becomes the end instead of the means. It has gotten to be a tough, vicious way of life.

The legislative leaders have amassed more power by controlling campaign purse strings and the means of reelection. They not only collect and distribute huge sums of campaign cash, but they shape and mobilize the staffs that provide expert political advice during legislative sessions and front-line management during the crucial months, weeks, and days before an election. When Governor Edgar sat down with the four legislative leaders to talk about school funding reform in 1997, he found himself in the company of three men – House Speaker Michael Madigan, Senate President James "Pate" Philip, and House Minority Leader Lee A. Daniels – who had headed their parties' caucuses longer than Jim Thompson served as governor – and Thompson's 14-year run had exceeded that of any other governor of the state of Illinois by six years! The rank-and-file, by looking to these seasoned leaders for job security, empower them. But the leaders also look to the rank-and-file for their own job security, knowing full well that coercing or even cajoling members to cast risky votes could ignite a caucus rebellion.

So, it was hardly shocking that the Republican leaders, Philip and Daniels, did not rally their members to Edgar's flanks in 1996 and 1997 when he proposed increasing state taxes to lower property taxes and funnel more dollars to property-poor school districts. Although both Philip and Daniels had supported him on many initiatives that did not appeal to their conservative constituencies and had often backed him in his battles with the Democratic legislative leaders, each had a track record of bucking Republican chief executives on some major issues. And in the spring of 1996, they recoiled from even allowing the people of Illinois to vote on a proposed state constitutional amendment that would facilitate Edgar's bold reform proposal. They and many of their members feared opponents in the November 1996 election would represent votes in favor of putting the measure on the ballot as votes to support an increase in the state income tax.

The less-than-lock-step loyalty wasn't unique to Jim Edgar. Indeed, Daniels and Philip had treated Edgar's Republican predecessor, Governor Thompson, much the same way when he proposed an income tax boost in 1983 to avoid fiscal and programmatic chaos in state government. Thompson publicly begged Philip to sponsor the measure. Philip ultimately agreed to put it in the Senate hopper but only in the most condescending way. For the one and only time in recent Illinois history, a bill sponsor indicated in writing he was doing so "by request." Not only that, but "sponsor" Philip told the media the bill would be approved by the Legislature "when hogs fly." In the end, however, Philip did come a long way from his initial position. He championed a permanent tax increase in legislation approved by the Senate. But then Thompson was undercut in the House by his other Republican leader, Representative Daniels, who refused to support anything but a truncated version of the governor's revenue initiative.

The Media and the Political Process

The media zoomed in on Thompson's difficulties in bringing his party's leaders into line – just as they were to do a decade later in reporting on Edgar's initiatives. That was understandable to an extent. Intraparty wrangling is clearly news, and obviously much had changed in relations between a governor and his party's legislative leaders since the Ogilvie years; indeed, Philip often cited Ogilvie's reelection defeat after enacting the income tax as cause for pause in supporting revenue enhancement measures.

But the media itself also had changed. In 1968, when Ogilvie was campaigning, the media did not press him or his opponent, Governor Samuel H. Shapiro, for an ironclad commitment on the possibility of increasing taxes. "Sam and I never had a formal understanding. But we just didn't talk much about it," Ogilvie later recalled, adding that the top journalists of the day were "smart enough not to pin anyone down" to the point a new governor would be hamstrung after the election. To be sure, the post-Ogilvie media have become a markedly different bunch. By the 1990s, most newspapers and television stations had scaled back significantly their coverage of government and politics. "Gotcha" journalism diluted legitimate, well-researched, meaty investigative reporting with superficial, sensational gruel. And, with some notable exceptions, the media only tangentially focused on the substance of issues when they did provide coverage. Who won? Who lost? Who outfoxed whom? Curiously, some journalists who had declared Daniels "the big winner" in 1983 when he embarrassed the Republican governor wondered aloud just a couple years later why he insisted on having his way when Thompson's Build Illinois program was hung up in the House.

Unintended Consequences of the Fall of Patronage

But as Governor Edgar's television blitz proved, the media, warts and all, have become increasingly important to a governor because of changes in other institutions. Given the persistent partisanship and the typical lawmaker's obsession with getting reelected, a chief executive can no longer count on a loyal opposition or even loyalty from a solid majority of fellow party members. Moreover, the patronage clout that Ogilvie and Daley had enjoyed in the late '60s has been substantially eroded by federal court decisions during the '70s and '80s. Although the decisions have curtailed the abuses that brought about the litigation, they also have blurred accountability and made it more difficult to govern. How can an elected official be held accountable for effecting policy and yet be strictly limited in whom he or she can hire to implement policy directives? How can an elective official stimulate action by inert or even recalcitrant bureaucrats protected not only by civil service but also by federal court rulings? Those are questions being posed not only by jobs-starved party faithful but by some of those interested in more responsive, effective government. Additionally, in a strictly practical sense, a governor has fewer carrots and sticks to use in dealing with legislative leaders and their members.

The Challenge of Leadership in the New Millennium

Does all this excuse a lack of leadership or success? Absolutely not. A governor must appoint the best and the brightest to his staff and cabinet. A governor must manage the state's finances well and rise to the occasion when natural disasters wreak their havoc. A governor must deliver honest, responsive, and responsible government – even if it means firing corrupt friends and taking on entrenched bureaucracies. A governor must be willing to brave temporary – or even permanent – unpopularity with the veto pen and the bully pulpit when principle and vision demand it. A governor must be willing to sit down and negotiate with legislative leaders and members of both parties, recognizing the legislature is a co-equal and often cantankerous branch of government. A governor must be willing and able to arouse public support – even if it means paying for the opportunity to talk directly to the people of Illinois – in order to convince legislative leaders and their members that they will be taking a greater political risk by opposing the governor than by supporting the governor.

Governors of Illinois today – and into the next millennium – must be good men and women. They must be competent men and women. They must also be effective communicators and master strategists if they are to lead the way in making a great state even greater.

Appendix A
Roster of Governors

Name	Inauguration Dates	County of Residence
Shadrach Bond	Oct. 6, 1818	St. Clair
Edward Coles	Dec. 5, 1822	Madison
Ninian Edwards	Dec. 6, 1826	Madison
John Reynolds,[1] Dem.	Dec. 6, 1830	St. Clair
Wm. L.D. Ewing,[2] Dem.	Nov. 17, 1834	Fayette
Joseph Duncan, Dem.	Dec. 3, 1834	Morgan
Thomas Carlin, Dem.	Dec. 7, 1838	Greene
Thomas Ford, Dem.	Dec. 8, 1842	Ogle
Augustus French,[3] Dem.	Dec. 9, 1846	Crawford
	Jan. 8, 1849	
Joel A. Matteson, Dem.	Jan. 10, 1853	Will
Wm. H. Bissell,[4] Rep.	Jan. 12, 1857	Monroe
John Wood,[5] Rep.	Mar. 21, 1860	Adams
Richard Yates, Rep.	Jan. 14, 1861	Morgan
Richard Oglesby, Rep.	Jan. 16, 1865	Macon
John M. Palmer, Rep.	Jan. 11, 1869	Macoupin
Richard Oglesby,[6] Rep.	Jan. 13, 1873	Macon
John Beveridge,[5] Rep.	Jan. 23, 1873	Cook
Shelby Cullom,[6] Rep.	Jan. 8, 1877	Sangamon
	Jan. 10, 1881	
John Hamilton,[5] Rep.	Feb. 16, 1883	McLean
Richard Oglesby, Rep.	Jan. 30, 1885	Macon
Joseph W. Fifer, Rep.	Jan. 14, 1889	McLean
John P. Altgeld, Dem.	Jan. 10, 1893	Cook
John R. Tanner, Rep.	Jan. 11, 1897	Clay
Richard Yates, Rep.	Jan. 14, 1901	Morgan
Charles S. Deneen, Rep.	Jan. 9, 1905	Cook
	Jan. 18, 1909	
Edward F. Dunne, Dem.	Feb. 3, 1913	Cook
Frank O. Lowden, Rep.	Jan. 8, 1917	Ogle
Len Small, Rep.	Jan. 10, 1921	Kankakee
	Jan. 12, 1925	
Louis L. Emmerson, Rep.	Jan. 14, 1929	Jefferson
Henry Horner,[4] Dem.	Jan. 9, 1933	Cook
	Jan. 4, 1937	
John H. Stelle,[5] Dem.	Oct. 6, 1940	Hamilton

Name	Inauguration Dates	County of Residence
Dwight H. Green, Rep.	Jan. 13, 1941 Jan. 8, 1945	Cook
Adlai E. Stevenson, Dem.	Jan. 10, 1949	Lake
William Stratton, Rep.	Jan. 12, 1953 Jan. 14, 1957	Grundy
Otto Kerner,[7] Dem	Jan. 9, 1961 Jan. 11, 1965	Cook
Samuel Shapiro,[5] Dem.	May 21, 1968	Kankakee
Richard B. Ogilvie, Rep.	Jan. 13, 1969	Cook
Daniel Walker, Dem.	Jan. 8, 1973	Lake
James R. Thompson,[8] Rep.	Jan. 10, 1977 Jan. 8, 1979 Jan. 10, 1983 Jan. 12, 1987	Cook
Jim Edgar, Rep.	Jan. 14, 1991 Jan. 9, 1995	Coles
George Ryan, Rep.	Jan. 11, 1999	Kankakee

[1]Resigned to become congressman.
[2]Senate president pro tem filled vacancy.
[3]Reelected under 1848 constitution.
[4]Died in office.
[5]Lieutenant governor filled vacancy.
[6]Resigned to become U.S. Senator.
[7]Resigned to become federal judge.
[8]First term was for two years due to a provision in the constitution of 1970

Appendix B
The Constitutions of Illinois and the Power of the Governor

The state of Illinois has operated under four constitutions. These documents are, naturally, a product of their times. They set the boundaries for governors' powers and describe the practices of the executive branch. They also reflect the people's attitudes toward investing power in the state's chief executive. Generally speaking, the succession of the state's constitutions have provided the governors with ever greater autonomy. Today, there are few impediments – on paper anyway – to a governor's ability to execute a political agenda in Illinois.

The Constitution of 1818

The governors had less authority than the legislature during the first 30 years of Illinois statehood. The state's first constitution set forth a "weak governor" system, giving more power to the legislative than to the executive branch. Provisions of the constitution that particularly hampered the governors were:

- A weak veto power – The four justices of the state Supreme Court along with the governor formed the Council of Revision, which could veto the legislature's bills. Acting collectively, the council could "revise all bills about to be passed into law" and send them with objections to the originating house. The chief executive could not act alone, and by a bare majority vote the legislature could override a veto, which it usually did.
- A self-succession prohibition – Governors could not be immediately reelected. Political agendas needed to be completed in one term.
- Limited authority to make appointments – The constitution invested the legislature – not the executive branch – with the ability to appoint the executive officers deemed "necessary."

Because of precedents set during the territorial period, the convention delegates who met at Kaskaskia to write the first constitution had no interest in strong governors. When Illinois was part of the Northwest Territory, Governor Arthur St. Clair had been deservedly unpopular. He had visited the scattered settlements on the Wabash and Mississippi rivers only three times and had shown little interest in their problems. William Henry Harrison, who became governor of Indiana Territory in 1800, had trouble with the powerful John Edgar, Robert Morrison, and W.L.D. Morrison faction at Kaskaskia when he discouraged their questionable land speculations. After 1809, when Illinois became a separate territory, there was no legitimate complaint about Ninian Edwards, the presidentially appointed governor during the next nine years. However, the factional enemies of Edwards included Jesse B. Thomas, who was president of the convention and who had ties with the Edgar-Morrison group.

Illinois copied the council of revision feature from the constitution that New York adopted during the Revolutionary War. The man responsible was Elias Kent Kane, a New York-born and Yale-educated lawyer who was a Thomas ally and the chief draftsman of the Illinois constitution. Half of the American states did not grant any veto power to their governors, which was due to the residual dislike of the unlimited authority held by the appointed colonial and territorial governors. Had it not been for Kane, Illinois might have been in the no-veto category.

The first constitution froze the salary limit for governors at $1,000, changeable only by constitutional amendment. The governor and other state officers were elected for four-year terms, twice the term of office set forth by some states, but they were not permitted to run for immediate reelection. As population increased, the low and inflexible pay scale became one of the reasons cited by advocates of change.

The preliminary draft of the constitution gave the chief executive the customary power to fill state and county offices by appointment. The delegates, however, knew that Shadrach Bond would be the first governor and probably would not appoint their choice for state auditor, Elijah C. Berry. As a result, they let that clause stand but added a confusing provision that gave the legislature the right to elect the auditor, attorney general, and "such other officers of the state as may be necessary." They didn't define necessity. It seemed clear that the governor could appoint the secretary of state, whose role was something like that of a confidential assistant. (But before many years, however, the relationship between the governor and the secretary of state became a major issue that involved the legislature.)

Joseph Duncan, who left the Jacksonian Democrats just before he was elected Illinois' sixth governor, was stripped of virtually all power to appoint. Thomas Ford, who became governor in 1842, was outspoken in his disapproval:

> Sometimes the legislature, feeling pleased with the governor, would give him some appointing power, which their successors would take away, if they happened to quarrel with him. This constant changing and shifting of power, from one coordinate branch of government to another...was one of the worst features of government. It led to innumerable intrigues and corruptions, and for a long time destroyed the harmony between the executive and legislative departments. And all of this was caused by the Constitution of 1818 in an attempt to get one man [Elijah C. Berry] into an office of no very considerable importance.

As a precondition for admission to statehood, the constitution was approved by Congress but was not submitted to the voters for ratification. They were allowed to elect only the governor, lieutenant governor, members of the legislature, sheriffs, and coroners.

Because the constitution became effective in 1818, the elections fell midway in presidential terms. The first election began the third Thursday of September and continued for two more days. After that first election, the constitution stipulated that elections were to be held on the first Monday of August. The chief executives were not required to live at the seat of government when the legislature was not in session. The constitution required that governors be at least 30 years old, citizens for 30 years, and residents of Illinois for two years.

Two of Illinois' strongest chief executives, Edward Coles and Thomas Ford, were in office while the "weak governor" system was in effect. Coles lost on the slavery issue when the legislature was in session but triumphed when the issue went before the voters. Ford dominated the lawmakers on the issue of state solvency. Other governors weren't as successful: Ninian Edwards battled the legislature valiantly, but Joseph Duncan was hit by a legislative steamroller.

The Constitution of 1848

The 1848 constitution was ratified March 6, 1848, and became effective April 1. Former Governor Thomas Ford and some other officials opposed it, for a number of reasons, but it had the support of Democrats because it ended lifetime appointments and of Whigs because it outlawed alien voting.

To allow governors to be elected in presidential years, Governor French's 1846 term was cut to two years. The state and federal synchronization was completed by shifting state balloting from August to November.

Some, but not enough, of the defects in Illinois' system of government were corrected by the new document. Notably the new constitution:

- Abolished the Council of Revision, and
- Gave the governor increased appointment powers.

Abolition of the Council of Revision removed the Supreme Court justices from the veto process and placed it exclusively in the hands of the governor. The change was largely meaningless, however, since the legislature by a majority vote could still override vetoes. During the Civil War, Governor Richard Yates blocked passage of anti-administration legislation by invoking a new proroguing provision that allowed him to prematurely terminate the 1861 legislative session.

The legislature was stripped of its much-abused power to appoint state, judicial, and county officers. Since statehood, public opinion had gradually shifted to the belief that power should be vested directly in the people, rather than in the legislative and executive branches of government. As a result, the roster of popularly elected officials was lengthened. Henceforth, the selection of subordinate state officials, such as the secretary of state, all judges, and local officers was made at polling places. Definite terms were fixed: four years for most officials, but nine years for Supreme Court justices. The long ballot meant that executive power was shared by the governor, secretary of state, and other officials. Public involvement in government also was increased by the provision that some decisions, such as banking law changes, had to be submitted to referendum. The governor retained the power to fill vacancies and make temporary appointments. The biggest gain was that the legislature no longer was politically dominant.

But a shortcoming in the 1848 constitution encouraged petty graft. Salaries, which could be changed only by statewide referendum, were set at poverty levels – $1,500 for the governor and less for others. A clause forbidding extra compensation led to subterfuges, such as an unnecessarily large appropriation to the governor for a gardener, payments to court clerks with the understanding that they be shared with judges, and authorization for officials to collect and pocket fees for routine transactions. At session after session, the legislature demonstrated that its ingenuity was equal to the need of officials for pay supplements.

Another economy move, intended to limit the duration of sessions, fixed the pay of legislators at two dollars a day for the first 42 days and one dollar a day thereafter.

The 1848 constitution, spawned during a series of Democratic-Whig compromises, included many verbose articles that were purely legislative in nature. A major loophole permitted wholesale passage of an increasing volume of personal and private bills for the benefit of corporations and local governments. They smelled of bribery; they overburdened Governors Richard J. Oglesby and John M. Palmer; and, they were a major reason why a third constitution was adopted in 1870.

The Constitution of 1870

After partisanship sunk an attempt to write a new constitution in 1862, the constitutional convention of 1869 produced a document that served the state for century. The 1870 constitution placed the executive and legislative departments in approximate equality.

The new constitution:

- Strengthened the governor's veto powers.
- Allowed the governor to succeed himself.
- Gave the legislature the power to set salaries.
- Defined the executive branch as seven popularly elected officials.
- Established three-member House districts and instituted cumulative voting, allowing for a relatively strong minority in the legislature.
- Prohibited special legislation that affected (or favored) only selected corporate or private constituents.

The authority of the governor was strengthened – and that of the lawmakers correspondingly weakened – by a provision that only by a two-thirds vote could a veto be overridden.

To eliminate a major abuse of legislative power, the new constitution included a triple prohibition of the special legislation that had placed the General Assembly in disrepute and had given Governor John M. Palmer the opportunity to write scholarly but ineffective veto messages. First, special laws could not be enacted if a general law could be made applicable. Next, the constitution specifically barred special laws involving 23 topics, including those that had led to scandalous situations. Last, for emphasis, it prohibited the granting of special or exclusive privileges, immunities, or franchises to corporations or individuals.

The legislature was given the authority to set and change official salaries, which the first two constitutions had frozen at unrealistically low levels. Governor Palmer promptly was given a pay raise from $1,500 to $5,000 a year.

For the first time, governors were permitted to run for immediate reelection. Except for Palmer, Frank O. Lowden, and Louis L. Emmerson, all governors since then have wanted second terms.

While the governor was given the constitutional duty "to take care that the laws be faithfully executed," he shared administrative authority with other state officers. The U. S. Constitution had specified that executive power is vested in the president, but the new Illinois basic law said that the executive department "shall consist of the governor, lieutenant governor, secretary of state, auditor of public accounts, treasurer, superintendent of public education, and the attorney general." Each was elected independently, not necessarily from the same political party. The legislature had authority to create additional commissions and agencies. As a result, Palmer regarded the office of governor as "a mere figurehead."

Easy ratification of the 1870 constitution soon was followed by agitation for further changes. An amendment in 1884 empowered the governor to veto line items in appropriation bills without rejecting the entire measure.

The constitutional convention, however, failed to anticipate future problems, including the growth of Chicago. An amendment in 1890 was required before the metropolis could finance the World's Columbian Exposition with a $5 million bond issue. Four years later, following an advertising campaign in downstate counties, a charter amendment for Chicago was adopted. By that time the governors' biennial messages to the legislature routinely asked that a convention be called or that revenue-raising restrictions be relaxed. In 1917 Governor Lowden also asked for a shorter ballot, which would concentrate more power in the chief executive.

The Constitution of 1970

Lowden wasn't alone in his desire for a new constitution. A convention met from 1920 to 1922, but it produced a document that was overwhelmingly rejected by voters. Absent a new constitution, a 1950 "gateway amendment" eliminated an immediate need for a new constitution by easing the amendment process. But, in 1968 the voters called for a constitutional convention by nearly a two-to-one majority. Because the Supreme Court had approved the new income tax law and an amendment reorganizing the court system had been ratified, the 1970 constitutional convention – with delegates elected on a nonpartisan basis – met without major controversy and produced a constitution that was easily ratified.

Regarding the powers of the governor, the 1970 constitution features the following provisions:

- Statewide executive officers are elected during nonpresidential election years.
- A party's candidates for governor and lieutenant governor are elected as a team.
- The governor retains the line-item veto, and receives the power to reduce any item of appropriations in a bill presented to him. The governor is also able to send a bill back to the legislature with specific revisions.
- The constitution abolishes the office of superintendent of public education as an elected executive office and places jurisdiction of education under a single board.

The shift to nonpresidential election years limited James R. Thompson to a two-year term upon his first election in 1976, and returned Illinois to the schedule in effect from 1818 to 1848.

The federal system of joint election of the president and vice president was adopted by requiring that the governor and lieutenant governor be elected together. In 1968 Republican Richard B. Ogilvie had been elected governor and Democrat Paul Simon lieutenant governor.

The delegates provoked a controversy by giving the governor amendatory authority to make changes in bills passed by the legislature, which could accept or reject the revisions. Intended to enable the correction of minor errors, the amendatory veto soon became a vehicle for major changes. Governor Walker used it to adjust the state's share of financial aid to the Regional Transit Authority.

The veto power was revised in other ways. On the theory that vetoes had been overused, the legislature was permitted to override a veto by a 60 percent vote, down from two-thirds. Also, the executive was given authority to reduce as well as to eliminate an appropriation item, but a reduction veto could be overridden by a majority vote.

The 1970 constitution clarifies the governor's power to make appointments. It specifies that the governor has supreme executive power and allows him to reorganize agencies by executive order, subject to legislative rejection.

On paper, the power of the executive branch – particularly the governor – has been greatly enhanced by the 1970 constitution. Coincidental to the passage of the constitution, Governor Ogilvie engineered an astounding restructuring of Illinois government by establishing numerous departments and state agencies that ultimately report to the governor. But, in practice, this power has been offset partly as the result of the first amendment to the 1970 constitution.

In 1980, the cutback amendment eliminated cumulative voting and the practice of having three representatives from each House district. This has reduced the power of the minority party, and, as illustrated in Mike Lawrence's chapter (pages 355 - 360), has concentrated legislative power to the party leaders in each house. Thus a test for modern governors is not how they deal with the general assembly as a whole, but how they deal with party leadership.

A 1988 call for a constitutional convention was rejected by vote by a vote of 900,109 for to 2,727,144 against.

Appendix C
Gubernatorial Vote Totals

	Vote	**%**	**Plurality**

1818

Shadrach Bond unopposed, returns lost.

1822

Edward Coles	2,854	33.2	167
Joseph Phillips	2,687	31.2	
Thomas C. Browne	2,443	28.4	
James B. Moore	622	7.2	

Total vote 8,606 (four candidates)

1826

| Ninian Edwards | 6,280 | 49.5 | 447 |
| Thomas Sloo, Jr. | 5,833 | 46.0 | |

Total vote 12,693 (three candidates)

1830

| John Reynolds | 12,837 | 59.0 | 3,899 |
| William Kinney | 8,938 | 41.0 | |

Total vote 21,776 (three candidates)

1834

Joseph Duncan, Whig	17,330	52.9	7,106
William Kinney, Dem.	10,224	31.2	
Robert K. McLaughlin, Dem.	4,315	13.2	

Total vote 32,771 (four candidates)

1838

| Thomas Carlin, Dem. | 30,648 | 50.8 | 926 |
| Cyrus Edwards, Whig | 29,722 | 49.2 | |

Total vote 60,370 (two candidates)

1842

| Thomas Ford, Dem. | 46,507 | 53.8 | 7,487 |
| Joseph Duncan, Whig | 39,020 | 45.1 | |

Total vote 86,440 (three candidates)

1846

Augustus C. French, Dem.	58,656	58.2	21,623
Thomas M. Kilpatrick, Whig	37,033	36.7	
Richard Eels, Liberty	5,157	5.1	

vote 100,846 (three candidates)

	Vote	%	Plurality

1848
Augustus C. French, Dem. . . . . . .67,828 . . . . .86.8 62,169
W. L. D. Morrison, Whig . . . . .5,659 . . . . .7.2
Charles V. Dyer, Free Soil 4,692 610
Total vote 78,179 (three candidates)

1852
Joel A. Matteson, Dem. . . . . .80,789 . . . . .52.4 16,381
E. B. Webb, Whig . . . . .64,408 . . . . .41.8
D. A. Knowlton, Free Soil . . . . . . .9,024 . . . . .5.9
Total vote 154,221 (three candidates)

1856
Wm. H. Bissell, Rep. . . . . .111,466 . . . . .47.0 4,787
Wm. A. Richardson, Dem. . . . . .106,679 . . . . .45.0
Buckner S. Morris, American . . . .19,088 . . . . .8.0
Total vote 237,233 (three candidates)

1860
Richard Yates, Rep. . . . . .172,196 . . . . .51.5 12,943
James C. Allen, Dem. . . . . .159,253 . . . . .47.6
Total vote 334,354 (six candidates)

1864
Richard J. Oglesby, Union . . . . .190,376 . . . . .54.5 31,675
James C. Robinson, Dem. . . . . . .158,701 . . . . .45.5
Total vote 349,077 (two candidates)

1868
John M. Palmer, Rep. . . . . .249,912 . . . . .55.6 50,099
John R. Eden, Dem. . . . . .199,813 . . . . .44.4
Total vote 449,725 (two candidates)

1872
Richard J. Oglesby, Rep. . . . . . . .237,774 . . . . .54.4 40,690
Gustave Koerner, Dem. . . . . . . .197,084 . . . . .45.1
Total vote 437,043 (three candidates)

1876
Shelby M. Cullom, Rep. . . . . . . .279,263 . . . . .50.6 6,798
Lewis Steward, Dem. . . . . .272,465 . . . . .49.4
Total vote 552,093 (four candidates)

1880
Shelby M. Cullom, Rep. . . . . . . .314,565 . . . . .50.6 37,033
Lyman Trumbull, Dem. . . . . . . .277,532 . . . . .44.7
Total vote 621,117 (four candidates)

	Vote	**%**	**Plurality**

1884
Richard J. Oglesby, Rep. ......334,234 ....49.6 14,599
Carter H. Harrison, Dem. ......319,635 ....47.5
Total vote 673,389 (four candidates)

1888
Joseph W. Fifer, Rep. ....367,860 ....49.1 12,547
John M. Palmer, Dem. ....355,313 ....47.5
Total vote 748,447 (four candidates)

1892
John P. Altgeld, Dem. ....425,558 ....48.7 22,872
Joseph W. Fifer, Rep. ....402,686 ....46.1
Total vote 873,155 (four candidates)

1896
John R. Tanner, Rep. ....587,637 ....54.1 113,381
John P. Altgeld, Dem. ....474,256 ....43.7
Total vote 1,086,272 (six candidates)

1900
Richard Yates, Rep. ....580,199 ....51.5 61,233
Samuel Alschuler, Dem. ....518,966 ....46.1
Total vote 1,126,828 (eight candidates)

1904
Charles S. Deneen, Rep. ......634,029 ....59.1 299,149
Lawrence B. Stringer, Dem. ....334,880 ....31.2
John Collins, Socialist .... 59,062 ....5.5
Total vote 1,072,934 (seven candidates)

1908
Charles S. Deneen, Rep. ....550,076 ....47.6 23,164
Adlai E. Stevenson, Dem. ......526,912 ....45.6
Total vote 1,154,612 (six candidates)

1912
Edward F. Dunne, Dem. ....443,120 ....38.1 124,651
Charles S. Deneen, Rep. ....318,469 ....27.4
Frank H. Funk, Progressive ....303,401 ....26.1
John C. Kennedy, Socialist ......78,679 ....6.8
Total vote 1,162,880 (six candidates)

1916
Frank O. Lowden, Rep. ....696,535 ....52.7 139,881
Edward F. Dunne, Dem. ......556,654 ....42.1
Total vote 1,322,553 (five candidates)

	Vote	**%**	**Plurality**

1920
Len Small, Rep. . . . . .1,243,148 . . . . .58.9 511,597
James Hamilton Lewis, Dem. . . .731,551 . . . . .34.6
        Total vote 2,111,605 (ten candidates)

1924
Len Small, Rep. . . . . .1,366,436 . . . . .56.7 345,028
Norman L. Jones, Dem. . . . . . .1,021,408 . . . . .42.4
        Total vote 2,409,121 (seven candidates)

1928
Louis L. Emmerson, Rep. . . . . .1,709,818 . . . . .56.8 424,921
Floyd E. Thompson, Dem. . . .1,284,897 . . . . .42.7
        Total vote 3,012,208 (five candidates)

1932
Henry Horner, Dem. . . . . .1,930,330 . . . . .57.6 566,287
Len Small, Rep. . . . . .1,364,043 . . . . .40.7
        Total vote 3,350,320 (six candidates)

1936
Henry Horner, Dem. . . . . .2,067,861 . . . . .53.1 385,176
C. Wayland Brooks, Rep. . . . .1,682,685 . . . . .43.2
        Total vote 3,891,976 (six candidates)

1940
Dwight H. Green, Rep. . . . . . .2,197,778 . . . . .52.9 256,945
Harry B. Hershey, Dem. . . . . .1,940,833 . . . . .46.7
        Total vote 4,152,622 (four candidates)

1944
Dwight H. Green, Rep. . . . . . .2,013,270 . . . . .50.8 72,271
Thomas J. Courtney, Dem. . . .1,940,999 . . . . .48.9
        Total vote 3,966,765 (four candidates)

1948
Adlai E. Stevenson, Dem. . . . .2,250,074 . . . . .57.1 572,067
Dwight H. Green, Rep. . . . . . .1,678,007 . . . . .42.6
        Total vote 3,940,257 (four candidates)

1952
William G. Stratton, Rep. . . . . .2,317,363 . . . . .52.5 227,642
Sherwood Dixon, Dem. . . . . . .2,089,721 . . . . .47.3
        Total vote 4,415,864 (three candidates)

1956
William G. Stratton, Rep. . . . . .2,171,786 . . . . .50.3 36,877
Richard B. Austin, Dem. . . . . .2,134,909 . . . . .49.5
        Total vote 4,314,611 (three candidates)

	Vote	**%**	**Plurality**

1960
Otto Kerner, Dem. . . . . .2,594,731 . . . . .55.5 524,252
William G. Stratton, Rep. . . . .2,070,479 . . . . .44.3
        Total vote 4,674,187 (three candidates)

1964
Otto Kerner, Dem. . . . . .2,418,394 . . . . .51.9 179,299
Charles H. Percy, Rep. . . . . .2,239,095 . . . . .48.1
        Total vote 4,657,500 (two candidates)

1968
Richard B. Ogilvie, Rep. . . . .2,307,295 . . . . .51.2 127,794
Samuel H. Shapiro, Dem. . . . .2,179,501 . . . . .48.4
        Total vote 4,506,000 (three candidates)

1972
Daniel Walker, Dem. . . . . . . .2,371,303 . . . . .50.7 77,494
Richard B. Ogilvie, Rep. . . . .2,293,809 . . . . .49.0
        Total vote 4,678,804 (four candidates)

1976
James R. Thompson, Rep. . . . .3,000,395 . . . . .64.7 1,390,137
Michael J. Howlett, Dem. . . . .1,610,258 . . . . .34.7
        Total vote 4,638,997 (seven candidates)

1978
James R. Thompson, Rep. . . . .1,859,684 . . . . .59.0 596,550
Michael J. Bakalis, Dem. . . . .1,263,134 . . . . .40.1
        Total vote 3,150,095 (five candidates)

1982
James R. Thompson, Rep. . . . .1,816,101 . . . . .49.4 5,074
Adlai E. Stevenson III, Dem. . .1,811,027 . . . . .49.3
        Total vote 3,673,681 (four candidates)

1986
James R. Thompson, Rep. . . . . . .1,655,849 . . . . .52.7 399,223
Adlai E. Stevenson III, Solidarity .1,256,626 . . . . .40.0
        Total vote 3,143,978 (five candidates)

1990
Jim Edgar, Rep. . . . . .1,653,126 . . . . .50.7 83,909
Neil Hartigan, Dem. . . . . .1,569,217 . . . . .48.2
        Total vote 3,257,410

1994
Jim Edgar, Rep. . . . . .1,984,318 . . . . .63.9 914,468
Dawn Clark Netsch, Dem. . . . .1,069,850 . . . . .34.4
        Total vote 3,106,556

	Vote	**%**	**Plurality**
1998			
George Ryan, Rep.	1,714,094	. . . . .51.0	119,903
Glenn Poshard, Dem.	1,594,191	. . . . .47.5	

Total vote 3,358,705 (nine candidates)

Candidates receiving 5 percent or less of vote are omitted.

Percentages are of total vote for gubernatorial candidates, not total vote cast at election.

Sources: 1818-1820, Theodore C. Pease, *The Story of Illinois*, appendix; 1920-1952, Samuel K. Gove, ed., *Illinois Votes: A Compilation of Illinois Election Statistics*, Urbana; 1953-1988 reports of Secretary of State and State Board of Elections; 1990, Craig A. Roberts and Paul Kleppner, *Almanac of Illinois Politics – 1994*, page 386; 1994, David A. Joens and Paul Kleppner, *Almanac of Illinois Politics – 1998*, page 374; 1998, State Board of Elections web site (http://www.state.il.us/election/), December 7, 1998.

Bibliographical Essay

Naturally, the major source for the second edition of *Mostly Good and Competent Men* is its first edition. Author Robert Howard spent the last years of his life researching the early governors and, for the modern governors, augmenting his private "archives" – a cache of tearsheets, news releases, official documents, clippings, and memoranda that he collected in his 50 years in Illinois.

In addition to the sources cited in the following bibliography, both Robert Howard, and later, the editorial staff at the Institute for Public Affairs used the biennially published *Illinois Blue Book* as a reliable resource for fact checking. Also, like Howard, the editorial staff found invaluable assistance from the administration and staff who oversee the collections of the Illinois State Historical Library, the State Archives, and Historical Societies throughout the state.

Also, like Howard, we drew on *Illinois Issues* magazine as a source of background information for matters relating to the Walker administration through the start of the Ryan administration. In her work on the Jim Thompson and Jim Edgar chapters, Peggy Boyer Long found 1981 through 1998 *Illinois Issues* articles by Charles N. Wheeler III, Michael D. Klemens, Al Manning, Harvey Berkman, and Jennifer Davis particularly useful.

Boyer Long also used numerous articles from the 1981 to 1998 editions of the *Chicago Tribune* and Springfield's *State Journal-Register* to research Edgar's career as secretary of state, his campaigns, his first six months as governor, and his response to the flood of 1993. The governor's office provided her with files containing Governor Edgar's State of the State speeches, his budget messages, and post-session press releases. She drew information from a tape recording of a speech the governor gave on September 11, 1998, in which Edgar recapped his political career. And she learned more about the governor when she sat down with him for an exclusive interview on October 28, 1998.

Peggy Boyer Long and the rest of the Institute for Public Affairs editorial team had an additional source that Robert Howard could not have conceived of: the Internet. Boyer Long found Edgar's official biography on the State of Illinois' homepage an initial source of background information. Ed Wojcicki used George Ryan's and Glenn Poshard's campaign web sites as well as

Ryan's Secretary of State web site as helpful starting points for his work. For fact checking, the editorial staff searched for a wide range of information including burial sites, civil war battles, Chicago mayors, and even the history of Mormons in Illinois, to name just a few.

Today, we are lucky to have information delivered directly to our computer screens. Of course, the new technology doesn't discriminate for us: That information can be wonderfully accurate, or it can be poorly researched propaganda.

It was ever thus. In the bibliographical essay in the first edition of *Mostly Good and Competent Men,* Robert Howard called the second Richard Yates' biography of his governor-father "shallow and incomplete." Historians such as Robert Howard, Peggy Boyer Long and Mike Lawrence must become the captains of the source material that they are often at the mercy of. They must make judgments on what scholarship is good and bad, whose eyewitness accounts can be trusted, and which authors are pushing what agendas. Historians become editors and framers of history.

The authors and editors of *Mostly Good and Competent Men* have taken their charge as framers of Illinois history seriously. We believe that this book, though surely imperfect, will stand up well to scrutiny; that novice and experienced Illinois historians will value it; and that it will, in a small way, advance the cause of preserving the rich heritage of our state.

Rodd Whelpley
Associate Editor
University of Illinois at Springfield
Institute for Public Affairs

Bibliography

Affleck, James. "William Kinney, A Brief Biographical Sketch," *Illinois State Historical Society Transactions* (1908), 209-211.

Akers, Milburn P. *Chicago Sun Times* (18 July 1982).

Allswang, John M. *A House for All Peoples: Ethnic Politics in Chicago, 1890-1936.* Lexington, 1971.

Altgeld, John P. *Live Questions.* Chicago, 1890.

Altgeld, John P. *Oratory, Its Requirements and Rewards.* Chicago, 1901.

Alvord, Clarence W., ed. *Governor Edward Coles.* Springfield, 1920.

Alvord, Clarence W., ed. *The Illinois Country, 1673-1818.* Springfield, 1920.

Angle, Paul M. "Ford's History of Illinois." *Illinois State Historical Society Journal* 38, no. 1 (March, 1945): 99-104.

Angle, Paul M. "Nathaniel Pope, 1784 1850, A Memoir." *Illinois State Historical Society Transactions*, vol. 43 (1936).

Arrington, Leonard J., and Davis Bitton. *The Mormon Experience: A History of the Latter-day Saints.* New York, 1979.

Avrich, Paul. *The Haymarket Tragedy.* Princeton, 1984.

Bakalis, Michael J. *Ninian Edwards and Territorial Politics in Illinois, 1775-1818.* Ann Arbor, Michigan, 1975.

Bakalis, Michael J. *Ninian Edwards and Territorial Politics in Illinois, 1775-1818,* Northwestern University doctoral dissertation, 1966.

Ballance, Charles. *The History of Peoria, Illinois.* Peoria, 1870.

Baringer, William E. *A House Dividing: Lincoln as President Elect.* Springfield, 1945.

Barnard, Harry. *Eagle Forgotten: The Life of John Peter Altgeld.* Indianapolis, 1938.

Barnhart, Bill, and Gene Schlickman. "Intangible Rights: ...Kerner's views on civil liberties, and how his views differed from those of the man who prosecuted him." *Illinois Issues* (July/August, 1998): 32-34.

Bateman, Newton, and Paul Selby. *Historical Encyclopedia of Illinois,* Cook County edition. 2 vols. Chicago, 1901.

Benneson, Cora Agnes. "The Work of Edward Everett of Quincy in the Quarter-Master's Department in Illinois During the First Years of the Civil War." *Illinois State Historical Society Transactions* (1909).

Bennett, James O'Donnell. *Private Joe Fifer.* Bloomington, 1936. (See also his four-day interview for the *Chicago Tribune* in 1933.)

Beveridge, Albert J. *Abraham Lincoln, 1809-1858.* New York, 1928.

Beveridge, Philo J. Typescript in Illinois State Historical Library vertical file.

Bird, Fred. *Fred Bird Memoir.* Sangamon State University, Oral History Office, Springfield, 1985.

Bogart, Ernest L., and Charles Manfred Thompson. *The Industrial State, 1870-1893.* Chicago, 1922.

Bogart, Ernest L., and John Mabry Mathews. *The Modern Commonwealth, 1893-1918.* Chicago, 1922.

Bohrer, Florence Fifer. Manuscript in the Bohrer-Fifer Papers. Illinois State Historical Library.

Bonham, Jeriah. *Fifty Years' Recollections, and Portrait and Biographical Album of Coles County.* Chicago, 1887.

Bonham, Jeriah. *Fifty Years' Recollections, With Observations and Recollections on Historical Events Giving Sketches of Eminent Citizens—Their Lives and Public Services.* Peoria, 1883.

Bowen, A. L. "Personal Reminiscences of Joseph W. Fifer, an Interview with the Former Governor and a Description of his Times." *Illinois Blue Book,* 1925-26.

Boyer, Peggy. "A Prologue to Governing: The Campaign Promises of Jim Edgar." *Tax Fax: The Newsletter of the Taxpayers' Federation of Illinois* (February, 1991).

Bradley, Ralph S. *Ralph S. Bradley Memoir.* Sangamon State University, Oral History Office, Springfield 1985.

Brasler Roy P., et al., eds. *The Collected Works of Abraham Lincoln,* 9 vols. New Brunswick, NJ, 1953-1955.

Broadwater, Jeff. *Adlai Stevenson and American Politics: The Odyssey of a Cold War Liberal.* New York and Ontario, 1994.

Brown, Mark. "A man for the Millennium? Republican George Ryan...." *Illinois Issues* (February, 1998): 20-25.

Browne, Waldo R. *Altgeld of Illinois: A Record of His Life and Work.* New York, 1924.

Browning, Orville Hickman. *The Diary of Orville Hickman Browning.* eds. Theodore C. Pease and James G. Randall. 2 vols. Springfield, 1915, 1933.

Buck, Solon J. *Illinois in 1818.* Springfield, 1918.

Buley, Carlyle R. *The Old Northwest: Pioneer Period 1815-1840.* 2 vols. Indianapolis, 1950.

Burtschi, Joseph C. *Documentary History of Vandalia, Illinois: The State Capital of Illinois from 1819 to 1839.* Vandalia, 1954: 17, 32.

Byrd, Cecil K. *A Bibliography of Illinois Imprints, 1814-1858.* Chicago, 1966.

Cappon, Lester J., ed. *The Adams-Jefferson Letters: The Complete Correspondence Between Thomas Jefferson and Abigail and John Adams,* 2 vols. Chapel Hill, 1959.

Carlson, Theodore L. *The Illinois Military Tract: A Study in Land Occupation, Utilization and Tenure.* Urbana, 1951.

Carr, Clark E. *The Illini: A Story of the Prairies.* Chicago, 1906.

Carter, Clarence E. *The Territory of Illinois.* Washington, D.C., 1950.

Carter, Clarence E. *The Territory of Indiana, 1800-1810.* Washington, D. C., 1939.

Casey, Robert, and W. A. S. Douglas. *The Midwesterner: The Story of Dwight H. Green.* Chicago, 1948.

Christman, Henry M., ed. *The Mind and Spirit of John Peter Altgeld.* Urbana, 1965.

Church, Charles A. *A History of the Republican Party in Illinois, 1854-1912.* Rockford, 1912.

Clendenin, Henry W. *The Autobiography of Henry W. Clendenin.* Springfield, 1926.

Cole, Arthur C. *The Era of the Civil War, 1848-1870.* Chicago, 1922.

Coles, Edward *History of the Ordinance of 1787.* Philadelphia, 1856.

Coles, William B. *The Coles Family of Virginia: Its Numerous Connections from its Immigration to America to the Year 1915.* New York, 1931.

Collins, William H. and Cicero F. Perry, *Past and Present of the City of Quincy and Adams County.* Chicago, 1905.

Converse, Henry W. "The Life and Services of Shelby M. Cullom." *Illinois State Historical Society Transactions.* (1914): 55-79.

Corneau, Octavia. *History of the Executive Mansion.* Typescript and research notes in the Octavia Roberts Corneau Papers, Illinois State Historical Library.

Cornelius, Janet. *A History of Constitution-Making in Illinois.* Urbana, 1969.

Court of Appeals Opinion 493, *Federal Reporter,* 2nd Series, 1124.

Cullom, Shelby M. *Fifty Years of Public Service: Personal Recollections of Shelby M. Cullom.* Chicago, 1911.

Davidson, Alexander, and Bernard Stuve. *A Complete History of Illinois from 1673 to 1873, Embracing the Physical Features of the Country; Its Early Explorations; Aboriginal Inhabitants; Conquest by Virginia; Territorial Condition and the Subsequent Civil, Military and Political Events of the State.* Springfield, 1874.

Davis, George Cullom. *Governor Shelby M. Cullom, 1877-1883.* University of Illinois master's thesis, 1961.

Davis, J. McCan. *The Breaking of the Deadlock, Being an Accurate and Authentic Account of the Contest of 1903-4 for the Republican Nomination for Governor....*Springfield, 1904.

Davis, Jennifer. "The Men Who Would Be Governor." *Illinois Issues* (September, 1998): 15 - 25.

Davis, Kenneth S. *A Prophet in His Own Country: The Triumphs and Defeats of Adlai E. Stevenson.* New York, 1950.

Davis, Kenneth S. *The Politics of Honor, a Biography.* New York, 1967.

Davis, Rodney O. "Illinois Legislators and Jacksonian Democracy, 1834-1841." University of Iowa doctoral dissertation, 1966.

Davis, Rodney O. "Judge Ford and the Regulators, 1841-1842," in *1981 Selected Papers in Illinois History.* Springfield, 1982: 25-36.

de Grazia, Victor. *Victor de Grazia Memoir.* Sangamon State University, Oral History Office, Springfield, 1984.

Dilliard, Irving. "Len Small Back to Prosperity." *The Nation.* (19 Oct. 1932): 352-353.

Downey, William. *William "Smokey" Downey Memoir.* Sangamon State University Oral History Office, Springfield, 1985.

Dowrie, George W. *The Development of Banking in Illinois, 1817-1863.* Urbana, 1913.

Dunne, Edward F. *Dunne: Judge, Mayor, Governor.* ed. William L. Sullivan. Chicago, 1916.

Dunne, Edward F. *Illinois, the Heart of the Nation.* 5 vols. Chicago, 1933.

Edward Coles Papers in the Princeton University Library.

Edwards, Ninian W. *History of Illinois from 1778 to 1833; and the Life and Times of Ninian Edwards.* Springfield, 1870.

Eversole, Mildred, ed. "Richard J. Oglesby: Forty-Niner. His Own Narrative." *Papers in Illinois History, 1938.* Springfield, 1939: 158-71.

Ewing, Presley Kittredge and Mary Ellen Williams Ewing. *Ewing Genealogy with Cognate Branches, A Survey of the Ewings and Their Kin in America.* Houston, 1919.

Flanders, Robert B. *Nauvoo: Kingdom on the Mississippi.* Urbana, 1965.

Ford, Thomas. *A History of Illinois, From Its Commencement in 1818 to 1847....* Chicago, 1854 and 1945-1946.

The French-Wicker Family Papers. Manuscripts Collection of the Illinois State Historical Library, Springfield.

Gillespie, Joseph. Introduction and appendix to *Reminiscences of the Early Bench and Bar.* Usher F. Linder, ed. Chicago, 1879.

Gosnell, Harold F. *Machine Politics: Chicago Model.* Chicago, 1937 and New York, 1969.

Gove, Samuel K., ed. *Illinois Votes, 1900-1958: A Compilation of Illinois Election Statistics.* Urbana, 1959.

"Governor Coles' Autobiography," *Illinois State Historical Society Journal* no. 3 (October, 1910).

Graham, James R. History of the Sangamon County Bar. Typescript in Illinois State Historical Library, January, 1931.

Gray, Wood. *The Hidden Civil War.* New York, 1942.

Green, Dwight H. Vertical file in the Illinois State Historical Library.

Green, Paul M., and Melvin G. Holli. *The Mayors.* Carbondale, 1987.

Greene, Evarts B., and Charles M. Thompson. *The Governors' Letter-Books, 1840-1853.* Springfield, 1911.

Greene, Evarts B., and Clarence W. Alvord, eds. *The Governors' Letter-Books, 1818-1834.* Springfield, 1909.

Harper, Josephine L. *John Reynolds, The Old Ranger of Illinois.* University of Illinois doctoral dissertation, 1949.

Hartley, Robert E. *Big Jim Thompson of Illinois.* Chicago, 1979.

Hesseltine, William B. *Lincoln and the War Governors.* New York, 1955.

Hicken, Victor. *Illinois in the Civil War.* Urbana, 1966.

Hicken, Victor. "The Virden and Pana Mine Wars of 1898." *Illinois State Historical Society Journal* 52 (Summer, 1959).

Hickey, James T. "An Illinois First Family: The Reminiscences of Clara Matteson Doolittle." *Illinois State Historical Society Journal* 69, no. 1 (February, 1976).

Hickey, James T. "Oglesby's Fence Rail Dealings and the 1860 Decatur Convention." *Illinois State Historical Society Journal* 54, no. 1 (Spring, 1961): 5-14.

Hiller, Mary Jane. *William H. Bissell and the Campaign and Election of 1856.* Southern Illinois University – Carbondale, master's thesis, 1964.

History of Greene County, Illinois. Chicago, 1879.

Holden, Robert J. "Governor Ninian Edwards and the War of 1812: The Military Role of a Territorial Governor," in *1980 Selected Papers in Illinois History.* Springfield, 1982.

Howard, Robert P. "A Thompson Scorecard: Compromise and Fiscal Prudence." *Illinois Issues* (January, 1980): 8-12.

Howard, Robert P. "Abraham Lincoln, William H. Bissell and Perjury." *Lincoln Herald* (Summer, 1985).

Howard, Robert P. *Illinois: A History of the Prairie State.* Grand Rapids, 1972 and 1986.

Howard, Robert P. *James R. Howard and the Farm Bureau.* Ames, 1983.

Howard, Robert P. "Mr. Sam of Illinois." *Chicago Tribune Magazine* (12 May 1968).

Howard, Robert P. "Old Dick Richardson: The Other Senator from Quincy." *Western Illinois Regional Studies* 7, no. 1 (Spring, 1984).

Howard, Robert P. "The Great Canal Scrip Fraud: The Downfall of Governor Joel A. Matteson," in *1980 Selected Papers in Illinois History*. Springfield, 1982.

Howard, Robert P. "Thompson vs. Stevenson: A Long View." *Illinois Issues* (October, 1982): 6-11.

Howard, Robert P. "Walker, a Lone Wolf Governor." *Illinois Issues* (January, 1977): 6-7.

Hutchinson, William T. *Lowden of Illinois: The Life of Governor Frank O. Lowden.* 2 vols. Chicago, 1957.

Ickes, Harold L. *Autobiography of a Curmudgeon.* New York, 1943.

Illinois Progress, 1921-1928, Len Small, Governor. 1928.

Illinois Reports, 1846. Springfield, 1847.

Illinois State of the State: 1977 - 1991 The Thompson Administration. James R. Thompson: Springfield, 1991.

Immel, Joseph, Johnson Kanady and Frederic B. Selcke. *Joseph Immel Memoir–Johnson Kanady Memoir–Frederic B. Selcke Memoir.* Sangamon State University Oral History Office, Springfield, 1985.

Johannsen, Robert ed. *Letters of Stephen A. Douglas.* Urbana, 1961.

Johannsen, Robert *Stephen A. Douglas.* New York, 1973.

Johnson, Allen. ed., *Dictionary of American Biography.* 22 vols. New York, 1973.

Johnson, Walter. *How We Drafted Adlai Stevenson.* New York, 1955.

Jones, Robert Huhn. "Three Days of Violence: The Regulators of the Rock River Valley." *Illinois State Historical Society Journal* 59, no 2 (Summer 1966): 132-3.

Keiser, John H. "Black Strikebreakers and Racism in Illinois, 1865-1900." *Illinois State Historical Society Journal* 63, no. 3 (Autumn, 1972): 310.

Keiser, John H. *Building for the Centuries: Illinois 1865-1898.* Urbana, 1977.

Kenney, David. *A Political Passage: The Career of Stratton of Illinois.* Carbondale, 1990.

Kenney, David. *Basic Illinois Government: A Systematic Explanation.* Carbondale, 1970.

Ketcham, Ralph L. "The Dictates of Conscience, Edward Coles and Slavery." *Virginia Quarterly Review* 36, no. 1 (Winter, 1960).

Kirby, Julia Smith. *Biographical Sketch of Joseph Duncan.* Chicago, 1888.

Klement, Frank L. *The Copperheads in the Middle West.* Chicago, 1960.

Kobler, John. *Capone: The Life and World of Al Capone.* New York, 1971.

Koerner, Gustave. *Memoirs of Gustave Koerner, 1809-1896: Life Sketches Written at the Suggestion of His Children.* ed. Thomas McCormack. Cedar Rapids, 1909.

Krenkel, John H. *Illinois Internal Improvements, 1818-1848.* Cedar Rapids, 1958.

Krenkel, John H. ed. *Richard Yates, Civil War Governor.* Danville, 1966.

Krenkel, John H. ed. *Serving the Republic: Richard Yates, Illinois Governor and Congressman, Son of Richard Yates, Civil War Governor: an Autobiography.* Danville, 1968.

Langhorne, Elizabeth. "Edward Coles, Thomas Jefferson and the Rights of Man." *Virginia Cavalcade* 23, no. 1 (Summer, 1973), 30-36.

Lawrence, Mike. "Ogilvie Revisited." *Illinois Issues* (December, 1982): 25-28.

Lawrence, Mike. "The Rematch, Thompson vs. Stevenson." *Illinois Issues* (October, 1986): 10-17.

Leckie, William H. and Shirley A. Leckie. *Unlikely Warriors, General Benjamin Grierson and His Family.* Norman, OK, 1984.

Leichtle, Kurt E. *Edward Coles, an Agrarian on the Frontier.* Ph.D. dissertation, University of Illinois-Chicago Circle, 1982.

Leithold, Esther M. *Genealogy of the Evans' Family, the "Virginia Biddles" and Other Related Families.* Woodland, California, 1940.

Lewis, Donald F. Collection of Deneen papers in the Illinois State Historical Library.

Lewis, Donald Fremont. The Philadelphia Years of Gov. Edward Coles of Illinois. Typescript in Illinois State Historical Library.

Littlewood, Thomas B. *Horner of Illinois.* Evanston, 1969.

Lutes, Terry, and Joseph P. Pisciotte. *Terry Lutes Memoir–Joseph P. Pisciotte Memoir.* Sangamon State University, Oral History Office, Springfield, 1985.

McCarter, John W. *John W. McCarter, Jr. Memoir.* Sangamon State University, Oral History Office, Springfield, 1985.

McDonald, Forrest. *Insull.* Chicago, 1962.

Manning, Al. "Dan Walker Meets the Public: The Accountability Sessions." *Illinois Issues.* (January, 1975): 12-14.

Mansfield, Frank C. "The Governor and the Anarchists." *Illinois Bar Journal* 65, no. 4 (May, 1977): 600-611;

Martin, John Bartlow. *Adlai Stevenson of Illinois.* New York, 1976.

Mauldin, William Henry. *Back Home.* New York, 1947.

"Memoirs of Speaker David Shanahan." *Illinois Blue Book.* Springfield, 1925.

Merriam, Charles E. *Chicago: A More Intimate View of Urban Politics.* New York, 1929.

Messick, Hank. *The Politics of Prosecution: Jim Thompson, Richard Nixon, Marge Everett and the Trial of Otto Kerner.* Ottawa, 1978.

Michaelson, Ron. *Ron Michaelson Memoir.* Sangamon State University, Oral History Office, Springfield, 1984.

Morgenstern, George *Chicago Tribune* (11 January 1948).

Morton, Richard A. *Justice and Humanity: Edward F. Dunne, Illinois Progressive* Carbondale, 1997.

Moses, John. *Illinois Historical and Statistical.* 2 vols. Chicago, 1889.

The National Cyclopedia of American Biography. Clifton, NJ, 1926.

Neely, Mark E., Jr. *The Abraham Lincoln Encyclopedia.* New York, 1982.

Neilson, James W. *Shelby M. Cullom: Prairie State Republican.* Urbana, 1962.

Nevins, Allan. *Ordeal of the Union,* 2 vols. New York, 1947.

Norton, W. T. *Edward Coles, Second Governor of Illinois.* Philadelphia, 1911.

Nortrup, Jack Junior. "A Western Whig in Washington." *Illinois State Historical Society Journal* 64, no. 4 (Winter, 1971): 419-441.

Nortrup, Jack Junior. "Governor Yates and President Lincoln." *Lincoln Herald* (Winter, 1968): 193-206.

Nortrup, Jack Junior. "Richard Yates: A Personal Glimpse of the Illinois Soldiers' Friend." *Illinois State Historical Society Journal* 56, no. 2 (Summer, 1963): 121-58.

Nortrup, Jack Junior. *Richard Yates, Civil War Governor of Illinois.* University of Illinois doctoral dissertation, 960.

Nortrup, Jack Junior. "Yates, the Prorogued Legislature, and the Constitutional Convention." *Illinois State Historical Society Journal* 62, no. 1 (Spring, 1969): 5-31.

Oral History Office, Sangamon State University. "Stories of the Governorship." *Illinois Issues* (December, 1982): 13-23.

Palmer, George Thomas. *A Conscientious Turncoat: The Story of John M. Palmer, 1817-1900.* New Haven, 1941.

Palmer, John M. *Personal Recollections: The Story of an Earnest Life.* Cincinnati, 1901.

Palmer, John M. *The Bench and Bar of Illinois, Historical and Reminiscent.* 2 vols. Chicago, 1899.

Park, Siyoung. "Land Speculation in Western Illinois: Pike County, 1821-35," *Illinois State Historical Society Journal* 77, no. 2 (Summer, 1984): 115-28.

Pease, Theodore Calvin. *Illinois Election Returns, 1818-1848.* Springfield, 1923.

Pease, Theodore Calvin. *The Frontier State, 1818-1848.* Chicago, 1918.

Pease, Theodore Calvin. *The Story of Illinois.* Rev. ed. by
   Marguerite Jenison Pease. Chicago, 1965.

Pensoneau, Taylor. *Governor Richard Ogilvie: In the Interest of the
   State.* Carbondale, 1990.

Pensoneau, Taylor "Walker, Ogilvie and Kerner Used Different
   Techniques in Dealing With Legislature." *Illinois Issues*
   (February, 1975): 51-53.

Pensoneau, Taylor and Bob Ellis. *Dan Walker: The Glory and the
   Tragedy.* Evansville, Indiana, 1993.

Philbrick, Francis S. *Laws of Indiana Territory, 1801-1809.*
   Springfield, 1930.

Phillips, Clarence. *Daily News.* Lawrenceville, Illinois, 5 February
   1962

Plummer, Mark A. "Governor Richard J. Oglesby and the
   Haymarket Anarchists." *1981 Selected Papers in Illinois History.*
   Springfield, 1982: 50-59.

Portrait and Biographical Album of Coles County, Illinois. Chicago, 1887.

Pree, Edward. *Edward Pree Memoir.* Sangamon State Oral History
   Office, Springfield, 1984.

Putnam, Elizabeth Duncan. "The Life and Services of Joseph
   Duncan." *Illinois State Historical Society Transactions* (1919).

Raines, Edgar F., Jr. "The Ku Klux Klan in Illinois, 1867-1875."
   Illinois Historical Journal 78 (Spring, 1985): 17-44.

Rakove, Milton. "Gov. Thompson: What Kind of a Politician is
   He?" *Illinois Issues* (October, 1977): 7-9.

Raum, Green B. *History of Illinois Republicanism.* Chicago, 1900.

Reynolds, John. *My Own Times, Embracing Also the History of My Life.* Belleville, 1855 and Chicago, 1879.

Reynolds, John. *The Pioneer History of Illinois.* Belleville, 1852 and Chicago, 1887.

Richardson, Eudora Ramsey. "The Virginian Who Made Illinois a Free State." *Journal of the Illinois State Historical Society* 45, no. 1 (Spring, 1952): 5-23.

Roberts, B. H. *The Rise and Fall of Nauvoo.* Salt Lake City, 1965.

Roberts, Sidney I. "The Municipal Voters' League and Chicago's Boodlers." *Illinois State Historical Society Journal* 53, no. 2 (Summer, 1960): 117-48.

Ross, Diane. "A Few Words from the Governor." *Illinois Issues* (January, 1985): 6-19.

Schlup, Leonard. "Adlai E. Stevenson and the Gubernatorial Campaign of 1908." *International Review of History and Political Science.* 13, no. 4 (November 1976).

Schlup, Leonard C. "Adlai E. Stevenson and the Presidential Election of 1896." *Social Science Journal* 14, no. 2 (April, 1977): 118-128.

Searles, William S. "Governor Cullom and the Pekin Whisky Ring Scandal." *Illinois State Historical Society Journal* 51, no. 1 (Spring, 1958): 28-41.

Shankman, Arnold. "Partisan Conflicts, 1839-1841, and the Illinois Constitution," *Illinois State Historical Society Journal* 63, no. 4 (Winter, 1970).

Small, Len. *Illinois Progress, 1921-1928.* Springfield, 1928.

Smith, George W. *History of Illinois and Her People.* 3 vols. Chicago, New York, 1927.

Snyder, John Francis. *Adam W. Snyder and His Period in Illinois History, 1817-1842.* Springfield, 1903.

Snyder, John Francis. "Governor Ford and His Family." *Illinois State Historical Society Journal* 3, no. 2 (July, 1910): 45-51.

Snyder, John Francis. "The Army Led by Col. George Rogers Clark in His Conquest of Illinois, 1778-9." *Transactions of the Illinois State Historical Society, Collections of the Illinois State Historical Library,* vol. 21 (1903).

Spenser, Donald S. "Edward Coles: Virginia Gentleman in Frontier Politics." *Illinois State Historical Society Journal* 61, no. 2 (Summer, 1968).

Stevenson, Adlai E. *Something of Men I Have Known.* Chicago, 1909.

Stover, John F. *History of the Illinois Central Railroad.* New York, 1975.

Stuart, William H. *The Twenty Incredible Years.* Chicago, 1935.

Suppiger, Joseph Edward. *Jesse Burgess Thomas, Illinois' Pro-Slavery Advocate.* University of Tennessee doctoral dissertation, 1970.

Tarr, Joel A. *A Study in Boss Politics.* Urbana, 1971.

Thiem, George. *The Hodge Scandal: A Pattern of American Political Corruption.* New York, 1963.

Thornburn, Neil. "John P. Altgeld: Promoter of Higher Education in Illinois." *Essays in Illinois History.* Carbondale, 1968.

Tinder, Usher F. *Reminiscences of the Early Bench and Bar.* Chicago, 1879: 77.

Tingley, Donald F. *The Structuring of a State: The History of Illinois, 1899-1928.* Urbana, 1980.

Tompkins, C. David. "John Peter Altgeld as a Candidate for Mayor of Chicago in 1899." *Illinois State Historical Society Journal* 56, no. 4 (Winter 1963): 654-76.

Townsend, Walter A., ed. *Illinois Democracy: A History of the Party and Its Representative Members, Past and Present.* Springfield, 1935.

Trutter, John Thomas and Edith English Trutter. *The Governor Takes a Bride.* Carbondale, 1977.

Villard, Henry. *Memoirs of Henry Villard.* Cambridge, 1904.

Walker, Dan. *Dan Walker Memoir. Sangamon State University,* Oral History Office, Springfield, n.d.

Walton, Clyde C., ed. *An Illinois Reader.* DeKalb, 1970.

Washburne, Elihu B. *Sketch of Edward Coles, Second Governor of Illinois, and of the Slavery Struggle of 1823-4.* Chicago, 1882.

Washburne, Elihu B., ed. *The Edwards Papers.* Chicago, 1884.

Watters, Mary. *Illinois in the Second World War.* 2 vols. Springfield, 1951, 1952.

West, Roy O. "Charles S. Deneen, 1863-1940." *Illinois State Historical Society Journal* 34, no. 1 (March, 1941): 7-23.

Wheeler, Charles N. III. "Gov. James R. Thompson, 1977 - 1991: The Complete Campaigner, the Pragmatic Centerist." *Illinois Issues* (December, 1990): 12-16.

Whitney, Ellen. *The Black Hawk War, 1831-1832.* Springfield, 1970.

Williams, Deloris. *The Administration of Thomas Carlin* University of Illinois master's thesis, 1936.

Wish, Harvey. "Governor Altgeld Pardons the Anarchists." *Illinois State Historical Society Journal* 31, no. 4 (December, 1938): 424-448.

Wish, Harvey. "John Peter Altgeld and Progressive Tradition." *American History Review* (July, 1941): 813-31.

Wish, Harvey. "The Pullman Strike: A Study in Industrial Warfare." *Illinois State Historical Society Journal* 32 (September, 1939): 288-312.

Wooddy, Carroll H. *The Case of Frank L. Smith: A Study in Representative Government.* Chicago, 1931.

Wrone, David R. "Illinois Pulls Out of the Mud." *Illinois State Historical Society Journal* 58 (Spring, 1965): 69 72.

Yates Speeches. 15 major speeches, bound, and in the collection of the Illinois State Historical Library.

Index

Pisgah, 48
Pollution Control Board, 299
polygamy, 142
Pontiac, 119
Pope County, 66, 73
Pope, John, 21
Pope, Nathaniel, 21, 22, 25
Poshard, Glenn, 352, 377
Powell, Paul, 264, 273, 289
Prairie du Rocher, 22
Price, Sterling, 135
Princeton University, 263
prisons, 6, 7, 80, 118, 298, 316,
    332, 340
"professional honest man",
    240, 280
Progressive Movement, 155,
    167, 193, 199, 200, 201,
    203, 204, 207, 211, 216,
    227
Progressive Party, 199, 203
Prohibition, 196, 235
Project Success, 340
property tax, 27, 56, 64, 80,
    189, 219, 242, 316, 327,
    335, 337, 342, 358
property tax caps, 339
public aid, 282
public aid commission, 256, 282
public aid department, 283
Public Service Company of
    Northern Illinois, 255
public utilities commission,
    210, 229
Pullman, Florence, 216, 217
Pullman, George M., 166, 216

Q

Quincy, 54, 65, 83, 90, 95-98,
    120, 274

R

Radical Republicans, 126
railroads, 44, 47, 48, 55, 62, 72,
    77, 78, 104, 118, 128, 140,
    142, 156, 160
Rainey, Henry T., 211
Ramsey, Rufus N., 164
Ray, Lyman B., 270
Reagan, Ronald, 299, 322
real estate tax, *see* property tax
reapportionment, 270, 283,
    290, 320
Red Cross, 221
redistricting, *see* reapportion-
    ment
reduction veto, 371
Regional Transit Authority,
    307, 371
Regional Transportation
    Authority, 330
regulators, 70, 73
Research Foundation for the
    Mentally Ill, 289
Reuben and Proctor, 300
Revolutionary War, 10, 40, 95,
    187, 365
Reynolds, John, 13, 14, 28, 30-
    37, 39, 41, 44, 46, 55, 73,
    362, 372
Richardson, William A., 90,
    97, 373

T

About the
Institute for Public Affairs

Because of its location in the state capital, the University of Illinois at Springfield has a special mission in public affairs. To fulfill its mission, the campus directs educational, research, and service efforts to help solve problems facing the state and nearby local communities. The Institute for Public Affairs is a primary vehicle through which the campus carries out these public affairs activities.

The Institute for Public Affairs houses the Springfield campus's major public affairs units: the Center for Legal Studies, the Graduate Public Service Internship Program, *Illinois Issues*, the Illinois Legislative Studies Center, the Office of Policy and Administrative Studies, the Survey Research Office, the Television Office, and radio stations WUIS/WIPA. These units are coordinated by the Institute's Central Office.

In cooperation with Institute for Public Affairs' Editorial Board, the Institute also oversees the publication and dissemination of works designed to enhance citizen awareness of issues, policy, and the history of Illinois government.

About the Authors

The late **Robert P. Howard** was a reporter and historian. He served a long tenure as the Springfield correspondent for the *Chicago Tribune* and covered gubernatorial campaigns for *Illinois Issues* magazine. He was president of the Illinois State Historical Society, a board member of the Abraham Lincoln Association, and the author of *Illinois: A History of the Prairie State.*

Peggy Boyer Long is the editor of *Illinois Issues* magazine. An Illinois native, she has a B.A. in English and an M.S. in Journalism from the University of Illinois. She also has an M.A. in History from Sangamon State University, now the University of Illinois at Springfield. Peggy has taught journalism at Northwestern University and Chicago's Columbia College. She has covered Illinois state government for magazines, newspapers, and public radio. As a reporter based in the Illinois Statehouse, she covered the administrations of Governors Dan Walker, Jim Thompson, and Jim Edgar.

Mike Lawrence is associate director of the Public Policy Institute at Southern Illinois University at Carbondale. He was born in Chicago, but grew up in Galesburg, Illinois, where he attended Knox College and started a journalism career after graduation. Mike was a newspaper reporter and syndicated columnist for 30 years, covering Illinois state government. Later, he was press secretary for Governor Jim Edgar.